Teacher Leadership

Studies in the
Postmodern Theory of Education

Shirley R. Steinberg
General Editor

Vol. 466

The Counterpoints series is part of the Peter Lang Education list.
Every volume is peer reviewed and meets
the highest quality standards for content and production.

PETER LANG
New York • Bern • Frankfurt • Berlin
Brussels • Vienna • Oxford • Warsaw

Teacher Leadership

The "New" Foundations of Teacher Education

A Reader

REVISED EDITION

Edited by Eleanor Blair

PETER LANG

New York • Bern • Frankfurt • Berlin
Brussels • Vienna • Oxford • Warsaw

Library of Congress Cataloging-in-Publication Data
Names: Blair, Eleanor, editor.
Title: Teacher leadership: the "new" foundations of teacher education:
a reader / edited by Eleanor Blair.
Description: Revised edition. | New York: Peter Lang, 2016.
Series: Counterpoints: studies in the postmodern theory of education; vol. 466 | ISSN 1058-1634
Includes bibliographical references.
Identifiers: LCCN 2015040524 | ISBN 978-1-4331-2790-8 (paperback alk. paper)
ISBN 978-1-4539-1799-2 (e-book)
Subjects: LCSH: Teachers—Professional relationships. | Teacher participation in administration.
Educational leadership. | Professional learning communities.
Classification: LCC LB1775.T4165 2016 | DDC 371.1—dc23
LC record available at http://lccn.loc.gov/2015040524

Bibliographic information published by **Die Deutsche Nationalbibliothek**.
Die Deutsche Nationalbibliothek lists this publication in the "Deutsche
Nationalbibliografie"; detailed bibliographic data are available
on the Internet at http://dnb.d-nb.de/.

The paper in this book meets the guidelines for permanence and durability
of the Committee on Production Guidelines for Book Longevity
of the Council of Library Resources.

As always, my work is dedicated to the thousands of teacher leaders who work tirelessly on behalf of children and their families in both Jamaica and the United States. Your valiant efforts to be leaders in classrooms, schools and communities are seldom recognized or granted status, and yet, it would be frightening to consider where education would be without you.

AND

To Julia Taylor Hilty Cannon, the pleasure of watching you emerge as a teacher leader is unmitigated. I was your first teacher, but now you have become the teacher; your passion and commitment to children is inspiring. Thank you for keeping me connected to 21st century schools.

Contents

SECTION 3
TEACHER LEADERS AS LEARNERS AND LEADERS

SECTION 4
TEACHER LEADERS IN ACTION

SECTION 5
TEACHER LEADERSHIP IN THE TWENTY-FIRST CENTURY:
CHANGING THE CULTURE OF SCHOOLS

Foreword

David Gabbard

The idea of teacher leadership, as it is now used in the language of the new *managerialism*, opens the door to a special kind of denial. It allows teachers to deny that they are not actually leading. We can plainly see that they are, for the most part, functionaries of the system that has now chosen them to help it lead. We can also see, however, other teachers who don't submit to their servitude as willingly or enthusiastically as others. Among this group, some may work to disguise their resistance by exploiting discursive regimes, such as the one responsible for the formation of a concept of teacher leadership that functions as aggressive compliance. Hence, we might find them serving in some role identified with teacher leadership. Some others may give more open expression to their resistance. By increasing the visibility of their resistance by drawing attention to themselves, they also increase their vulnerability to various forms of exclusion, marginalization, and/or punishment. Perhaps it was the lessons learned from those stories that led some resisters to disguise their resistance, which constitutes its own kind of denial. In any case, I believe it is crucial to remain mindful of how the notion of teacher leadership creates an opportunity for some resisters to deny their resistance and for those who identify with and as "teacher leaders" to deny their compliance. They aren't resisting, and they aren't complying; they are leading!

Even a cursory glance at "Teacher Leadership Standards," however, reveals the "impossibility" of teacher leadership. Those standards associate leadership with the following:

- Fostering a Collaborative Culture to Support Educator Development and Student Learning (Domain 1),

- Promoting Professional Learning for Continuous Improvement, Facilitating Improvements in Instruction and Student Learning (Domain 3),

- Facilitating Improvements in Instruction and Student Learning (Domain 4),

- Improving Outreach and Collaboration with Families and Community (Domain 6), and

- Advocating for Student Learning and the Profession (Domain 7).

Looking at them more carefully, we see they actually negate leadership through the clear intent to expand the scope and the amount of compliance. Teacher leaders bring more students, teachers, parents, and community into compliance, and they work to improve everyone's knowledge, including their own, of how to do *what* they are told to do. Domains 2 and 5 cover that *what*:

- Accessing and Using Research to Improve Practice and Student Learning, and

- Promoting the Use of Assessments and Data for School and District Improvement.

Most fundamentally, it would not matter what ends are pursued. The problem for teacher leaders and the concept of teacher leadership stems from those ends having been determined *for* them, not *by* them. I don't want to suggest that the kinds of work described under the teacher leadership standards aren't important, but we should ask ourselves whether such work is representative of leadership or an inspired form of followership? Again, I do not mean to denigrate followership or obedience to something that one deems worthy of pursuing. As such, that would, at the very least, trivialize the idea of vocation as a calling to serve some larger purpose, but that purpose may or may not have been determined by oneself. Leadership implies both the autonomy/agency of a subject and a form of authority/influence that flows from the exercise of that autonomy/agency. The ideas or acts that are products of these actions must inspire followership and, frequently if not always, some form of change promised or offered by the vision.

On Educational Leadership More Generally

Scott Eacott has written in very similar terms about the more common notion of educational leadership. Apart from problematizing the practice of equating educational leadership with one's positional status within the hierarchical bureaucracy of what was once called educational administration and, then, school management, Eacott also challenges the leadership label when applied to those (e.g., principals, superintendents, etc.) whose primary role relates to school and district operations. We shouldn't diminish this work either, but, with Eacott, we should question whether or not it truly qualifies as leadership.

Elsewhere (Gabbard, 2013), I have also questioned the leadership of people in those positions, though my focus was more squarely placed on academia (schools and colleges of education). Most of these academic departments now refer to themselves as "educational leadership." My colleague Vachel Miller works in one such department, and I had been asked to write a reply to an essay in which he expressed alarm over the growing influence of Eli Broad and his corporate model for training district and school administrators (Miller, 2012). While I do share those concerns, I remain unconvinced that the traditional university-based educational leadership programs that he seeks to defend from the likes of Broad have ever offered anything substantively different from what is being taught in Broad's Superintendents Academy. In fact, I've always viewed educational leadership to be one of the great oxymorons of our time, at least in terms of how it's actually been practiced by those in positions of authority. For example, how many educational leadership faculty within those university-based programs made Berliner and Biddle's *The Manufactured Crisis* (1996) required reading in the 1980s and 1990s? How many faculty within those programs openly and publicly challenged the ridiculous claims of the 1983 *A Nation at Risk* report? More recently, who within the Association for Supervision and Curriculum Development (ASCD) or the American Association of Colleges for Teacher Education (AACTE) challenged the 2010 Blue Ribbon Report from the National Council for the Accreditation of Teacher

Education (NCATE) entitled Transforming Teacher Education through Clinical Practice: A National Strategy to Prepare Effective Teachers?

Challenging the Medical Model and More

Should teacher-training programs really operate more like medical schools and require more hours of clinical experience? Rhetorically, such a prescription might sound appealing. It certainly plays on the prestige that our culture ascribes to medical doctors, but is that prestige really based on the actual performance of the medical community? Or is it based on our culture's materialism that gives doctors their esteemed social status because of their income? Did anyone in a position of educational leadership ask any of these questions? Did any of them consider the ramifications of a study published just prior to the NCATE report by the U.S. Health and Human Services Office of the Inspector General detailing how mistakes by medical care providers lead to around 15,000 deaths every month? Those same mistakes cost U.S. taxpayers about $4.4 billion each year (U.S. Department of Health and Human Services, 2010).

Why did no educational "leaders" tie these failures back to the professional preparation of doctors and nurses in the same way that low student test scores are tied to the preparation of teachers? Why is no one screaming for our nation's medical schools to be placed under greater scrutiny and held more accountable? While medical schools do require students to spend much more time in clinical experiences than do colleges of education, how many of those 15,000 deaths each month can we attribute to the excessive demands placed on medical students during their clinical experiences that drive so many of them to exhaustion, burnout, depression, and substance abuse?

Is this really the model that teacher education needs to follow? Is more clinical experience always better? Given the rate of errors leading to patient deaths, too much clinical experience might not be what's best for medical students or their patients. According to another study published in the same year as NCATE's "blue ribbon" report, we should all avoid being hospitalized any time during the month of July. According to statistics described in that report, July is the deadliest month to be admitted to a hospital. It also happens to be the month when most graduating MDs begin their residency programs (Rice, 2010). But almost no one within the educational leadership community raises these issues or challenges the dominant logic. Given their status, our educational leaders within higher education have been remarkably compliant in the face of the corporate assault on schools, and this compliance with an economistic and corporatist vision of education essentially spans the entire history of compulsory schooling.

Will Teacher Leaders Be Any Less Compliant?

Earlier, I claimed that "leadership implies both the autonomy/agency of a subject and a form of authority/ influence that flows from her exercise of that autonomy/agency. The ideas or acts that she creates must inspire followership and, frequently if not always, some form of change promised or offered by their vision." In other words, leadership always entails what Teresa Amabile identifies as "creativity relevant processes." Some of these processes, she explains, give expression to elements of a person's cognitive qualities, while others relate more directly to their personality. Cognitively, creative persons demonstrate "the ability to use wide, flexible categories for synthesizing information and the ability to break out of perceptual and performance 'scripts'" (Amabile, 2012, p. 4). Personality-wise, they demonstrate a great deal of self-discipline and, because creative tasks are open-ended by their very nature, "a tolerance for ambiguity" (Ibid). In combination, these two dimensions of creativity-relevant processes allow people to work independently, to take risks, and to bring fresh perspectives on problems that allow them to create new ideas. These qualities lay the foundation for creativity, which Amabile defines as "the production of a novel and appropriate response, product, or solution to an open-ended task" (p. 3). Creativity-related processes make up one third of components of creativity that she identifies as internal to the individual. The second entails domain-specific skills that contribute, I would argue, toward our becoming recognized as leaders in our fields when we demonstrate significant creativity in those fields. And finally, Amabile explains why she calls the "intrinsic motivation principle of creativity," which posits that people are most creative when they feel motivated primarily by the interest, enjoyment, satisfaction, and challenge of the work itself—and not by extrinsic motivators" (p. 4).

Domain-specific skills, the cognitive and personality dimensions of creativity-relevant processes, and intrinsic task motivation make up three of the components of Amabile's theory. They do not, however, exhaust it. They constitute only the internal (internal to the individual) components. She also identifies a fourth component essential to creative work that is external to the individual, namely, the social environment. To maximally nurture creative work, the social environment should stimulate a sense of positive challenge in the work, and it should include (a) work teams that are collaborative, diversely skilled, and idea-focused; (b) freedom in carrying out the work; (c) supervisors who encourage the development of new ideas; (d) top management that supports innovation through a clearly articulated creativity-encouraging vision and through appropriate recognition for creative work; (e) mechanisms for developing new ideas; and norms of actively sharing ideas across the organization (Amabile, 2012, p. 4).

These traits, however, seldom characterize the social environment of schools to encourage creative work among teachers, particularly since the rise of high-stakes testing and accountability in the 1980s. Under those pressures, an increasing number of districts have imposed scripted lesson plans on teachers, further restricting the professional autonomy they may have ever enjoyed in their work environments. Even more frequently have those traits been missing from the classroom learning environments created by teachers for students.

As Westby and Dawson (1995) explain, "One of the most consistent findings in educational studies of creativity has been that teachers dislike personality traits associated with creativity" (p. 1), Instead, "teachers prefer traits that seem to run counter to creativity, such as conformity and unquestioning acceptance of authority" (p. 1). These hardly represent the dispositions we'd associate with leadership, but Westby and Dawson help us recognize that there is a rich tradition of research supporting their conclusion. Among the studies they cite, we find works by Bachtold (1974), Cropley (1992), Dettmer (1981), Getzels and Jackson (1962), as well as Meyers and Torrance (1961).

In addition to citing Westby and Dawson, Kyung Hee Kim (2008) draws upon an equally impressive body of literature to support her conclusion that "research has shown that teachers are apt to prefer students who are achievers and teacher pleasers rather than disruptive or unconventional creative students" (p. 236). As she elaborates, Scott reported that teachers see creative children as a source of interference and disruption. Westby and Dawson found that teachers' judgment of their favorite students was negatively correlated with creativity. Teachers prefer students to exhibit traits such as unquestioning acceptance of authority, conformity, logical thinking, and responsibility that make students easy to manage in the classroom. Teachers' images of the ideal student emphasize traits that were conformist and socially acceptable (p. 236). All in all, due to the negative attitudes among a majority of teachers toward creativity, the environment of schools does little to encourage or reward leadership.

Hagen (1962), Myers and Torrance (1962), and Urick and Frymier (1963) help us extend beyond recognizing how teachers' attitudes have historically contributed to the creation of classroom norms that are hostile toward creativity as well as leadership. Their work helps us understand why those same attitudes work to ensure that the learning environments in our nation's system of compulsory schooling will likely never change. The majority of teachers deplore and resist change—and the teacher leadership that might foster it—as much as they deplore and punish creativity.

With regard to people's attitudes toward change, Hagen (1962) distinguished between two different personality types: innovational and authoritarian. His account of innovational personalities, it turns out, aligns neatly with Amabile's componential theory of creativity as well as the autonomy/agency dimension of leadership through which one gains authority/influence. Hagen described the innovational personality as demonstrating "an openness to experience, a confidence in one's own evaluations, a satisfaction in facing and resolving confusion or ambiguity, and a feeling that the world is orderly, and that the phenomenon of life can be understood and explained" (cited in Urick and Frymier, 1963, p. 109). Conversely, Urick and Frymier explain, Hagen viewed the authoritarian personality, the one most frequently demonstrated by teachers, as "characterized by a fear of using his initiative, an uncertainty concerning the quality of his own judgment, and tendency to avoid frustration and anxiety, an uneasiness in facing unresolved situations, and a tendency to see the world as arbitrary and capricious" (and therefore in dire need of management) (p. 109). If a leader viewed the world in this way, on what basis would they pursue innovation in hope of making positive change? How could they ever become recognized as a leader?

Studies by Myers and Torrance (1962) reveal that teachers who resist change demonstrated the characteristics of "authoritarianism, defensiveness, insensitivity to pupil needs, preoccupation with information-giving functions, intellectual inertness, disinterest in promoting initiative in pupils, and preoccupation with discipline" (cited in Urick and Frymier, 1963, p. 109). This latter authoritarian preoccupation with discipline reveals itself in the feedback received by teacher education programs on surveys of their graduates in response to the question, "If you could have had more instruction in one area during your years spent in teacher training, what would that area have been?" Invariably, in my twenty years of experience in teacher education, across four different institutions in four different states, the most frequent response to that question has always been "classroom management."

This tells me, in light of all the research revealing their authoritarian personality, that most teachers must view the work they demand of students as being a kind of necessary drudgery. They also view it as immutable. The nature of the work is not up for questioning or challenge. It's a given. It's not going to change, but why should it? The program worked for them when they were students in school. They went along with it, and their teachers rewarded them with gold stars and praise and, ultimately, high grades. How could there be anything wrong with the program? The problem must be with the students, particularly their motivation. Perhaps the gold stars don't work to motivate these students. We need to increase the extrinsic rewards to get them to work harder at completing their assigned tasks. Unfortunately, as Amabile and Kramer's (2010) research demonstrates, people tend not to be motivated by extrinsic rewards:

> Ask leaders what they think makes employees enthusiastic about work, and they'll tell you in no uncertain terms. In a recent survey we invited more than 600 managers from dozens of companies to rank the impact on employee motivation and emotions of five workplace factors commonly considered significant: recognition, incentives, interpersonal support, support for making progress, and clear goals. "Recognition for good work (either public or private)" came out number one. (Amabile and Kramer, 2010, p. 1)

Unfortunately, those managers are wrong.

Likewise, most teachers also believe that motivational issues need to be managed by external stimuli rather than addressed through the intrinsic qualities of the work they ask students to undertake. They, too, are wrong, and the learning/working environments they create in their classrooms frequently reflect many of the same traits Amabile (1998) associates with creativityand leadership-killing environments.

Conclusion: The Cycle of Compliance

Earlier, I stated that the idea of teacher leadership, as it is now used in the language of the new managerialism, involves a kind of denial. It allows teachers to deny that they are not actually leading. It creates an opportunity for them to deny acting in compliance, rather than leadership.

In Melissa Engleman's (2007) study of 213 graduate students in education with a median of 4 years of classroom teaching experience, for example, she found that more than half of her respondents fell into either the ISFJ (25%) or ESFJ (28%) personality type on the Humanetrics "Jung Typology" Test. Another 6% fell into the ESTJ type and 10% fell into the ISTJ type, for a total of 69% of the teachers fitting the SJ temperament profile. Keith Golay (1982) characterized SJs as "Actual Routine Learners" (ARLs). These people feel a need to establish and preserve social units, which fits with their demand for clear expectations and specific, clearly defined procedures for accomplishing a task. These traits align with their tendency to be meticulous as well as highly industrious. As students, ARLs also display a very strong need to please and receive approval from authority figures, including and especially their teachers. In turn, they hold authority figures in reverence, deferring to that authority through obedience and conformity (Golay, 1982, n.p.).

If we can accept Engleman's numbers as fairly representative of the broader population of those people who chose to enter teaching as a career, we can hypothesize that 70% of the classroom learning environments in America's system of compulsory schooling are created and maintained by Actual Routine Teachers (followers, mimickers). We can further hypothesize that those environments most heavily reward children who learn to revere the authority of teachers and who work diligently at their assigned tasks to win their approval through their obedience to and their conformity with the teacher's values and expectations. Because they experience these rewards from their teachers in these environments, ARLs/SJs might be more disposed toward choosing teaching as a career. In this case, they may embrace the notion and standards of teacher leadership, because they hear that they should, and they want to please the authority of those above them in the hierarchy. All the while, however, they will deny their own compliance while demanding compliance from others.

References

Amabile, T. M. (1998). How to kill creativity. *Harvard Business Review, 76*(5), 76–87.

Amabile, T. M. (2012). Componential theory of creativity. Harvard Business School. Working Paper Number 12–096. http://hbswk.hbs.edu/item/7011.html

Amabile, T. M., & Kramer, S. J. (2010, January). What really motivates workers? *Harvard Business Review, 88*(1), 44–45. http://www.hbs.edu/faculty/Pages/item.aspx? num=37331

Bachtold, L. (1974). The creative personality and the ideal pupil revisited. *Journal of Creative Behavior, 8*, 47–54.

Berliner, D. C., & Biddle, B. J. (1996). *The manufactured crisis: Myths, fraud, and the attack on America's public schools.* New York: Basic Books.

Cropley, A. J. (1992). *More ways than one: Fostering creativity.* Norwood, NJ: Ablex.

Dettmer, P. (1981). Improving teacher attitudes toward characteristics of the creatively gifted. *Gifted Child Quarterly, 25*, 11–16.

Eacott, S. (2014). *Educational leadership relationally: A theory and methodology for educational leadership, management and administration.* Rotterdam: Sense.

Engleman, M. (2007). Applying learning styles and personality preference information to online teaching pedagogy. *Journal of Interactive Instruction Development, 19*(3), 3–10.

Gabbard, D. (2013). Educational leadership or followership? *Democracy and Education, 21*(1), Article 8.

Getzels, J. W., & Jackson, P. W. (1962). *Creativity and intelligence.* New York: Wiley.

Golay, K. (1982). *Learning patterns and temperament styles.* Newport Beach, CA: Manas Systems.

Hagen, E. E. (1962). *On the theory of social change: How economic growth begins.* Belmont, CA: Dorsey Press.

Kim, K. L. (2008). "Underachievement and creativity: Are gifted underachievers highly creative?" *Creativity Research Journal, 20*(2), 235–242.

Miller, V. W. (2012). The broad challenge to democratic leadership: The other crisis in education. *Democracy and Education, 20*(2), Article 1.

Myers, R. E., & Torrance, E. P. (1961). Can teachers encourage creative thinking? *Educational Leadership, 19*, 156–159.

Rice, S. (2010, July 7). Are hospitals deadlier in July? CNN Health. http://articles.cnn.com/2010-07-07/health/hospital.deaths.july_1_medical-residents -medication-errors-medical-school?_s=PM:HEALTH

Torrance, E. P. (1963). The creative personality and the ideal pupil. *Teachers College Record, 65*, 220–226.

Torrance, E. P. (1965). *Rewarding creative behavior: Experiments in classroom creativity.* Englewood Cliffs, NJ: Prentice-Hall.

Urick R., & Frymier, J. R. (1963). Personalities, teachers and curriculum change. *Educational Leadership, 21*(2), 107–111.

U.S. Department of Health and Human Services. (2010). *Adverse events in hospitals: National incidence among Medicare beneficiaries.* Retrieved from http://oig.hhs.gov/oei/reports/oei-06-09-00090.pdf

Westby, E. L., & Dawson, V. L. (1995). Creativity: Asset of Burden in the Classroom. *Creativity Research Journal, 8*(1), 1–10.

Introduction to Second Edition

Eleanor J. Blair

When the best leader's work is done, the people say, "We did it ourselves!"—LAO-TZU

The concepts of *teacher leaders*, *teacher leadership*, and *leadership capacity building* are not new in the field of education. These terms began to emerge in the mid-1990s as the importance of principals and teachers working together on school improvement began to be recognized (Katzenmeyer & Moller, 2009; Lambert, 2003). Today, however, these concepts are dominating discussions regarding the roles and responsibilities of teachers in educational reform. Sweeping across the country are teacher leader courses that have, in effect, become the "new" foundations of education in both the undergraduate and graduate teacher education programs. Teacher leader courses, as they are currently conceptualized, include the study of the social, historical, and philosophical foundations of education as well as curriculum studies and leadership theory. These courses appear, on the surface, to be a fairly benign rendering of foundational information within the context of an examination of teacher leadership. However, I believe that the concept of teacher leaders is a radical notion that has the potential to profoundly impact the growth of a stronger, more resilient teaching profession.

Teachers, today, are committed professionals who are better educated than ever before, and yet they often enter a profession where their talents and enthusiasm are marginalized in the pursuit of higher test scores. Teachers know how to teach, and most have an understanding of student learning and classroom dynamics that far exceeds the knowledge base of the politicians, lobbyists, and even the administrators who seem intent on dictating the processes and procedures that will shape the daily lives of children and teachers. If teachers can be prepared to enter schools and embrace new opportunities to lead and collaborate with individuals both within and beyond the classroom, the possibilities for increased student learning are endless, and the reform of schools will simultaneously include a much overdue reform of the teaching profession.

Any discussion of teacher leadership must acknowledge the historical foundations of the profession of teaching. As Warren (1985), poignantly argued, "To call teaching a career in the nineteenth century would be misleading … for most, it was a part-time job taken up temporarily. School terms could be measured in weeks and those who taught tended to move on to other occupations or to marriage after a few years" (Finkelstein, 1970, qtd. in Warren, 1985, p. 6). In the twentieth century, the educational requirements for teachers increased, but the profession was seen, nevertheless, as a semi-profession (Lortie, 2002). Teacher salaries were notoriously low, and the status and autonomy granted to teachers were limited. In most schools, the teachers were primarily women, and the administrators were men. These gender differences were often accompanied by differentiated roles and responsibilities for teachers and administrators: administrators had power and authority over entire schools; teachers had *very limited* power and authority in their classrooms. This phenomenon led Tyack (1974) to refer to schools as "pedagogical harems" where male administrators ruled and teachers unquestioningly performed the tasks assigned to them. Within this context, teacher leadership was seen by many teachers as a noble term used to assign many mundane and decidedly "unnoble" duties to teachers in order to "free" the administrators to "lead" the schools. In these settings, teacher hostility often led to petty acts of rebellion that tended to reinforce the patriarchal role of administrators and the childlike dependency of female teachers. Teaching would never be a "real" profession as long as teachers were not granted the same respect and autonomy that other professionals routinely expect and enjoy. Indeed, herein lies the problem with teacher leadership: It is often misunderstood by teachers and administrators, and thus teachers are reluctant to seek out leadership roles, and administrators prefer to retain all of the power and authority that they now have in schools. Instead of seeing teaching and leadership as "two sides of the same coin," these skills are seen as separate and distinct entities that seldom exist in one individual. As one teacher recently asked, "Can I teach kindergarten and still be seen as a competent leader of both adults and children of all ages?" The answer should be yes, but the response to this question is usually accompanied by numerous caveats suggesting that a love of small children is not consistent with our ideas about whom we will allow to lead us.

Teacher leaders, as discussed by contemporary writers in the field of education, are defined quite differently. Katzenmeyer and Moller (2009) define teacher leaders as those who "lead within and beyond the classroom; identify with and contribute to a community of teacher learners and leaders; influence others toward improved educational practice; and accept responsibility for achieving the outcomes of their leadership" (p. 6). Lambert (2003) expands this definition by elaborating upon the idea of "leadership capacity" as a cornerstone of teacher leadership that involves "broad-based, skillful participation in the work of leadership" (p. 4). Taken together these two concepts set the parameters for a "new" kind of teaching profession where "professional development is as much about *adult* learning as student learning," and "teacher leadership does not replace, but rather augments, principal leadership" (Lieberman, 2003, p. viii). Thinking about teaching in these ways represents a revisioning of the teaching profession as a place where teachers can begin to confront the obstacles that have impeded the growth of the teaching profession: "Some of these obstacles are related to gender bias, but others are more personal, related to narrow definitions of leadership roles and responsibilities within schools and communities" (Hilty, 1999, p. 167). If teacher leaders and leadership capacity building were seriously embraced by schools and communities across the nation, our ability to work thoughtfully and collaboratively to reform the schools would be radically enhanced. The voices of all major stakeholders, teachers, administrators, parents, and students would be a part of the conversation and the effort to change schools today. Rather than piecemeal, disconnected efforts to reform the schools, teachers would "step up" and lead efforts that are based on the knowledge and skills of experienced teachers and reflect the needs and desires of our most important constituents: parents and students.

The second edition of this book expands on the ideas presented in the first edition with the addition of an entire section on teacher leadership and social justice. Too often, educators talk about leadership generally and teacher leadership specifically as if it is a set of skills, knowledge, and dispositions that operate in a vacuum with no ideological foundation, and that is a mistake. Twenty-first-century teacher leadership has the potential to transform both schools and the teaching profession; however, this vision must be shaped by a set of beliefs and values that define what is most important in our work. Roland Barth (2001) makes reference to one simple definition of teacher leadership, "Making happen what you believe in" (p. 446). Knowing what you believe in as a teacher, knowing what you want to make happen in schools and classrooms is fundamental to transformative and sustainable change initiated by teachers acting as leaders in schools and classrooms.

In addition to the material on teacher leadership and social justice, the second edition is reorganized and presents new work being published on teacher leadership. Teacher leadership is an accepted part of most school reform efforts, and the writers presented in this book are key players in that discussion. The second edition of the book is divided into five sections, and each section includes an introduction and questions for critical reflection on the essays. This book presents a variety of perspectives on the changing roles and responsibilities of teacher leaders and the potential of teacher leadership to transform the teaching profession as well as the quality of teaching and learning in all schools. Thus, it is hoped that the reading of these essays will be accompanied by a lively, and critical, discussion of the roles and responsibilities of teacher leaders in twenty-first-century schools.

References

Barth, R. (2001). Teacher leader. *Phi Delta Kappan, 82*(6), 443–449.

Finkelstein, B. J. (1970). *Governing the young: Teacher behavior in American primary schools, 1820–1880.* Unpublished doctoral dissertation, Teachers College, Columbia University.

Hilty, E. B. (1999). Southern schools, southern teachers: Redefining leadership in rural communities. In D. Chalker (Ed.), *Leadership for rural schools: Lessons for all educators* (pp. 157–171). Lancaster, PA: Technomic.

Katzenmeyer, M., & Moller, G. (2009). *Awakening the sleeping giant* (3rd ed.). Thousand Oaks, CA: Corwin.

Lambert, L. (2003). *Leadership capacity for lasting school improvement.* Alexandria, VA: Association for Supervision and Curriculum Development.

Lieberman, A. (2003). Foreword. In L. Lambert, *Leadership capacity for lasting school improvement.* Alexandria, VA: Association for Supervision and Curriculum Development.

Lortie, D. (2002). *Schoolteacher* (2nd ed.). Chicago: University of Chicago Press.

Tyack, D. (1974). *The one best system: A history of American urban education.* Cambridge, MA: Harvard University Press.

Warren, D. (1985). Learning from experience: History and teacher education. *Educational Researcher, 14*(10), 5–12.

SECTION 1

Teacher Leadership and Social Justice

Introduction

Teacher leaders working to make social justice an essential part of twenty-first-century schools inevitably confront political and social agendas that are in direct conflict with efforts to create educational contexts that are responsive to the needs of diverse students and their families. These efforts are often lost in the myriad roadblocks created by politicians and bureaucrats who focus on self-interests rather than the broader needs of society. This conflict is obvious in the daily, and all too familiar, struggles surrounding power, authority, and advocacy in the increasingly bureaucratic school–industrial complex. In Weiler's (1988) study of women teachers and administrators, she found:

> They inherit positions in already existing, highly complex institutions … . Feminist and antiracist teachers and administrators who seek to redefine curriculum and social relationships inside and outside the classroom find themselves in conflict with existing patriarchal ideology and hierarchical relationships. (p. 101)

Since 1988, little has changed. The same conservative patriarchal ideologies and hierarchical relationships are alive and well in schools today and impact every level of pedagogical decision-making. However, today's teachers are better educated than ever before and uniquely qualified to assume leadership roles that have an ideological component that would shape the direction of discussions regarding how, what, and where we teach as well as notions about teachers' roles and responsibilities as leaders in the reform of twenty-first-century schools.

Cochran-Smith (1991) conceptualized the notion of "teaching against the grain" in the following way:

> Teaching against the grain stems from, but also generates, critical perspectives on the macro-level relationships of power, labor, and ideology-relationships that are perhaps best examined at the university, where sustained and systematic study is possible. But teaching against the grain is also deeply embedded in the culture and history of teaching at individual schools and in the biographies of particular teachers

and their individual or collaborative efforts to alter curricula, raise questions about common practices, and resist inappropriate decisions. These relationships can only be explored in schools in the company of experienced teachers who are themselves engaged in complex, situation-specific, and sometimes losing struggles to work against the grain. (p. 280)

Thus, for teachers acting as leaders, the tasks are not easy. Teacher leaders are not the norm, and their efforts require a combination of skill, courage, and ideological commitment to "lead against the grain," both within and beyond the school. However, in effect, a teacher leader must see herself as a change agent, not just in the classroom, but in the many different venues associated with the role of teacher. Teachers must challenge current thinking about schools and "push" to get major stakeholders to "make the familiar strange, and the strange familiar" in the examination of *how* and *what* occurs in the name of public education. Knowledge is politically influenced, and therefore objectivity is limited in most educational decision-making. Public schools clearly work better for some populations of students than others; and so, ideologically committed teacher leaders are required to guide our discussions of what needs to happen to make schools work better for everyone, but especially for those children who depend most heavily on the public schools for the provision of fair and equitable educational opportunities. A commitment to equity, justice, and advocacy for all students is nonnegotiable; there is no middle ground or place in public education for anything else. Our schools have the opportunity, resources, knowledge, and skills to create a model system of education, and yet we have grown accustomed to routinely accepting a pervasive mediocrity that does nothing to intervene and shift the rising tide of school failure. Teachers who "lead against the grain" will demand a "school culture" that encourages critical pedagogical innovations that require teachers to be both scholars and researchers when it comes to defining what works and what does not work in schools and classrooms that are committed to overturning school failure and promoting success for all students.

Many "voices" must contribute to the meaningful reform of schools, and the voices of teacher leaders are an essential conduit between societal needs and the needs of children and their families. Teacher knowledge regarding the chasm between the values, beliefs, and attitudes of the school and those of the community is a key piece of information that is important to any serious efforts to facilitate a critical examination of schools and simultaneously encourage the examination of the familiar, but often strange, policies and procedures that guide how we "do schools." This kind of understanding is fundamental to changing the schools, and ultimately it has the potential to initiate the kind of thinking that will revolutionize efforts to provide a quality education for ALL children in ALL schools.

The four essays in this section of the book represent a consideration of ideas that connect the political and philosophical ideals associated with social justice to the work done by teacher leaders. As stated at the beginning of this introduction, teachers' work is political, and for many novice teachers, there is an absence of discussion regarding the gap between their commitment to social justice ideals and the realities of their work in public schools. The essays by Cambron-McCabe and McCarthy, Carr, Kose, and Picower offer a range of views from the theoretical to the practical regarding the relationship between social justice and leadership. These authors define and provide examples of social justice in practice and place it within the context of teacher leadership in a way that is seldom encountered in the educational literature. As such, the addition of this section to the book reflects a personal belief that effective and meaningful teacher leadership must reflect ideological commitments to justice, equity, and advocacy; commitments that ultimately have the potential to transform the lives of students and their families through public education.

References

Cochran-Smith, M. (1991). Learning to teach against the grain. *Harvard Educational Review, 61*(3), 279–307.
Weiler, K. (1988). *Women teaching for change: Gender, class and power.* South Hadley, MA: Bergin & Garvey.

CHAPTER 1

Educating School Leaders for Social Justice

Nelda Cambron-McCabe and Martha M. McCarthy

G rave concerns exist about leadership preparation programs' lack of relevance in preparing school leaders to address the crisis conditions facing many children and schools in this country. As the efficacy of existing preparation programs is questioned, specific concerns also are raised about the extent to which social justice issues are being considered in the development of new approaches and standards for preparing leaders. Although policy makers express a concern for creating more just, equitable schools, new standards and licensure requirements do not explicitly encompass social justice concerns (Marshall, 2001; Oliva, 2001).

The prevalence of social justice language in educational settings and scholarship portends a new movement with as many meanings as actors on the scene. This visibility is cause for celebration as well as unease. With popular use, both liberals and conservatives have embraced the term social justice to rationalize similar as well as polar opposite strategies. In the policy arena, educational accountability policies tend to construct the meaning of social justice in narrow market-based terms that attempt to remedy the so-called deficits students from diverse backgrounds bring to school (Marshall & Parker, 2009). When policy makers are asked to identify social justice elements in their states, they point to high academic standards and stringent assessment strategies (Cambron-McCabe, 2009; Marshall & McCarthy, 2002). Consequently, elimination of the achievement gap between Caucasian students and students of color has become the signifier for the political commitment to fairness and equal educational opportunity. The by-product of this policy discourse of accountability, standards, and quality is safe language that eschews more controversial confrontations about race, class, gender, sexual orientation, and systemic inequities (Cambron-McCabe, 2009). In this climate, school administrators desiring to create inclusive, just schools find themselves constrained by rules, regulations, and state controls (Foster, 2004).

Within a social justice context, school leaders are being called on to take up the role of transformative intellectuals, public intellectuals, or critical intellectuals—that is, individuals who engage in critical analysis of conditions that have perpetuated historical inequities in schools and who work to change institutional structures and culture (Burrello, Lashley, & Beatty, 2001; Dantley & Tillman, 2009; Foster, 2004; Giroux, 1997). But traditional leadership preparation programs and licensure requirements give only token consideration to social justice concerns (Marshall, 2004). In this chapter we examine the emerging social justice discourse in the educational administration field and discuss its implications for reconceptualizing preparation programs for more just schooling. We begin by delineating the multiple dimensions of social justice leadership, particularly noting its broad construction not only as the identification of institutional and societal inequities affecting race, gender, sexual orientation, and disability but also as the assumption of an activist role for school and social change. Next, we explore several issues that are significant in preparing school leaders for social justice critique and activism. We conclude with a discussion of the implications for educational administration faculties and programs.

An Emergent Social Justice Discourse

Social justice scholarship and conversations have become prominent in leadership journals and conferences. Momentum intensified in the educational administration field in 1999 when 140 scholars convened by Catherine Marshall organized as Leadership for Social Justice. These scholars targeted their research and practice on creating an understanding and capacity to do social justice work. An impressive body of work has amassed during 4 years that gives educational administration programs grounding to articulate more clearly what social justice means and how the field might move these ideas into the practice of leadership.[1]

Social justice is informed by multidisciplinary inquiry that struggles to accommodate distinct ontological and epistemological foundations. Tensions arise as some perspectives are validated and others are excluded. In creating a new social justice discourse for leadership, we argue that educational administration scholars must engage in an ongoing critical dialogue drawing on diverse theoretical perspectives. Although structural-functional and positivist research paradigms continue to influence inquiry in educational administration, alternative social justice perspectives have emerged under the banners of multicultural leadership, feminist leadership, critical African American and Latino leadership traditions, and so on (Dantley, 2003; Larson & Murtadha, 2002; Lopez, 2003). These critiques move us from merely an examination and naming of inequities to intentional action to make radical, fundamental changes in societal structures, including schools.

Social justice scholarship in educational leadership exhibits some broad, common themes. Scholars emphasize moral values, justice, respect, care, and equity; always in the forefront is a consciousness about the impact of race, class, gender, sexual orientation, and disability on schools and students' learning (Dantley & Tillman, 2009).[2] Foster's (1986) early work in critical theory echoes through this emerging social justice discourse. The crucial questions for Foster involved what ends are being pursued, whom do they benefit, and whom do they harm. The unmasking of the distortions around us, however, was only the beginning of his critique. He maintained that leadership must be critically educative: "It can not only look at the conditions in which we live, but it also must decide how to change them" (Foster, 1986, p. 185). This call for activism to challenge entrenched institutional structures reproduced by the dominant culture unites a number of other scholars (Bogotch, 2002; Goldfarb & Grinberg, 2002; Grogan, 2004; Gruenewald, 2003; Marshall, 2004).

In deepening and expanding the social justice discourse, some educational leadership scholars argue that race and racism in society must become a central and integral aspect of the leadership knowledge base (Donmoyer, Imber, & Scheurich, 1995; Lopez, 2003; Parker, Deyhle, & Villanas, 1999). When race is included in preparation programs, typically the emphasis focuses on a surface level of inequitable treatment as opposed to probing the pervasive and systemic nature of racism in society (Donmoyer et al., 1995; Lopez, 2003). Critiques of racism too often lead to "decontextualized and deracialized political theory of conflict, yielding a sanitized view of racial politics in the United States" (Lopez, 2003, p. 77) that produces racially neutral understandings of policies and schools. New legal scholarship in critical race theory (CRT) directs attention to the invisibility of racism and through counternarratives portrays racial realities rather than the dominant privileged stories (Delgado & Stefancic, 2001; Lopez, 2003; Parker et al., 1999). This scholarship adds an important dimension to the social justice discourse; CRT stresses that laws alone will not alter racism and that the values and knowledge underpinning a racially neutral construction of democracy work to maintain racism.

Other contested terrain with implications for a social justice discourse includes gender and sexual orientation. Today's battles in statehouses over gay marriages point to the deeply contentious issues in this arena. News reports highlight how devastating the violence and harassment can be for queer students in public schools. Courts grapple with defining rights in the absence of specific constitutional language. Lugg (2003) reminded the educational administration field that protecting students and educators from harassment because of gender or sexual orientation, although important, is not social justice. Drawing on queer legal theory, she attempted to illuminate legal and regulatory systems that privilege and enforce heterosexuality and other forms of oppression. Again, school leaders and scholars are urged to take an activist stance in making deep structural issues around gender and sexual orientation explicit as they work to change them.

The emerging social justice discourse calls on school leaders to question the assumptions that drive school policies and practices to create more equitable schooling. To meet this challenge, school leadership programs must prepare new leaders to critically inquire into the taken-for-granted structures and norms that often pose insurmountable barriers to many students' academic success.

Issues Affecting Leadership for Social Justice

From our perspective, four broad issues must be carefully considered in any serious attempt to reconceptualize what it means to lead with a concern for social justice in today's schools. School conditions reveal that expectations for leaders have shifted substantially, but we continue to prepare administrators for traditional roles in traditional school settings (see Hess & Kelly, 2005). At this juncture, educational administration scholars can help shape radically new roles and expectations for school leaders; inequitable practices and conditions demand fundamental changes in the ways we think about school reform and leadership. Reform issues around the standards movement, selection of leaders, student achievement gap, and privatization of education may simply reinforce and tighten the present system that marginalizes many students and educators.

The Standards Movement

Standards-based reforms create new challenges regarding both the assessment of leadership preparation programs and the alignment of these programs with social justice commitments. The standards movement, accompanied by high-stakes testing, affects virtually every level of education from K–12 schooling to teacher and administrator preparation. The standards drive the curriculum, and standards-based tests are used as prerequisites to grade promotion, high school graduation, and teacher and administrator licensure. This movement has evoked substantial controversy. Some view these reforms as the best strategy to ensure that no child is left behind (see Paige, 2003). They contend that equal educational opportunities will be realized if schools are held accountable for all students achieving the standards, but others argue that these developments are hindering the creation of vibrant and intellectually challenging education programs at all levels (see Gronn, 2002). These critics assert that standards-based school reforms have replaced efforts to achieve diverse student populations.

Standards-based reforms for school leaders focus on the standards developed by the Interstate School Leaders Licensure Consortium (ISLLC). The ISLLC standards address the school leader's role in connection with developing a shared vision of learning; sustaining a school culture conducive to learning; ensuring appropriate management of school operations and resources; facilitating collaboration with families to respond to diverse needs; acting with integrity and fairness; and responding to the schools' political, social, economic, legal, and cultural context. As of 2004, about four-fifths of the states had adopted the ISLLC standards for administrative licensure or had developed their own standards based on ISLLC.

Standards for school leaders have been proposed by various professional organizations and government agencies over time, but the current standards movement, based on the ISLLC model, differs in several respects. First, these standards focus attention on the centrality of student learning as each begins with the notation that school administrators are school leaders who promote success for all students (Council of Chief State School Officers, 1996).

Second, there has been surprising agreement among educators and policy makers on the validity of the ISLLC standards. Many state policy makers view ISLLC and other standards-based reforms as the solution to problems associated with school leadership and university preparation programs (Marshall & McCarthy, 2002). National and state criteria for the accreditation of educational leadership preparation programs, including the *Standards for Advanced Programs in Educational Leadership* of the National Council for Accreditation of Teacher Education (NCATE), reflect the ISLLC standards. In fact, the Educational Leadership Constituent Council (ELCC), which includes representatives from all national practitioner organizations focusing on school leadership, has merged its standards with ISLLC and NCATE for use in accrediting leadership preparation programs. The major thrust of this consolidation is for leadership preparation program accreditation and administrative licensure to be based on performance measures in line with the ISLLC standards (Cibulka, 2004; National Policy Board for Educational Administration, 2000). By 2004, ELCC had reviewed 178 educational leadership programs, of which 137 (77%) achieved "national recognition" status (Cibulka, 2004, p. 3).

Despite the consensus among policy makers regarding the merits of standards-based education reforms, this movement also has critics (Bracey, 2000; Merrow, 2001). The very act of creating standards, noted Gronn (2002), is an inherently biased process in which preference is given to a particular perspective and other points of view are silenced. The ISLLC standards have not been universally embraced in the field of educational administration (English, 2000; Furman, 2000; Maxcy, 2000). Specifically, questions have been raised about whether the standards give sufficient attention to social justice issues such as diversity and whether they represent a negative reduction toward a single correct method (English, 2004).

Standards, of course, lack significant meaning without valid mechanisms to determine that the standards have been met. The assessments used to determine that standards are satisfied, however, do not necessarily produce fair results whether for K-12 students or for teacher and administrator licensure. For example, studies indicate that African Americans score an average of one standard deviation below Caucasians on teacher licensure tests (Hedges & Nowell, 1998; Mitchell, Robinson, Plake, & Knowles, 2001). Similarly, slightly more than 40% of the Caucasian applicants receive certification from the National Board for Professional Teaching Standards, whereas only about 11% of African American applicants are successful (Bond, 1998). These data have dramatic implications for the racial composition of public school personnel in our nation. At a time when student bodies are becoming increasingly diverse, the opposite trend may occur among public educators, partially as a result of assessment tests used as a prerequisite to licensure.

A standards-driven paper-and-pencil test is the most popular strategy used to assess that school leaders meet the ISLLC standards. Thirteen states condition administrative licensure on the passage of the School Leaders Licensure Assessment (SLLA), a performance-based assessment developed by the Education Testing Service (ETS). A number of other states are considering the adoption of the SLLA. This instrument consists of a set of vignettes to which individuals respond. The test is then evaluated by a national group of trained assessors based on predetermined criteria. In some states professional standards boards link accreditation of leadership preparation programs to how well their students perform on the SLLA. Thus, the stakes are extremely high for everyone involved.

In the near future, across most states, the successful passage of SLLA may very well become a prerequisite to administrative licensure, an exit examination in university preparation programs, and/

or a criterion for program accreditation. If so, the ETS instrument will greatly influence the content and components of school leadership preparation programs. Universities will be forced to align their admissions process and curriculum with the high-stakes test. This does not necessarily mean that preparation programs will be narrowed or negatively affected if we are certain that SLLA measures what is considered essential for moral leaders who can guide schools toward becoming humane, challenging, learning-centered communities (McCarthy, 2002b).

Yet, many critics are concerned that current assessment instruments, like SLLA, do not give individuals the opportunity to demonstrate some important leadership behaviors such as tolerance, creativity, vision, and commitment to social justice (Bracey, 2000). Merrow (2001) declared that "bad tests, used to make high-stakes decisions, are the enemy of good (i.e., high) standards" (p. 653). In short, assuming the standards are appropriate (which continues to be debated), if the tests that assess whether they are met are poorly written, biased, or not aligned with the intent of the standards, the process will not be effective. Fears are voiced that reliance on SLLA and similar tests to judge both individuals and leadership preparation programs could take educational leadership preparation in detrimental directions and impede efforts to increase diversity among our public school educators (English, 2000, 2004).

Nonetheless, the standards movement, and its direct link to high-stakes testing, is the dominant strategy to improve the quality of education at the present time. Indeed, high-stakes assessments of students, teachers, and school leaders currently are being used to judge the value of pre-K–12 schools and their school personnel, issue school rankings and report cards, determine which schools must provide their students other educational options, and make personnel decisions. Foster (2004) has urged scholars to problematize this metanarrative that is defining the story of how and why schools exist in terms of global competitiveness and economic dominance. School leaders and those preparing them must create counternarratives that emphasize social justice and provide a space for local initiatives and for reinventing democratic processes (Foster, 2004).

Selection of Leaders

Who will lead schools may be one of the most critical challenges and one of the most important opportunities to influence social justice. Marshall (2004) characterized the current turnover in school administrators as "never a better time" to prepare new leaders for social justice (p. 10). She noted that by 2010 numerous surveys show that the profession will essentially be repopulated. This raises questions about who will fill the positions, what they will do, and how will they do it?

Faced with a short supply of qualified administrator candidates in the pipeline in many school systems as well as an interest in recruiting more minority and women applicants, states are exploring a range of strategies such as removing barriers for noneducators and recent retirees to assume these roles, establishing administrative internship programs for teachers, redesigning administrative positions, providing financial and other incentives, and recruiting administrators from other states. Florida, for example, has omitted the credentialing process for school administrators (see Herrington & Wills, 2005). California has considered a bill to expedite the credentialing process. The California fast-track program proposes to enable individuals to demonstrate their administrative skills through rigorous testing rather than by completing extensive university coursework. Little is known, however, about whether such expedited programs adequately prepare future administrators to identify systemic inequities and engage in their eradication (see Hess & Kelly, 2005).

Some school districts are establishing partnerships with universities to develop collaborative training programs for aspiring principals to increase the pool of qualified candidates and to ensure a stronger practitioner voice in the nature of the preparation (see Goldring & Sims, 2005). Often collaboration not only involves joint development of the courses and experiences but also shared delivery of the courses (see Cambron-McCabe, Cunningham, Harvey, & Koff, 2005). Such efforts offer the potential to confront embedded injustices that may exist in specific school sites. Collecting and analyzing data related to a particular school and school district enables educators to actually do equity-focused work (Skrla, Scheurich, Garcia, & Nolly, 2004). These collaborative programs, however, are not numerous and are found primarily in urban areas.

Central to the question of who will lead is what do we mean by leadership? If we accept that a school leader's role is developing and maintaining a clear focus on a core purpose embedded in student learning and that the leader engages directly in the improvement of teaching and learning, it is reasonable to posit that expertise in instructional practices and curriculum content must be central in our selection of leaders. Aggressive and intentional recruitment of teachers who possess demonstrated high-quality instructional skills can expand the candidate pool for administrative positions and provide greater potential for increasing the number of women and administrators of color in leadership positions.

Elmore (2000) asserted, "If public schools survive, leaders will look very different from the way they presently look, both in who leads and what these leaders do" (p. 3). The present ferment over this new conception of leadership provides an opportunity to reconsider within a social justice discourse what it means to lead in schools where student learning, rather than the management of daily operations, is the heart of the work. Thus far we have only tinkered around the edges of this dilemma by attempting to incorporate elements of instructional leadership into the traditional principal role. What if we start with inventing new roles directed at student learning (Boris-Schacter & Langer, 2002)? This would help us avoid the trap of responding to these new challenges with old approaches and traditional roles. Buchen (2000) has argued that it is time to give up on "trying to save or keep intact roles and institutions that no longer are fluid, aspirational, and future driven" (p. 35). If we desire to create learning organizations "where people continually expand their capacity to create the results they truly desire, where new and expansive patterns of thinking are nurtured, where collective aspiration is set free, and where people are continually learning how to learn together" (Senge, 1990, p. 3), radical action is required.

From a social justice perspective, the greatest challenge for the educational administration field may be to shift its mental model of what it means to be a school leader rather than a school administrator. Usdan (2002) has posed several questions that are helpful in reframing the roles and responsibilities of school leaders:

> If the criteria for success have changed in terms of our expectations of school administrators, how can we meaningfully reshape the substance and role of preparatory programs? If principals and superintendents are to be assessed on the basis of their ability to raise test scores, how can the jobs be constructively and realistically reconfigured? For example, could successful teachers begin to serve as instructional leaders enabling principals to discharge their important customary responsibilities as leaders who work with parents and the community on political and management issues that certainly cannot be ignored in schools? Is it time to rethink the assumption that one individual can or should handle such diverse administrative responsibilities? (p. 302)

Clearly, this reconceptualization of who will lead and what they will do reaches far beyond university administrator preparation programs to teacher preparation, school communities, and state policy makers as teachers' roles are also redefined. Goodlad (1990) has asserted that a critical moral dimension of schooling requires teachers as well as principals to provide responsible moral stewardship of schools. That is, if student learning and the school site are pivotal points for renewal, teachers play a central role in creating and sustaining school-wide change, not simply improving efforts in their own classrooms. This reconceptualization of roles involves more than improving current practice; it requires rethinking those practices and taking action to implement new ones within a more just, democratic context. Accordingly, it represents a significant shift regarding who will fill leadership roles and what they will do in those roles.

The Achievement Gap

The focus on educational accountability has revealed the startlingly large performance gap between African American, Latino, and economically disadvantaged students and Caucasian students, particularly from middle- and upper-income families. For example, Haycock (2001) has noted that African American and Latino students' mean 12th-grade math and reading skills are comparable to those of Caucasian eighth graders. Substantial differences exist among groups not only in achievement but also in completion of high school and college. And, these gaps are wider than they were a decade ago (Fuller, 1998). Haycock has maintained that the gaps exist because "we take the students who have less to begin with and then systematically give them less in school" (p. 8). The differences show up in the curriculum taught, the resources spent, how teachers are assigned, and achievement expected.

Despite its critics, the school accountability movement has focused attention on the widening achievement gap among students and related equity concerns. It is no longer possible to conceal through aggregate data reports what we have known all along—achievement patterns vary markedly among different groups of students. The inability of schools to close this gap prompted Congress to pass the No Child Left Behind Act (2002). The Act tightens the assessment side of schooling and provides options for children stuck in failing schools. Under intense pressure from both the federal and state levels, school leaders are struggling with substantive and strategic approaches to achieve equity for poor and minority children.

Marshall (2001) noted in her North Carolina study of administrative licensure that state officials see the closing of the achievement gap as the way to address social justice. Some research has shown that illuminating the achievement gap is an important step in challenging the so-called deficit-thinking of school leaders by clearly showing that all children are not being served well (Reyes, Scribner, & Paredes Scribner, 1999; Skrla & Scheurich, 2001).[3] But critics assert that simply disaggregating test scores by race and class will not ensure a better education for poor and minority children. McNeil (2000), for example, cautioned that the intense emphasis on the achievement gap may actually worsen the current inequities for minority students as schools focus on test results and narrow educational opportunities. Anderson (2004) echoed this perspective, noting that if equity is locally lodged in classrooms and schools "we may end up legitimating the larger persistent social inequities [thereby] distracting attention and energy from the larger political movements needed to bring about real social change" (p. 255).

Confounding the social justice issues related to student achievement is a recent report showing that school districts educating the largest number of poor and minority children receive less state and local money than school districts educating the least number of poor and minority children (Orlofsky, 2002). At a time when it is imperative to provide a rigorous curriculum, quality teachers, intense professional development, and more instructional time, many school districts do not have adequate resources to meet the higher standards. The funding gap represents a major state-policy issue that cannot be separated from the efforts to close the achievement gap in school districts facing the greatest disparities (Dantley & Cambron-McCabe, 2001; Rusch, 2001).

In the face of the growing social inequality in the nation, how do we link educational equity and social equity? What skills do leaders need to engage the school and the community in confronting social justice issues? How do we avoid the trap of confusing gains in test scores with substantive educational improvement?

Privatization of Education

Schools naturally are a place where values and ideas are transmitted to youth. The original intent of the American common school was to ensure an educated citizenry and to inculcate democratic values in its students. Although the promise of the common school has not been fully realized, political rhetoric has maintained a national commitment to safeguarding the collective welfare of our children through public education. In reality, however, the trend toward privatizing education poses a significant threat to the fulfillment of public education's promise. This recent shift toward privatization presents noteworthy challenges for schools, their leaders, and those preparing school leaders, and it has important social justice implications. Bauman (1996) has contended that greater consumer control of education entails a reduced governmental role in providing services and "a belief in efficiency and individuality over equity and community" (p. 627). Commenting that schools increasingly are seen as a private rather than public good, Giroux (2003) observed that schools, therefore, "are concerned less with demands of equity, justice, and social citizenship than with the imperatives of the marketplace, skill-based learning, and the needs of the individual" (p. 76).

Educational-choice strategies range from purely public models (e.g., theme-based magnet programs that remain public schools) to purely private models (e.g., state-supported vouchers available for private-school tuition). Regardless of the approach, each of these choice options has significant implications for the values and ideas that our schools transmit to students. School leaders and those preparing them need to understand these implications and be involved in policy discussions about strategies to open education to the marketplace.

Recent federal initiatives show increased support for a marketplace model of education, including public support for private schools. The federal government's current emphasis on providing educational options for families in the No Child Left Behind Act (2002) is based on the premise that competition, including private options, can improve educational opportunities and ultimately the academic performance of all children. Indeed, $77 million in the Bush administration's discretionary fund, which does not have to be approved by Congress, is channeled toward organizations that champion private education, including homeschooling (Merrow, 2004).

States have also shown an increased interest in providing greater education options for parents, particularly low-income parents, through various marketplace models of schooling. Murphy (1999) has argued that consumer-based control of education can be viewed as a logical next stage in the evolution of school governance. With confidence in public-sector educational monopolies dwindling, the public pressure for opening education to the marketplace is increasing (see Boyd & Miretzky, 2003; Hill, 2002; Lewis, 1993; Richards, Shore, & Sawicky, 1996). The marketplace is viewed by some as the only way to provide options for the poor that the rich traditionally have enjoyed. In fact, schoolchoice initiatives in some locales have created strange bedfellows in that conservative citizen groups have joined forces with parents of color to support efforts to open education to the marketplace.

Despite mounting public interest, critics of marketplace models of education argue that consumer choices should not drive the educational enterprise. More specifically, some fear that the privatization of education will hinder efforts to diversify and democratize American schools (Fowler, 1991). Because families will select schools with staff members and students who look like them and think as they do, this will decrease diversity within schools. Giroux (2003) has further argued that the corporatized model of education "cancels out the democratic ideals and practices of civil society by either devaluing or absorbing them within the logic of the market" (p. 79).

Substantial current attention focuses on various voucher proposals under which families would receive a state voucher of a designated amount per child that can be redeemed at a public or private school of their choice.[4] States may be reluctant to adopt voucher plans to fund all education because students currently supported by their families in private schools or home education programs would receive state support under a general voucher program. However, targeted voucher plans, focusing on disadvantaged students or those attending deficient public schools, are likely to increase and are currently being considered in about half of the states.

Unlike states' hesitation to adopt comprehensive voucher systems to fund education, most have enthusiastically enacted charter school legislation during the past few years. In 1992 only two states—Minnesota and California—had passed charter school legislation, but by December, 2003, charter school legislation had been passed in 40 states, Washington, D. C., and Puerto Rico (Education Commission of the States, 2002; U.S. Charter Schools, 2003). Charter school laws vary greatly across states, but most relax state regulations for schools that are granted charters by state or local education agencies or state universities. Most charter school laws place a cap on the number of charters that will be awarded, and some place restrictions on the types of entities that can apply (e.g., nonsectarian and nonprofit groups).

Private companies presently manage about 10% of the charter schools nationally, and several virtual or online charter schools have been established. Critics of corporate involvement in schools contend that some important features of the school program, including the values and desires of the local community, may be neglected with so much riding on the companies' reaching their target objectives (McCarthy, 2002a).

School leaders, those preparing them, and policy makers need to understand the values guiding various models to privatize education because current decisions in this regard will affect the next generation of students and beyond. Consumer-driven education, with its focus on individual choice and advancement, differs greatly from the government-run common school that focuses on promoting the nation's general welfare. Moreover, these privatization strategies have important social justice implications for education as individual schools will become more homogeneous because they are designed to appeal to only a portion of the market. This could have a negative impact on efforts to promote diversity and respect for those with different backgrounds and beliefs. Clearly, each of these choice-based models provides a vision for our educational system; these competing visions must be questioned and carefully examined.

School leaders will face very different educational environments and challenges in the age of school privatization. Leadership preparation programs need to explore the potential for the school privatization movement to alter the purposes and basic structure of schooling in our nation. If school privatization becomes dominant, the change in the nature of education in our nation could be as momentous as the common school movement in the 1800s.

Implications for the Preparation of School Leaders

As our field debates how school leaders should be prepared, attention often focuses primarily on the effectiveness and efficiency of schools. This narrow conversation results in the identification of specific skills and performances that potential administrators must exhibit—frequently ignoring knowledge that cannot be quantified. We are not contesting the importance of technical expertise; however, failure to prepare administrators to engage in difficult work that requires a shift in values, attitudes, and behaviors within the school community severely limits their ability to address fundamental social justice issues. Giroux (1993) has urged educational leadership faculty to create "a new language capable of asking new questions and generating more critical practices" (p. 37). He has noted that "such a language would have to reformulate traditional notions of authority, ethics, power, culture, and pedagogy" (p. 37). The emerging social justice discourse provides a means to create this language and to focus directly on concerns about equity, student achievement, diversity, privilege, and social responsibility.

For educational leadership preparation programs to promote a social justice orientation, they must develop in their students what McKenzie and Scheurich (2004) have called *practiced reflexivity*, where individuals consciously take responsibility for their actions—recognizing that all actions have an impact on the community. McKenzie and Scheurich further have noted that the school leader's job requires a constant, vigilant critical perspective that always asks these questions:

> What are we doing? Why are we doing it? What do we value? Why do we value what we do? How are our values evident or not evident in our practice? How is what we're doing affecting all students? Is what we're doing privileging one group over another? Is what we're doing working for all students, why or why not? Are our practices transparent? Is our leadership transparent? (p. 3)

Such critical discourse calls for preparation experiences that are very different from traditional university programs. Pounder, Reitzug, and Young (2002) noted that this means that leaders must be provided with new analytical skills, knowledge, and dispositions to promote social justice in schools. Among their recommendations they suggested a range of ideas: participating in field-based inquiry focused on oppression and discrimination, analyzing empirical data regarding racism in schools, examining stereotypes related to oppression, facilitating the creation of a rigorous and inclusive curriculum, and developing socially just practices among all individuals within the school community.

The social justice leadership discourse means that administrative preparation programs must encourage future school leaders to think very differently about organizational structures and leadership roles. Instead of continuing with incremental reforms that simply add more layers to existing structures, it is imperative to reconstruct roles and relationships at the school level around a vibrant core purpose focused on social justice and directed at improving student learning. This cannot be accomplished without concentrated expertise in teaching and learning. School leaders must possess high-quality instructional skills, be able to support the learning of both students and adults in the school, raise critical issues concerning equity and privilege, and be able to provide leadership for collective responsibility for school improvement. A growing number of leadership preparation programs are attempting to meet these challenges with coursework and teaching strategies directed at educating leaders to do social justice work (see Hafner, 2009, for a rich discussion of teaching strategies, programs, and resources).

The interdependent nature of education requires all segments of the educational enterprise—local schools, state licensure boards, higher education, professional associations—to collaborate in the preparation of a new type of school leader who is strongly committed to achieving social justice, one who draws on wide-ranging fields including educational leadership, curriculum, instruction, learning theory, communication, political theory, cultural studies, early childhood education, and systems theory. A challenge at the forefront of the papers commissioned by the National Commission for the Advancement of Educational Leadership Preparation is the assertion that substantive change in leadership preparation requires collaboration among all segments of the schooling enterprise (Young, Petersen, & Short, 2002). New structures are needed to enable this deliberation. The disconnect among the groups that influence or are responsible for school leadership impedes thoughtful reconsideration of leadership preparation. At both state and federal levels, processes must be established to facilitate conversations leading to reconceptualizing leadership for social justice. At the state level, departments of education could begin the work by serving as conveners of such sessions. From ongoing dialogue, a broader vision could be forged for creating new leadership roles for social justice and the requisite preparation and licensure requirements.

At the preparation level, recognition of the inextricable link between practitioners and the academy signals the need for close collaboration in the design and delivery of leadership programs. This is particularly important because school leaders generally find the academy irrelevant to their work (Cambron-McCabe & Cunningham, 2002; Hess & Kelly, 2005). For the most part, the formal preparation of preservice administrators resides in the academy with minimal input from practice. These programs are developed and taught primarily by professors under the strong influence of state licensure requirements. A few districts, particularly urban districts, are forging new partnerships with higher education faculty to jointly design alternative preparation programs that meet their special needs. We think this form of collaboration can be paramount in redefining leadership roles if it is framed around an emphasis on social justice using a school district's own context. This could provide a means to develop the new analytical skills Pounder et al. (2002) identified.

Furthermore, higher education faculty must model the kinds of organizations they expect their graduates to create. This challenges faculty to reflect on their pedagogy and program content to determine if their efforts represent the social justice questions and actions that they urge practitioners to embrace. Modeling becomes particularly important in the context of the tremendous struggle school leaders confront in reforming their practice. Too often, the academy is viewed as incapable of altering its own programs and as having little potential for informing school reform. Kottkamp (2002) has cautioned that "the largest problem in changing our programs, making them more effective, lies in changing ourselves" (p. 3). Faculty cannot teach about creating and leading socially just schools with credibility if they are not modeling these principles in their own departments, which includes working with practitioners on the front lines to reform schools.

Perhaps it is most important for professors to undertake an advocacy role in influencing educational policy to achieve social justice (Cambron-McCabe & Cunningham, 2002). School leaders and those preparing them will need to be creative and proactive to address current challenges, drawing on the past as well as multiple disciplines for new perspectives to shift their thinking. Blaming school problems on children's characteristics, lack of resources, politics, societal conditions, and myriad other issues simply incapacitates our efforts to achieve substantive transformation of schools. Instead of simply responding to criticisms and calls for change, school leaders need to influence the direction of education in our nation. If graduates of educational administration programs are expected to take on new roles, faculty must be active participants in the political arena when state policies affect social justice issues; mentoring from a distance does not prepare educational leaders for this difficult work.

Social justice discourse in educational leadership is being defined by its inclusiveness and activism. Through a language of critique, public intellectuals are shaping a new discourse with profound implications for social justice and the education of school leaders. This new language may move us closer to Foster's (1986) dream of educating leaders "to develop, challenge, and liberate human souls" (p. 18).

Notes

1. Numerous presentations have been made at annual meetings of the American Education Research Association, National Council for Professors of Educational Administration, and University Council of Educational Administration. *Leadership for Social Justice: Making Revolutions in Education* (Marshall and Oliva, 2009), has been created as a textbook for leadership preparation programs. Also, special issues of the *Journal of School Leadership* and *Educational Administration Quarterly* have been devoted to the social justice challenges facing educational administration.
2. See Furman and Gruenewald (2004) for an ecological critique of the current social justice discourse. They have argued that social justice must also consider the link between social and ecological systems and the impact on the future of humans, nonhumans, and habitats globally.
3. Deficit-thinking posits that students' academic failure results from the deficiencies they bring to school (i.e., poor, dysfunctional family, etc.). Consequently, this thinking leads to assignment in low-level classes, identification as special education, harsher discipline, and dropping out.
4. The Supreme Court found no federal constitutional barrier to voucher programs—under which state vouchers can be redeemed at public or private schools—including religious schools (*Zelman v. Simmons-Harris*, 2002). However, such programs still may abridge stronger antiestablishment provisions in the constitutions of 36 states (see *Davey v. Locke*, 2004).

References

Anderson, G. (2004). William Foster's legacy: Learning from the past and reconstructing the future. *Educational Administration Quarterly, 40*(2), 240–258.

Bauman, P. C. (1996). Governing education in an antigovernment environment. *Journal of School Leadership, 6*(6), 625–643.

Bogotch, I. E. (2002). Educational leadership and social justice: Practice into theory. *Journal of School Leadership, 12*(2), 138–156.

Bond, L. (1998). Disparate impact and teacher certification. *Journal of Personnel Evaluation in Education, 12*(2), 211–220.

Boris-Schacter, S., & Langer, S. (2002, February 6). Caught between nostalgia and utopia: The plight of the modern principal. *Education Week, 34*, 36–37.

Boyd, W. L., & Miretzky, D. (Eds.). (2003). *American educational governance on trial: Change and challenges.* Chicago: University of Chicago Press.

Bracey, G. (2000). *High stakes testing.* Retrieved from University of Wisconsin–Milwaukee, Education Policy Project, Center for Education Research, Analysis, and Innovation Web site: http://www.uwm.edu/Dept/CERAI/

Buchen, I. H. (2000, May 31). The myth of school leadership. *Education Week*, pp. 35–36.

Burrello, L. C., Lashley, C., & Beatty, E. E. (2001). *Educating all students together: How school leaders create unified systems.* Thousand Oaks, CA: Corwin Press.

Cambron-McCabe, N. (2009). Preparation and development of school leaders: Implications for social justice policies. In C. Marshall & M. Oliva (Eds.), *Leadership for social justice: Making revolutions in education.* Boston: Allyn & Bacon.

Cambron-McCabe, N., & Cunningham, L. (2002). National Commission for the Advancement of Educational Leadership: Opportunity for transformation. *Educational Administration Quarterly, 38*(2), 289–299.

Cambron-McCabe, N., Cunningham, L., Harvey, J., & Koff, R. (2005). *The superintendent's fieldbook: A guide for leaders of learning*. Thousand Oaks, CA: Corwin Press.

Cibulka, J. (2004, Spring). The case for academic program standards in educational administration: Toward a mature profession. *UCEA Review*, pp. 1–5.

Council of Chief State School Officers. (1996). *Interstate School Leaders Licensure Consortium: Standards for school leaders*. Washington, DC: Author.

Dantley, M. E. (2003). Principled, pragmatic, and purposive leadership: Reimagining educational leadership through prophetic spirituality. *Journal of School Leadership, 13*(2), 181–198.

Dantley, M., & Cambron-McCabe, N. (2001, April). *Administrative preparation and social justice concerns in Ohio*. Paper presented at the American Educational Research Association Annual Meeting, Seattle, WA.

Dantley, M. E., & Tillman, L. C. (2009). Social justice and moral/transformative leadership. In C. Marshall & M. Oliva (Eds.), *Leadership for social justice: Making revolutions in education*. Boston: Allyn & Bacon. *Davey v. Locke*, 540 U.S. 712 (2004).

Delgado, R., & Stefancic, J. (2001). *Critical race theory: An introduction*. New York: New York University Press.

Donmoyer, R., Imber, M., & Scheurich, J. (1995). *The knowledge base in educational administration: Multiple perspectives*. Albany, NY: SUNY Press.

Education Commission of the States. (2002, August). *State notes on charter schools*. Retrieved from http://www.ecs.org/ecs-main.asp?page=/html/issues.asp?am=1

Elmore, R. (2000). *Building a new structure for school leadership*. Washington, DC: The Albert Shanker Institute and Consortium for Policy Research in Education.

English, F. (2000, April). *The ghostbusters search for Frederick Taylor in the ISLLC standards*. Paper presented at the American Educational Research Association Annual Meeting, New Orleans, LA.

English, F. (2004, Spring). Undoing the "done deal": Reductionism, ahistoricity, and pseudoscience in the knowledge base and standards for educational administration. *UCEA Review*, pp. 6–7.

Foster, W. (1986). *Paradigms and promises: New approaches to educational administration*. Buffalo, NY: Prometheus Books.

Foster, W. (2004). The decline of the local: A challenge to educational leadership. *Educational Administration Quarterly, 40*(2), 176–191.

Fowler, F. C. (1991). The shocking ideological integrity of Chubb and Moe. *Journal of Education, 173*, 119–129.

Fuller, H. (1998). Transforming learning: The struggle to save urban education. *UCEA Review*, pp. 1–3.

Furman, G. (2000, November). *The ISLLC rendition of community: Contradiction and control?* Paper presented at the annual convention of the University Council for Educational Administration, Albuquerque, NM.

Furman, G., & Gruenewald, D. (2004). Expanding the landscape of social justice: A critical ecological analysis. *Educational Administration Quarterly, 40*(1), 49–78.

Giroux, H. A. (1993). Educational leadership and school administrators: Rethinking the meaning of democratic public cultures. In T. A. Mulkeen, N. Cambron-McCabe, & B. J. Anderson (Eds.), *Democratic leadership: The changing context of administrator preparation*. Norwood, NJ: Ablex.

Giroux, H. A. (1997). *Pedagogy and the politics of hope: Theory, culture, and schooling*. Boulder, CO: Westview Press.

Giroux, H. A. (2003). *The abandoned generation: Democracy beyond the culture of fear*. New York: Palgrave Macmillan.

Goldfarb, K. P., & Grinberg, J. (2002). Leadership for social justice. *Journal of School Leadership, 12*(2), 157–173.

Goldring, E., & Sims, P. (2005). Modeling creative and courageous school leadership through district-community-university partnerships. *Educational Policy, 19*, 223–249.

Goodlad, J. (1990). *Teachers for our nation's schools*. San Francisco: Jossey-Bass.

Grogan, M. (2004). Keeping a critical, postmodern eye on educational leadership in the United States: In appreciation of Bill Foster. *Educational Administration Quarterly, 40*(2), 222–239.

Gronn, P. (2002). Designer leadership: The emerging global adoption of preparation standards. *Journal of School Leadership, 12*(5), 552–578.

Gruenewald, D. (2003). Foundations of place: A multidisciplinary framework for place-conscious education. *American Educational Research Journal, 40*(3), 619–654.

Hafner, M. M. (2009). Teaching strategies for developing leaders for social justice. In C. Marshall & M. Oliva (Eds.), *Leadership for social justice: Making revolutions in education*. Boston: Allyn & Bacon.

Haycock, K. (2001). Closing the achievement gap. *Educational Leadership, 58*(6). Retrieved from http://www.ascd.org/readingroom/edlead/0103/haycock.html

Hedges, L. V., & Nowell, A. (1998). Black-white test score convergence since 1965. In C. Jencks and A. Phillips (Eds.), *The black-white test score gap* (pp. 149–181). Washington, DC: Brookings.

Herrington, C. D., & Wills, B. K. (2005). Decertifying the principalship: The politics of administrator preparation in Florida. *Educational Policy, 19*, 181–200.

Hess, F., & Kelly, A. (2005). An innovative look, a recalcitrant reality: The politics of principal preparation reform. *Educational Policy, 19*, 155–180.

Hill, P. T. (Ed.). (2002). *Choice and equity*. Stanford, CA: Hoover Institution Press.

Kottkamp, R. (2002). What makes a difference in developing effective school leaders? A challenge to the field. *TEA/SIG: Teaching in Educational Administration, 9*(2), 1, 3.

Larson, C., & Murtadha, K. (2002). Leadership for social justice. In J. Murphy (Ed.), *The educational leadership challenge: Redefining leadership for the 21st century* (pp. 134–161). Chicago: National Society for the Study of Education.

Lewis, D. A. (1993). Deinstitutionalization and school decentralization: Making the same mistake twice. In J. Hannaway & M. Carnoy (Eds.), *Decentralization and school improvement* (pp. 84–101). San Francisco: JosseyBass.

Lopez, G. R. (2003). The (racially neutral) politics of education: A critical race theory perspective. *Educational Administration Quarterly, 39*(1), 68–94.

Lugg, C. A. (2003). Sissies, faggots, lezzies, and dykes: Gender, sexual orientation, and a new politics of education. *Educational Administration Quarterly, 39*(1), 95–134.

Marshall, C. (2001, April). *School administration licensure policy in North Carolina.* Paper presented at the American Educational Research Association Annual Meeting, Seattle, WA.

Marshall, C. (2004). Social justice challenges to educational administration: Introduction to a special issue. *Educational Administration Quarterly, 40*(1), 5–15.

Marshall, C., & McCarthy, M. (2002). School leadership reforms: Filtering social justice through dominant discourses. *Journal of School Leadership, 12*(5), 480–502.

Marshall, C., & Oliva, M. (Eds.). (2009). *Leadership for social justice: Making it happen.* Boston: Allyn & Bacon.

Marshall, C., & Parker, L. (in press). Vignettes of leaders' social justice dilemmas. In C. Marshall & M. Oliva (Eds.), *Leadership for social justice: Making revolutions in education.* Boston: Allyn & Bacon.

Maxcy, S. (2000, November). *Leadership clones, copies and mutations: Scientific management and leadership philosophy in educational administration.* Paper presented at the American Educational Research Association Annual Meeting, New Orleans, LA.

McCarthy, M. (2002a). The changing environment for school leaders: Market forces. In G. Perreault & F. Lunenburg (Eds.), *The changing world of school administration* (pp. 91–108). Lanham, MD: Scarecrow Press.

McCarthy, M. (2002b). Educational leadership preparation programs: A glance at the past with an eye toward the future. *Leadership and Policy in Schools, 1*, 202–221.

McKenzie, K., & Scheurich, J. (2004, July). Position paper for Miami University Education Summit, Oxford, Ohio.

McNeil, L. (2000). *Contradictions of school reform: The educational costs of standardized testing.* New York: Routledge.

Merrow, J. (2001). Undermining standards. *Phi Delta Kappan, 82*, 653–659.

Merrow, J. (2004, March 26). *The Merrow report* [Television broadcast]. New York: Public Broadcasting Service.

Mitchell, K. J., Robinson, D. Z., Plake, B. S., & Knowles, K. T. (Eds.). (2001). *Testing teacher candidates.* Washington, DC: National Academy Press.

Murphy, J. (1999). New consumerism: Evolving market dynamics in the institutional dimension of schooling. In J. Murphy & K. Seashore-Lewis (Eds.), *The handbook of research on educational administration* (2nd ed., pp. 405–419). San Francisco: Jossey-Bass.

National Policy Board for Educational Administration. (2000). *Standards for advanced programs in educational leadership.* Arlington, VA: Author.

No Child Left Behind Act, 20 U.S.C. § 6301 *et seq.* (2002).

Oliva, M. (2001, April). *Texas educator certification and social justice.* Paper presented at the American Educational Research Association Annual Meeting, Seattle, WA.

Orlofsky, G. (2002). *The funding gap: Low-income and minority students receive fewer dollars.* Retrieved from http://www.edtrust.org/main/documents/investment.pdf

Paige, R. (2003, Fall). Under the microscope: Educational progress in Houston. *The Beacon: Journal of Special Education and Practice, 2*(2), 1–8.

Parker, L., Deyhle, D., & Villanas, S. (1999). *Race is … race isn't: Critical race theory and qualitative studies in education.* Boulder, CO: Westview.

Pounder, D., Reitzug, U., & Young, M. (2002). Preparing school leaders for school improvement, social justice, and community. In J. Murphy (Ed.), *The educational leadership challenge: Redefining leadership for the 21st century* (pp. 261–288). Chicago: University of Chicago Press.

Reyes, P., Scribner, J., & Paredes Scribner, A. (1999). *Lessons from high performing Hispanic schools: Creating learning communities.* New York: Teachers College Press.

Richards, C. E., Shore, R., & Sawicky, M. B. (1996). *Risky business: Private management of public schools.* Washington, DC: Economic Policy Institute.

Rusch, E. (2001, April). *Preparing leaders for social justice in New Jersey.* Paper presented at the American Educational Research Association Annual Meeting, Seattle, WA.

Senge, P. (1990). *The fifth discipline: The art and practice of the learning organization.* New York: Doubleday.

Skrla, L., & Scheurich, J. (2001). Displacing deficit thinking in superintendent leadership. *Education and Urban Society, 33*(3), 235–259.

Skrla, L., Scheurich, J., Garcia, J., & Nolly, G. (2004). Equity audits: A practical leadership tool for developing equitable and excellent schools. *Educational Administration Quarterly, 40*(1), 135–163.

U.S. Charter Schools. (2003). *State info.* Retrieved from http://www.uscharterschools.org/pub/uscs_docs/sp/index.htm

Usdan, M. (2002). Reactions to articles commissioned by the National Commission for the Advancement of Education Leadership Preparation. *Educational Administration Quarterly, 38*(2), 300–307.

Young, M., Petersen, G., & Short, P. (2002). The complexity of substantive reform: A call for interdependence among key stakeholders. *Educational Administration Quarterly, 38*(2), 137–175.

Zelman v. Simmons-Harris, 536 U.S. 639 (2002).

CHAPTER 2

Transforming Educational Leadership Without Social Justice?

Looking at Critical Pedagogy as More Than a Critique, and a Way Toward "Democracy"[1]

Paul Carr

One thing we know for sure, as common wisdom has it, is that you can always count on change. *Change is everywhere,* we are told constantly. *We are about change,* political parties extoll. *If you don't change, you'll be left behind,* is what we are taught. While advertisers, business gurus, pundits, and highly remunerated futurists all agree that change is in the air, that progress is the way to go, and that evolution means embracing change, I'm left wondering: what type of change, defined by whom, for whom, contextualized, understood, and embraced in what manner, by whom, and why? If change is a certainty, as we are led to believe, then why is there still poverty? One would think that social inequities—including racism, sexism, income gaps, homelessness, religious intolerance, discrimination of all forms, and so on—would be history; that, with all of the change going on, there would be no room for such anti-change variables. While, undoubtedly, much *has* changed—and there is evidence of this—social inequities, in many regards, are widening, not dissipating. This, I would argue, relates to power and how it is exercised, challenged, and considered. This chapter on transformative leadership, building on the work of Carolyn Shields (2004, 2010), takes the posture that power is directly related to the educational project and, moreover, that it can only take place within a broad framework that acknowledges social inequities (Kincheloe, 2007, 2008a, 2008b; Macrine, 2009). Critical pedagogy provides such a framework, and I will use that framework here to position an argument in favour of a more engaged, politically meaningful, and counter-hegemonic transformative leadership, one that deemphasizes neo-liberalism, the reproduction of social relations, and the solidification of a rigid educational system that too willingly weeds out those with lower cultural capital, incongruent lived experiences, and divergent identities (see the work of Paulo Freire, 1973, 1985, 1998, 2004, 1973/2005).

In discussing the transformative leadership project, I will focus on democracy as a means of reframing a way of understanding change in education within a critical pedagogy pedagogical perspective (Carr, 2007, 2008a, 2008b, 2008c, 2010; Lund & Carr, 2008). Democracy is key to this debate because if democracy is not an objective of education, then what is its purpose (Westheimer, 2008; Westheimer & Kahne, 2003, 2004)?[2] Principals and vice-principals, along with superintendents and other senior

education officials, form a group that I, and others, call administrators, and they are the focus of the first line of implementation in the quest for transformative leadership. Added to this group, we must also consider policymakers, decisionmakers, and other leaders, who have a direct stake in what happens in schools. Interest groups, think-tanks, teachers' federations, parents' groups, and others are also enmeshed in how we define, orchestrate, evaluate, and produce education. Transformative leadership, therefore, involves many sectors, interests, concepts, and realities (Shields & Edwards, 2005). Significantly, it is something that is a product of society; is socially, economically, and politically constructed, and is an appendage of the power structures in which it exists. For this chapter, I will argue that democracy is a useful concept to guide our thinking here because it forces us to acknowledge the broader macro-portrait of society, something that inevitably impinges on the individual actions of administrators and, moreover, is shaped by the concerns and priorities of various groups in society. Thus, the critical pedagogy of democracy in relation to transformative leadership is the focus of this chapter and will guide the analysis and discussion throughout. The chapter presents thoughts, concepts, and research related to democracy, critical pedagogy, and the critical pedagogy of democracy, and concludes with some proposals for more engaged, critical, and meaningful transformative change in education, with particular attention being paid to the leadership role.

Democracy and Transformative Leadership

What can be done to contribute to democracy in and through education, and how does leadership fit into the equation? Clearly, there is no one answer, especially not an easy or simplistic one. A fundamental, and perhaps obvious, argument is that democracy and education must be inextricably linked. One might ask: What kind of education? Part of the formulation of a response comes in the form of how we choose to elucidate what we mean by *democracy*. My interpretation surpasses the electoral politics (representative) model, embracing a *thicker* version of inclusion, participation, dialog, interrogation, and critical engagement, which is underpinned by a vigorously and humbly formulated critical pedagogy (Carr, 2008c). This form of democratic education seeks to embrace the experiences and perspectives of diverse peoples, including those traditionally marginalized from the national narratives that have enshrined a partisan allegiance to patriotism; these narratives were not often included and accepted military conquest as a normative value, and, conversely, often excluded and rejected those groups and actions that ran counter to hegemonic reasoning (Carr, 2010). It is problematic, therefore, to consider democracy in exclusion of a meaningful analysis of inequitable power relations, and this links directly with the notion of transformative leadership as opposed to traditional forms of leadership that privilege maintaining the status quo (Kincheloe & Steinberg, 2006; Macrine, 2009; McLaren & Kincheloe, 2007).

I caution that there is no one thing, menu, or recipe that can be produced to inculcate a democratic state, government, citizen, or education system (Carr, 2008a). Indeed, even addressing an amalgam of concerns is no guarantee of reinforcing democracy. However, the desire for a more meaningful, just, and decent form of democracy is something that requires—borrowing from the contemporary vernacular within mainstream politics—a certain measure of *hope*. One must remain confident and strident in order to improve the current situation, because to simply endorse it uncritically is to further entrench vast swaths of the landscape, figuratively and literally, to a permanently deceptive existence in which the quest for human rights becomes a mere fictional legal manoeuvre reserved largely for those with their hands firmly on the economic levers of power.

Ultimately, seeking a more democratic society in and through education is tantamount to seeking the truth. Never comfortable, nor easily achieved, such a proposition requires a multitude of measures as well as the belief that people can, ultimately, function together without self-destruction. War is not the answer, nor is violence. Corruption and greed are also areas that can be addressed, provided that the will of the people is respected. Racism, sexism, and poverty are not virtues—they are man and woman-made, and can be addressed. Cycles of disenfranchisement do not mesh well with the oft-repeated mantra of American "greatness" and the superiority of a highly-developed, advanced nation, one often invoked as being blessed by God. Rather than reducing inequities, society is actually (according to all of the standard measures used to demonstrate development and superiority) becoming less united, less equal, less resolutely inclusive, and ultimately, I would argue, less democratic. The space provided for elections has usurped the place of education in many regards (Carr, 2010; Denzin, 2009).

Critical Pedagogy and Democratic (Sur)Realities

Can we have democracy without democratic literacy? Without democratic engagement? Is critical pedagogy an appropriate means for achieving democratic literacy and democratic engagement? Relying, in large part, on the critical pedagogical foundation of Paulo Freire, it is helpful here to highlight the epistemological salience of Freire's work, which Au (2007) argues is steeped in the Marxist tradition. Epistemological interrogation is a necessary function in the quest for transformative change in education. Although the terminology may change from context to context, Freire's "conscientization" has meaning across diverse milieus and environments. Achieving meaningful experiences in and through education, cognizant of differential power relations, is the core of a critical pedagogical, democratic education. Whether or not a critical Marxist perspective is germane in nurturing democratic education should not obfuscate the reality that critical pedagogy can lead to the process of personal and collective transformation.

Brosio (2003), in citing leading radical political philosopher Michael Parenti, highlights that normative neo-liberal, capitalistic structures have, and continue to have, a significant effect on people and societal development:

> What we need is a 180-degree shift away from unilateral global domination and toward equitable and sustainable development among the peoples of the world. This means U.S. leaders would have to stop acting like self-willed unaccountable rulers of the planet. They must stop supporting despots, and stop opposing those democratic movements and governments that challenge the status quo. The struggle is between those who believe that the land, labor, capital, technology, markets, and natural resources of society should be used as expendable resources for transnational profit accumulation, and those who believe that such things should be used for the mutual benefit of the populace. What we need is to move away from liberal complaints about how bad things are and toward a radical analysis that explains why they are so, away from treating every situation as a perfectly new and befuddling happening unrelated to broader politico-economic interests and class power structures. What we need is a global anti-imperialist movement that can challenge the dominant paradigm with an alternative one that circumvents the monopoly ideological control of officialdom and corporate America. (Brosio, 2003)

Bellamy Foster, Holleman, and McChesney (2008) support this perspective, arguing for a more comprehensive, critical, and global analysis of the American empire, suggesting that the degree to which U.S. society is controlled by militarization is poorly understood by the population, which then leads to the military having far-reaching potential to dominate, marginalize, and diminish the vibrancy of vast swaths of society. Willinsky (1998) further addresses the need to critique empire as a necessary step in bringing forth the prospect for change, which relates to Freire's (1973/2005) oppressor-oppressed dichotomy. Anticolonial education should, therefore, not be uniquely a discussion reserved for the archives, as the historical is intertwined with the present, and appreciating how current problems and issues are connected with previous actions is pivotal to avoiding simplistic, essentialized education responses.

Taking account of the dialectical relationship between hegemony and ideology (Fischman & McLaren, 2005) is a fundamental part of the critical pedagogical equation. As highlighted in the first section of their book, critical epistemological interrogation is fundamental to the dissection and unravelling of how power is infused in and through (supposed) democratic processes. The relevance for education, therefore, is clear:

> Critical pedagogy problematizes the relationship between education and politics, between sociopolitical relations and pedagogical practices, between the reproduction of dependent hierarchies of power and privilege in the domain of everyday social life and that of the classroom and institutions. In doing so, it advances an agenda for educational transformation by encouraging educators to understand the sociopolitical contexts of educative acts and the importance of radically democratizing both educational and larger social formations. In such processes, educators take on intellectual roles by adapting to, resisting, and challenging curriculum, school policy, educational philosophies, and pedagogical traditions. (Fischman & McLaren, 2005, p. 425)

A critical pedagogy of democracy can cultivate a vigorous and meaningful interrogation of the various strands underpinning power structures, including the functioning of the military, the limited but populism-laden visions of politics, and the infusion of right-wing Christian fundamentalism into decision-making (Giroux, 2005; Steinberg & Kincheloe, 2009). Giroux and Giroux (2006) provide a thoughtful synthesis of critical democratic pedagogy:

> The democratic character of critical pedagogy is defined largely through a set of basic assumptions, which holds that power, values, and institutions must be made available to critical scrutiny, be understood as a product of human labor (as opposed to God-given), and evaluated in terms of how they might open up or close down democratic practices and experiences. Yet, critical pedagogy is about more than simply holding authority accountable through the close reading of texts, the creation of radical classroom practices, or the promotion of critical literacy. It is also about linking learning to social change, education to democracy, and knowledge to acts of intervention in public life. Critical pedagogy encourages students to learn to register dissent as well as to take risks in creating the conditions for forms of individual and social agency that are conducive to a substantive democracy. (p. 28)

Challenging neo-liberalism is a central feature to this project, shining a light on nefarious practices, marginalization, and conservative interpretations of success that serve to blame the victim rather than critique the trappings and inner-working of power (Giroux & Giroux, 2006). Decoding signals, omissions, directives, and the meaning of rhetoric is a key component of the critical pedagogy of democracy (Engels, 2007; Kellner & Share, 2007; Macedo & Steinberg, 2007). State authority is not obliged to be oppressive, and ingratiating students with a critical pedagogy of democracy can lead to thicker experiences and interpretations of democracy.

A radical democratic pedagogy, as outlined by Denzin (2009), speaks to hope: "Hope is ethical. Hope is moral. Hope is peaceful and nonviolent. Hope seeks truth of life's sufferings. Hope gives meaning to the struggles to change the world. Hope is grounded in concrete performative practices, in struggles and interventions that espouse sacred values of love, care, community, trust, and well-being" (p. 385).

Compelling arguments can be made for a more deliberately conscious, engaged, and loving connection to others (Darder & Miron, 2006). Freire spoke of radical love and the inescapable prospect of indignation, which need not be considered weakness, cynicism, or hopelessness (Freire, 2004). The capacity, and necessity, to love is entrenched in the very essence of the human condition. Accepting human and humane interactions and relations, without exploitation and discrimination, is a fundamental consideration for a critical pedagogy of democracy. Darder and Miron (2006) emphasize that our experiences are not disconnected from the broader politico-economic context but, as Brosio (2003) maintains, are interwoven into a socially constructed narrative:

> Capitalism disembodies and alienates our daily existence. As our consciousness becomes more and more abstracted, we become more and more detached from our bodies. For this reason, it is absolutely imperative that critical educators and scholars acknowledge that the origin of emancipator possibility and human solidarity resides in our body. (p. 16)

As Darder and Miron (2006) argue, everyone is capable of contesting, resisting, and challenging nefarious neo-liberal policies and manifestations:

If we, as citizens of the Empire, do not use every opportunity to voice our dissent, we shamefully leave the great task of dissent to our brothers and sisters around the world who daily suffer greater conditions of social, political, and economic impoverishment and uncertainty than we will ever know. For how long will our teaching and politics fail to address the relevant and concrete issues that affect people's daily lives? (p. 18)

Not every action or gesture need be representative of a grandiose, sweepingly transformative manifestation. For transformative leadership to be meaningful, individuals can, and must, make their voices heard: They can resist imperialism, hegemony, and patriotic oppression, and, importantly, they can choose love over hate, peace over war, and humanity over inhumanity. This may seem abstract and outside of the boundaries of the proverbial three Rs, student-based learning, high academic standards, No Child Left Behind–like system reforms, and the like, but, as argued throughout this chapter, there is a direct, visceral relation between power and change, and transformative leadership is hinged, according to this thinking, on a broad platform of macro-level thinking combined with micro-level transformative leadership within school and educational sites.

Fifty Proposals That Could Contribute to Democracy Through Education

Building on the backdrop outlined above—at the risk of being criticized for including some ideas that may not mesh with a democratic education focus, or others that seem to be superfluous to the debate or that may not seem too original or innovative—what follows is a list of 50 proposals that could contribute to a thicker democratic education. Importantly, these proposals should be considered as an ensemble, not as disparate, individual efforts at reform. Within the spirit of this chapter and book, all of these proposals would require a vigorous, engaged, and critical transformative leadership. Based on a critical pedagogical conceptualization of education, change, and democracy, these proposals are offered as an alternative to the neo-liberal, hegemonic reform models currently in place, which have largely overlooked and underplayed social justice.

1. Make education a *societal* responsibility, removing the false narrative of it somehow being only a *local* responsibility. The nation-state should undertake a public education campaign to acknowledge and promote public education as the engine behind societal growth, development, harmony, and ingenuity.

2. Democratic conscientization should be integrated into educational planning, and political, critical, and media-centric forms of literacy should become mandatory aspects of teaching and learning.

3. Eradicate the mainstream representation of education as being neutral and devoid of politics. Emphasize that education can lead to change and that regressive forms of education can lead to docile, compliant citizens, the antithesis of thick democracy.

4. Redefine the notion of accountability in education to more centrally focus on ethics, bona fide diversity, social justice, and thick democracy. Just because No Child Left Behind (NCLB) declares that there is greater accountability does not necessarily mean that this is true.

5. The state should only fund public education, and charters, vouchers, private schools, and other offshoots should be discouraged and not be eligible for public support. Public education is a public good, benefitting all of society, and it should be viewed as a collective, global responsibility.

6. End the ranking of schools and school boards. Such efforts are divisive, punish the marginalized, are not appropriately contextualized, and serve to disintegrate rather than integrate, thus diminishing the possibility of enhancing the public good and the notion of

education being a fundamental pillar to solidifying the thicker and more humane elements of a democracy.

7. Do not let high cultural capital areas—those with high property values and other advantages—graduate their high schools without having them work closely with schools in their areas that are facing serious challenges. The notion here is that all schools will see that they are part of a common struggle, existence, and society, and are not simply, as within the neo-liberal mindset, individuals demonstrating how hard they work as opposed to others who are supposedly not committed.

8. All subject areas of the curriculum should explicitly diagnose how power works as well as the meaning of social justice. This should include a critical pedagogical analysis of whiteness; racial, gender, and class inequities; and other forms of marginalization, discrimination, and disenfranchisement. It may be considered impolite to discuss such matters, but to avoid them is only to further entrench and ingratiate harm, damage, and the antithesis of democracy.

9. Education-systems and educators should embrace the following saying: *"The more I know, the less I know."* If education is to sincerely be about life-long learning, then it should involve an endless process of critical interrogation, lived experiences, and dialectical questioning and dialog, which far overshadows the notion of standards, high-stakes testing, and a prescriptive curriculum.

10. Men and women of all origins, races, ethnicities, and backgrounds should be involved in teaching and education. Some elementary schools lack male teachers, and some schools have no racial minorities or no females in leadership positions, which can further lead to false stereotypes about leadership, role models, and learning.

11. Educational policymaking and curriculum development should involve more consultation and collaboration with diverse groups and interests, and the decision-making process should necessarily become more transparent. Educators, parents, students, and the broader community should be able to understand how decisions are made and why, and they should be involved in these processes that will, ultimately, have an effect on all of society.

12. All schools should be twinned within local areas (for example, an urban school could be twinned with a suburban school, and a suburban school twinned with a rural school, or schools from different demographic areas could be twinned in the same area). This twinning would involve bona fide academic and curriculum work in addition to cultural exchange. No student should be allowed to say that they do not know, understand, or experience diversity because "everyone in their school is white," which does not sufficiently encapsulate a thicker version of critical thinking and engagement with pluralism.

13. School boards should use technology to twin classrooms in the United States with those around the world so that educators can exchange language and culture with colleagues in other countries. The government should provide seed funding to schools that require it in order to undertake this program.

14. If there must be standards in education, there should be standards for democratic education, citizenship education, peace education, media literacy, and social justice. Standards should be focused on building a more decent society, not on testing basic skills that are predefined largely because of cultural capital.

15. Teachers should not be remunerated on how well their students do. Teachers' salaries should be increased and other measures of acknowledgement for their contributions should be pursued.

The objective should not be to diminish those working in more challenging situations or those whose students have lower levels of cultural capital. The role of the teacher has to be understood in a broader societal context, not simply related to mercantilist outcomes.

16. The curriculum should be significantly revamped. Freire's generative themes and Dewey's constructivism should be incorporated into classrooms at all levels, instilling values of respect, critical interrogation, engagement, and appreciation of how power works.

17. All schools should emphasize deliberative democracy and young people should learn how to listen, articulate, debate, and diagnose difference. Significantly, students should learn how to respectfully seek to construct further knowledge in a peaceful way. Condemning those with critical opinions needs to be stopped as group-think can lead to societal paralysis and a nefarious form of patriotism.

18. Rather than protecting students from controversial subject matter, they should be encouraged to critically understand not only the *what* but also the *how* and *why* behind significant events, issues, and concerns. The mythology that politics is about Democrats and Republicans needs to be rectified, and students need to learn that critical reflection can lead to more appropriate and effective resolutions of systemic problems and conflicts than the use of force, whether it be wars, racial profiling, or the neglect of impoverished groups.

19. Peace and peace education should become centerpieces of the educational project. If peace is not a fundamental part of education, what then is its purpose?

20. A thicker interpretation of the environment and environmental education should be taught throughout the educational program. The effects of war and military conflict on the environment, for example, should be explored.

21. Poorer areas should not be punished because of wealth concentration, and everyone should be able to enjoy the outdoors without cost.

22. Accessible, fair-play, sportsmanlike values should be reasserted in place of a win-at-all-costs mission and the drive for notoriety and the supremacy of money.

23. All students should be introduced to critical service learning. The experiences should be accompanied by courses and debriefings on why societal problems exist. To do a service-learning placement without some sociopolitical contextualization may only reinforce the opposite of what is sought through the actual experience.

24. Contracts for superintendents of education and principals should contain a clause that they will be evaluated on how well they inculcate democratic education, political literacy, and social justice. Their renewal should hinge, in part, on how well they address these matters within their educational institutions.

25. There should be no place in schools for military recruitment, especially not in schools in poorer areas. All students should be afforded the possibility of higher education, not just those with higher levels of cultural capital, and the message should not be transmitted, either explicitly or implicitly, that poor people have no other option than to join the army.

26. All American students should learn at least one foreign language starting in first grade and then be introduced to a second language in high school. The notion that English will get Americans everywhere they wish to go at all times and will lead to inter-cultural development, not to mention the visible concern of achieving peace and good relations with the world, must be recast in a more holistic and democratic form of education.

27. The enticement to enter into contracts with for-profit enterprises as a way of funding schools should be eliminated. Communities should be made aware of economic situations that pressure and coerce some localities more than others, and should also be invited to critique the role of marketing, advertising, and the drive to capture market-share within schools. Educational policymaking should also address this area. Programs such as Channel One should be prohibited from schools. They are not benevolent services; moreover, they come with strings attached, and are not problematized.

28. The differentiated experiences of schools that have a larger wealth-base, as compared to poorer districts, should be addressed. The research on this reality, including the social context, should be concisely and critically presented to parents, students, educators, and the broader community. The approach should not be to illustrate blame, pity, guilt, or incompetence but, rather, to seek to underscore systemic problems, resource allocation, and ineffectual curriculum and policy development.

29. The limited accessibility to field trips to museums, cultural events, and even foreign countries only serves to further increase the educational, cultural, and political gap between Americans. Governments should provide an appropriate level of funding so that all schools can benefit from such indispensable activities.

30. Parents should be required, except in extraordinary circumstances, to provide one-half day of service per month to their children's schools. The objective is to make all parents knowledgeable of what happens at school, to create support for progressive activities, and to provide a vehicle to discuss education and democracy. Legislation should be passed to ensure that no parent would be penalized for participating in such a program (and these days would not count as formal vacation-days). School principals should be supported in finding the appropriate ways to liaise with parents.

31. Teacher-education programs should focus on qualitative teaching and learning experiences and develop assessment schemes that monitor and support innovation, engagement, collaboration, and critical pedagogical work that emphasizes learning and the *construction* of knowledge over the *acquisition* of knowledge. Similarly, these programs should forge meaningful relationships with local school boards. All education faculty should have some type of formal relationship with their schools.

32. All schools should implement a guest program, whereby a range of professionals, academics, and people with diverse experiences could liaise with students. The access to a diversity of guests should be distributed equally throughout all schools, and no schools should be without some form of a regular, regimented, and engaging program in place. Special attention should be paid to diversity and the public good (i.e., high cultural-capital schools should not be the only ones exposed to leading business and political figures; conversely, critical alternative movements and grass-roots figures should not be invited only to working-class schools).

33. Public officials, including politicians, diplomats, and mainstream media, should be invited into schools to dialog with students, all the while being open to critical questions about social justice, bias, patriotism, propaganda, and why systemic issues exist, in addition to the traditional reasons that such figures visit schools (e.g., to extol the virtues of democracy, to sell support for a particular platform, to discuss career choices, how to be a good citizen, etc.).

34. All schools should embark on a range of community projects that could count for credit toward graduation. These projects could involve service-learning, undertaking research, writing

narratives and ethnographies, and making presentations on how social problems might be addressed.

35. State departments of education, overseen by a board of professionals and activists, should gather data on inputs and outputs of the education system, and report on how diversity, social justice, media literacy, democracy, and other program areas are relevant. These reports should be available online, free of cost, through the state's Department of Education website.

36. The study of democracy and elections should not be concentrated within a single course (often labelled as a Civics or Government course). Democracy must be demonstrated, acted upon, and lived, not relegated to a course that focuses on encouraging voting.

37. Require school boards and schools to implement participatory budgeting in an inclusive and meaningful fashion, involving diverse interests in determining the allocation of funds for education.

38. Prohibit fundraising within schools, and have educators focus exclusively on critical teaching, learning, and engagement. If schools are not concerned with raising funds they will then be able to freely target the best interests of the students and also to not be beholden to any outside interests.

39. Schools should focus on the prevention of bullying and violence, and work with communities, families, and students at various levels to establish a conducive environment for learning, and, at the same time, seek to avoid the nefarious zero-tolerance, criminalization route.

40. Schools should undertake community violence and criminality projects, examining the form, substance, and degree of violence and criminality in their localities. The data-collection and analysis should include white-collar crime, corruption, racial profiling, and un-and under-documented crimes, including abuse against women, gang activities, and police misconduct. The results, which would form part of a process of critical interrogation, could be publicly presented on an ongoing basis in order to lead to a more rigorous understanding of how and why criminal activities and violence take place, and, moreover, what is done about it.

41. Similar to point 40, schools should undertake community health projects to determine the types of diseases, infections, and illnesses that exist in local communities, with a view to undertaking critical comparative analyses. Are poorer people more at risk, do they live shorter lives, do they have access to adequate health care, do they contribute equally to the formulation of health policy, and so on? The ongoing results of the research should be exposed, and acted upon.

42. Students should be invited, as per Lawrence Kohlberg's moral-development model, to determine some of the rules, guidelines, and conditions of their school experience. Students should not be uniquely the recipients of the formal education experience but should also be full participants in shaping their knowledge and reality.

43. No child should be placed in special education without a full determination of the socioeconomic context, thus diminishing the possibility of marginalized and racialized communities being disproportionately streamed into these programs. Despite formal procedures outlined in present processes, there is still wide-spread concern about the types of children directed to special education.

44. Make humility a virtue for teaching and learning, and downgrade the emphasis placed on economic gain accrued by business leaders, actors and professional athletes.

45. All schools should have a garden that produces fruits and vegetables. While working one to two hours a week on the garden, students will also learn, and will have opportunities to make concrete curricular connections to the environment, agriculture, nutrition, the economics of food, and globalization. The fruits and vegetables produced could also be consumed by the students.

46. All schools should have music, arts, and physical education programs. Funding and wealth should not be an impediment to children having access to a broad liberal arts education.

47. A war tax of 20% should be applied to all spending on the military and militarization, and the resultant funding should be applied to education. In present times, with approximately $1 trillion being spent annually on the military in the United States, the government would be obligated to allocate an additional $200 billion to the education section. Education should not be used to subsidize war, nor should poorer people be forced into fighting other people's battles.

48. The federal government should organize an annual education summit, in which diverse civil society, educational, and *alter-mondialiste/counter-globalization* organizations could contribute to a debate on the formal measures, data, policies, resources, and goals of public education. This education summit could be considered as an accountability forum for governments and education authorities. The summit would generate a detailed annual report and plan, which would be reviewed the following year.

49. Humility should be emphasized over nationalism and patriotism.

50. Radical love should be the starting point for the conceptualization of education. Whether or not the above proposals appear to be realistic is not the fundamental question.

The reality that there are diverse proposals, movements, interests, and people seeking a different kind of democracy should be kept in mind. Transformative leadership, being ideologically positioned to engage and act upon inequitable power relations, is afforded unique and meaningful access to formal educational structures in which myriad dialogs, debates, and decisions are hashed out. The above set of proposals could be considered and massaged by transformative leaders, who might be able to shift some portions of the bedrock underpinning the neo-liberal monopoly within mainstream education circles that prevents many progressive and social-justice–based reforms from making it to the table.

A Democratic Education Planning Model

This democratic education planning model (Figure 2.1) can assist in mapping what individuals, schools, and communities are thinking and experiencing in relation to democracy and democratic engagement. Schools could document the context, content, experiences, and outcomes of what takes place within the realm of education. There are many ways of promoting constructive collaboration, and I would encourage critical, dialectical, and harmonious efforts aimed at understanding and constructing more meaningful experiences, rather than imposing haphazard, incongruent, and inauthentic ones. For this model, schools could work with diverse interests—or stakeholders, in public-policy jargon—who are not, to use the neoliberal terminology, clients. Involving teachers, parents, students, members of the community, and others, and being cognizant of differential power relations, may facilitate some important synergetic planning as well as the formulation of proposals. This approach is inspired by the participatory budget planning process (Gandin & Apple, 2005), established in Porto Alegre, Brazil, in which the community comes together to consider how portions of the budget will be spent. Using a critical pedagogical analysis, participants in the democratic education planning model should be highly sensitized to systemic and institutional barriers to change and should also consider the *lived* experiences of individuals and groups, being vigilant to grasp the nuanced existence of marginalized interests.

	Context	Content	Experiences	Outcomes
Individual				
School				
Community				

Figure 2.1: Democratic Education Planning Model

This model does not seek the typical (supposed) accountability report that is skewed toward illustrating the virtue of the funder or the institutional interest. Rather, the focus should be on bona fide, tangible critical engagement, questioning why policies and programs have been developed, in whose interest, and to what end. For example, how do individuals, the school, and the community contribute to the democratic foundation, growth, and tension of what takes place locally within an educational site?

One way to use this model would be to chart out the context for democratic education: to define it, to highlight the historic and contemporary achievement, issues, and challenges, and to address fundamental concerns, such as those related to patriotism, socioeconomic development, and political participation, in an inclusive and thick way. The notion is not to draft volumes here but, rather, to attempt to link to our actions the epistemological and philosophical foundation of what we know, and how we know and believe it (Kincheloe, 2008b). Often, education policies seem to drop from the sky, disconnected from the lived realities of students, and are inconsistent with scientific research—although NCLB specifically prescribes that reforms be based on scientific research, can educational leaders enumerate the literature that has informed their philosophies? (Gordon, Smyth, & Diehl, 2008).

Concluding Thoughts

In focusing on democracy, it is clear that a thicker, more critical version of democracy—outside of representative, electoral politics—necessarily involves an inter-disciplinary approach (touching on sociology, history, philosophy, political science, economics, education, cultural studies, and the social sciences in general), and close consideration should be given to a number of directly related subjects and issues (peace studies, media literacy, environmental education, intercultural relations, etc.). There is no set answer, list, or menu to the question of how to *do* democracy, or how to create a *thicker* democracy. Rather, as suggested in the earlier list of what might be done, an amalgam of thinking, interrogation, critical analysis, experience, and humility may lead to a more meaningful and sustainable democracy, one that seeks to inspire and cultivate critical engagement of all people and interests. A more radical determination toward a more radical democracy requires thinking well outside of constricted, hegemonic boundaries, and must address how power works (Hill & Boxley, 2007).

How does transformative leadership fit into this discussion? One might argue that the discussion would remain theoretical, conceptual, and academic without considering the real-world problems and challenges that encapsulate the educational arena, experience, and institution. How do we actually promote change—not just the discourse of change, which is surely important—but the actual process of change? For it to be transformative, it would be important to consider diverse epistemologies, values, strategies, and variables, and, especially, to understand how power works (Shields, 2010). Power is not neutral, nor is democracy, and change of a transformative type can only happen when there is serious, critical engagement. Thus, for the purposes of this chapter, the administrative class must be attuned to the power dynamic. Administrators are not employed simply to carry out orders: They are not soldiers on the battle-field. They provide, one would hope, insight, knowledge, intelligence, and compassion as to how to consider change.

If administrators, individually and as a group, are dissuaded from considering alternative perspectives, as was once the case when women were not taken seriously within the leadership realm, then meaningful transformative change in and though education would be almost impossible. Transformative leaders must be courageous to point out institutional deficiencies that harm groups and populations, and they must be open to that which they do not know. How they are taught, trained, cultivated, and promoted are important pieces of the equation. I have argued that critical pedagogy may be one area in which administrators could benefit a great deal, even if they, at first, react negatively. In a nutshell, administrators are a necessary piece of the puzzle of promoting change in formal education. The issue of whether change is transformative or not depends on how we evaluate power, from what angle, and who is doing the evaluating.

Regarding the 50 proposals enunciated earlier, it is clear that administrators would have an important role to play in endorsing, debating, accepting, shaping, implementing, and evaluating the implications, ramifications, and measures related to them. Such change requires vision and transformative leadership, not merely leaders who oversee incremental change. Are the proposals too radical or not radical enough; too precipitous, too poorly conceived, too costly, too jarring, and so on? I can only answer that they form part of what I call the critical pedagogy of democracy, and they could lead to transformative change. Are they the only proposals to transform education? Most certainly not, but, given the history, political economy, traditions, and context of education, I believe that they are certainly worth considering.

Neither Paulo Freire, nor Joe Kincheloe, nor other well-known critical pedagogues, I believe, would want students, educators, and others to simply replicate what they've done or to simply believe that what they've experienced and developed in theory and in praxis is the ultimate answer. The quest for critical humility and radical love encourages all of us to seek new, innovative, and reflective thoughts and actions in the quest for a more decent society. What Freire, Kincheloe, and others offer us, however, is an enormous wealth and insightful archive of *constructed* knowledge, something that is, I would argue, of tremendous value to those wishing to have a more conscious connection to what society was, is, and is evolving into. The critical pedagogy of democracy is not about counting votes, but relates more fundamentally to an unending critical interrogation of the human experience, focused on humane encounters, social justice, peace, a more equitable and respectful distribution of resources, a more dignified and just recognition of indigenous cultures, and an acknowledgement that hegemonic forces exist that marginalize peoples at home and abroad. *Does your vote count?* (Or we might ask, *Are our schools democratic?*) It might (or they might be), but there are a multitude of other factors that are most likely more germane—not to mention that voting, in and of itself, does not make a democracy. As argued throughout my book, any definition of democracy that omits a central place for a meaningful, engaged, and critical education is problematic. *People* construct a democracy, not political parties and institutions (albeit they are relevant), and, therefore, *people* must construct their political, economic, social, cultural, and philosophic destinies. The people are the ones who define their circumstances, values, affiliations, interpersonal relations, and essence to live. Yet, as per the central hypothesis of this book, the people must also be vigilant and suspicious of how power affects their daily lives, their abilities, their relations, and their connection to the world. Education is the key intersecting vehicle that can reinforce or, conversely, interrupt patriotic bondage, racialized marginalization, essentialized visions of poverty and impoverishment, and an uncritical assessment of how power works. Freire and Kincheloe offer much inspiration for this journey, and their willingness to question and accept questions provides for a vibrant, dynamic, and engaged democracy within the spirit of critical pedagogy. Alongside the mantra of the *alter-mondialiste* movement that *another world is possible*, I would like to conclude by suggesting that *another democracy is possible*.

Postscript: Good People in Difficult Jobs

For five years, from 2005 to 2010, I had the pleasure to teach in an educational leadership doctoral program at Youngstown State University. I taught three of the mandatory courses—Qualitative Methods, Theories of Inquiry, and Diversity and Leadership—providing me with significant exposure to the students, in addition to sitting on dissertation committees. The students, who were largely white, with a majority being male, and were, for the most part, principals and superintendents, came from rural, suburban, and urban schools boards within a roughly two-hour radius. My learning experience in working with the students was not only important but also transformative. I learned that my views, concerns, opinions, beliefs, values, ideology, proclivities, idiosyncrasies, and way of being may not be common, shared, accepted, and embraced by others.

I learned that sustained and meaningful critical analysis, discussion, and engagement can help transform thinking. I refer to myself because I learned a great deal from the students, from their questions, critiques, presentations, papers, justifications, and positioning as students, people, and colleagues. Much of the material I presented was not necessarily what might come quickly to mind when thinking of educational leadership; for instance, we focused on epistemology and what we do not know, which is not easy for educational leaders, when thinking about theory. We started with what we did and did not know about Cuba, and why, and what the signification was for us in deconstructing political reality and intercultural relations; and when we started to study diversity, I had them focus on white power and privilege rather than the much-vaunted benefits of a heterogeneous society. In both cases, the initial reaction was: *Why this?* and *What does this have to do with what we're all about?*

I recall a professor of political science from my undergraduate studies warning that we should not focus too narrowly on the target, lest we miss the framework. Thus for me, during this period, the objective was to engage and accept, with humility, that we were limited in our knowledge, and, moreover, that knowledge is socially constructed. We also sought to ingratiate ourselves in the comfort that we could change, perhaps not as radically and quickly as we would like, but for the better, in seeking to refocus our comprehension of our limitations. Ultimately, the process of dialectical engagement in this way aimed to liberate us from the strictures and structures that are ensconced in hegemonic relations, which limit how we consider and address social justice.

Did the students benefit? I can only speak for myself, but the experience was one that instilled in me the notion that transformative leadership requires a process, humility, and a rejection of rubrics, matrices, tools, instruments, and measures that provide one answer only (or, rather, one hegemonic viewpoint only). Administrators are surely a fundamental part of the change equation, and engaging them in ways that encourage transverse thinking can help facilitate change. As important as this is, the next and even more transformative step involves confronting power, not sustaining it, and transformative leadership will reach its full potential when this becomes a central feature of the educational debate, not a peripheral one.

Notes

1.   Parts of this chapter borrow from a book I recently completed: Carr, P. (2010). *Does Your Vote Count? Democracy and Critical Pedagogy.* New York: Peter Lang.
2.   As elaborated in Carr (2010), formal, normative, hegemonic interpretations of democracy based on electoral processes to the behest of critical, meaningful engagement through education can be understood through a thin to thick spectrum of democracy, with the former (electoral processes) being more at the thin end, and the latter (critical engagement) being more at the thick end.

References

Au, W. (2007). Epistemology of the oppressed: The dialectics of Paulo Freire's *Theory of knowledge. Journal for Critical Education Policy Studies, 5*(2). Retrieved from http://www.jceps.com/index.php?pageID= article&articleID=100

Bellamy Foster, J., Holleman, H., & McChesney, R. (2008). The U.S. imperial triangle and military spending. *Monthly Review, 60*(5), 1–19.

Brosio, R. (2003). High-stakes tests: Reasons to strive for better Marx. *Journal for Critical Education Policy Studies, 1*(2). Retrieved from http://www.jceps.com/index.php?pageID= home&issueID=17

Carr, P. R. (2007). Experiencing democracy through neo-liberalism: The role of social justice in education. *Journal of Critical Education Policy Studies, 5*(2). Retrieved from http://www.jceps.com/index. php?pageID= article&articleID=104

Carr, P. R. (2008a). "But what can I do?": Fifteen things education students can do to transform themselves in/through/with education. *International Journal of Critical Pedagogy, 1*(2), 81–97. Retrieved from http://freire.mcgill.ca/ojs/index.php/home/article/view/56/31

Carr, P. R. (2008b). Educating for democracy: With or without social justice? *Teacher Education Quarterly*, fall, 117–136.

Carr, P. R. (2008c). Educators and education for democracy: Moving beyond "thin" democracy. *Inter-American Journal of Education and Democracy, 1*(2), 147–165. Retrieved from http://www.riedijed.org/english/articulo.php?idRevista= 4&idArticulo=16

Carr, P. R. (2010). *Does your vote count? Democracy and critical pedagogy.* New York: Peter Lang.

Darder, A., & Miron, L. F. (2006). Critical pedagogy in a time of uncertainty: A call to action. *Cultural Studies—Critical Methodologies, 6*(1), 5–20.

Denzin, N. K. (2009). Critical pedagogy and democratic life or a radical democratic pedagogy. *Cultural Studies—Critical Methodologies, 9*(3), 379–397.

Engels, J. (2007). Floating bombs encircling our shores: Post–9/11 rhetorics of piracy and terrorism. *Cultural Studies—Critical Methodologies, 7*(3), 326–349.

Fischman, G. E., & McLaren, P. (2005). Rethinking critical pedagogy and the Gramscian and Freirean legacies: From organic to committed intellectuals or critical pedagogy, commitment, and praxis. *Cultural Studies—Critical Methodologies, 5*(4), 425–447.

Freire, P. (1973). *Education for critical consciousness.* New York: The Continuum Publishing Company. Freire, P. (1985). *The Politics of education.* South Hadley, MA: Bergin & Garvey Publishers.

Freire, P. (1998). *Pedagogy of freedom: Ethics, democracy, and civic courage.* Lanham, MD: Rowman & Littlefield.

Freire, P. (2004). *Pedagogy of indignation.* Boulder, CO: Paradigm Publishers.

Freire, P. (1973/2005). *Pedagogy of the oppressed.* New York: Continuum.

Gandin, L. A., & Apple, M. (2005). Thin versus thick democracy in education: Porto Alegre and the creation of alternatives to neo-liberalism. *International Studies in Sociology of Education, 12*(2), 99–116.

Giroux, H. (2005). The passion of the right: Religious fundamentalism and the crisis of democracy. *Cultural Studies—Critical Methodologies, 5*(3), 309–317.

Giroux, H., & Giroux, S. S. (2006). Challenging neo-liberalism's new world order: The promise of critical pedagogy. *Cultural Studies—Critical Methodologies, 6*(1), 21–32.

Gordon, S. P., Smyth, J., & Diehl, J. (2008). The Iraq war, "sound science," and "evidence-based" educational reform: How the Bush administration uses deception, manipulation, and subterfuge to advance its chosen ideology. *Journal for Critical Education Policy Studies, 6*(2), 173–204. Retrieved from http://www.jceps.com/PDFs/6-2–10.pdf

Hill, D., & Boxley, S. (2007). Critical teacher education for economic, environmental and social justice: An ecosocialist manifesto. *Journal for Critical Education Policy Studies, 5*(2). Retrieved from http://www. jceps.com/index.php?pageID= article&articleID=96

Kellner, D., & Share, J. (2007). Critical media literacy, democracy, and the reconstruction of education. In Macedo, D., and Steinberg, S. (Eds.), *Media literacy: A reader* (pp. 3–23). New York: Peter Lang.

Kincheloe, J. L. (2007). Critical pedagogy in the twenty-first century. In McLaren, P., & Kincheloe J. (Eds.), *Critical pedagogy: Where are we now?* (pp. 9–42). New York: Peter Lang.

Kincheloe, J. L. (2008a). *Critical pedagogy: Primer.* New York: Peter Lang.

Kincheloe, J. L. (2008b). *Knowledge and critical pedagogy: An introduction.* London: Springer.

Kincheloe, J. L., & Steinberg, S. R. (2006). An ideology of miseducation: Countering the pedagogy of empire. *Cultural Studies—Critical Methodologies, 6*(1), 33–51.

Lund, D. E., & Carr, P. R. (Eds.). (2008). *"Doing" democracy: Striving for political literacy and social justice.* New York: Peter Lang.

Macedo, D., & Steinberg, S. (2007). *Media literacy: A reader.* New York: Peter Lang.

Macrine, S. (Ed.). (2009). *Critical pedagogy in uncertain times: Hopes and possibilities.* New York: Palgrave Macmillan.

McLaren, P., & Kincheloe, J. L. (Eds.). (2007). *Critical pedagogy: Where are we now?* New York: Peter Lang.

Shields, C. M. (2004). Dialogic leadership for social justice: Overcoming pathologies of silence. *Educational Administration Quarterly, 40*(1), 109–113.

Shields, C. M. (2010). Transformative leadership: Working for equity in diverse contexts. *Educational Administration Quarterly, 46*(4), 558–589.

Shields, C. M., & Edwards, M. M. (2005). *Dialogue is not just talk: A new ground for educational leadership.* New York: Peter Lang.

Steinberg, S., & Kincheloe, J. (Eds.). (2009). *Christotainment: Selling Jesus through popular culture.* Boulder, CO: Westview Press.

Westheimer, J. (2008). *No child left thinking: Democracy at-risk in American schools* (Democratic Dialog series, no. 17). Ottawa, Canada: Democratic Dialog, University of Ottawa.

Westheimer, J., & Kahne, J. (2003). Reconnecting education to democracy: Democratic dialogs. *Phi Delta Kappan, 85*(1), 9–14.

Westheimer, J., & Kahne, J. (2004). What kind of citizen? The politics of educating for democracy. *American Educational Research Journal, 41*(2), 237–269.

Willinsky, J. (1998). *Learning to divide the world: Education at empire's end.* Minneapolis: University of Minnesota Press.

CHAPTER 3

One Principal's Influence on Sustained, Systematic, and Differentiated Professional Development for Social Justice

Brad W. Kose

Purpose defines success.—*David Allen*

I hate the phrase, "All kids can learn." To me, that's an insult to educators and to kids because of course all kids can learn. The question is, "What are they learning?"—*Audrey Union, Principal of Integration Middle School*

In this article, I explore the promising practices of Audrey Union (all names in this article are pseudonyms), a white principal of Integration Middle School (IMS), which served nearly 400 students in sixth through ninth grades. Approximately 40% of the students were of color and a similar percentage qualified for free and reduced lunch. In particular, I examine her influence in creating systemic, sustained, and differentiated professional development for social justice in her school. This is a critical case study (Yin, 2003) in that her practices offer in-depth insights for addressing at least two crucial challenges faced by middle level principals.

The first challenge concerns providing quality professional development opportunities for all teachers to enhance their practice for all students, a core component of school improvement (Elmore, 2002). Several authors have provided models of or demonstrated the crucial role principals play in creating these opportunities (Bredeson, 2003; Lindstrom & Speck, 2004; Tallerico, 2005; Youngs & King, 2002). However, documented principal practice is needed for creating a more comprehensive understanding of how they differentiate professional learning for individual teaching needs, especially considering the next challenge. A second, related challenge, despite its importance, has received much less attention. It is also the challenge that set Principal Union apart from most principals: providing professional development that encourages teachers to prepare students as citizens who understand and address community, national, and global social issues. In other words, Principal Union's practices not only demonstrated commitment to professional development for equity and academic excellence

(Scheurich & Skrla, 2003), but also commitment to professional development driven by student learning for diversity and social action.

Certainly, students face a number of complex and inescapable 21st century social challenges, some of which are longstanding, while others are just emerging. As Banks and Banks (2005) suggested, "The world's greatest problems ... result from people in the world—from different cultures, races, religions, and nations—being unable to get along and work together to solve world problems" (p. 5). Some of these realities include a "flattening" and more competitive global economy (Friedman, 2005), multiple threats to the realization of a democratic society (West, 2004), global warming (Oreskes, 2004), other pressing environmental issues (Worldwatch Institute, 2005, 2006), and social injustices such as poverty, discrimination, and violence that extends from hate crimes to terrorism to genocide. Preparing students to understand and engage these challenges in developmentally appropriate ways positions the unusual development of justice-oriented citizenship (Westheimer & Kahne, 2004) as a central purpose of education. Thus, the purpose, goals, and enactment of professional development aim higher than the ubiquitous and important goal of improved and equitable standardized test scores.

Recent scholarship has advanced theories of leadership for social justice (see Grogan, 2002a, 2002b) and frameworks devoted to a comprehensive understanding of leadership for learning (see Knapp, Copland, & Talbert, 2003; Waters, Marzano, & McNulty, 2003), but there has been relatively little discussion of school leadership that seeks to evoke student learning to understand and address social issues (for exceptions, see Furman & Gruenewald, 2004; Theoharis, 2004). Marshall and Ward (2004) have further suggested the need for constructive or real-life models of leaders for social justice.

Although principals cannot assume total responsibility for addressing social issues within or outside of school, the practices delineated in this article provide evidence that principals can play an important role in this endeavor. Without principal leadership, systemic school change for equitable and critical student learning is unlikely. Just as educators likely vary greatly in the extent to which they have considered what 21st century realities mean for their practice, principals who embrace these realities must assess their teachers' relevant levels of practice and ways to meet their individual and collective learning needs.

Methods

This article stems from a larger study that provides a more detailed account of the rationale, conceptual framework, and data collection and analysis methods (Kose, 2005). In essence, after principals were nominated by peers, they were asked to participate in a voluntary pre-screening interview, used to identify principals for social justice. Principal Union was one of three principals selected for an in-depth, five-month qualitative study, which entailed more than 20 half- to full-day observations, formal and informal interviews with her and her staff, and document collection.

The nomination process and screening criteria assessed principals' beliefs and commitment to what I termed "socially just learning" and "socially just classrooms." Socially just learning entailed equitable student learning in high subject matter achievement (often, academic); personal development (e.g., intrapersonal and interpersonal development); diversity development—growth in affirming one's own and others' diversity (e.g., race/ethnicity, gender, ability); and sociopolitical development—increasing understanding and ability to address local, national, and global social issues. Socially just classrooms involve five components: (a) rigorous subject matter content; (b) differentiated pedagogy—teachers design classrooms and teaching to meet all student needs; (c) an ethic of care—positive relationships as a central part of the classroom environment; (d) equitable inclusion—all students are treated fairly (not necessarily the same), and students with special needs are included and served in the classroom rather than pulled out for various programs (with rare exceptions); and (e) social reconstructionist pedagogy, teaching that encourages the development of democratic citizens who understand and engage social issues.

Sustained, systemic, and differentiated professional learning

These high expectations for teaching and learning create a strong need to support teachers with high quality sustained and individualized professional development. After I spent significant time at IMS, Principal Union turned to me one day and said she hoped I had learned the importance of differentiating professional learning. She explained that she thought about professional development much like she thought about her extensive history of teaching—it needed to be differentiated according to three levels. In short, professional development was designed for the whole staff (the core of what everyone should know), certain groups of teachers, and individual teachers. These three organizers help reveal her influence on meeting collective and individual teaching needs. As will become clear, differentiated professional learning was inextricably tied to sustained and systemic professional learning.

Whole-staff learning

At least three areas established the core of what all staff should know: (a) vision, (b) school-wide program coherence, and (c) complementary professional development. After I describe these areas and Principal Union's influence on them, I gradually reveal how this collective learning was vital to reinforcing and differentiating teacher learning needs, particularly in group and individual professional development contexts.

Vision

Professional learning efforts were grounded, often implicitly, in IMS's vision. Principal Union, in her fifth year as principal, communicated the extensive and collective community and staff participation in creating and enacting their vision, which centered on bringing suburban and urban students together, cultivating individual talents and needs, and developing students as global citizens and environmental stewards in an interdisciplinary school. Stated differently, Principal Union and other school leaders not only provided opportunities for everyone to understand the vision of Integration Middle School, but they also used this vision to mobilize a collective agreement for school and professional learning efforts. The vision was substantiated, in part, through three collaboratively developed school goals that were tracked with a new and sophisticated data system: (a) improving standardized test scores in each student sub-group, (b) lowering disaggregated disruptive behavior, and (c) increasing disaggregated attendance rates.

School-wide program coherence

Two broad school-wide programs provided the curricular framework from which teachers planned, taught, and, therefore, had reason to learn from one another: the Responsive Classroom (RC) and the Middle Years International Baccalaureate Program (IB). After describing each program, I will discuss how Principal Union helped influence relevant whole-staff learning opportunities.

The Responsive Classroom and International Baccalaureate Program. The school model that guides classroom relationships and expectations was the Responsive Classroom, which Principal Union explained is based on "the idea of building a community with a very diverse group of kids. ... It's basically a model to help to teach kids social skills, and to set up learning so that everyone can be successful." Principal Union described the Middle Years International Baccalaureate Program as a global, worldwide curriculum based on high expectations that fits well with the interdisciplinary mission and vision of Integration. She further explained:

> I see IB as a way to justify spending time helping teachers learn how to do social justice teaching. IB absolutely promotes that idea ... to have kids involved in making the world a better place, to promote global awareness, and community service learning being integrated in every subject area. ... It gave us a very specific thing to guide what we are doing. It's a credibility, it allows our staff development

committee to look at these IB schools and say, "Yes, it is important for our teachers to be at that fourth level of James Banks' hierarchy" … our wonderful ideas … need credibility and a backbone so we aren't constantly defending ourselves. Having that IB model gives us that foundation from having to be contested about what we are doing.

The curricular and assessment structure of IB prompted teachers to shift from focusing on activities to focusing on in-depth student learning, in part, because, as one teacher put it, "IB scoring is based on what students know and are able to do. … It is not based on 10 points for this assignment, or turning in homework."

Building enthusiasm and providing training. Principal Union's role in this professional development at the whole-staff level was largely two-fold. One aspect of her role concerned influencing gradual collective motivation and agreement for these school-wide adoptions. She brought her successful experiences with Responsive Classroom to IMS and with the encouragement of a few other teachers, convinced an initial wave of teachers to take the RC training several years ago. Principal Union said what "really sold" RC to the staff was one teacher's longtime success with RC, which "dramatically changed" her teaching.

Although Principal Union knew about the International Baccalaureate for many years, it was a teacher from Integration Middle School who initiated the conversation. This teacher, whose previous school was rejected by IB, told Principal Union that IMS already was doing many of the most difficult things about IB. For example, Principal Union had used the work of Wiggins and McTighe (1998) as one guide for helping teachers develop "backward design" units that began with rigorous student learning expectations. Principal Union encouraged this teacher to take further responsibility in researching and discussing IB. Principal Union and others first had to remove one decisive barrier: the perception held by many that IB was for middle to upper class white students. They eventually convinced a critical mass of faculty and stakeholders that IB was compatible with the vision and student demographics of IMS. Momentum for the program snowballed, and after a task force gave its approval, the school board accepted it. One of the teachers trained in IB implied the importance of its legitimacy:

I mean it's a little weird that it came up initially, but now that I know a lot more about it, I feel very strongly that it's about creating a quality consistent program without limits that we don't want.

The general manner in which Principal Union and teacher leaders approached RC and IB implementation with other staff members also was important. In short, they stated: "We expect you to implement IB, but do so at your own professional discretion, and we are here to support your needs."

Principal Union's second relevant task was to provide resources for training. Principal Union allocated funds to train teachers and educational assistants in Responsive Classroom and provided stipends to support their work. Here is one teacher's experience with RC training:

I took Responsive Classroom this August, and the only reason I took it was because they offered to pay me to go. So not only was my tuition paid, but they paid my time to be there. It was the most fantastic experience of my life. I learned more about classroom management during that time than I probably did in the four years I was in college and then the two years that I was, you know, floundering in teaching. I really learned [what] language [to] use when you talk to kids … what is effective and what's not.

Principal Union allocated funds for IB, but because the training was expensive, Principal Union and the IB committee decided to use a "train-the-trainer" model of professional development. The IB committee was composed of several strategically located members who were encouraged or who volunteered to take different levels of the training and then provide training to various groups of teachers. Principal Union often structured staff meetings to provide time for the International Baccalaureate training. IB topics at staff meetings included general information, student assessment guidelines, assessment of teacher implementation stages, and distribution of IB materials.

Complementary staff development

The International Baccalaureate program, in particular, provided a broad framework in which to situate other types of professional development. At the whole-staff level, professional development remained comprehensive and sufficiently general to provide multiple points of entry for all teachers, regardless of their teaching assignments. Three examples help demonstrate complementary staff development.

Differentiating instruction. Principal Union facilitated a discussion in one staff meeting that focused on brainstorming ways in which to accomplish school goals by meeting different student needs. During this meeting, Principal Union provided models of differentiating instruction for student needs, one of which included a matrix of high/low skill and high/low will. She explained students with low skill need more intensive learning support, whereas students with low will need to develop stronger relationships with their teachers and peers.

Diversity discussions. One parent volunteered to provide diversity consultation professional development services, because she was "immediately impressed" the first time she met Principal Union. Principal Union had already begun using her services to encourage extensive diversity conversations with students, parents, and teachers. During the current study, this parent, along with a district curriculum specialist, guided the staff through an intense presentation and discussion of a developmental model of intercultural sensitivity (Bennett, 2004).

Staff members were helped to interpret the results of their Intercultural Developmental Inventories (Hammer, Bennett, & Wiseman, 2003). One of the crucial discussion points was the strengths and limitations of a worldview that minimized differences or masked diversity by remaining "color-blind." By minimizing students' (or others') diversity, teachers risked overlooking or misinterpreting important cultural differences that could be interpreted as behavioral problems. Both Principal Union and this parent mentioned that diversity professional development was relevant for all staff members, but particularly for a predominantly white teaching staff and especially for teachers with little previous experience teaching students from diverse backgrounds.

Teaching for social justice. Principal Union also devoted one staff meeting to social justice teaching, frameworks, and literature. Prior to the meeting, she provided staff members with copies of an article that distinguished levels of multicultural education in schools, the exemplary school being one that called students to affirm diversity, critique social injustices, and take action (Nieto, 2002). The media specialist began the meeting by sharing children's literature relevant to social justice. The majority of the staff meeting was facilitated by a district diversity specialist invited by Principal Union. This facilitator provided an engaging overview of James Banks' four levels of multicultural education (Banks, 1988), which was closely aligned with the assigned readings (the fourth level is "social action"). Teachers and other staff members had opportunities to critique curricula through this multicultural lens and reflect upon how their practices aligned with these frameworks.

Principal Union brought the meeting to a close by highlighting a number of relevant curricular resource books available in the school and in her office (e.g., Christensen, 2000). As with the Responsive Classroom and International Baccalaureate professional development, teachers reported that allowing them to integrate teaching for social justice into their practice at their own pace and discretion was important in their willingness to take risks and try these new ideas. Principal Union considered teaching for social justice to be an advanced and sophisticated level of teaching. She said about one-quarter of her staff taught for social justice, half understood it and were working toward it, and the remainder were so new they were just working on classroom management and implementing basic curriculum:

I think you've got to be really comfortable in your own skin and in other people's skins, you know, just to be able to go out there and do that. ... I would say that community service learning is a part of our school and it's a part of the IB model, and so everyone is expected to do that. But a lot of it is still at a very superficial level; ... some teachers get this faster than others.

Group learning

Although Principal Union helped create multiple group learning opportunities, such as book clubs and task forces, I highlight three of the most important structured group contexts that provided teachers with further chances to learn according to their own needs and areas of specialty: core teams, specialist groups, and a mentor group.

Core teams

Principal Union had the opportunity to help design IMS's new facility several years prior to this study. Part of the structural design incorporated large offices to provide a shared space for interdisciplinary teams of four core teachers (language arts, math, science, and social studies), a special education teacher, and special education assistants who shared the same team of students.

In addition to providing training for newly formed teams, Principal Union scheduled daily common planning and preparation time for these teams to plan integrated units, discuss strategies for meeting students' needs, and share teaching methods. Collaboration was an implicit non-negotiable expectation for the team. The IB program provided common curricular and assessment guidelines, language, and tools for teachers to learn from one another in job-embedded and "just in-time" professional development (i.e., professional learning embedded in the daily practice of teaching and learning). Therefore, teachers had sustained formal and informal learning opportunities for their common and idiosyncratic needs, which included classroom management, developing IB assessments, and learning how to connect with a particular student or parent. In short, this team context created a rich differentiated learning environment.

As Principal Union inferred in an above quote, several "social action" units had been developed by teams and were being adapted within the IB framework. For example, Principal Union told me about one student who collected community member signatures and contacted legislators to successfully lower noise in her neighborhood (thereby allowing her to sleep at night) as her class project. One teacher described a "huge diversity unit" Principal Union helped create a few years prior to this study (and prior to the IB adoption):

I have never had eighth graders, and still to this day haven't had eighth graders that talked about racism and cultural diversity on the level that they did, and it stemmed from the question of "What is normal?" And that was a question that Principal Union and [the assistant principal], I think, came up with from our whole year long theme of diversity. We spent a quarter understanding who we are and where we come from.

Not only did teachers learn through collaborative, sustained, job-embedded, and differentiated curriculum development, but they also simultaneously developed and deepened their abilities to nurture justice-oriented citizens.

Additionally, the rich daily learning opportunities between general education and special education teachers afforded by sharing students with special needs and planning together should not be overlooked. The entire core team benefited from sustained formal and informal opportunities to explicitly and tacitly understand and meet individual student needs as well as student group similarities and differences, such as working with students with disabilities, students of color, and students from upper class backgrounds.

Subject area and specialist teams

At least weekly, subject area teams (e.g., social studies) and the specialist team (art, music, special education) held meetings in which teachers had opportunities to deepen their content expertise. Again, the IB framework provided the substance of many of these learning opportunities. For example, many subject area teams spent considerable effort developing, backward mapping, and aligning IB grade-level assessments with state standards.

Mentor group

Besides IB discussions, during this study the mentor/mentee group, consisting of 28 people, decided to learn about multiple intelligences, which according to several teachers helped both veteran and novice teachers gain different levels of insight into differentiating their teaching to meet a greater range of student learning styles. Everyone I spoke to about the mentor program said it greatly improved since Principal Union hired a part-time mentor facilitator to create a formal structure for scaffolding activities to various teachers' learning curves. Teachers told me the mentor program two to three years prior to the study was "not helpful" to "nonexistent" because they rarely met as a large group and seldom saw their mentors.

Implicitly, this section reveals another indirect influence of Principal Union: designing different groups and deciding appropriate ways of determining team members. Many of these decisions were made democratically.

Individual learning

Principal Union helped to create three contexts that provided individualized professional learning opportunities. These contexts included formal and informal one-on-one conversations, a self-selected professional development day, and strategically placed specialists.

One-on-one conversations

Principal Union, who considered herself to be a teacher of teachers, created individualized learning opportunities by encouraging teachers to see her and by actively meeting with teachers. During my observations, many teachers stopped in her open door for brief or extended conversations about students, teaching, curricula, parents, or personal matters. One teacher told me that Principal Union gradually and continuously nurtured, but never forced her to teach students about social issues by providing articles in her mailbox and holding informal conversations. She noted that it took her a few years to feel truly comfortable teaching in that way.

Whenever possible, Principal Union made it part of her daily routine to visit teachers' classrooms to understand their teaching, understand their students, provide feedback, and establish comfort and trust in being observed. She used the evaluation process to provide extensive feedback on areas of strength and encouraged teachers to identify areas in which they had questions or would like to grow. Principal Union also used this time to encourage greater responsibility for teacher leadership, particularly for intermediate and veteran teachers. Besides providing specific feedback and ideas, Principal Union also used these formal and informal opportunities to highlight and encourage external professional development activities that may be of interest. Based on teacher feedback and interest levels, Principal Union sometimes recommended colleagues to observe or speak with for a particular expertise area.

A good example of this indirect influence occurred when she encouraged two language arts teachers to attend an intensive state writing conference. Since that time, they have planned together, observed each other teach, attended other conferences, backward mapped language arts curriculum and assessments to IB criteria on one of their breaks, and have sometimes even carpooled to school. As one of these teachers explained:

I learn stuff from her, and I get her advice and sometimes vice versa, but not as much. I watch her class during prep too because we had different schedules. The equivalent knowledge and time of that would be, you know, $20,000 in staff development money [laughs].

Self-selected professional development day

Another opportunity Principal Union and the professional development committee helped create was an on-site professional development day led by teachers. They realized they had enough expertise in the building to allow teachers to provide workshops on various topic areas that other teachers could choose. Teachers self-selected into workshops that met their individual learning needs.

Strategic placement of specialists

Principal Union was also instrumental in hiring, training, or placing at least three learning specialists in the building: an IB/mentor leader; a creative writing teacher who also served as a valued resource for planning with and observing teachers, teaching students about diversity and social action, and implementing International Baccalaureate; and a lead teacher trained as a trainer in the Responsive Classroom. I expand on the latter example.

Principal Union negotiated with the person in charge of Responsive Classroom training to allow Deb Bell, a part-time lead teacher, to become a trainer under the conditions she could coach students, parents, and teachers at IMS. "That was the only way I was willing to pay for this one teacher to get all this extended training." Here is one example of the return on Deb's professional development, which created sustained, just-in-time, individualized learning opportunities:

> Deb: [Teachers] just come into my room whenever, and say, "Can I just stop in?" [to see RC in action.] People stop in all the time. Sometimes I'll [sense] teachers just hanging outside the door where I can't even see them [laughs]. They just come in to listen to what's going on in the classrooms, hear the language, feel the flow of the class. ... I would say probably a couple of teachers from each team throughout the course of a year, and, you know, we're talking about a staff of probably 50 people, so probably 10 to 15.

Discussion

Principals face challenges in creating quality, differentiated professional development for different teacher needs regarding equitable learning and preparing students to be 21st century social change agents. Although this article is limited to focusing on one principal's practice and further studies are needed to fully understand how these practices affect student learning, several insights seem noteworthy.

The first is that to provide quality differentiated professional development, the entire school as a learning system needs to be considered (i.e., systemic professional development). When principals assess the expansive array of teacher learning needs (especially with expectations to teach for social justice), they should help ensure that professional development content and processes appropriately address the different and sustained professional development needs in whole-staff, group, and individual contexts.

The second point of curricular coherence should be clear by now. The adoption and implementation of the Responsive Classroom and the International Baccalaureate program provided school-wide frameworks that connected whole-staff, group, and individual learning opportunities. One can easily imagine that without this coherence, there would be substantially less reason for teachers to learn from each other. Additionally, integrating the IB framework with diversity and social action curriculum and assessments was critical for organizational learning.

An associated implication is that principals should articulate the importance of curricular coherence and provide the encouragement, opportunities, and available resources for their schools to develop this coherence. Although Principal Union helped to successfully mesh the adoption of RC and IB with her school, other frameworks or programs may better fit the needs and interests of different schools.

Flexibility for innovation (e.g., to develop social action projects) appears to be a critical consideration in this adoption. Principals should avoid overly prescriptive programs that may constrain teachers' creativity and abilities to adapt to student needs. Additionally, principals and schools may wish to take more of an organic approach to program coherence for philosophical, expertise, or fiscal reasons and develop their own programs. However, even in these scenarios, principals likely want to consult content-free frameworks such as Understanding by Design (Wiggins & McTighe, 2005).

Finally, a number of Principal Union's practices provide subtle clues that are important for guiding professional development related to preparing students to affirm diversity and understand and address social issues. Her involvement in developing, articulating, and communicating the school's vision (for professional development) suggests that principals should cultivate the development of a school mission that creates a fertile context in which discussions such as teaching for social justice can grow. Principal Union's influence on the diversity discussions further implies that principals should assess and address their own and teachers' identity needs (e.g., racial identity) before expecting teachers to teach students about diversity. Additionally, Principal Union's selection of and influence on providing frameworks of diversity and social justice indicates that principals should offer similar frameworks for staff members to visualize and interpret what these big ideas look like in practice. Finally, and consistent with other approaches to professional learning in this article, Principal Union's practice of allowing teachers time and discretion to develop this more critical pedagogy seems paramount for teachers' willingness and ability to transform new ideas into teaching and learning.

References

Banks, J. A. (1988). Approaches to multicultural curriculum reform. *Multicultural Leader, 1*(2), 1–3.

Banks, J. A., & Banks, C. A. M. (Eds.). (2005). *Multicultural education*: Issues and perspectives (5th ed.). Hoboken, NJ: John Wiley & Sons.

Bennett, M. J. (2004). Becoming interculturally competent. In J. Wurzel (Ed.), *Toward multiculturalism: A reader in multicultural education* (2nd ed., pp. 62–77). Newton, MA: Intercultural Resource Corporation.

Bredeson, P. (2003). *Designs for learning: A new architecture for professional development in schools.* Thousand Oaks, CA: Corwin Press.

Christensen, L. (2000). *Reading, writing, and rising up: Teaching about social justice and the power of the written word.* Milwaukee, WI: Rethinking Schools, Ltd.

Elmore, R. F. (2002). *Bridging the gap between standards and achievement: The imperative for professional development in education.* Washington, DC: Albert Shanker Institute.

Friedman, T. L. (2005). *The world is flat: A brief history of the twenty first century.* New York: Farrar, Straus and Giroux.

Furman, G. C., & Gruenewald, D. A. (2004). Expanding the landscape of social justice: A critical ecological analysis. *Educational Administration Quarterly, 40,* 47–76.

Grogan, M. (2002a). Leadership for social justice [Special Issue]. *Journal of School Leadership, 12*(3).

Grogan, M. (2002b). Leadership for social justice [Special Issue], *Journal of School Leadership, 12*(2).

Hammer, M. R., Bennett, M. J., & Wiseman, R. (2003). Measuring intercultural sensitivity: The intercultural developmental inventory. *International Journal of Intercultural Relations, 27,* 421–443.

Knapp, M. S., Copland, M. A., & Talbert, J. E. (2003). *Leading for learning: Reflective tools for school and district leaders.* Seattle, WA: Center for the Study of Teaching and Policy.

Kose, B. W. (2005). *Leadership and professional development for social justice: A multi-case study of the role of school principals.* Unpublished dissertation, University of Wisconsin, Madison, WI.

Lindstrom, P. H., & Speck, M. (2004). *The principal as professional development leader.* Thousand Oaks, CA: Corwin Press.

Marshall, C., & Ward, M. (2004). "Yes, but..." Education leaders discuss social justice. *Journal of School Leadership, 14*(3), 530–563.

Nieto, S. (2002). Affirmation, solidarity and critique: Moving beyond tolerance in education. In E. Lee, D. Menkart, & M. Okazawa-Rey (Eds.), *Beyond heroes and holidays: A practical guide to K-12 anti-racist, multicultural education and staff development* (2nd ed., pp. 7–18). Washington, DC: Teaching for Change.

Oreskes, N. (2004). Beyond the ivory tower: The scientific consensus on climate change. *Science, 306,* 1686.

Scheurich, J. J., & Skrla, L. (2003). *Leadership for equity and excellence.* Thousand Oaks, CA: Corwin Press.

Tallerico, M. (2005). Supporting and sustaining teachers' professional development: A principal's guide. Thousand Oaks, CA: Corwin Press.

Theoharis, G. T. (2004). At no small cost: Social justice leaders and their response to resistance. Unpublished dissertation, University of Wisconsin-Madison, Madison, WI.

Waters, T., Marzano, R. J., & McNulty, B. (2003). *Balanced leadership: What 30 years of research tell us about the effect of leadership on student achievement.* Aurora, CO: Mid-continent Research for Education and Learning.

West, C. (2004). *Democracy matters: Winning the fight against imperialism.* New York: The Penguin Press.

Westheimer.J., Be Kahne, J. (2004). What kind of citizen? The politics of educating for democracy. *American Educational Research Journal, 41*(2), 237–269.

Wiggins, G., & McTighe, J. (1998). *Understanding by design.* Alexandria, VA: Association for Supervision and Curriculum Development.

Wiggins, G., & McTighe, J. (2005). *Understanding by design* (Expanded 2nd ed.). Alexandria, VA: Association for Supervision and Curriculum Development.

Worldwatch Institute. (2005). *State of the world 2006: Redefining global security.* New York: W. W. Norton.

Worldwatch Institute. (2006). *State of the world 2006: Special focus, China and India.* New York: W. W. Norton.

Yin, R. K. (2003). *Case study research: Design and methods* (3rd ed., vol. 5). Thousand Oaks, CA: Sage.

Youngs, P., & King, M. B. (2002). Principal leadership for professional development to build school capacity. *Educational Administration Quarterly, 38*, 643–670.

CHAPTER 4

Learning to Teach and Teaching to Learn

Supporting the Development of New Social Justice Educators

Bree Picower

Introduction

Beginning teachers are more likely to leave the profession than seasoned counterparts; 14 percent of new teachers leave after their first year, 33 percent leave within three years, and almost 50 percent leave in five years (Alliance for Quality Education, 2004). Research on teacher attrition shows many educators who are part of this "revolving door" (Ingersoll, 2001) are "service oriented" and "idealistic" teachers (Miech & Elder, 1996). These teachers enter the profession to "mak[e] a difference" and contribute to positive change in society. The constraints they face within public schools, however, make it difficult to realize their idealism, leading to attrition. With fewer teachers in the field teaching from this perspective to serve as mentors, how can emerging teachers, dedicated to social justice education (SJE), find the support needed to develop as professionals and remain in the field?

This study explored the role that participating in a critical inquiry project (CIP) played on the development of new educators who aspire to teach from a social justice perspective. The study also examined how relationships between the first and second-year teacher participants shaped their development as social justice educators, learners, and leaders. Findings contribute to understanding two areas: new teacher induction and peer and near-peer mentorship. Unlike most new teacher support groups, CIP was specifically geared to support teachers in their pursuit of SJE. It provided induction designed to combat the attrition of "idealistic" teachers, a group often not targeted through professional development literature. Additionally, little research in the field examines how peer and near-peer relationships between teachers at varying stages of teaching impact their development as social justice educators and leaders.

Literature Review

The National Commission on Teaching and America's Future (2003) contends that one strategy to support teachers professionally is to prepare teachers for the challenges they will face in urban schools.

Darling-Hammond and McLaughlin (1995) argue that quality professional development must "provide teachers opportunities to share what they know, discuss what they want to learn, and connect new concepts and strategies to their own unique contexts" (p. 597). Quality mentoring by veteran teachers and access to networks of educators who share similar concerns are strategies that are often promoted (Alliance for Quality Education, 2004; Achinstein & Athanases, 2006).

While there is much research on general support for new teachers (Achinstein & Athanases, 2006; NCTAF, 2003), there is less research on how to meet the needs of what Miech and Elder (1996) call "idealistic" teachers "who seek to make a significant impact on society" (p. 239). Idealistic teachers place less importance on a job's extrinsic rewards, such as income and prestige (Mortimer & Lorence, 1979; Rosenberg, 1981) and instead have a "desire to help people" (Simpson et al., 1979). Unlike teachers who enter the field without this service orientation, these teachers have a higher rate of attrition due to working in an "environment that offers them little guidance on the goals, means, and evaluation of their work" (p. 249). By introducing such teachers to the goals and skills of the field of SJE, projects such as CIP are spaces that can provide guidance to such educators with a specific focus on the service nature of teaching that attracted them to the profession in the first place.

There is a rich tradition of teachers who also approach education from this perspective, seeing it as a vehicle for freedom and liberation (Ayers, Hunt, & Quinn, 1998; Freire, 1993; Greene, 1988; Payne, 2008). Westheimer and Kahne (2007) assert, "For many, a commitment to social justice also involves a critique of current inequities in society and experimentation with ways to create socially just conditions within schools that model the equality of educational access and equity of educational outcomes we want for the larger society" (p. 97). Like Dewey (1932), Counts (1932), and scholars that have followed them (Anyon, 1981; Ayers, 2004; Banks, 2006; Giroux, 1995), social justice educators contest the notion that teaching is a neutral enterprise, and in contrast embrace the political nature of education that is situated in the cultural, racial, economic, and political tensions of the time. Such teachers are concerned with providing their students with opportunities to develop a political analysis, to link that analysis to academic skills and to provide opportunities to take social action (Cochran-Smith, 2004; Oakes & Lipton, 2006). To combat the attrition of idealistic teachers, projects that help them gain these skills, improve their pedagogy, and take action can help them feel empowered rather than defeated (Duncan-Andrade, 2004; Picower, 2007).

Duncan-Andrade shows that critical inquiry groups support such teachers in the difficult work of creating classroom environments in which students are engaged in critical analysis of and take action to improve the world around them. Critical inquiry groups he facilitated "work to powerfully address the needs of [the participating teachers'] students while [participating teachers] are engaged in their own professional growth" (Duncan-Andrade, 2004, p. 340). Research at the University of California Los Angeles's Center X, a program that explicitly works to develop social justice educators, found that the relationships created as novice teachers worked toward equity positioned them as valued leaders at their school sites and kept them in the profession longer than average (Quartz, 2003). In a pilot study, Picower (2007) found that the CIP project provided first-year teachers with ongoing support, culturally relevant curriculum development, and accountability to continue to teach SJE. Without likeminded veteran teachers at their school sites to turn to for the mentorship suggested by the literature, these teachers turned to each other for support.

Method

In an attempt to learn about educational innovation in everyday settings (Bell, 2004; Sandoval & Bell, 2004), I designed the Social Justice Critical Inquiry Project as an environment in which to collect phenomenological data that uncovered how participating in CIP supported the development of new social justice educators. CIP is a multi-year study in which data are collected from audio-taped, bimonthly meetings, annual individual interviews, limited classroom observation, K-5 student work, and field notes. While the content, tone, and activities of the CIP meetings are driven by the participants, I focus on a different research question every year based on my observations and assessment of what is happening within the group at the time. For example, a prior study that emerged was the strategies that the participants used to teach SJE in hostile climates (Picower, 2011).

The present study aimed to assess the role that the group, as well as the role that peer-to-peer relationship, played in their sense of their development as social justice educators. The annual 60–90 minute ethnographic interviews that were conducted at the end of the academic school year were designed to elicit a sense of their experiences, perceptions, feelings, and knowledge of these roles (Lofland & Lofland, 1984). Open-ended questions allowed participants to reflect upon the prior two years and how they believed the group and group relationships impacted their development as social justice teachers and emerging leaders. An example of such a question was "Given that CIP is made up of 1st and 2nd year teachers and graduate students, how has this contributed to your development as a social justice educator?" The findings were compared with data from the previous yearly studies to provide a sense of growth over time.

All interviews and meeting sessions were transcribed and the data were analyzed using grounded theory, allowing the data to inform the analysis, rather than forcing it into *a priori* categories. I read through all interview and session transcriptions looking for examples of the role of the group and peer-to-peer relationships and wrote codes in the margins, creating short line-by-line units, staying as close to the participants' words as possible (Foss & Waters, 2007). I then physically cut these line-by-line units, with only a color-coded system as to who said what, and created piles of data that shared similar themes. These piles were checked for consistency and put into envelopes, each titled with a label that described the phenomenon within. As I arranged these labels and thought about the relationship between them, my conceptual framework of the norms and collaboration that supported the teachers' development emerged as the story these labels told together (Foss & Waters, 2007). Glaser and Strauss (1967) contend that this approach ensures that the theory fits the phenomenon studied, that it does not include any forced elements.

Participants

As a professor of a two-course sequence on social justice education, I offered the opportunity to participate in CIP to students before graduation. Two years in a row, students inspired by the courses volunteered based on their desire to enact social justice education. Eleven of the 12 participants graduated from 2007 and 2008 cohorts of the undergraduate program.[1]

Table 1 shows the diversity of race, grade, specialty, and experience of the teacher participants. The teachers taught in nine different schools in a variety of communities in New York City (with the exception of Luis, who taught in urban New Jersey) that served predominantly students of color who qualified for free and reduced lunch. Several were in schools that had a high percentage of English Language Learners. While each school provided a range of professional development opportunities, the teachers reported that most of the in-services and mentoring they received focused more on technical aspects of teaching (i.e., filling out report cards, data analysis, training on specific curricular programs) than on issues pertaining to critical pedagogy, culturally relevant teaching, or social justice education.

CIP met biweekly at the university from which the teachers graduated for two-hour dinner meetings. Kicking-off with a full-day retreat in September, participants set goals and decided on how to structure the subsequent meetings. As the researcher/facilitator of the group, I facilitated the retreat, and then created a structure in which the participants took turns creating the agendas and facilitating the remainder of the meetings in pairs. Most sessions opened with check-ins with critical friends trios, which remained constant for the year, in which they talked about issues they faced in their classrooms or schools. Every session closed with teachers appreciating something they learned from another group member. Other than that, the sessions often varied and included a range of activities: responding to

Member	Race/Ethnicity	Teacher of	Type of School	Years Teaching	Years in CIP
Stephanie	White	5th Grade	Public	2	2
Jonathan	White	5th Grade, Special Ed CTT	Public	2	2
Hally	White	Kindergarten	Catholic	2	2
Nina	African-Amer.	Pre-K	Independent	2	1.5
Nick	White	2nd Grade, bilingual ASL	Public	I	I
Luis	Latino	6th, 7th, 8th Grade, Sp. Ed.	Public	2	I
Chantale	Black/Haitian descent	6th Grade, Math, Science	Public	1.5	I
Reina	Jewish/White	5th Grade	Public	I	I
Dana	Jewish/White	4th Grade	Public	I	I
Vanessa	Latina	4th Grade	Public	I	.5
Shama	Indian	Ass't Teacher, Special Ed.	Independent	I	I
Beth	White	Ass't Teacher, Special Ed.	Independent	I	I

Table I Participant Information

readings, developing curriculum on social justice topics (child labor, Iraq war, historical racism, genocide), sharing and troubleshooting enacted curriculum, examining student work to see how students were understanding themes of social justice, researching and learning about specific topics they identified as knowledge gaps in their own learning (Malcolm X, service learning), listening to guest speakers on social justice pedagogy, preparing for presentations on their work, creating blogs of their projects, and more.[3] They also presented at local and national conferences and presented to current pre-service teachers in multiple courses at their alma mater. The teachers received no credit or financial incentives to participate; they chose to participate solely because of their desire to continue to develop as social justice educators.

As the facilitator and researcher of the group, I had a variety of roles. I handled most of the logistics such as ordering dinner, reserving space, gathering materials, etc. While some of my roles shifted from professor to facilitator, I still was looked to as the "expert" when it came to issues of SJE. I identified and shared readings, resources, and speakers connected to topics that the participants decided to learn more about or develop lessons on. I was often turned to for an empathetic ear, listening and giving advice to situations that overwhelmed the teachers in their schools. I reviewed the agenda that the facilitating teachers planned prior to the meeting and gave feedback on content, continuity, and time, and often debriefed their facilitation with them afterwards. As taskmaster, I often kept them on time, and redirected when they got stuck or didn't follow through on their responsibilities. I believe my most important role was to raise critical questions connecting them back to the social justice goals they set.[4]

Findings and Discussion

CIP was made up of first and second-year teachers going through similar teaching experiences who shared commitments to social justice education. These factors led to the creation of a collaborative space characterized by several unspoken norms: (1) members were expected to be full participants, no matter experience level; (2) to expect difference and explore multiple perspectives; (3) that members should allow for a certain level of tension; and (4) CIP was a place to discuss 'taboo' issues that aren't typically possible in mainstream conversations.

The collaborative space coupled with these unspoken norms paved the way for collaboration characterized by an exchange of ideas, resources, and feedback. This supported the teachers' development in three ways. First, members became role models to each other and were able to learn from each other's experiences and projects. Second, collaboration improved members' ability to actualize social justice education in their classrooms. Third, the collaboration taught members necessary social justice leadership skills.

Participation resulted in members becoming reflective of their journey and remaining committed to teaching and social justice. The members learned to "have each other's backs," began presenting to other educators, and felt a sense of pride in their accomplishments. These results kept them on their social justice teaching journey, which also contributed to deepening their political analysis.

Unspoken Group Norms

The make-up and tone of the group set the stage for four unspoken norms that supported members' development as social justice educators. The first norm was that CIP expected, even pushed, members to be active participants. Second, the participants understood that even though they had shared goals, they were not going to agree on every issue; therefore, they created an expectation for difference and multiple perspectives. Because of this, the group allowed for tension in a way that challenged and furthered their thinking, rather than damaged the cohesion of the group. This third norm challenged them intellectually and created a space for them to unpack complex issues. As a result, the fourth norm of the group was that there was a different way of talking in CIP; they could discuss topics that were taboo in general company and do so in ways that might have resulted in conflict outside of CIP.

Norm One: Expectation of Full Participation. Members understood CIP was not a place to sit back and observe; that it was acceptable, even desirable, to participate even if you didn't have all the answers. There was an unspoken expectation that if you were there, you were going to contribute. As Hally said:

> It's not competitive, but it is. If you have nothing to bring up, what are you doing, just sitting there? You have to have something to talk about … you *want* to say what's going on in your classroom, that's a good part of it.

The members recognized the sense of pressure in the group, but felt that it contributed positively to their development. Instead of being positioned as beginning teachers with no professional knowledge, CIP framed members as intelligent people who had every reason to participate. This norm set the stage for rich collaboration that supported their development.

Another factor that increased participation was the sense that members need not 'have all the answers' to contribute. Members felt free to take risks no matter their level of experience. Being on the same plane allowed CIP members to explore, as equals, a new way of thinking. As Chantale stated:

> We're humble enough to be on the same plane and knowing that we don't know all the answers but that we can get help from anyone. The fact that … I am just like a first-year in CIP, but that someone would ask my opinion about something it was great.

Not feeling compelled to have all the answers allowed people to be more fully involved. The participation was made easier because even though they were expected to contribute, no one felt judged; rather there was an equal exchange of ideas.

Norm Two: Expectations of Difference and Multiple Perspectives. Members understood that topics discussed would sometimes be uncomfortable. Therefore, there was an unspoken expectation that people might come from different perspectives, and these must be respected. Members characterized CIP as a place that has "tolerance of other people and other views" and where "most of the people in the group are not going to take offense easily." As Stephanie explained:

> We all know that nothing in CIP is ever going to cause us not to be friends or be nasty to each other. Any disagreement is taken with the sense that we're social justice educators. We know that we're going to have different views on topics. I think having a lively discussion about it is important, and that these discussions are vital for us to understand them more deeply.

Here Stephanie demonstrated that to not agree is a vital part of being a social justice educator. Unlike polite circles where disagreement is swept under the rug, CIP members actively sought out lively discussions that pushed them to think.

CIP members relied on these multiple perspectives as a way to broaden their understandings of different issues. They identified the racial and cultural diversity of the group as a key factor in helping them find alternative perspectives they would have trouble getting outside of the group. Reina, a White Jewish member explained, "There's not too many places in society you can go and ask somebody 'as a Black woman, how do you feel about this,' right? So that's been really good." The members' understandings that were deepened through the norm of expected differences set the stage for them to have difficult and often unresolved discussions that supported their development.

Norm Three: Allowance for Tension. The fact that CIP was a diverse group, coupled with their openness to different perspectives, paved the way for intense discussions marked by some level of tension. This norm took three forms: it was acceptable for issues to remain unresolved; there was room to unpack complexity; and it was desirable to be challenged intellectually. As an example of unresolved issues, almost all members referenced a discussion about what Obama's election meant for race relations between Chantale, a Black woman of Haitian descent, and Jonathan, a White man. Both members talked about how they felt that their racial and economic background had shaped their status and achievements.

> *Chantale:* [Success is] … all mental. … We all have the same opportunity.
>
> *Jonathan:* We do not.
>
> *Chantale:* Yes we do. Jonathan, I grew up in a neighborhood where I'm telling you a lot of people think the way that you're saying 'oh no, my mom did it like this so I'm gonna do it just like this.' My mom worked in a factory, ok? … She didn't go to college; she only has a third grade education. Look at me … My mom said 'I'm working hard so you can become somebody. You do it. Don't use me as an excuse.' So I did it and I kept going forward and I've never looked back. I don't knock the people in my neighborhood who didn't move forward in their lives. I just said that's not gonna be me.
>
> *Jonathan:* Do you think that works for everyone?
>
> *Chantale:* It can if you just decide to. It can.
>
> *Jonathan:* Cause I'll tell you why I'm here. I'm here because I came from a middle class White family that sent me to private school and had the money to send me to NYU and had the money to buy me lawyers

when I needed them and to shave me and get me a haircut when I needed to go to a job and that woke me up for school and that made me do my homework. It wasn't because I wanted to I wholeheartedly believe that if I didn't have the parents or the money or the morals that my family tried to instill in me, I wouldn't be here. And I don't think that has to do necessarily with me having given it my all cause I definitely didn't … Like you had to overcome your things and I slept through a lot of my things. But we're doing the same thing now.

Chantale: Well that's you're talking from your standpoint. I'm telling it from my standpoint... For me personally for me I don't think about it in the sense of 'oh its just so much tougher for me as a Black woman' you know. It just is. That's the world we live in; therefore I have to push that away and just focus on me and what I need to do. I don't have to think about anybody else; I'm running my race. You run your race, you run your race, and I'm running my race.

Jonathan: I think this is a great conversation and I just want to, I know we're far over time and I wanna tell you Chantale that I appreciate you engaging in this with me and with us and you know I feel safe to go head to head with you here and I hope you do and it's not personal. Or is it? But you know I think we need to have these conversations. (Picower, 2008, Transcript)

What characterized the unspoken norm in this discussion was the group's ability to allow tension to exist, and to learn from each other's viewpoints, rather than to attempt to come to agreement and "all just get along." As Chantale reflected months later:

There was a lot of tension there but we heard each other out, even though we had strong opinions about something. I think we were both willing to say: "Okay, that makes sense." I may not agree with it, but it's okay to disagree with that, so I think that was good for me. Not that I'm a confrontational person, but I'm a bold and honest person, and I think I expected a big blow up. It was great to see someone handle it the way he did.

Although the majority of other members did not actively speak during the exchange, they also learned from the nature of the give and take. As Shama explained:

To be part of a group where we are supposed to expose our kids to these kinds of issues, to just see that tension made me realize, okay, well, we can talk about it. … We left kind of agreeing to disagree … there was still respect towards the person making the argument.

Typical models for cross-cultural discussions on race are tense, unfriendly, and usually end poorly. In contrast, CIP's ability to hear the multiple perspectives and not seek resolution allowed for deeper understanding of a complex issue.

The allowance for tension provided opportunities to unpack complicated issues that members might not otherwise know about based on their own lives. This allowed them to challenge their previous assumptions and think about situations differently. For example, one evening a member suggested that CIP learn more about the conflict between Israel and Palestine after Israel launched a wave of air strikes against targets within the Gaza Strip in December 2008. One Jewish member who was not in attendance that evening had a strong pro-Israel stance, while the majority of the other members professed to know less about the situation but had a pro-Palestinian stance. The group engaged in an intense discussion about whether or not they should use CIP as a space to learn more about the conflict. Unlike most topics discussed in meetings, such as the civil rights movement, the holocaust, or child obesity which had a 'target' or 'enemy' that they all identified, the group did not agree on which country was on the side of justice. The group ultimately decided that it would be too divisive to approach it in depth, but during the evening they respectfully listened to each other's perspectives in the group and agreed to disagree (Picower, 2009, Transcript). Dana, a Jewish member, was even able to challenge her taken-for-granted assumptions about the conflict by listening to the perspectives of her peers:

Maybe I would have taken a pro-Israel stance, because that's what I have been surrounded by my whole life, without ever thinking that there is a very real pro-Palestine stance. I might have automatically come into a situation assuming that my opinion is in the right, and I think CIP having the conversation reminded me just how sensitive it was.

By having a space that allowed for tension, Dana was able to recognize that some of her previously uninterrogated stances might originate from her upbringing, and CIP provided her a space to examine them. The group's allowance for tension permitted members to explore issues more deeply because they let the complexity of the issues guide them rather than the tension inherent in such discussions.

Norm Four: Different Kind of Talk. The tolerance, safety, and desire to hear multiple perspectives allowed the participants to talk to each other in ways that aren't typical of mainstream discussion. As Luis said, "The rest of the team is so open-minded that it is comfortable to put those issues out there that are kind of taboo." Typically, when tension arises during "taboo" discussions, it is interpreted as hostile. The CIP talks stood out to members as qualitatively different because, when people with different opinions disagreed, it didn't affect their relationships. These discussions taught members ways of engaging in positive cross-cultural dialogue. Reina observed:

Hearing Chantale speak made me think about how you can talk to people when you want to ask them a personal question about their background, their lifestyle, their culture, but you don't want to be demeaning or disrespectful. I think that she proved that there are ways to do it, and to make the person feel like you're actually honoring them by asking and talking, versus attacking them.

The conversations in CIP were perceived as skill building, allowing members to learn how to express themselves and to recognize the value of having difficult talks.

Style of Collaboration

The group make-up and norms facilitated a motivating collaboration within CIP. Despite their years teaching, all members felt they had something to contribute. This sense of efficacy fostered a reciprocal exchange of feedback, ideas, and resources. This give and take stayed with them even when apart. As a second-year teacher, Stephanie reflected:

The fact that [Dana] was coming to me showed that she respected my opinion and she valued it and that made me feel like she sees me as somebody that knows what I'm doing ... There are times when I've felt like a leader, people are looking to me for guidance or an example, or advice and it made me feel like I have something to contribute, and I am a professional, and I am good at this, and so it's bringing forth confidence in myself.

Often times, beginning teachers feel they are at the bottom of the pecking order and have little professional knowledge. By being able to contribute and feeling well received within CIP, the teachers gained confidence that they were growing leaders with advice to share.

From feedback to resources, what most characterized their collaboration was that of a reciprocal exchange. This contributed to a unique space in which they mentored and served as role models, while gaining confidence and receiving ideas. Unlike traditional professional development in which there is an "expert" leading "learners," in CIP everyone played both roles at different times, allowing them to benefit from each other's assistance, while simultaneously developing as leaders. A specific type of give and take happened during feedback time, particularly on classroom issues and curricular plans. Having people to provide feedback helped them to feel less alone by having a community of like-minded people to support their ideas. Because they often didn't have other places to turn to discuss issues of SJE, CIP provided them with critical space to get valued advice, making them feel less alone. Another benefit was that the feedback members gave each other continued after meetings. They internalized the process and learned to think about each other's perspectives when they developed their curriculum on their own. As Stephanie planned she said, "I'll think: 'Oh what would Val say about this?' or 'What would Chantale say?'" This feedback helped them think about multiple perspectives when creating curriculum independently.

Ideas were not the only thing that CIP members shared. Often members referenced, brought in, or emailed each other tangible resources that connected to units mentioned in sessions. The materials often "saved the day" for these new teachers who might not have found time to research them. It also strengthened their sense of teamwork. Chantale described, "I remember I was doing ratios and I was telling Jonathan and he was like: 'Oh, I have an article for you.'" Jonathan gave her a class set of *Indy Kids,* an independent student newspaper that focuses on progressive topics. The cover story was on the mortgage crisis and provided her with data and statistics that transformed her textbook driven ratio lesson into one that allowed students to use mathematics to better understand the economic crisis and the rise in homelessness (Picower, 2008, Classroom). She continued, "He gives me the article and it was perfect … I was like 'Ahhh.' Suddenly the heavens opened up!" These exchanges provided them resources that moved their teaching toward social justice and created a resource for future projects. Through the give and take of feedback, ideas and resources, CIP expanded the knowledge and strategies of each of the individual members.

Collaboration Supports Their Development

The style of collaboration the teachers engaged in supported their development in three main areas that are explored in this section. First, members provided each other with models of what it looked like to be social justice educators. Second, the collaboration provided concrete plans that increased their ability to actualize SJE in their classrooms. Third, through collaboration members developed leadership skills.

Collaboration Led to Models of Social Justice Education. By acting as models, members provided each other with inspiration and motivation. The more experienced teachers gave a sense of what was coming next and their projects helped newer members understand how to get started, and sparked ideas for new projects for everyone. Additionally, listening to each other's experiences helped them all to better analyze their own contexts.

CIP members inspired each other by providing models of what was possible for people who are going through similar experiences. As Chantale shared:

> It gives me something to aspire to. I get the opportunity to see Jonathan and Stephanie and how they work together really hard to integrate social justice inside the curriculum. They're very passionate about it and I think you have to be loony not to have that pass on to you.

Often new teachers are acculturated into an atmosphere of compliance or teaching only the mandated curriculum (Picower, 2011). By setting a different example, one of deep commitment to SJE and the work it entails, members created another culture, and a new orientation of being a first-year teacher. The accomplishments of the second-year group members became models of aspiration, guiding the newer members into a culture of teaching for social justice from the beginning of their careers. The second-year teachers' experiences and strategies served as models to know what to expect. Beth explained:

> Hearing from other people and seeing their progress lets me have a catalog of what can happen, and later on if something like that comes up, I have a reference for how to deal with it … I do realize it's going to be hard, so just knowing that they did it makes me feel better, and it gives me lots of ideas.

Often, the only thing new teachers hear is how hard and overwhelming the first year is. Hearing success stories directly from people who had the same preparation, were teaching at similar schools, and had successfully implemented SJE provided a sense of relief.

Collaboration Improved Ability to Teach for Social Justice. The ways in which members collaborated also improved their SJE practice by triggering their thinking, helping them get work done, and preparing them for multiple contexts. Often, the nature and content of CIP meetings translated to members' classrooms because they practiced discussing complex issues and had time to think about how they would introduce them to their students. The members were adapting their willingness to allow for tension into their ability to facilitate discussions with students. Additionally, CIP gave them a space to workout and examine some of their own beliefs prior to presenting a topic to their students. For Stephanie, it also prepared her to better respect the multiple perspectives of her students:

> We have respected each other's opinions and feelings, and I apply that to my classroom. Because my kids are going to think something different than I think most of the time, I need to keep in mind that it's their opinions, and I need to respect them just as much as I would respect Reina, or Chantale. My kids are people, and knowing how to practice that with adults, that backing-off or knowing when to push, having that skill is really important to have in the classroom.

Critics of SJE (Labaree, 2004; Stem, 2006) often claim that such teachers are indoctrinating their students to a particular ideology. Stephanie clearly demonstrated her role as the antithesis of that. Rather than forcing all students to share one stance, members actively worked to respect their students' multiple opinions.

CIP also provided a space to get concrete work done. Newer teachers are often overwhelmed by how to manage their time and responsibilities. As Jonathan stated, "When you get home from work, [social justice curriculum planning is] just not something you're going to jump on. We are all busy people, and there needs to be time for those things." A key component of CIP sessions was time to develop and get feedback on curriculum. During this time members planned units and lessons on topics ranging from genocide, to the Iraq War, to child obesity. The teachers often shared the units with each other. For example, Stephanie and Reina exchanged units on the Holocaust and on school segregation, which cut their planning time in half while increasing the amount of time students learned about issues of justice. By providing time and space for collaborative planning, members developed SJE projects that they could implement the next day.

The different contexts in which members taught (public school, Catholic school, special and general education, multiple grade levels) exposed them to what SJE looked like in multiple settings. Teachers often think that certain ways of teaching aren't realistic for their setting and make excuses for why it can't be done. Jonathan admitted, "I think a lot of times I make excuses for my kids or my school and say: 'They won't get it.'" By seeing his peers' projects in different contexts, his mindset was challenged.

> Look at Nick, he's teaching ASL and teaching really tough topics with absolutely no sacrifice of content at all. And this sticks its tongue out at those mind-sets, because who are you to say they aren't going to get it. Because all signs point to that you can do this almost anywhere, at any age, and with any ability or disability.

Seeing Nick in action reminded the other members to question the excuses they might bring to the table.

Collaboration Developed Leadership and Mentoring Skills. Finally, the third result of collaboration was to develop members' ability to lead for SJE. By taking turns setting agendas and facilitating meetings, the participants learned to lead a group of adults, which provided leadership practice for other settings. While teachers may be expected to exhibit leadership when promoted to coaches, cooperating teachers, or administrators, their leadership skills are rarely *consciously developed*. CIP explicitly built in opportunities for practice at leadership, and members were given feedback about their style. By providing practice in facilitating and presenting, members felt more confident in themselves, their skills and their ability to be leaders in the field. As Stephanie shared:

> I had the chance to facilitate, and people actually used what I did in their classrooms. It's such a boost of confidence because they took what I did … Just getting that chance to plan a meeting and an agenda, now I feel like I could do that for any meeting; I can take leadership.

Rather than feeling like fledglings, CIP experiences helped them to perceive themselves as leaders, confident to act in a variety of settings. For those concerned with social justice, the ability to step up and lead in multiple contexts is a required skill with which they now have practice.

The skills and resources that members brought back to their schools positioned them as leaders with expertise in issues pertaining to SJE. Through the exchange in sessions, members were equipped with an arsenal of resources and the ability to share them with colleagues in collaborative ways. Nick, a first-year, became the "go-to-guy" on social justice issues for his principal and other colleagues because of the projects and leadership he had exhibited.

> My principal asked *me:* 'Should we do professional development on this?' And so I gave her my feedback … People at my school are like: 'Oh wow! You're doing this and this; You're so involved.' So it's cool. Some of the other teachers come to me now.

While many new teachers are perceived as needy, the confidence, knowledge and skills gained at CIP positioned members as leaders with tangible resources to contribute. This helped to give credibility to the SJE units that they integrated into their classrooms and, in many cases, caused colleagues to want to do similar projects.

Tangible Results

Four tangible benefits to the members emerged from the data. First, members were able to reflect on their journey of developing as social justice educators, seeing where they started and where they were still heading. This ongoing reflection and their own perception of their development kept them committed to the group and to the goal of SJE. Second, members demonstrated some of the mindsets and skill sets of social justice activism by the ways in which they "had each others' backs" when they faced challenging circumstances. Third, by publically sharing their work, members began to spread social justice education to others. Finally, the culmination of these results increased their confidence and their motivation to remain teaching.

By having opportunities to present to current students in the program from which they graduated, members were able to see how far they had come in their journey of thinking about teaching and social justice. After leading a workshop for freshman, Reina said, "We used to be like the freshman … I would have answered the same way … That was awesome to see we've come so far in the way we think about society, education, everything. I think it was cool to see the transition, to prove how far we've come." Seeing how far they had come served to keep them motivated and to realize that they were on a trajectory of learning that is ongoing.

CIP played a profound role in keeping members committed to teaching. Without CIP many members felt they would not have been as successful, or might not have even attempted to teach for social justice. When asked what their year would be like had they not been in CIP, Chantale's emotionally charged response was:

> I'd have quit teaching. I think I'm going to cry … [CIP] inspires me to keep being a teacher, because I know that you've got to start somewhere. I really love being [at CIP] … I just see now that being a teacher is not about teaching this, this and this. It's is about preparing our kids for being knowledgeable human beings that understand the way of the world, and to understand not just their cause, but all causes … It keeps me going, it definitely keeps me going.

With over 50 percent of new teachers leaving within the first five years, CIP played a role in helping members put their vision of preparing human beings who understand the way of the world into practice. The satisfaction they gain by teaching with a purpose and being able to improve their craft in a community of peers kept them going.

Another tangible result was how members learned to have each other's backs. In many ways, they exemplified some of the tenets of SJE by being ready and willing to take action on each other's behalves. For example, Nick learned that his American Sign Language school was being threatened with closure. Nick turned to the group and their encouragement bolstered his efforts to save his school. The CIP members learned the power of collective support by having each other's backs. While most teachers feel isolated and alienated, members learned how power in numbers further sustained their social justice efforts. They also realized that this level of unity is personally rewarding as well.

A third result was that CIP gave members opportunities to teach SJE to others. Through leading workshops for students in their former program to presenting at national conferences and writing a book chapter about CIP, members grew as leaders by passing on their knowledge and encouraging others to teach SJE. Stephanie stated, "If people like it and read it and are inspired by it, then I want to continue to write. It makes me feel like I'm really doing it and it's not like; 'oh when I get it together.' I have it together! I can do it and I am doing it." By having the opportunity to spread their knowledge, members gained confidence and a sense of expertise. This kept the teachers connected to the reasons they went into teaching. Rather than feeling like cogs in the system, or getting bogged down in the daily grind, CIP members were having positive experiences spreading their vision of what education should be.

Finally, members felt a tremendous sense of accomplishment. The sense of pride they felt boosted their confidence and motivated them to keep learning and teaching SJE. When Nick learned their book chapter had been accepted, "I told my old cooperating teacher and he was so proud of me, and just hearing him like: 'Ah, you're doing so great, I can't believe you are doing this!' … It built my self esteem." For these young teachers, their successes in CIP represented some of their first professional accomplishments. Without the opportunities presented in CIP, they might not have had other chances to stand out from the crowd. These experiences left them excited and motivated to take on more challenges while furthering their dedication to CIP.

Implications

These findings indicate that collaboration within CIP furthered the development of new social justice educators. While it may appear that it was the activities of the project that led to their increased capacity, the data show that more significant was the norms and tone of the group. While the activities of lesson planning and presenting were key elements, without the four norms that expected participation, encouraged multiple perspectives, allowed for tension, and encouraged "taboo" talk, the stage would not have been set for participants to push each other towards growth. This has implications for those interested in replicating critical inquiry groups for new teachers. Copying the agendas of CIP sessions will be insufficient; it is necessary to create the collaborative space that allows for critical discussions that aren't always resolved. These findings also demonstrate how traditional models of professional development may not be successful in supporting the development of new social justice educators. Often characterized by large groups that meet once or twice led by an "expert," these traditional models do not allow for the relationship building, participation or kinds of discussion necessary to create critical collaboration. Not as simple as gathering many teachers in a room for two hours, the findings in this study demonstrate that true teacher development requires long-term and intense investments in the relationships and well-being of aspiring social justice educators.

Notes

1. The 12th participant had been a graduate student at the same university. She was also a former student of mine, received similar preservice education, and taught at the same school with three other participants.
2. There is less data reported on Vanessa and Nina because they only participated in CIP for half the year because of schedule conflicts and therefore were not interviewed.
3. For more information on the logistics of CIP, see Picower, B. (2007), Supporting new educators to teach for social justice: The critical inquiry model. *Penn Perspectives on Urban Education*. Vol 5(1). This previous article describes a pilot project of CIP.
4. As their former professor/facilitator of the group, it is very likely that I had an influence on the participants. However, this article is a review of the role that the group members played on the members' development.

References

Achinstein, B., & Athanases, S. (2006). *Mentors in the making: Developing new leaders for new teachers.* New York: Teachers College Press.

Alliance for Excellent Education. (2004). *Tapping the potential: Retaining and developing high-quality new teachers.* Washington, DC: Author.

Anyon, J. (1981). Social class and school knowledge. *Curriculum Inquiry, 11*(1), 3–40.

Ayers, W. (2004). *Teaching toward freedom: Moral commitment and ethical action in the classroom.* New York: Beacon Press.

Ayers, W., Hunt, J. A., & Quinn, T. (1998). *Teaching for social justice: A democracy and education reader.* New York: Teachers College Press.

Banks, J. (2006). Democracy, diversity, and social justice: Educating citizens for the public interest in a global age. In G. Ladson-Billings & W. F. Tate (Eds.), *Education research in the public interest.* New York: Teachers College Press.

Bell, P. (2004). On the theoretical breadth of design-based research in education. *Educational Psychologist, 39*(4), 243–253.

Cochran-Smith, M. (2004). *Walking the road: Race, diversity, and social justice in teacher education.* New York: Teachers College Press.

Counts, G. (1932). *Dare the school build a new social order?* New York: Derek Day.

Darling-Hammond, L., & McLaughlin, M. W. (1995). Policies that support professional development in an era of reform. *Phi Delta Kappan, 76*(8), 597–604.

Dewey, J. (1932). *The school and society.* Chicago: University of Chicago Press.

Duncan-Andrade, J. M. R. (2004). Toward teacher development for the urban in urban teaching. *Teaching Education, 15*(4), 339–350.

Foss, S., & Waters, W. (2007). *Destination dissertation: A traveler's guide to a done dissertation.* Lanham, MD: Rowman & Littlefield.

Freire, P. (1993). *Pedagogy of the oppressed.* New York: Continuum.

Giroux, H. (1995). Teachers, public life, and curriculum reform. In A. C. Ornstein & L. S. Behar-Hornstein (Eds.), *Contemporary issues in curriculum* (2nd Ed.). Needham Heights, MA: Allyn & Bacon.

Glaser, B. G., & Strauss, A. L. (1967). *The discovery of grounded theory: Strategies for qualitative research.* Chicago: Aldine.

Greene, M. (1988). *The dialectic of freedom.* New York: Teachers College Press.

Ingersoll, R. (2001). *Teacher turnover, teacher shortages, and the organization of schools.* Seattle, WA: Center for the Study of Teaching and Policy.

Labaree, D. F. (2004). *The trouble with ed schools.* New Haven, CT: Yale University Press.

Lofland, J., & Lofland, L. H. (1984). *Analyzing social settings: A guide to qualitative observation and analysis* (2nd Ed.). Belmont, CA: Wadsworth.

Miech, R. A., & Elder, G. H. (1996). The service ethic and teaching. *Sociology of Education, 69*(3), 237–253.

Mortimer, J., & Lorence, T. (1979). Work experience and occupational value socialization: A longitudinal study. *American Journal of Sociology, 84,* 1361–1385.

National Commission on Teaching and America's Future. (2003). *No dream denied: A pledge to America's children.* Washington, DC: Author.

Oakes, J., & Lipton, M. (2006). *Teaching to change the world* (3rd Ed.). Boston: McGraw Hill Higher Education.

Payne, C. M., & Strickland, C. S. (2008). *Teach freedom: Education for liberation in the African American tradition.* New York: Teachers College Press.

Picower, B. (2007). Teacher education does not end at graduation: Supporting new teachers to teach for social justice. *Penn GSE Perspectives on Urban Education, 5*(1).

Picower, B. (2008). [Transcript of CIP Session, November 13th, 2008]. Unpublished raw data.

Picower, B. (2008). [Classroom Observation, November 25th, 2008]. Unpublished raw data.

Picower, B. (2009). [Transcript of CIP Session, February 9th, 2009]. Unpublished raw data.

Picower, B. (2011). Resisting compliance: Learning to teach for social justice in a neoliberal context. *Teachers College Record, 113*(5).

Quartz, K. (2003). "Too angry to leave": Supporting new teachers' commitment to transform urban schools. *Journal of Teacher Education 54*(2), 99–111.

Rosenberg, M. (1981). *Occupations and values.* New York: Arno Press.

Sandoval, W. A., & Bell, P. (2004). Design-based research methods for studying learning in context: Introduction. *Educational Psychologist, 39*(4), 199–201.

Simpson, I., Back, K., Ingles, T., Kerckhoff, A., & McKinney, J. (1979). *From student to nurse: A longitudinal study of socialization.* Cambridge, UK: Cambridge University Press.

Stem, S. (2006). The ed schools' latest-and worst-humbug. *The City Journal, 16*(4).

Westheimer, J., & Kahne, J. Introduction, *Equity & Excellence in Education, 40*(2), 97–100.

Questions for Reflection and Application

After reading the essays in Section One, answer the following questions:

1. How we define the problems/issues in our schools often determines the kinds of solutions that we consider to be viable. Do a brief situation analysis of the context where you work or intend to work; for example, demographics, geography, economics, politics, etc. Identify the major stakeholders and their perspectives regarding major problems/issues. What types of issues would a social justice leader identify and seek to solve within this context?

2. Consider the obstacles to becoming a social justice leader in your school. Within each of the following four dimensions of your work, consider the associated obstacles: self-interests, school, district, and/or profession. Within each category (as appropriate), list the relevant factors that get in the way of teacher leadership operating within a social justice framework.

3. As you consider your personal plan for teacher leadership, what additional skills, knowledge, or attitudes will you need in order to achieve your desired image of teacher leader? How will you develop these skills, knowledge, and attitudes?

Answer these questions using both the ideas from the essays that we are considering as well as your personal experiences with the schools you have encountered during your life: as a student, parent, and/or teacher. References to specific ideas found in the Section One essays are expected.

SECTION 2
Teacher Leadership and Teachers' Work

Introduction

Teaching has traditionally attracted individuals who come to the profession for the right reasons but find the public schools are the wrong institutions for their dreams and aspirations. Teachers express dissatisfaction with the profession for many reasons, but most complaints focus on the dissatisfactions associated with a low salary, status, autonomy, and limited decision-making. Attempts to improve the status of the profession have generally focused on increasing the educational requirements for entry into the profession, raising salaries, and encouraging collaboration and shared decision-making among major stakeholders. These efforts to recognize the various levels of skill, education, and expertise of teachers often "open the door" to opportunities for teachers to assume important leadership roles beyond the classroom, roles that challenge traditional notions of school leadership, and ultimately provide opportunities for teacher leaders to practice independent decision-making. A renewed interest in teacher leadership as a cornerstone of most teacher education programs in the twenty-first century is an important indicator that the public is ready to put teachers on the front line of school reform efforts and acknowledge the essential knowledge and skills that they bring to schools and communities.

Contemporary discussions of teacher leadership in the research literature rely on conceptions of teachers' work as focusing on student achievement goals and building on a professional trilogy: teaching, learning, leading. Katzenmeyer and Moller (2009) described teacher leaders as those who "lead within and beyond the classroom; identify with and contribute to a community of teacher leaders and learners; influence others toward improved educational practice; and accept responsibility for achieving the outcomes of their leadership" (p. 6). However, Barth (2001) considers the contradictions inherent to teachers' work:

> A profound ambivalence about teachers pervades our profession. On the one hand, teachers are viewed—and treated by many—as semiskilled workers who need to be more technically trained and retrained, more closely monitored, more regulated, and more frequently evaluated against ever more prescriptive requirements and standards. On the other hand, teachers are viewed by others as

grownups—professionals—deserving greater opportunity for more leadership, more participation in important decisions, and greater self-governance. (p. 449)

While most definitions of teacher leadership describe aspects of teachers' work that encompass work within and beyond the classroom to facilitate student learning, few consider the relationship of teacher leadership to a broader examination of how teachers function in a larger bureaucratic scheme that is structured in such a way that teachers are relatively powerless, marginalized workers who have little voice in the day-to-day decisions that govern and direct teachers' work. Considering teachers' work within a larger philosophical and ideological context is almost nonexistent in the literature, but individuals like Anderson (2009) and Giroux (2012) have laid the groundwork for these discussions. Challenging the status quo of teachers' work and professing a vision of teachers that defines their work as having an ideological purpose that propels them into different kinds of roles will require an ongoing struggle to realign the political power arrangements in most schools. However, it is work that must be done if teaching is to become a "real" profession that can then play a pivotal role in articulating a vision for the progress and direction of substantive school reforms. This vision for teacher leadership must be conceptualized as a piece of a larger theoretical and ideological vision if it is to ultimately have the potential to transform the profession and, ultimately, the schools. Teacher leadership, in this context, is a radical departure from previous ideas about teachers' work, roles, and responsibilities.

The five essays in this section of the book lay the groundwork for a consideration of the challenges that teachers face when making teacher leadership an important element of the roles and responsibilities of all teachers. Allen and Topolka-Jorissen, Richardson, Schlechty, Steel and Craig, and Thornton consider different aspects of teacher leadership in relationship to teachers' work. In each of these essays, the challenges faced by teachers moving into leadership roles are highlighted as part of the process of renegotiating a school culture that promotes and facilitates the emergence of teacher leadership as an essential element of both school improvement and teaching as a full-fledged profession. The role of teachers as advocates for all students requires that all teachers recognize that their leadership is a required part of their work that extends beyond individual classrooms to the school and the community. These essays provide a context for discussions of the ways in which individual teachers can address their strengths and weaknesses as leaders and seek to develop the professional dispositions, skills, and knowledge that will foster their evolution as teacher leaders.

References

Anderson, G. (2009). *Advocacy leadership: Toward a post-reform agenda in education.* New York: Routledge.

Barth, R. (2001). Teacher leader. *Phi Delta Kappan, 82*(6), 443–449.

Giroux, H. (2012). *Education and the crisis of public values: Challenging the assault on teachers, students, and public education.* New York: Peter Lang.

Katzenmeyer, M., & Moller, G. (2009). *Awakening the sleeping giant: Helping teachers develop as leaders* (3rd ed.). Thousand Oaks, CA: Corwin.

CHAPTER 5

Teacher Leadership Continuum

How Principals Develop and Support Teacher Leaders

Ann S. Allen and Kathleen Topolka-Jorissen

Imagine the excitement as you begin your new teaching assignment. You arrive in a small rural town; the mayor, the preacher, and the president of the bank greet you at the train station. You are the town's new teacher. You have been selected from a pool of enthusiastic, educated, and morally sound graduates from the state's Normal School. Young and idealistic, you venture far from home to fulfill a lifelong dream. The town's one-room schoolhouse is your stage. The town's school age children become your pupils to teach, love, and lead. Your place in the town's social order depends on your ability to organize and assess appropriate lessons and curricula, prepare students for the academic demands of their chosen vocations, manage discipline of students ranging from age 5 to 16, keep the schoolhouse and outhouse clean, oversee playground and lunchtime activities, insure that there is enough wood cut to keep the building warm, and inform parents of students' progress or struggles. If your pay is determined by the number of students attending, then you are also charged with recruitment and retention of students.

The responsibilities set forth by the townsfolk for a young adult with dreams and ideals of a smooth-running school near the turn of the 19th century challenged teachers not only to provide instruction but also to provide leadership. Teacher leadership began when tutors were hired to educate young men from powerful families. The tutors were charged not only to teach curricula but also to teach thinking, moral decision making, and social skills. Responsibility for all aspects of the school rested with the teacher of the one-room schoolhouse. The industrialization of the nation led to larger schools with many teachers and one principal teacher, who was responsible for assisting with the managerial tasks associated with a larger facility, staff, and student body. The current age of accountability requires teachers, principals, students, and parents to respond to a myriad of dilemmas ranging from discipline to curriculum to health concerns. Teachers can no longer meet the needs of all students single-handedly. All teachers must provide leadership.

What Is Leadership?

Leadership has been defined in many ways. Many definitions and theories focus on leadership traits (McClelland, 1985; Stogdill, 1981; Yukl, 2002). Others focus on skills (Northouse, 2004; Mumford,

Zaccaro, Harding, Jacobs, & Fleishman, 2000; Yukl, 2002). What trait and skill theories have in common is a focus on individuals in formal leadership roles. However, in the context of a model in which leadership is shared across an organization or school, the definition of leadership takes on a more diffuse nature. Spillane (2006) defines leadership this way:

> *Leadership* refers to activities tied to the core work of the organization that are designed by organizational members to influence the motivation, knowledge, affect, or practices of other organizational members or that are understood by organizational members as intended to influence their motivation, knowledge, affect, or practices. (2006, pp. 11–12, emphasis in original)

The primary purpose of this kind of influence, according to Elmore (2004) must be the "improvement of instruction and practice" (p. 66). Furthermore, because leadership aims to improve practice, it requires continuous learning and modeling. (Elmore, 2004, p. 67). Actions that are directed toward the improvement of instructional practice, then, may be categorized as leadership practices, regardless of the role of the person engaging in those practices. What is the role of the principal in schools where adults in a range of roles engage in influencing "the motivation, knowledge, affect, or practices" of other members of the school community, with the intention of improving instructional practice? According to Lambert (1998), the role of the principal becomes more critical than ever in a shared leadership school community. A primary goal of a principal committed to collective work as the key to student growth across the school will be to develop the leadership capacity of everyone in the school. Lambert says:

> Viewing leadership as a collective learning process leads to the recognition that the dispositions, knowledge, and skills of capacity building are the same as those of leadership. Leadership capacity building, then, can be defined as broad-based, skillful participation in the *work of leadership*. (Lambert, 1998, p. 12)

A principal committed to building leadership capacity will engage teachers and others in the school community in the work of leadership in several ways.

Hiring Teachers Capable of Leadership Work

In schools developing leadership capacity, principals seek teachers who value collaborative learning and work and who see their responsibilities as extending to all the students in the school, not just to their own classes. Principals look for teachers who are a good "fit" for the school culture. In preparing to interview for entry-level teaching positions, teachers need to be prepared to respond to questions such as:

1. Describe a time when you worked on a team to solve a problem. What was the problem? How did your team approach the problem? What role did you play on the team?

2. Assume that you collect data from your first unit test, using the common assessment that your team has developed. You see that your students have scored lower on one section than those of the other teachers on your team. What will you do?

3. Think of a time when you were working with another person or team, and the group was unable to agree upon a course of action. Describe that situation. What did you do?

Just as teachers need to be prepared to answer questions, they also need to be prepared to ask good questions and to share work samples. In preparing a file of materials to share with prospective employers, teachers should select at least one project that reflects the work of a collaborative effort and be prepared to describe their roles in developing the project. Questions teachers might ask to determine whether a school is committed to shared leadership include:

- How often does the (third-grade team or math department) meet to work on instructional issues?

- What are the current priorities for the (third-grade team or math department)?

- In reviewing your Web site, I noticed that math scores have been steadily rising for the past three years. What has caused this significant improvement?

Participation Through Leadership Structures

Teachers in leadership capacity building schools can expect many opportunities to participate in leadership and to engage in the shaping of structures and processes that facilitate participation. For example, schools in which leadership capacity is developing are likely to use a School Improvement Team or School Leadership Team as a key structure that involves representatives from each grade level or subject, as well as parents and support staff, in reviewing data, establishing short and long term goals, implementing action research, monitoring progress, and communicating across the school. Flowing from the School Improvement Team will be grade level, subject area, or interdisciplinary work teams, focused on discrete aspects of more global school goals. For example, a third grade team may target fluency as a means of improving student achievement in reading, using a variety of agreed-upon methods for ensuring the success of all third graders.

Engaging in Collaborative Inquiry

Traditionally, teachers have practiced in isolation from each other. In schools where developing leadership capacity is a goal, teachers expect to collaboratively investigate their practice. This dynamic involves going beyond simply sharing materials and ideas to exploring together to find solutions to shared problems of practice. Nelson (2009), points out:

> Dialogically, teachers' interactions shift from sharing teaching activities to critically questioning relationships between common activities, learning goals, and student learning. The essential characteristic in this shift is teacher learning through the analysis of student work, teaching artifacts, and relevant professional resources. Teachers generate knowledge that can inform larger school and district initiatives. (pp. 551–552)

Because such inquiry requires time for reflection, dialogue, data review, and discussion among team members, principals building leadership capacity will develop schedules that provide sufficient time for teachers to work together. For example, Glenn Marlow Elementary School in Hendersonville, NC, allocates common planning time each week for each grade level team. Over a two-year period, teachers have identified needs for more active engaged student learning strategies, studied learning styles, and developed differentiated lessons geared to a range of student learning styles.

In schools where leadership is the lever for school improvement, the role of the principal becomes vastly different from traditional views of the formal school leader. Principals assume the role of steward, entrusting all members of the educational community who are committed to achieving the collective goals and vision with respect and with support and assistance.

What are some of the specific strategies principals promote and support in order to build school and leadership capacity? In our work with schools, we have observed that savvy principals use their understanding of the school culture and developmental readiness of their teachers to design collaborative learning processes that best match teachers' orientation to professional inquiry and learning. Similar observations have been noted by Copland (2003). Moving along a continuum from novice to advanced, principals create opportunities for teachers to begin by analyzing data and helping each other learn and develop strategies to address learning problems. As teachers become increasingly comfortable with their participation in the work of leadership, they move into deeper inquiry, studying teaching and learning through direct observation. Schools and teachers at advanced levels become concerned with internal accountability and methods of integrating change initiatives across the entire school. Table 1 illustrates the continuum with examples of teacher leadership at each stage. To illustrate the continuum of participation in the work of leadership, we will present examples of strategies that represent each stage.

Novice	Intermediate	Advanced
Book study	Train the trainer	Shared examination of student work
Individual classroom level action research	Group action research	Development of common assessments
Teacher-led professional development activities	Mentoring (with protégé' observations)	Direct observation
		Teacher learning walks

Table 1. Continuum of Teacher Leadership in Collaborative Learning

Book Study as a Strategy for Novice Professional Learning Communities

In schools where teachers are accustomed to working in isolation, strategies such as book studies are effective in bringing teachers together to focus on a topic of common interest. Glenn Marlow Elementary School in Hendersonville, North Carolina, is a good example of a school that used a common concern about student learning as a catalyst for collaboration through book study. In examining their student achievement data, the teachers noticed a dip in learning for students transitioning from second to third grade and from fifth grade to middle school. They decided to learn more about their students as learners and more about themselves as teachers. As Principal Jan King explained, "The teachers wondered why their students weren't more engaged. After all, the teachers were planning these great lessons!" The teachers explored two questions:

- How do our learning styles affect our instructional decisions?
- How do styles-based lessons affect student engagement and performance?

To answer the first question, teachers assessed their own learning and teaching styles and the learning styles of their students, using a small grant to purchase teaching and learning style inventories. They also purchased copies of a book to study together, in order to learn about teaching and learning styles. This initiative enabled the teachers to transform their grade-level teams into professional learning communities (PLCs), in which the teachers identified a student learning problem and worked together to identify strategies for addressing the problem. This approach illustrates the power of teacher leadership, even in its novice stages. As Lieberman and Miller (2008) say, "Much of current professional development activity rests on the assumption that there are best practices *out there*. In professional learning communities, this belief is replaced by the conviction that the best practices are *in here*; they can be uncovered by mining inside knowledge" (Lieberman & Miller, 2008, p. 22). Through sharing their self-assessment data and their perspectives on the ideas presented in the book, the teachers began to lead each other in learning.

Moving to the Intermediate Stage with Action Research

As they used their common planning time to examine the data from the inventories, the Glenn Marlow teachers discovered that they had been designing lessons that matched the way *they* learned best—instead of considering the way *the children* preferred to learn. That provided sufficient motivation for the teachers to move into action research. Their grade-level meetings became action research meetings, in which they worked together to design lessons and to commit to trying strategies that would better engage their students. Together the teachers used the ideas they had learned in their book study to develop lessons that gave students many options for active, engaged learning. To assess the impact of the new strategies they were implementing, teachers began to bring samples of student work to their grade-level/PLC meetings, thus breaking down the barriers of isolation further and developing norms of trust. As Lieberman and Miller (2008) point out, "Professional learning communities … offer an alternative to the norms of privacy and secrecy and build the capacity of teachers to make their work public" (p. 24). In order to perform the work of leadership, teacher leaders need to progress to this level of trust.

Advanced Stage Teacher Leaders Learning Through Direct Observation

The idea for teacher learning walks emerged from a supervisory practice commonly referred to as classroom walk-throughs. Principals began to see the benefit of teachers visiting other classrooms to seek ideas, strategies, and find common ground to begin discussions surrounding pedagogy and best practices. Learning walks can be simple informal visits shared between two or three colleagues seeking particular information such as student engagement techniques, use of a specific teaching tool such a learning map, or they can be more organized and engage the entire faculty and staff in formal professional development. In this model, the entire school becomes the context for teachers as leaders and learners. The focus is always on learning, not evaluating, and reflection is a key learning process at every stage of the process.

The more formal version of teacher learning walks includes the staff in a planning meeting which is led by any willing facilitator. The staff identifies shared goals or needs frequently taken from school report cards or school improvement plans. They then generate a list of indicators or "look fors" to guide the three-to five-minute snapshot visits. A schedule that involves all teachers being observed by at least one group and all teachers visiting at least three classrooms with at least one other teacher provides the necessary structure for using this process as school-wide professional development.

Teams of two to five teachers visit a classroom together, observe the action using the agreed-upon indicators for three to five minutes, and then step into the hall to discuss what they saw. The hallway conversation centers on what was observed, what was seen that is included on the indicator list, and any other positive ideas that one of the observers would like to borrow. The team decides on a question or two to ask later when the whole faculty meets for reflective dialogue and then moves on to the next class. After school the visitors have an opportunity to provide only positive feedback to those they observed and ask questions to help deepen their understanding of the techniques or approaches they saw.

The after-school conversations are where professional dialogue begins in earnest. Teachers are recognized for the hard work that occurs in each classroom. We have heard comments such as, "I knew we had a good school, but after visiting several classrooms today, I am really proud to say that we have some fantastic teachers here!" A physical education teacher commented, "No one ever came to see me teach before. It was nice to connect on an instructional level with other teachers." He went on to say that after visiting a third-grade classroom during a spelling lesson he planned to get the weekly spelling lists from teachers to use as students did calisthenics at the beginning of his class each day. He planned to have them do push-ups and jumping jacks while spelling!

Less formal teacher learning walks include visiting teachers in one grade level or content area and just picking up skills and ideas by watching for a short period of time. Visiting in a team of two or more helps teachers work together to develop ways to immediately apply in their own classrooms the good strategies they observe in their colleagues' classrooms. As learning walks become a professional norm in a school, teachers invite each other to come to see a "special" lesson or a new strategy to address a student learning goal.

Integrating a Continuum of Strategies to Build School Capacity

As teachers become increasingly comfortable with shared inquiry and collaboration, they will naturally integrate novice, intermediate, and advanced strategies. One way to integrate levels of teacher leadership is to combine a "train the trainer" model of professional learning with site-based PLC work and learning walks.

Frequently teachers attend professional development events that teach how to present materials, support adoption of a specific program or curriculum, or even provide new tools to deliver instruction. These events are usually costly to the district and not practical for the entire staff to attend. If only one or two teachers attend, they may have difficulty implementing what they have learned, because they have no site-based support for their efforts. Sending one or two teachers to promising professional development sessions may be practical and contribute to school improvement, provided that those teachers assume leadership in sharing new information with colleagues.

One of the schools we have worked with has used a specific workshop—"Worksheets Don't Grow Dendrites"—to create a year-long focus, integrating teacher leaders presenting new material to all the other teachers (novice stage), all teachers adapting strategies for engagement into their lessons (intermediate), and using the teacher learning walk process for all teachers to see the strategies in practice and then engage in dialogue to analyze their practices and impact on student learning (advanced stage). Three teachers from the school attended a regional workshop and followed up by sharing two or three strategies a month during regular faculty meetings. Each month the teachers used the examples presented at the workshop as their indicators during teacher learning walk days. Their after school discussions focused on successful uses of the strategies, extensions they had discovered, and future plans to implement the skills and techniques they were developing.

An example of this integrated approach at the high school level is a school where the School Improvement Team had established the goal of integrating technology across the curriculum. The school had received a grant for ELMO tools Smart Boards, and Promethean boards. Many teachers had the technology in place in their classroom but were unsure of how to use it effectively. One Smart Board sat in a hallway, unused for three months. During teacher learning walks, all teachers saw some of their colleagues using technology in ways that inspired their own lesson designs. Within a matter of weeks, most of the Promethean boards were being used every period of the day. The once-lonely Smart Board became a vital tool in the Spanish teacher's classroom, helping her move vocabulary practice at a faster pace than a chalkboard ever could. Some of the older tools continued to be used because teachers saw that the tools supported student learning and made their teaching practice more efficient.

Summary

Although there is no prescription or recipe for engaging teachers in the work of school leadership, the momentum for teacher engagement in the work of leadership is increasingly evident in schools. When teachers begin to meet to focus on student learning and their deep-seated commitment to improve their own professional practice, in order to ensure success for all students, teacher leadership has the potential to build school capacity. Lambert's (2003) assertion, "It is what people learn and do together, rather than what any particular leader does alone, that creates the fabric of the school" (p. 20) captures the essence of distributed leadership. When educators learn and work together to improve instruction and practice, schools develop the capacity to fulfill their mission for students.

Discussion Topics

Assessing Readiness and Planning for Teacher Leadership

Imagine how teachers in your school might begin to share their wealth of knowledge. Building communities of practice involves engaging the members of your school in authentic activities which connect their knowledge, skills, and practice to each other.

- How would you assess your school's current level of readiness for teacher leadership—novice, intermediate, advanced?

- What strategies would you recommend to engage teachers in the work of leadership?

- What ideas do you have that could build communities of practice?

Case study

Your school buzzes with the excitement and bustle of a new school year. The annual "welcome back" teacher meetings this year offered a new twist. Your principal has organized several new committees that need teacher leaders to serve as committee chairpersons. There are also leadership opportunities in other positions. Select one of the following committees or leadership opportunities and describe your qualifications for the position, how you envision this committee addressing student learning needs, and what you would do to facilitate the group to define and achieve its goals.

School Improvement	Student intervention process
Grade level leader	Department chair (content specific)
Literacy initiative	Professional learning community
Textbook adoption	Mentor for entry year teacher
Community outreach	Testing coordination
District Science Fair	School to Work representative

References

Copland, M. A. (2003). Leadership of inquiry: Building and sustaining capacity for school improvement. *Educational Evaluation and Policy Analysis, 25*(4), 375–395.

Elmore, R. F. (2004). Building a new structure for school leadership. In R. F. Elmore, *School reform from the inside out: Policy, practice, and performance.* Cambridge, MA: Harvard University Press.

Lambert, L. (1998). *Building leadership capacity in schools.* Alexandria, VA: Association for Supervision and Curriculum Development.

Lambert, L. (2003). *Leadership capacity for lasting school improvement.* Alexandria, VA: ASCD.

Lieberman, A., & Miller, L. (2008). Developing capacities. In A. Lieberman & L. Miller (Eds.), *Teachers in professional communities: Improving teaching and learning* (pp. 18–28). New York, NY: Teachers College Press.

McClelland, D. C. (1985). *Human motivation.* Glenview, IL: Scott, Foresman.

Mumford, M. D., Zaccaro, S. J., Harding, F. D., Jacobs, T. O., & Fleishman, E. A. (2000). Leadership skills for a changing world: Solving complex social problems. *Leadership Quarterly, 11*(1), 11–35.

Nelson, T. H. (2009). Teachers' collaborative inquiry and professional growth: Should we be optimistic? *Science Education, 93,* 548–580. DOI: 10.1002/sce.20302.

Northouse, P. G. (2004). *Leadership: Theory and practice* (3rd ed.). Thousand Oaks, CA: Sage.

Sergiovanni, T. J. (2007). Administering as a moral craft. In T. J. Sergiovanni, *Rethinking leadership: A collection of articles* (2nd ed.). Thousand Oaks, CA: Corwin.

Spillane, J. P. (2006). *Distributed leadership.* San Francisco, CA: Jossey-Bass.

Stogdill, R. M. (1981). Traits of leadership: A follow-up to 1970. In B. M. Bass (Ed.), *Stogdill's handbook of leadership* (pp. 73–97). New York: Free Press.

Yukl, G. A. (2002). *Leadership in organizations* (5th ed.). Upper Saddle River, NJ: Prentice Hall.

CHAPTER 6

Helping Teachers Participate Competently in School Leadership

Lystra M. Richardson

Traditionally, schools have been large, impersonal systems with decision making centralized at the highest levels. Today, with collaborative leadership, teachers are being asked to engage as leaders.

Distributive leadership (Firestone 1996; Heller and Firestone 1995; Ogawa and Bossert 1995; Spillane, Halverson, and Diamond 2001) stresses the importance of leadership that is distributed and performed by several people including the formal leader. The Institute for Educational Leadership (2001) points out that teacher leadership is becoming increasingly present and that it can contribute to improving school health and performance.

In this article I will examine the expectation for teachers to participate in school leadership and, based on results of a recent study, draw conclusions and make recommendations regarding the kinds of professional development that would engender competent and effective involvement of teachers in the leadership of schools. Because this decision-making role is new and somewhat uncomfortable for many teachers (Conley 1999), the expectation for teacher participation should be accompanied by empowerment through knowledge and skill acquisition.

Expectations for Participation

Several questions come to mind regarding teachers' preparedness and ability to participate competently in leadership: Where do they learn the skills necessary for leadership? When and how do teachers gain an understanding of schools as complex systems? Who helps them understand the nature of leadership? Are teachers really prepared to provide effective leadership? Answers to these questions and others are vital to making teachers' contributions meaningful and substantive.

Keiffer (1981) describes empowerment as a process through which people develop competence in meeting their own needs. By developing the skills they need to participate in their social and political worlds individuals gain control of their lives.

Usually, prospective school leaders engage in some type of preparation during which they gain deeper understanding of schools as organizations, the change process, and the context in which schools operate. They also hone their communication, problem-solving, and decision-making skills, and develop or refine attitudes necessary for effective leadership. The teacher leadership role, by contrast, is not currently preceded by any such training. Interestingly, large numbers of teachers complete leadership preparation programs and do not enter the ranks of formal school leadership. Consequently, those teachers exist within schools as valuable resources for leadership.

My study was designed to determine the extent to which preparation in educational leadership benefits graduates who remain as teachers. I was particularly interested in identifying ways in which teachers with this preparation use the knowledge, skills, and dispositions in their roles as teachers.

Method

The study combined quantitative and qualitative methods to better understand participants' perceptions of their professional responsibility as delineated in the Connecticut Common Core of Teaching (CCT). The sample consisted of graduates of the Educational Leadership Department at Southern Connecticut State University from 1995 to 2000. Of the 600 individuals who received the three-part survey by mail, 170 returned usable responses (28 percent). Of this total, 110 indicated they were teachers and 60 administrators or other personnel.

Part 1 of the survey contained demographic data. Part 2 consisted of seven questions developed from the professional responsibility category of the CCI, directed to graduates who have assumed administrative positions. A set of 19 questions for those graduates who have remained as teachers made up part 3 of the survey.

I also included three write-in items in which I asked participants to indicate additional ways in which their training in educational leadership benefited them in their roles as teachers.

I coded and analyzed the qualitative data I collected from the write-in items using the constant comparative method of quantitative analysis (Glaser and Strauss 1967). Each response was coded into as many categories as possible. I constructed some categories as they emerged from the data, and took some categories from the literature on teacher responsibility. I analyzed the third question, "Would you recommend preparation in educational leadership for teachers who do not plan to become administrators? Why or why not?" by frequency of yes or no answers and coded each explanation of "Why?" or "Why not?" using the constant comparative method of analysis.

This exploratory study was limited in several ways. First, population validity is reduced when generalizing to the same set of subjects at another time, or to similar population in another area. Generalizability, then, is minimized. Second, this study was not intended to study the nature of teacher leadership, but to explore the ways in which program graduates who remain as teachers use their knowledge in carrying out their professional responsibility. In spite of these and other limitations, the qualitative aspect of the study yielded some insightful data regarding how teachers use leadership training in their work.

The majority of respondents indicated they would recommend preparation in educational leadership for teachers who do not plan on becoming administrators. Acquisition of an expanded knowledge base, seeing the big picture, improving teaching, improving communication skills, and better positioning for teacher leadership were among the primary benefits teachers reported.

Expanded Knowledge Base

Teachers reported using their new knowledge in curriculum work, working on teams and committees, fostering collegiality and collaboration, and facilitating change in their department or school. The knowledge helps them to view issues in school life more globally. Specifically, they gained better understanding of legal issues, appreciated the difficult role of the administrator, became professional development facilitators, dealt more effectively with displeased parents and students, and better understood the politics in schools. One teacher stated that the knowledge helped her "better understand problems administrators face and be more effective in helping administration when needed."

Seeing the Big Picture

Teachers noted that preparation in educational leadership enables them to see another side of education. One teacher commented,

> There is great value in seeing the overall picture of a school and a school system that you don't see as a classroom teacher. The educational leadership program helps in that way. You become more aware of the mechanics of school politics and leadership. It breaks you out of the smaller classroom box and opens you up to greater awareness of the influences which affect your teaching. You stay competitive in learning strategies and can network with others who believe in strong leadership and effective teaching.

Another teacher explained, "It gives you a better understanding of how administrators in your building are making the decisions they do, and implementing the strategies they do."

Improved Teaching and Communication Skills

"Confident" and "knowledgeable" were the primary descriptors teachers used in explaining some of the benefits of their preparation in educational leadership. They noted that they were better prepared to face daily challenges, working differently with groups of professionals, maintaining a professional attitude after thirty years, remaining a caring, open-minded teacher to all students, and as one teacher responded, "I understand the impossible, stress-filled job done by my principal, and I take care to give constructive criticism to this poor man."

Improving teaching was frequently mentioned as a reason for recommending teachers for preparation in educational leadership. Specifically, teachers said they gained valuable understanding of curriculum, school culture, effective teaching practice, and the process of teaching and learning. They said that such training helps to make the school better and the profession better, as illustrated by statements such as these: "Courses in curriculum and effective teaching make me a better teacher and more valuable to my students"; "Provides background and training to become a more reflective teacher and therefore more effective"; "It broadens the scope of practice, and helps you understand teaching better." "It enhances your knowledge of how to perform as a professional, enables you to assess curriculum, and it provides nonsubjective perspectives which help to further the growth and learning of your students," was a comment that effectively summed up the program's impact on teaching.

Teachers also reported developing their interpersonal skills. A class on relationships and handling conflict helps in everyday situations, particularly in dealing with parents and peers.

Several graduates made the following comments recommending the educational leadership preparation program:

> Because teachers can be the most important educational leaders in a school.

> The program offers strategies that can be used by teachers, counselors, or administrators. I have been invigorated by the program. The program helps with problem solving and how to be a change agent.

> Since completing my sixth year I have taken on more of a leadership role within the visual arts department. I have mentored new teachers, taken student teachers, and I am currently creating assessment tools for the department.

Conclusions

Based on the foregoing, formal preparation in educational leadership may be an important form of professional development for teachers (Jacobs 1994). Leadership skills are, for the most part, learned skills. However, even with the present emphasis on promoting the professionalization of all teachers, little training is provided for teachers as instructional leaders, as noted by Fessler and Ungaretti (1994). If teachers are to contribute meaningfully and substantively to the leadership of the school, the development of teachers as leaders should be a substantial investment for school districts. Results of my study (Richardson 2002) reveal some insights into the training teachers would need to carry out their professional responsibilities more effectively. I concur with Barth (2001), who asserts that teacher leadership is about mobilizing the still largely untapped attributes of teachers.

Recommendations

I would like to make three major recommendations. First, because significant numbers of teachers undergo school leadership training and remain as teachers, it may be prudent and practical for preparation programs to incorporate training on the dimensions of teacher leadership. In this way, whether graduates become administrators or remain as teachers, they will be better equipped to engage in collaborative leadership.

The differences in the training for teacher leaders and administrators would be a matter of the perspective from which leadership is viewed and position from which leadership is exercised. Although the basic leadership training would remain intact, the key difference in the perspective taken by administrators would be how to empower teachers and how to engage teachers in the leadership of the school. For teacher leaders the key difference in perspective would be how to contribute to collaborative leadership.

Second, it may also be prudent for teacher preparation programs to incorporate teacher leadership as one aspect of preservice preparation. This could enable teachers to see that their role in contributing to overall school improvement goes beyond the classroom.

Administrative response to this level of empowerment for teachers may vary. Although administrators with more autocratic styles of leadership may not fully use this aspect of teacher preparation, administrators who practice collaborative or distributive leadership are likely to welcome the increased awareness and skill in their teachers. This level of preparation for teachers holds potential to contribute to the overall functioning of the school.

Third, having taught hundreds of teachers in a leadership preparation program over the last several years, it is evident that although teachers bring solid classroom experience with them, their knowledge and understanding of the context in which schools operate and of the challenges facing school leaders is often minimal. There is a dire need to build the knowledge of teachers regarding the external and some of the internal realities of public schooling. Teacher leaders must understand how and why change occurs in schools. With this in mind, principals may also want to focus some professional development activities on effective teacher participation in decision making. Principals must keep themselves informed to provide teachers with relevant background, contextual information and must function as staff developers for their faculty.

Helping teachers to understand the broader context of public schooling and to develop leadership skills, attitudes, and dispositions will empower them to participate much more competently in school leadership.

Key words: school leadership, training programs, teacher preparation, development

References

Barth, R. 2001. Teacher leader. *Phi Delta Kappan*, 82(February), 443–49.

Conley, D. T. 1999. *Roadmap to restructuring: Charting the course of change in American education.* University of Oregon, Eugene, OR: ERIC Clearinghouse on Educational Management.

Fessler, R., and A. Ungaretti. 1994. Expanding opportunities for teacher leadership. In *Teachers as leaders,* ed. D. R. Walling, Bloomington, IN: Phi Delta Kappa Educational Foundation.

Firestone, W. A. 1996. Leadership: Roles or functions? In *International handbook of educational leadership and administration,* ed. K. Leithwood, J. Chapman, D. Corson, P. Hallinger, and A. Hart, (pp. 395–418). Dordrecht, The Netherlands: Kluwer.

Glaser, B., and A. Strauss. 1967. *The discovery of grounded theory: Strategies for qualitative research.* Chicago, IL: Aldine.

Heller, M. F., and W. A. Firestone. 1995. Who's in charge here? Sources of leadership for change. *Elementary School Journal* 96, 65–67.

Institute for Educational Leadership. 2001. *Leadership for student learning: Redefining the teacher as leader.* Washington, DC: Institute for Educational Leadership.

Jacobs, H. 1994. Assessment of program effects on graduates of the Department of Educational Leadership. Unpublished.

Keiffer, H. 1981. Domination, power and empowerment. In *Transforming power,* S. Kreisberg, New York: State University of New York Press.

Ogawa, R. T., and S. T. Bossert. 1995. Leadership as an organizational quality. *Educational Administration Quarterly* 31, 224–243.

Richardson, L. 2002. Benefits of educational leadership preparation to teachers and their schools. Paper presented at the Annual Meeting of the American Educational Research Association, New Orleans, LA.

Spillane, J., R. Halverson., and J. B. Diamond. 2001. Investigating school leadership practice: A distributed perspective. *Educational Researcher 30*(3), 23–28.

CHAPTER 7

On the Frontier of School Reform with Trailblazers, Pioneers, and Settlers

Phillip C. Schlechty

Improvement focuses on doing the same things better with the intent of changing and enhancing the performance of individuals within existing systems. Restructuring is aimed at changing systems so that new types of performances will be possible and encouraged and new or different outcomes can be produced.

Educational leaders and those in charge of training and development activities in schools have had much more experience in trying to improve things than they have had in trying to restructure. As a result, the training and support which is provided to encourage and facilitate restructuring isoften inappropriate.

Distinctions between improvement and restructuring are significant and have implications for those who lead restructuring efforts and for those who provide training and support to participants in the restructuring process. Unfortunately, too few educational leaders and staff developers seem to appreciate the significance of the distinction. In this article, I share some of the lessons I have learned about providing training and support to those who are trying to restructure schools.

Differences That Make a Difference

Staff development which is aimed at improvement is typically based on prior experience and research. This is seldom the case with staff development aimed at encouraging or supporting restructuring. Restructuring creates new conditions which neither the staff developer nor the participants have experienced. Restructuring, therefore, always requires one to be willing to act beyond the data and without benefit of guidance from empirical research. Creating new systems, which is what restructuring is about, calls for faith, logic, wisdom, and intuition, at least to the degree that it calls for disciplining action with facts.

Most staff developers have been taught to place experience and research at the center of their agenda. They are often not prepared to proceed in areas where faith and a new vision, more than research and prior experience, must serve as a guide to action. Yet, this is what they must do if staff development is to be relevant for the restructuring effort.

Four Key Questions

Four key questions must be answered if the process of restructuring is to move forward effectively. These questions suggest four different types of "lessons" that must be taught by leaders and need to be learned by all if the restructuring process is to be properly directed. The content and structure differs for each of the four lessons.

1. What is the new circumstance or system that we are trying to create? This question asks that a vision, direction, or intention be clearly articulated. It must be articulated in a way that the person asking the question understands the answer and in a way that is appealing and compels action. This requires a *concept development* lesson.

Those who are best at concept development often seem to rely heavily on Socratic dialogue, focused discussion, and pointed questions, combined with the use of metaphors and counter examples intended to distinguish the concept of concern from other notions with which it might be confused. (For example, I began this discussion with a distinction between improvement and restructuring, and now I am using that distinction as an example of another concept—the concept of a concept development lesson.)

2. Can it be done? This question is a request for real-life, hands-on experience or testimony from those who have had such experience. This requires a *demonstration* lesson.

Demonstration lessons require models and exemplars which are real or contrived, empirically demonstrable, or theoretically described. Those who ask the question "Can it be done?" seek assurance that what they are being called on to do is possible and that, if they commit effort to the task, it is likely that they can do what the concept or vision calls them to do.

Modeling and illustrating are techniques associated with demonstration lessons. Where real life situations do not yet exist, simulating actions based on theoretically derived models are often used.

3. Should we do it? This question calls for the analysis of values, beliefs, commitments, context, studies of the past, and anticipation of the future. This requires a *values clarification* lesson.

Value clarification lessons, like concept development lessons, rely heavily on dialogue, discussion, and logical analysis. Such lessons require detailed attention to the values which participants bring to the discussion, the values which the proposed change promises to enhance or serve, and the values which the change is likely to threaten. For example, the value of security is most likely to be threatened by any radical change. Thus, those who promote restructuring must be carefully attuned to the significance various actors give to security, for it is in protecting this value that some of the greatest resistance to change can occur.

4. How do we do it? The last question is a request for assistance in developing the skills and habits required to do the job. This requires a *skill development* lesson.

Skill development lessons, like demonstration lessons, usually rely heavily on modeling and simulation. But skill development lessons are more likely to be active and involve opportunities to practice, coaching, experimental efforts, and corrective feedback. Demonstration lessons are intended to be persuasive, to show that things can be done. Skill development lessons are intended to develop understandings, skills, attitudes, and habits of mind that permit one to do with confidence and ease that which is at first exceedingly difficult, awkward, and, perhaps, even threatening and frightening.

Five Types of Roles

There are five types of roles that become activated in the restructuring process. Each of these role types requires support from staff developers and other school leaders. Some of these roles are more prominent at some stages of restructuring than at others. Further, those who play these roles have vastly different training and support needs related to the lessons for the four key questions previously posed. It is, therefore, critical that staff developers understand who they are addressing at distinct stages in the process, for the needs of different actors will be different from time to time.

1. Trailblazers. Paradigm-breaking journeys are not for the timid, and one should not expect everyone to volunteer to undertake such a journey. Those who take the first steps in restructuring are trail blazers, for they are willing to go—in terms understood by *Star Trek* fans—without maps to places where no person has gone before them, without the benefit of empirically based models, and with little to guide them except belief in themselves, a desire for novelty, the freedom to try, and a vision that motivates and guides them.

The most important requirement for trailblazers is a clear guiding vision. Trailblazers want to know that there is someplace to go that is different; they are motivated by novelty and excited by risks. Once trailblazers have found a vision in which they believe, all they want and need is encouragement and support for that pursuit. Most of all, they want to be recognized for their unique brand of courage, and they want to be celebrated, recognized, praised, and honored—at least most of them do. Staff developers and school leaders must, therefore, find ways to celebrate the trailblazers among them.

Trailblazers are not egomaniacs but they are often monomaniacs with a mission. They know where they are going, even if they are not quite sure how they are going to get there or what obstacles they will confront on the way. When they confront obstacles, they are likely to view them in highly personal terms, for the vision of the trailblazer is a personal vision, and anything that stands in the way of the pursuit of that vision is a personal threat. Thus, trailblazers need much personal and personalized support.

Staff developers and other school leaders should be sensitive to the fact that trailblazers need to be constantly reinforced that the vision they are pursuing is worth the quest and that others, especially powerful others, see that what they are about is important. It is important enough, in fact, that the trailblazers should receive unusual latitude and unconventional forms of support (e.g., non-categorical funding, flexible schedules, and special access to the human and physical resources of the system).

Equally important, trailblazers need to be constantly reminded that it is a community quest they are on, not a private venture. Because the vision the trailblazer pursues is a private vision, it is up to other leaders in the system to link it to a larger shared vision. For example, Lewis and Clark were motivated by the excitement of exploring new frontiers, and Thomas Jefferson linked their quest to a vision of America that spread from shore to shore. Teachers who become enthusiastic about one curriculum innovation or another also often need leaders to help them see the linkage between their private adventures and the common good.

Since trailblazers lead the way into a new world, whether that world is a physical frontier or the creation of a new way of doing business, they do not have access to a body of research and experience to guide them. What then do trailblazers use as guides?

First, they use experiences they and others have gained in circumstances that are analogous to those they are about to confront. For instance, it is not coincidental, I think, that the language of space travel is laced with language which refers to early explorers who took voyages on the ocean, just as space ships now take voyages to the moon. And names of spacecraft often refer to explorers in other times.

Trailblazers need the opportunity to read about and visit with trailblazers from other fields (e.g., business, the military, medical services, and so on). They also need time to discuss and assimilate what they learn from these encounters. It is from such experiences that relevant analogies are discovered and come to be understood. I have found that leaders whose language is rich with metaphors and who argue by analogy are particularly good at inspiring and directing trailblazers.

A second source of guidance for trailblazers is the experiences of other trailblazers who are moving in roughly the same direction and over the same terrain. The rendezvous was one of the ways early trailblazers on America's frontier got information from other trailblazers. Today, we refer to such rendezvous as "networks" where people who are moving in a common direction develop mechanisms to ensure regular interactions. Providing opportunities for such networking is one of the primary contributions staff developers can make to the continuing growth and development of trailblazers.

It is important to understand that networks and rendezvous do much more than provide opportunities for the sharing of information. Such networking provides opportunities for self-affirmation and more than a bit of bragging and storytelling. Networking turns lonely ordeals into shared ordeals. Lonely ordeals debilitate; shared ordeals inspire and motivate.

Alert staff developers and trainers who listen to these stories can learn much that will be of value to pioneers (the second type of role). Furthermore, if staff developers watch carefully, they can get some insight concerning which of the trailblazers have the temperament and the style to be guides as well as trailblazers. After all, the pioneers and settlers who come later will need guides as well.

Leaders and staff developers need to create conditions so that what is learned by the trailblazers is not lost. Trailblazers tell stories. Unfortunately, they seldom turn the stories into lessons for others. It is up to the staff developers, therefore, to turn the stories of trailblazers into lessons that can serve as sources of guidance for those who would follow. This is much like the map makers of the early Fourteenth Century who translated the tales and reports of the early explorers into crude maps which in turn were rendered more accurate and refined with further exploration.

Trailblazers need public acknowledgment for their efforts. They need the opportunity to tell others about places they have been and about what they have done. Such story-telling not only serves as source of information for others, but it also serves as a continuing source of motivation for the trailblazers. Futhermore, telling stories also gives one the opportunity to listen to the stories of others and thus to learn from others as well, especially from other trailblazers.

Staff development budgets that do not make provision for sending trailblazers to conferences where they can brag a bit are not adequate budgets. And staff developers are not doing their job if they do not seek every opportunity to put local trailblazers out in front, including helping them write proposals that will get support for their work and that will permit the trailblazers to share their work at conferences.

2. Pioneers. Closely following the trailblazers are the pioneers. Like the trailblazers, pioneers are an adventurous and hardy lot and are willing to take considerable risks.

Pioneers have many of the same needs as trailblazers. Like trailblazers, concept development lessons (i.e., the development of a vision that links a personal quest to a larger agenda) are the most important lessons they must learn. But the pioneers also have considerable need for assurance that the trip upon which they will embark is worthwhile. More than the trailblazers, pioneers need demonstrations to provide assurances that the journey can, in fact, be made. But pioneers understand that there are really few people who can teach them "how to do it" since only the trailblazers have gone to the frontiers which they are set to explore.

Thus, pioneers need concept development lessons, value clarification lessons, and demonstration lessons. They do not need skill development lessons, and staff developers would be ill-advised to try to provide them. Why does all of this mean in practical terms? First, it means that when staff developers approach pioneers, or are attempting to recruit them, their best allies are those who write about trailblazers (e.g., Fiske, 1991, *Smart Schools, Smart Kids;* Sizer, 1992, *Horace's School).* Such writings do not provide research data, but they do provide anecdotal accounts, reports, and stories. Such stories can inspire prospective pioneers to take the journey. These stories contain some possible lessons regarding what one must know and be able to do to survive the rigors of the journey.

Trailblazers can help motivate pioneers, especially if they are colorful and good storytellers. Davy Crockett did much more to inspire pioneers than he did as a true trailblazer. Indeed, one could argue that Davy Crockett was a staff developer rather than a trailblazer since he often took the stories of others and embellished them a bit, making himself the hero. He used the stories to inspire others to act. Thus, an effective trailblazer may provide needed assurances to encourage pioneers.

I have found that trailblazer teachers and administrators are invaluable sources of inspiration and direction for pioneers, and even for settlers (which are discussed next). But a caution is in order. Too often staff development specialists, in their quest for authenticity, remove trailblazers from their natural habitat on the "frontier" and move them into the central office, or worse to the university campus, in the hope that the stories they will tell will reach a wider audience.

Sometimes this works, but more frequently it is a bad experience for both the trailblazers and for those with whom they work. The teamwork that it takes to "build community," which is what pioneers must do, requires a different style than does the early explorations of new frontiers.

Monomaniacs with a mission can quickly come to appear to others to be egomaniacs whose only mission is to advance themselves. Trailblazers are needed, but they are not easy to live with in the more sedate environments of committee meetings and seminar rooms.

3. Settlers. After the trailblazers and pioneers come the settlers. Settlers need to know what is expected of them and where they are going to go. They need much more detail and more carefully drawn maps than do those who have gone before them. Settlers are bold, but they are not adventurers. They need to be persuaded that the venture upon which they are being asked to embark is worthwhile. Thus, staff developers must provide value clarification lessons that help the settlers understand why the change is needed.

Settlers also want assurance that the task can be accomplished and that they are not set on a fool's mission. Thus, settlers have considerable need for demonstration lessons (e.g., site visits where pioneering work is already under way, conversations with pioneers and trailblazers, testimonials from those who have tried, books and articles that provide rich descriptions of what can be expected, and so on).

Much more than either pioneers or trailblazers, settlers want skill development lessons. They want to be sure they know how to do what will be required of them. Indeed, many potential settlers will not move until they have assurance that the requisite knowledge and support are available to them.

School leaders and staff developers who support them must, therefore, give attention to providing systematic training which is supported by coaching, opportunities for feedback and critique, and, above all, protection from negative consequences for failed efforts.

Perhaps the most critical thing to remember about settlers is that they need strong, constant, and reassuring leadership that inspires them to keep going when they are tempted to turn back. Change of the sort envisioned in an honest restructuring agenda is likely to create uncertainty, doubt, and confusion. The new practices called for are likely to be frightening and demanding, and the results may be no better—at least in the short run—than doing things the "old way." Fullan's (Fullan with Stiegelbauer, 1991) notion of the "implementation dip" comes to mind here; he assumes that a natural part of the change process is short-term deterioration in performance capacity. This occurs because the new way is unfamiliar and requires learning and practice. While the old way of doing things may not be as good as the new way, at least it is familiar and people know how to do it.

Without persistent leadership by people who have been there and without encouragement from others who are going there (settlers traveled in wagon trains and were not isolated travelers), it is unlikely that settlers will stay the course. Thus, it is critical that staff developers and leaders understand the terrain well enough that they can point out progress when settlers become discouraged. Benchmarks of progress and feedback regarding progress toward these benchmarks are essential. To this extent, assessment and constant monitoring, coupled with public appraisals of progress toward restructuring goals (as opposed to the goals of restructuring), are important. For example, a restructuring goal might be to have teachers and building administrators become more systematic in the use of data regarding student performance as a means of evaluating the merit and worth of decisions the administrators and teachers make. But, informed student performance would be a goal of restructuring.

Helping settlers learn how to use evidence of progress is a necessary antecedent to answering the question "Does restructuring improve student performance?" Until restructuring has occurred, this question cannot be answered. Therefore, the first-order assessment question is "What evidence is there that we (those who are engaged in restructuring) are, in fact, doing our business differently today than we did business yesterday, and why do we think the new way of doing business will improve our results?" Settlers need the answers to such questions to keep them going and also to provide assurance that where they are going is worth the effort.

4. *Stay-at-Homes.* There are two conditions that motivate change. First, present conditions are so intolerable or dangerous to one's interests and values that the only alternative is to do something. The Separatists who left England to settle in America were driven by such motives. Second, there is a new and compelling vision—one that so inspires hope of a new day, a better life, or a fuller realization of existing values—that causes risks to seem tolerable when measured against rewards. The Utopian settlements on the American frontier are examples of such vision-driven change.

However, as the Declaration of Independence states so eloquently, fundamental changes are not lightly undertaken, and people will tolerate a great deal rather than give up what is known. Furthermore, intolerable or threatening conditions, which can serve as an initial impetus for change, cannot sustain change. In fact, negative forces are seldom adequate to motivate fundamental change and are almost never adequate to sustain it.

The Mayflower Separatists—who had among them some trailblazers, some pioneers, and a substantial number of reluctant and frightened settlers—may have left England because of oppression, but it did not take their leaders long to recognize that a new and compelling vision would be required to sustain them. This new vision, expressed first in the Mayflower Compact and reinforced by visions based in religious symbols, was as important to the settlement of the new world as were the oppressive conditions that started the movement to that world.

Stay-at-homes are not bad people. Indeed, in the long-view of history, they are inconsequential people for no one remembers the stay-at-homes after the change has occurred. How many Tory supporters of King George are American students expected to recall?

At the time a change is being contemplated, however, stay-at-homes receive a great deal—I think too much—of attention.

This is because most leaders need approval from those they want to lead, which is usually everybody in their sphere of influence. Thus, those who do not respond enthusiastically—or at least compliantly—with the desires of change leaders are often viewed as problems.

Effective leaders seem to understand that early in the change process it is probably not wise to spend too much energy trying to convince the stay-at-homes that they, too, need to move to the frontier. These leaders accept the fact that some will never come along, and those who do change will only do so after the pioneers and settlers have done their work very well. Of course, some will only come to the new land for a visit.

One of the greatest dangers when dealing with stay-at-homes in the restructuring process is that the strategies used to entice them to change may backfire and thus may convert these relatively benign actors into supporters of the saboteurs discussed below. Saboteurs' favorite strategy is to sow distrust through rumors and disinformation, and they will destroy even the best organized wagon train if they can gain enough followers. The most likely source of recruits for the saboteurs are the stay-at-homes and the more timid settlers who feel pressured to move before they have the assurances they need and before they have identified leaders they trust.

I have found the best strategy to use with stay-at-homes, at least in the early stages of the restructuring process, is benign neglect coupled with as much generosity of spirit as is possible. One must remember that those who do not particularly want to change are not necessarily opposed to others changing if they choose to do so. Many stay-at-homes stay at home because they truly love the place. As John Dewey has observed, "Familiarity breeds contempt, but it also breeds something like affection. We get used to the chains we wear, and through custom we finally embrace what at first wore a hideous mien."

And there are, of course, those who are simply too timid to go to unfamiliar places. Such persons are not likely to be encouraged to move by direct assaults on what they currently value or by threats to what little security they now enjoy. Rather they will join with the saboteurs who do not want to change for other reasons.

5. *Saboteurs.* Saboteurs are actively committed to stopping change. Not only do they refuse to take the trip, but they do not want others to go either.

Many of those who take on the role of saboteurs do so because they receive benefits from this role which are not provided if they were to support change. I have also been struck by the fact that some of the most effective saboteurs have many qualities and needs which are similar to trailblazers.

Saboteurs are often lone rangers. They are not afraid of taking risks. The difference is that while the trailblazers will go to places that others fear to go, saboteurs are likely to remain in place when others are beginning to feel afraid to stay. Loneliness does not have the same meaning to them as it has to the settlers, and isolation often inspires the saboteur to even greater effort. To be persecuted, it seems, is to be appreciated, and, in a perverse way, to be isolated or excluded is to be honored.

Saboteurs can cause trouble, no matter where they are. But I have found that the best place to have them is on the inside where they can be watched rather than on the outside where they can cause trouble without its being detected until the effects are felt. Certainly, saboteurs can be disruptive, and some will not cooperate even enough to communicate their concerns.

If, however, change leaders continue to reach out to saboteurs and critics and try hard to hear what they are saying, sometimes there is much to be learned. It might be learned that some saboteurs were once trailblazers and pioneers who at some time in the past had the misfortune to follow leaders who did not give them the support they needed and abandoned them at the first sign of trouble.

A Concluding Comment

Creating commitment to change is not the same thing as overcoming resistance to change. To create commitment, one must understand motives. Trailblazers are motivated by novelty, excitement, and sometimes by the possibility of fame and glory. Pioneers sometimes begin their journey because of intolerable conditions, but they will stay the course only if they become convinced that the new world is really better.

Settlers need to know, almost for certain, that the world they are being asked to move to is better than the one they are leaving and that the way to get there is known. And, most of all, they need to know that they are not taking the trip alone.

Stay-at-homes will only move when all or nearly all—of their friends and neighbors have deserted them or when they muster the courage to "come for a visit" and find that they prefer it.

Some saboteurs will never come along, and if they do, they will make the trip as difficult as possible. Saboteurs, however, are people who in some prior movement to another frontier, behaved as trailblazers and pioneers, but were betrayed by their leaders. As a result, they became cynical about the prospects of change. Most of all, they want to be assured that those who are sounding the latest call to move to a new frontier will stay the course rather than turn around and go back.

Whether the present demand that our schools be restructured will be responded to positively remains to be seen. But of one thing I am confident: Without leaders who will stay the course and without staff developers who understand what draws men and women to the frontier and what these people need to keep on going, all our efforts to reform schools will fail.

References

Fiske, E. (1991). *Smart schools, smart kids.* New York: Simon & Schuster.
Fullan, M. with Stiegelbauer, S. (1991). *The new meaning of educational change* (2nd ed.) New York: Teachers College Press.
Sizer, T. (1992). *Horace's school.* New York: Houghton Mifflin.

CHAPTER 8

Reworking Industrial Models, Exploring Contemporary Ideas, and Fostering Teacher Leadership

Christopher Steel and Elizabeth Craig

Ask any American to describe the basic operational structure of a typical public school in the United States, and he or she can probably do it with great accuracy. The systems and processes of schooling in this country are remarkably standardized and make education perhaps the most familiar of public institutions. One could also reasonably claim that, until recently, public education has been the nation's most unchanging entity.

For over a century, public schools have conformed to an industrial production model.[1] No sooner had Henry Ford discovered the efficiency of the assembly line than educators began to apply similar logic to the "production" of educated citizens. As a society, we came to believe that students could be placed on a metaphorical conveyor belt at the start of their school years and, provided the machine was properly constructed, would step off at the end with all the necessary skills and knowledge to enter adulthood. The role of the teacher was quickly equated with that of the assembly-line worker, who would add some small subset of the requisite educational "parts" to the student/product.

For better or worse, this industrial model of education became the basis for how all those involved in the educational enterprise viewed the role of teachers. The marvel of the assembly line is that each worker needs to perfect only his or her own assigned task for the final product to be accurately built. The application of this concept to education led swiftly to the "egg-crate model" of schooling, under which a powerful culture of teacher autonomy and isolation was allowed to thrive.[2] Certainly teachers recognized themselves as being part of a larger system, but for the most part they could do their work with the classroom door closed and with little interruption from others who worked around them.

In the same way that the industrial model has been widely applied to the roles of teachers, it has also been a powerful force in defining the roles of the education system's traditional leaders, those individuals in school and district administrative positions. Often, the chief responsibility of these instructional leaders is to ensure that the education machine continues to function smoothly. In many situations, the teachers who work in schools appreciate this approach. When a problem arises, a teacher can go to somebody and get it fixed. However, this technical, managerial approach to leadership further reinforces the schools' isolated, egg-crate mode of operation.

Directly related to this operational structure is an extraordinary level of attrition. Teacher turnover is at an all-time high. Nearly half of all new teachers in public schools quit within the first five years.[3] Indeed, recent research has shown that as many as 30% of new teachers leave by the end of their third year of service.[4] Researchers have pointed to uncompetitive salaries, high levels of teacher isolation, and unfavorable working conditions as among the possible causes. Surely the lack of opportunities for professional growth is a significant factor as well. In many cases, teachers are given highly structured, scripted curriculum materials for use in their classrooms, and systems of districtwide assessment and accountability procedures necessarily limit the professional autonomy of educators. These fully trained, certified professionals are, in effect, required to simply "press play" to do their jobs. Small wonder many choose to leave the profession. School administrators, who are in a position to effect change, must seriously consider why teachers are leaving the profession and then respond by reassessing their own role in the empowerment and professional development of teachers.

Reframing Leadership: Lessons from Teachers

Although many aspects of teachers' work can still be compared to participation in an assembly line, the experiences of those who have chosen to stay in the classroom and have managed to thrive there can be instructive. In a potentially limiting professional environment, some administrators have worked to counteract the trend of undervaluing teachers. From interviews that we conducted with teacher leaders during the spring of 2004 and interviews with teachers reported in recent studies by Susan Moore Johnson and the Project for the Next Generation of Teachers (NGT) at Harvard University, we have derived a number of recommendations for administrators seeking to support teachers as authentic professionals.

1. **Trust: show confidence in teachers' professional judgment**. Teachers who know that they are trusted by administrators have a sense of increased credibility and are more open to taking risks and, in turn, to pursuing professional growth. One teacher whom we interviewed referred to the "opportunity for individual leadership" as the decisive reason for his staying in the profession. "It's a question of leadership," he said. "I've more experience now, more credibility. … I'm a bit more of a risk-taker now; the principal trusts and listens to me." Without a doubt, such trust must be earned. But once that trust is established, it is critical that leaders articulate it in order to enhance teachers' confidence and commitment and to engage them meaningfully in the improvement process.

2. **Listen: acknowledge the relational nature of schools**. In her 2001 book, *You Just Don't Understand: Women and Men in Conversation,* Deborah Tannen discusses the power of "intentional interpersonal relationships" in the workplace. She offers one example of a high-ranking corporate executive who deliberately set out each workday to have a nonbusiness conversation with each member of her department. Through these seemingly small exchanges, Tannen argues, this supervisor ultimately created an environment in which the staff felt acknowledged and valued as people and came to view their individual importance as central to the success of the larger company. These intentional connections also served to cultivate the employees' respect for their supervisor, which increased her degree of effectiveness as the corporate leader. This proved particularly beneficial when she had to take unpleasant or undesirable actions. If the staff did not embrace a particular corporate decision, says Tannen, the decision was nevertheless respected and executed in light of the relationships, achievements, and personal rapport that had been built.

By making individual efforts to become better acquainted with teachers, administrators simultaneously accomplish two things. First, they communicate their understanding that teachers are people whose lives extend beyond their roles as educators, thus making it more likely that teachers will feel connected to and sustained in the workplace. Second, they establish a relational context in which they can more effectively garner support for their decisions and actions as school leaders. All members of such school communities feel vested in administrative decisions and, regardless of outcome or personal conviction, remain engaged contributors.

3. **Validate: recognize contributions from all levels**. One teacher, upon learning that a major restructuring of the curriculum was imminent, considered leaving in the middle of the year but changed his mind after the administrative team called him to the principal's office and acknowledged much of the unofficial work he had contributed to the school community. "This was a pretty powerful experience," he said. "It seemed that they knew that, if they weren't careful, they would lose me. That helped me realize that, wow, they do care, they do listen." This teacher came away from the interaction feeling validated in his work—and not a moment too soon.

All too often, recognition and appreciation go unstated, or accomplishments are indirectly credited to those in formal leadership roles. Validation of the type that this teacher experienced can have a tremendous impact. It serves as a positive signal from the administration and motivates teachers by making them feel that they are integral parts of the system. Fresh bagels in the teachers' lounge on a Friday morning, words of encouragement and thanks on the daily bulletin, and a bouquet of flowers for the director of the school musical may be mere tokens when compared to the actual amount of work and commitment they acknowledge, but they can validate teachers in a powerful way and provide them with important sustenance.

4. **Communicate support: give feedback other than criticism**. One NGT teacher, Victoria, identified positive, noncritical feedback from administrators as strengthening her commitment to staying in the classroom. She described "classroom visits from the principal and vice principal which she experienced as supportive rather than threatening." Such visits made her aware that administrators were not just interested in what she was doing wrong. When administrators fail to provide positive feedback regularly or to engage in informal conversation regarding teaching practice (which can happen innocently, given the immense demands on school leaders' time), teachers quickly learn to interpret any communication from administrators as critical rather than supportive. Victoria's experience reveals the importance of positive feedback and of a diverse range of communication between teachers and those in administrative roles.

If school administrators are serious about supporting improved teaching practices in their schools, they will also be intentional about providing input that teachers can use to reflect on and develop their expertise. Without clear, consistent feedback on new classroom practices, teachers can justifiably become jaded when they encounter administrators' calls for improvement and directives for change. In effect they come to think, "If my principal was serious about what he's asking me to do, he would follow up and help make sure I'm doing it well." It is up to administrators to remain aware of this potential pitfall and to provide the feedback that will help avoid it. Doing so will confirm for teachers that they are supported in their efforts, with the additional benefit of enhancing the likelihood of sustainable improvement.

5. **Expect growth: support teachers as learners**. With an ever-growing emphasis on accountability that connects details of student progress and achievement to individual teachers, a school administrator must be able to recognize the limitations of or gaps in teachers' content and pedagogical knowledge and must foster an atmosphere in which growth in these areas becomes a priority. As NGT teacher Fred commented, doing so creates a culture in which continuous growth and development of one's teaching practice is assumed, and no one is expected to have mastered instructional techniques on the first day in the classroom. Instead, everyone is expected to be adding to his or her skills consistently over time.

One key to creating such a culture of teachers as learners is for administrators to support professional development activities consistently and to make them part of the regular, ongoing work of teachers. Such an approach is considerably more valuable than the traditional one-shot, daylong seminars that are separated from the core of teachers' work. These activities rarely affect actual practice.[5] Professional development that is ongoing also helps increase teachers' sense of upward mobility in the profession, a key factor in reducing turnover.[6] Continuous learning counteracts the deadly tendency toward professional stagnation that so desperately needs to be eliminated from the profession. Expecting professional growth cultivates an environment in which faculty members feel consistently challenged and motivated to develop their individual capacity.

6. **Facilitate collaboration: work to reduce teacher isolation.** Closely related to administrators' efforts to support the professional development of each teacher is the need to create more effective systems and structures for professional collaboration and in the process to consciously break down the isolation of teachers that persists in most school settings. One teacher whom we interviewed spoke of the implementation of team-teaching practices at her junior high school: "To do it right, they had to incorporate teamteaching in the design of the master schedule." Such significant restructuring of a school's regular operation is no small endeavor, but for this teacher, such explicit organizational administrative support made change possible, and the benefits proved to outweigh the initial investment of effort. After the changes had been made, the teacher reported, "I felt like I was finally creating the actual environment I always wanted for my students. I now had someone helping me, offering me feedback early and often, and just letting me run with it all!" As this teacher's situation makes clear, the success of collaboration between teachers can hinge on the efforts of leaders to align a school's overall operating procedures with the stated goals for the collaborative effort.

Time is undoubtedly a teacher's scarcest resource, so specific changes to make new approaches effective—especially because collaboration almost always requires more time from everyone—must be carefully executed. As Vivian Troen and Katherine Boles note in a description of their Millennium School, initiating teacher collaboration takes more than just providing "time to talk about teaching, learning, and thinking."[7] Setting up teaching arrangements that actively support classroom partnerships, offering released time as needed, and orchestrating course schedules to enhance the exchange of ideas all place an increased cultural emphasis on collaboration rather than individual work.

But beyond supporting such structural adjustments, administrators also need to work to align their own practices more closely with the collaborative approach. For example, most teachers are observed and evaluated individually, and the central evaluation question pertains to the individual and whether he or she is doing the job well, not to the overall outcomes produced by the system as a whole. For a school environment to become truly collaborative, however, at least part of each individual's performance needs to be assessed in relation to the broader role that he or she plays within the organization.

7. **Empower: encourage leadership beyond the classroom.** For administrators, genuine efforts to empower teachers are perhaps the most critical component in promoting true teacher leadership and the resultant improvement of the education system. Many of today's most talented teachers envision themselves developing as professionals over the course of their careers, and that vision includes their having a hand in such processes as curriculum writing, mentorship, and professional development. It is up to the new generation of administrators to devise innovative ways in which teachers can fulfill these aspirations and continue to teach.

If empowerment can be defined as the connection between a sense of personal competence and a desire for and a willingness to take action in the public domain,[8] then many teachers are, without a doubt, already empowered. When considering the idea of empowerment in relation to school leadership, we believe that an additional component must be added to the definition: administrators must provide teachers with permission and genuine encouragement to take on active roles beyond the classroom. Teachers need to hear and understand that their participation and leadership beyond the classroom are essential, and administrators need to act with diligence in making the structural and operational changes in schools that make these roles sustainable.

Beyond that, administrators must let go of the obsolete notion of a "classroom teacher" and come to view those whose work includes classroom teaching as professional colleagues in a broader sense. It is only when administrators make this final shift that teachers will feel the sense of empowerment that comes with being recognized as major contributors to the school community, with knowing that one's work has value and significance to those outside of the classroom, and with the expectation of even greater contributions in the future.

Reframing of School Leadership

In an age of heightened accountability, school leaders can no longer define their role through technical competencies, even if the dominance of the industrial model still makes the administrative role at least partly procedural. The challenges that contemporary administrators face, spurred by the urgent need for improvement in most of the nation's schools, require them to acknowledge the political dynamics that surround their efforts, to be responsive to the human resource needs of the various players involved, and to be aware of the symbolic dimensions of effective leadership.[9] These areas were not originally accounted for in Henry Ford's logical and efficient industrial design. However, they are crucial to promoting leadership at the most fundamental level of the educational assembly line—the teacher.

Administrators need to trust, listen to, and validate the teachers in their schools and give them frequent and constructive feedback on their efforts. As adaptive leaders, they need to expect growth and facilitate teachers' participation in the collaborative processes that have the power to change the way schools work. By doing these things, they will empower teachers more fully and promote their sustained commitment to the work of teaching.

If education in America has so far been shaped by the energies and philosophies of the Industrial Age, then innovative thinking, awareness of the bigger picture, and new goals of the instructional enterprise should characterize the modern effort. The scope and efficiency of the work of teachers have necessarily expanded, yet purposeful, distributed leadership from the administrative level is the only approach that can sustain the benefits of this expansion. This approach has the power to begin to reverse current trends in teacher turnover and rebuild the profession as one characterized by strong, highly aware, committed teacher leaders who are capable of making educational improvement a reality.

Notes

1   Nancy Hoffman, *Woman's "True" Profession* (New York: The Feminist Press at CUNY, 2003); Vivian Troen and Katherine C. Boles, *Who's Teaching Your Children?: Why the Teacher Crisis Is Worse Than You Think and What Can Be Done About It* (New Haven, CT: Yale University Press, 2003).

2   Jennifer A. O'Day, "Complexity, Accountability, and School Improvement," *Harvard Educational Review,* vol. 72, 2002, pp. 293–329; and Troen and Boles, op. cit.

3   Linda Darling-Hammond, "Teachers and Teaching: Testing Policy Hypotheses from a National Commission Report," *Educational Researcher,* January/February 1998, pp. 5–15.

4   Susan Moore Johnson and the Project on the Next Generation of Teachers, *Finders and Keepers: Helping New Teachers Survive and Thrive in Our Schools* (San Francisco: Jossey-Bass, 2004); Richard Ingersoll, "The Teacher Shortage: A Case of Wrong Diagnosis and Wrong Prescription," *NASSP Bulletin,* June 2002, pp. 16–31; and idem, "A Different Approach to Solving the Teacher Shortage Problem," Teaching Quality Policy Brief Number 3, Center for the Study of Teaching and Policy, University of Washington, Seattle, 2001.

5   Sonia Nieto, *What Keeps Teachers Going?* (New York: Teachers College Press, 2003).

6   Roland Barth, *Improving Schools from Within* (San Francisco: Jossey-Bass, 1990); Nieto, op. cit.; and Troen and Boles, op. cit.

7   Troen and Boles, p. 15.

8   Marc A. Zimmerman and Julian Rappaport, "Citizen Participation, Perceived Control, and Psychological Empowerment," *American Journal of Community Psychology,* vol. 16, 1988, pp. 725–750.

9   Lee G. Bolman and Terry E. Deal, "Leading with Soul and Spirit," *School Administrator,* February 2002, pp. 21–26.

CHAPTER 9

Excellent Teachers Leading the Way
How to Cultivate Teacher Leadership

Holly J. Thornton

P olicy changes and mandates that may be at odds with middle school philosophy continue to come from state legislatures and departments of education. Increased emphasis on content coverage and test scores can be an obstacle to many middle level practices, such as curriculum integration and differentiated instruction. As this situation continues, it becomes increasingly difficult for middle grades educators to meet students' needs as individual learners, to develop their voices and ownership in learning, and to explore students' questions and concerns about the world around them (Kohn, 2000).

While an increasing number of well-prepared, exemplary middle grades educators know and understand this situation, these educators are often not the ones leading school change. Teachers are at the center of all reform movements, and without their full participation and leadership, any effort to reform education is doomed to failure. Real change cannot be mandated, even by well intentioned policymakers (Lieberman & Miller, 1999). Given this, why is it that teachers are not taking the lead in current reform, and how can they best be supported as leaders of school improvement? A grassroots movement by teachers reinforcing the notion that "every teacher is a leader" may be vital to the continued success of middle level schools in this challenging time.

Benefits of teacher leadership

Middle schools benefit in numerous ways by increasing opportunities for teacher leadership. Teacher leaders serve as mentors and encourage their peers; they influence policies in their schools; they assist in improving instructional practice; and they help develop the leadership capacity and improve retention of other teachers (Katzenmeyer & Moller, 2001). As these teacher leaders work to help others develop skills and practices, they frequently hone their own teaching skills and improve their classroom performance (Ovando, 1994). The ultimate benefit is improved practice and increased student performance for all (Katzenmeyer & Moller). Higher student achievement, even as defined by traditional measures, increases in schools with strong teacher leaders (Lambert, 2003). Teacher leadership allows excellent teachers to impact their colleagues and the students in their classrooms, and this serves as an incentive for them to remain in the classroom. Given these benefits, it may be worth asking, *What is the current status of teacher leadership?* and *How can we cultivate it in our middle level schools?* In the spirit of teacher leadership, let us ask teachers to answer these questions.

Are teacher leaders in our schools?

Teachers enrolled in graduate programs that included a focus on action research and teacher leadership designed and implemented studies within their home schools. These teacher researchers used action research projects to examine teacher leadership in 44 middle level schools in 13 counties. All were rural or small community schools, identifying themselves as middle schools or middle schools within a P–8 setting. Most schools housed grades 6–8, with others housing grades 7–8 or P–8. All included elements of middle school organization such as teaching teams, common planning time, a verbalized commitment to teachers who are knowledgeable about young adolescents, and some implementation of integrated curriculum and exploratory classes. They included a range of educators in terms of experience, typically predominantly female, with 10%–15% males. Both male and female principals were included in the study, and the gender of the principal did not correlate with any findings. The schools ranged in size from 160 to 908 students, with the majority falling within the 500–749 range. The schools varied in terms of students' ethnic diversity, with the majority serving less than 25% students of color. Half of the schools identified more than 50% of students as economically disadvantaged. In terms of student achievement test scores, the majority of the study schools were identified as meeting expected state growth goals (Figure 1).

School Size/ Number of Students		Grade Configuration		Student Achievement		Economically Disadvantaged Students		Minority Student Population	
0–249	2%	P–8	11%	Exceeded school goal by 10%	32%	0–24%	9%	0–24%	66%
250–499	27%	7–8	11%	Met school goal	52%	25–49%	41%	25–49%	27%
500–749	48%	6–8	78%	Did not meet school goal	16%	50–74%	45%	50–74%	5%
750–1000	23%					75–100%	5%	75–100%	2%

Figure 1. Action research project settings and populations

The teacher researchers gathered data from multiple sources, including school mission statements, school and district policy documents, school improvement plans, and student achievement data. They also distributed surveys to all building teachers and administrators, with an average return rate of 35%. They conducted follow-up interviews with a subgroup of five to ten survey respondents.

All of the data were analyzed using two frameworks. The first was a "leading structural change" schema (Knoster, 1991) which focused on elements necessary to sustain change (Figure 2). The second was Lambert's (2003, p. 5) teacher leadership capacity matrix. Lambert described a school's capacity for teacher leadership in terms of four quadrants running along two continuums—skillfulness of teachers to act as leaders and levels of teacher leadership participation. Quadrant one schools have low skillfulness and low participation levels and are characterized by the following.

• Principal as autocratic manager

• One-way flow of information; no shared vision

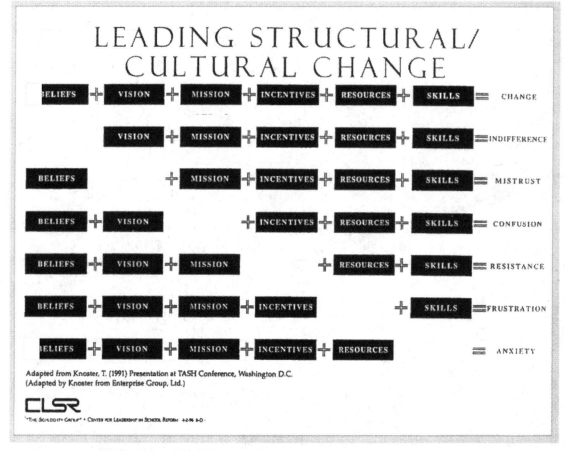

Figure 2. Leading structural/cultural change schema

- Codependent, paternal/maternal relationships; rigidly defined roles
- Norms of compliance and blame; technical and superficial program coherence
- Little innovation in teaching and learning
- Poor student achievement or only short-term improvements on standardized tests

Quadrant two schools, which have low skillfulness and higher participation, display the following characteristics.

- Principal as laissez-faire manager; many teachers develop unrelated programs
- Fragmented information that lacks coherence; programs that lack shared purpose
- Norms of individualism; no collective responsibility
- Undefined roles and responsibilities
- Both excellent and poor classrooms
- "Spotty" innovation; some classrooms are excellent while others are poor
- Static overall student achievement (unless data are disaggregated)

Quadrant three schools have low leadership participation, but high skills. Schools in this quadrant may exhibit the following.

- Principal and key teachers as purposeful leadership team

- Limited uses of school-wide data, information flow within designated leadership groups

- Polarized staff with pockets of strong resistance

- Efficient designated leaders; others serve in traditional roles

- Strong innovation, reflection skills, and teaching excellence; weak program coherence

- Student achievement is static or shows slight improvement

Quadrant four schools have high levels of both skillfulness and participation in terms of teacher leadership. These schools are considered the target and may possess the following traits.

- Principals, teachers, parents, and students as skillful leaders

- Shared vision resulting in program coherence

- Inquiry-based use of information to inform decisions and practice

- Broad involvement, collaboration, and collective responsibility reflected in roles and actions

- Reflective practice that leads consistently to innovation

- High or steadily improving student achievement

The survey and interview questions were designed to elicit teacher input related to the quadrant descriptors and to allow teachers and administrators to place their schools within the matrix. Follow-up interviews examined the rationale for the placement, revealing barriers to increased skill and participation. Teacher leaders are disposed to work collegially toward change and improvement at the team level, school level, and beyond (Danielson, 2007). The researchers' own understandings of their schools, relationships with participants, and commitment to change within their schools were all considered as teachers worked together in cohort groups to analyze their data. Finally, the teacher researchers devised action plans based on their specific schools' potential and concerns. These plans were shared with administrators and, in some cases, implemented.

What is the status of teacher leadership?

Data from the participating schools indicated the following placements of schools within Lambert's (2003) leadership capacity matrix: quadrant one 14%, quadrant two 18%, quadrant three 59%, and quadrant four 9%. Overwhelmingly, the data indicated that schools had a predominance of teachers who were highly skilled in leadership but had low participation of teachers in leadership roles and activities. Even though the schools had school improvement teams and multiple committees where teachers were often assigned "leadership" roles, these were not synonymous with the presence and cultivation of teacher leadership in the school. The defining characteristics of a school in quadrant three—limited use of school wide data, polarized staff, pockets of excellence, and innovation with relatively static student achievement—were the norm in 26 schools. Only four schools in the study were reported to have a predominance of both teachers highly skilled in leadership and teacher participation in leadership roles. Data analysis revealed why more schools were not in quadrant four.

What are the barriers?

Time. Lack of time was consistently found to be a barrier to developing teacher leadership. Multiple demands kept the teachers in the study from committing the time necessary to act as leaders. These demands included individual and team planning, meeting the needs of the whole child, collaboration with parents and other professionals, completing paperwork and other administrative duties, committee involvement, and fulfilling new requirements for accountability and testing. Those who wanted to get more involved in leading change in their schools and districts felt they were not able to add yet another item to their already full plates, and they felt they did not have the time necessary to collaborate with and lead other teachers.

Formal leadership structures. At first glance, the teacher researchers viewed formal structures for participation on committees and school improvement teams as beneficial to cultivating teacher leadership. However, a closer look at the data revealed that teachers tended to view these leadership roles as perfunctory—more of a "rubber stamp" on decisions that had already been made. Further, teachers in the study reported that these "leadership" positions were often assigned to the same teachers over and over again. Those not included viewed this as cliquish, as if only individuals who agreed with the movement afoot were chosen. Teachers who found themselves on such committees reported they often felt saturated by too much involvement and, therefore, could not do the job well enough to make their participation worthwhile. They also reported collegial "jealousy" from those not selected (typically by the principal). At times, teachers were on these committees by default, when no one else wanted to do it. Even when change resulted from work on curriculum committees, parent councils, and teaching teams, participants reported they did not feel they were the ones setting the agenda. The vision and incentive to participate—two elements key to implementing change—were missing in these schools.

Communication and fragmentation of faculty. Ironically, middle school structures designed to promote connections and identity were reported as potential barriers to cultivating teacher leadership. The close knit team identities and focus on grade levels as units of instruction often led to communication barriers and a sense of fragmentation of the faculty as a whole. Teachers spent so much time with their own teams or grade level colleagues that they often lost focus on the needs and concerns of the whole school. Regular school wide communication was limited, creating feelings of disconnect among teams and grade levels. Respondents in some schools reported that principals' actions did little to address these communication issues within buildings. Sometimes teachers felt that by keeping them apart, it was easier for the principal to maintain building level control and make decisions without negotiating and compromising across many leaders.

Principal leadership style. It may come as no surprise that principal leadership was either a clear asset to the development of teacher leadership or a powerful barrier. The issue most frequently reported as impacting the cultivation of teacher leadership was the principal's leadership style. The principal's primary role is to be an instructional leader who mobilizes the energy and capacities of teachers by supporting them in their endeavors to increase student achievement and learning (Fullan, 2002). To sustain school improvement, teachers and administrators need to work and create meaning together. Principals who were reported as engaging in collaborative leadership were seen as better equipped to both understand and support the leadership of others in the school. Those who were more authoritative and those who were laissez-faire proved to be the most troublesome. In schools where the principal was authoritative and preferred to make decisions alone, teacher leadership was relegated to service on committees and other formal structures where teachers felt they were merely there to implement predetermined plans. A limited number of teachers may have been part of the decision-making circle. Those not in that circle felt that the principal played favorites, thus causing division in the faculty. In schools where the principal was more hands-off with very little visual presence, teachers reported that there was confusion, lack of "buy-in," and occasional in-fighting among teachers trying to take charge of the situation. These situations undermine the collective efforts and ownership of a school with strong teacher leadership and the benefits derived from those leaders.

Support for change. For real change to occur, teachers must become agents of change (Fullan, 1993). According to Knoster (1991), several elements must be in place and aligned to support and sustain change and improvement. In each of the school studies teacher researchers used Knoster's model. The model included six elements, namely shared beliefs, vision, mission, incentives, resources, and skills. They looked for evidence of these elements through the analysis of surveys, interview data, and artifacts found in the school, such as mission statements, school improvement plans, schedules, professional development plans, and faculty meeting minutes.

The most frequently missing change elements across all types of schools in the study were mission and incentives, while vision, shared beliefs, and resources were the next most often reported missing. Even when schools had a vision grounded in shared beliefs, they often lacked a mission as a way to actualize that vision. In these situations, teachers felt that change did not occur as a result of acting on their vision and beliefs. Change was seen as mandated or handed down from others. In schools with low leadership skills, teachers did not work toward developing the mission. These teachers no longer wanted to take part in leadership that led to no results or results that sometimes ran counter to their beliefs. When incentives were lacking, teachers felt that their time and energy were limited, and they needed to focus on direct contact with students. They felt there was little intrinsic pay-off for their work, and there was no other tangible compensation. Without the elements necessary to support change, teacher leadership cannot be fully supported and realized within the school.

What action can we take?

Exemplary teachers who wish to remain in the classroom while leading school reform must find ways to take action. The teacher researchers developed action plans to address the primary barriers identified in each of their studies. Within each plan, they presented a timeline for implementation and identified key participants. They shared the plans with these participants, who often included building level administrators. Some plans were implemented immediately. Others led to dialogue, which called attention to the need for teacher leadership and to barriers that may have been present in the schools. The teacher researchers themselves acted as teacher leaders as they engaged in this action research. Overviews of some of the plans follow.

- ***Making time: staff meetings, PLCs, teaming***
  Some action plans institutionalized time to develop teacher leaders within these middle schools. The plans included opportunities for teachers to meet and problem solve in staff meetings and to create professional learning communities (PLCs) as a way to empower teachers, set goals, and develop action plans. Plans also dedicated team time to give teachers a vehicle for voice and change. While staff meetings, learning communities, and teams were all present and part of the time structure of the schools, they were not being used to cultivate teacher leadership.

- ***Communication: A new approach to staff meetings***
  The research frequently revealed that staff meetings were an underused means for developing teacher leadership. In one action plan, teachers set up and led staff meetings with the principal's support, and in other plans, teachers used staff meetings as opportunities to share best practices and exchange ideas related to school improvement and changes in district policy. Teachers often felt traditional meetings were not very productive, so allowing them to take the lead in restructuring the purpose and function of staff meetings gave them a sense of renewal and collective ownership.

- ***PLCs as teacher leadership***
  The term *professional learning community* (PLC) is frequently misused to describe every imaginable combination of individuals with an interest in education (DuFour, 2004); however, true PLCs are collaborative cultures in which groups of teachers meet to lead change by focusing on student learning, making changes to improve their teaching practices, and evaluating the success of these changes. This allows PLCs to act as ideal situations for developing teacher leaders.

Many schools in the study were implementing PLCs (DuFour, 2007; DuFour, Eaker, & DuFour, 2005), but these PLCs often operated with predetermined topics and agendas rather than being opportunities for teachers to engage in inquiry and implement changes related to issues they deemed important. Teachers may have been interested in the topics, but they did not fully own and engage in the process of developing the PLC in a way that could capitalize on widespread teacher leadership.

- ***Rethinking structures: Crossing team and grade level boundaries***
  By emphasizing teams and team identity, some middle schools inadvertently foster competition and teacher isolation, especially across grade levels. Action plans included a specific focus on team time to regularly share and collaborate across teams and grade levels. Some schools planned to use "houses" in which students remain together across grade levels. This allows teachers in different grades to collaborate to meet students' needs over their entire middle grades experience.

- ***Shared vision in action vs. the mission statement on the wall***
  Research participants often felt school mission statements were created for accreditation purposes, not for guiding and reflecting lived experiences of faculty and students. Many action plans revisited the schools' mission statements, aligning them with Knoster's (1991) change schema.

- ***Recognition and sharing as incentives***
  Publicly sharing thoughts, practices, and accomplishments is an important way to recognize individual teachers as school leaders. Some action plans provided opportunities for such sharing at staff meetings, through bulletin boards, or by e-mail. This public recognition provided an incentive for teachers to take action in leading school improvement and change. Instead of spending money on speakers or consultants, the plans reallocated this money to teacher leaders who could facilitate professional development owned and determined by teachers. When monies for financial compensation were scarce, teachers were rewarded with small incentives donated by the school community, such as dinner certificates, spa coupons, or breakfast brought to the school.

Conclusion

As we face challenges to middle level education from many fronts, it is encouraging that we have so many exemplary teachers who can act as our guides to meaningful student-centered reform. To capitalize on the strengths and commitment of these educators, we must find ways to tap into and support their leadership. Teachers, themselves, can act as researchers to help identify barriers and challenges to cultivating teacher leadership in their schools, and they can develop action plans to address these barriers as they build a community of learners and leaders within the school. In this manner, they can continue the hard work of the middle level movement—taking steps to move forward. Finding ways to empower teacher leaders to take these steps may be crucial to the retention of excellent teachers (Thornton, 2004). As excellent teachers enable young adolescents to achieve their greatest potential, it is a win-win situation for all involved. Strong principals who are willing and able to truly share leadership with their teachers will recognize this, but it is likely they already know.

The author describes Lambert's framework for classifying leadership capacity in schools.

In which of Lambert's four quadrants of leadership capacity would your school be located? What data support your judgement?

What are some potential barriers to cultivating strong teacher leadership in your school? What actions can your school take to overcome these barriers?

References

Danielson, C. (2007). The many faces of leadership. *Education Leadership, 65*(1), 14–19.

DuFour, R. (2004). What is a professional learning community? *Educational Leadership, 6*(8), 6–11.

DuFour, R. (2007). Professional learning communities: A bandwagon, an idea worth considering, or our best hope for high levels of learning? *Middle School Journal, 39*(1), 4–8.

DuFour, R., Eaker, R., & DuFour, R. (2005). *On common ground: The power of professional learning communities.* Bloomington, IN: National Education Service.

Fullan, M. (1993). Why teachers must become change agents. *Educational Leadership, 50*(6), 12–17.

Fullan, M. (2002). The change leader. *Educational Leadership, 59*(8), 16–20.

Katzenmeyer, M., & Moller, G. (2001). *Awakening the sleeping giant: Helping teachers develop as leaders.* Thousand Oaks, CA: Corwin Press.

Knoster, T. (1991, October). Paper presented at the annual meeting of the National Conference for the Association for Persons with Severe Handicaps, Washington DC.

Kohn, A. (2000). *The case against standardized testing: Raising the scores, ruining the schools.* Portsmouth, NH: Heinemann.

Lambert, L. (2003). *Leadership capacity for lasting school improvement.* Alexandria, VA: Association for Supervision and Curriculum Development.

Lieberman, A., & Miller, L. (1999). *Teachers—Transforming their word and their work.* New York: Teachers College Press.

Ovando, M. N. (1994, October). Effects of teachers' leadership on their teaching practices. Paper presented at the annual conference of the University Council of Educational Administration, Philadelphia, PA.

Thornton, H. (2004). What can we learn about retaining teachers from PDS teachers' voices? *Middle School Journal, 35*(4), 5–12.

Questions for Reflection and Application

After reading the essays in Section Two, answer the following questions:

1. Everything that happens in a school should focus on the well-being and success of all students. Changing the expectations for the roles and responsibilities of teachers assumes that all teachers are committed professionals. How does one go about addressing the lack of teaching and learning effectiveness in some teachers' classrooms without challenging a colleague's competence or questioning his or her professional commitment?

2. Is there a role for teacher leaders in this scenario? What are the different kinds of roles that teacher leaders/learners might assume in a setting focused on student learning, not just student testing?

3. Discuss these different roles within the context of a continuum that focuses on different skill levels and developmental differences among teachers, for example, different teachers may be at different places with regard to experience, skill, and personal commitments.

4. And finally, what kinds of changes have to occur in teachers' work, both in the classroom and in the larger school/institutional environment, for teachers to be seen (and treated) as professionals equal in stature with other educational leaders and administrators?

Answer these questions using both the ideas from the essays that we are considering as well as your personal experiences with the schools you have encountered during your life: as a student, parent, and/or teacher. References to specific ideas found in the Section Two essays are expected.

SECTION 3

Teacher Leaders as Learners and Leaders

Introduction

The roles of teachers have traditionally been confined by narrow definitions of what good teachers do. While "teacher leadership" has been a term tossed around for several decades, the term is most often used to define roles and responsibilities for teachers that serve the needs of others, for example, administrators and politicians. "Others" define what needs to be done and teacher leaders make it happen. Teacher leaders are often named as key actors in school improvement efforts, but the voices of teachers seldom determine the process and product of those efforts.

Meaningful teacher leadership in the twenty-first century depends on an in-depth understanding of how teachers acting as leaders must, by necessity, integrate a variety of roles within a context of reform, school improvement, and transformation—teacher leaders are learners and leaders. The conception of teachers as lifelong learners is not new. However, a consideration of how this role intersects with teachers as leaders is prerequisite to an understanding of how the notions of teacher leadership discussed in this book differ from previously held ideas of teacher leadership as simply one piece of the school improvement equation. Teachers functioning as autonomous decision-makers and educational leaders who define their own unique agendas are important dimensions of a "new and improved" twenty-first-century version of the teaching profession. Yet, moving beyond this vision to an understanding of how teacher leaders overcome the myriad obstacles to this potential transformation of the profession is the critical next step in the process of making teacher leadership an accepted, and necessary, part of the work of all teachers.

Paulo Freire's (2000) ideas can be used to discuss and analyze the oppression and inequitable relationships that have traditionally characterized teacher's work. His ideas force us to look beyond the rhetoric about school reform and consider the possibilities for praxis and a reinvention of the ways in which we view the roles and responsibilities associated with teacher leadership in schools and classrooms. Just as Freire criticized the idea of narrative education in which teachers participated in the facilitation of student passivity within a context that was devoid of critical thinking and/or reconsiderations of notions of truth and knowledge, so are teachers treated in similar ways where school improvement efforts often encourage teacher passivity in contexts that are devoid of action informed by an examination of the forces that lead to the oppressive practices that characterize the work of teachers. Regardless of their training and education, important formal and informal roles, and responsibilities, teachers are repeatedly rewarded for implementing policies, programs, and testing protocols where their concerns and issues are ignored if they contradict or challenge the status quo. There is little time or attention devoted to "reading" school culture and understanding the narrative that is woven throughout discussions of teachers' work.

Thus, it is important to consider how teacher leaders disrupt a dominant school culture that discourages teacher reflection and scholarship and rewards blind adherence to norms and standards that are a contradiction to reform efforts and behavior that represents compliance to the rules and regulations established by managers working outside of the spaces where teachers' work occurs. Teaching and learning are clearly political acts where the actors, that is, the teachers, have very little control over the politics that govern their lives and work. And yet discussions of teacher leadership frequently focus upon the benefits of teacher leadership to the aims and purposes of the organization—a focus that moves the discussion to a level that ignores the realities associated with how teachers experience their work on a personal level and how students, parents, and communities are affected by the various roles of teachers.

In this section of the book, teacher leadership as a key component of teacher roles and responsibilities is discussed by scholars who have attempted to define the parameters of teacher leadership and describe how teachers must function as both leaders and learners. Angelle, Barth, Helterbran, Katzenmeyer and Moller, Lambert, and Lieberman each contribute to the construction of a bridge that connects the realities of teachers' work with the vision of teacher leadership as an essential part of that reality. Highlighted in this work is a consideration of multiple definitions of teacher leadership that include both the "what" and "how" of teachers' work as leaders and learners.

Reference

Freire, P. (2000). *Pedagogy of the Oppressed*. New York: Bloomsbury Academic.

CHAPTER 10

Teachers as Leaders

Collaborative Leadership for Learning Communities

Pamela S. Angelle

This We Believe Characteristics
- Educators who value working with this age group and are prepared to do so
- Collaborative, courageous leadership
- A shared vision that guides decisions
- High expectations for every member of the learning community
- Organizational structures that support meaningful relationships and learning

The idea of leadership is recognized throughout the school reform literature as critical to school improvement (Hallinger & Heck, 1996; Leithwood, Jantzi, Earl, Watson, Levin, & Fullan, 2004). Through increased understanding of the nature of leadership, the definition of this concept has expanded to include leadership at the teacher level. Given the scope of federal and district mandates that fall upon schools, schoolwide learning and the development of learning communities are essential. If schools are to operate as learning communities, then they cannot do so with the leadership of a single person or with a singular leadership strategy (Harris, 2002). Therefore, teacher leadership becomes imperative to the success of any school reform movement (Crowther, Kaagan, Ferguson, & Hann, 2002; Frost, Durrant, Head, & Holden, 2000; Katzenmeyer & Moller, 2001; Murphy, 2005). If mandates for accountability and improvement are not seen as valuable or are not implemented at the classroom level, they are doomed to mediocrity at best or complete failure at worst. Logically, embracing teacher leaders as part of a vision for improvement is a key to success. The purpose of this article is to examine the role of teacher leadership in schools. To accomplish this end, areas which will be considered include:

- The concept of teacher leadership: definitions, roles, self-perceptions
- The relationship between principal leadership and teacher leadership
- The school culture necessary to support teacher leadership
- The organizational structures that support or challenge teacher leadership.

The Concept of Teacher Leadership

A review of current literature reveals inconsistency in defining teacher leadership due to a myriad of concept variations, from leading by example to assuming a specific leadership position (Bowman, 2004; Crowther, Kaagan, Ferguson, Hann, 2002; Frost, Durrant, Head, & Holden, 2000; Katzenmeyer & Moller, 2001; Murphy, 2005; Wasley, 1991). Most teachers who take on leadership roles do not see themselves as leaders, reserving the term leader for those who take on formal roles, such as principals or district supervisors. Instead, they perceive that most of their work is done informally through collaboration (Moller, Childs-Bowen, & Scrivner, 2001). While definitions of teacher leadership differ, a commonly held notion is the expanded view of leadership beyond traditional classroom boundaries (Beachum & Dentith, 2004). Teacher leadership reflects teacher agency, through establishing relationships, breaking down barriers, and marshalling resources throughout the organization in an effort to improve students' educational experiences and outcomes (York-Barr & Duke, 2004).

Definitions and Roles of Teacher Leadership

Teacher leaders are those teachers who maintain focus on student learning, seek lifelong learning for themselves, use facilitation and presentation skills, engage others in shared vision and meaning, develop and maintain relationships with other organization members, work with a sense of integrity, and plan and organize (Bowman, 2004; Moller, Childs-Bowen, & Scrivner, 2001). Snell and Swanson (2000) maintain, however, that expertise is the foundation of a respected teacher leader because the level of expertise establishes credibility with colleagues. The literature alternately suggests that teacher leaders are those who have the ability to "encourage colleagues to change" (Wasley, 1991, p. 23) and have the willingness to "lead beyond the classroom and contribute to the community of learners" (Katzenmeyer & Moller, 2001, p. 17). Teacher leadership has also been discussed as an issue of density where a larger number of people throughout the organization are involved in decision making and creating knowledge (Sergiovanni, 2001).

The duties of teacher leaders typically have more to do with a focus on teaching and learning, rather than a focus on the management of the school (Katzenmeyer & Moller, 2001). Specifically, teacher leaders may visit and observe other teachers, provide demonstrations and feedback to colleagues, attend conferences to re-deliver knowledge to their peers, and develop curriculum (Feiler, Heritage, & Gallimore, 2000). Collegiality, collaboration, and communication are skills listed as necessary for teacher leadership and are frequently found in the literature (Andrews & Lewis, 2002; Davidson & Dell, 2003; Fennell, 1999; Harris, 2002; Silins & Mulford, 2004; Thornton, Langrall, Jones, & Swafford, 2001). Hatch, White, and Faigenbaum (2005) examined teacher leadership beyond the school building level and found that teacher leaders can be effective at influencing policy outside of their school, including the district level and wider audiences through presentations and publications.

Just as the definition and duties of teacher leaders are ill-defined in the literature, so also are the roles, though Ogawa and Bossert (1995) argued that leadership is a quality embedded in relationships, not roles. Harris (2003) referred to both the informal roles and formal roles of the teacher leader. Informal roles encompass classroom-related functions such as planning, communicating goals, and regulating activities, while formal roles entail specific positions, including department head or subject coordinator—positions that remove the leader from the classroom. Teacher leadership roles are defined by Thornton, Langrall, Jones, and Swafford (2001) with a focus on change—in planning and initiating professional development, facilitating communication about the change, or in addressing curriculum development or problems.

The evolution of teacher leadership is discussed by Silva, Gimbert, and Nolan (2000) in terms of their roles. The development of the teacher leader role includes teacher as manager (e.g., department heads or master teachers), teacher as instructional leader (e.g., team leader and curriculum coordinator), and teacher as re-culture agent (e.g., reformers of goals and norms, proponents of collegiality) (Silva, Gimbert, & Nolan, 2000). Reform coaching is another role taken on by teacher leaders—a role that includes building capacity, serving as a bridge between administrators and teachers, and using knowledge to assist others in changing their practice (Coggins, Stoddard, & Cutler, 2003). Coaching roles, including reform coaches and content coaches, emphasize the traits of trust, determination, innovation, perseverance, and calm (Guiney, 2001).

Self-perceptions of Teacher Leaders

A focused characterization of teacher leadership is further muddied by their self-perception, which often differs from the perceptions of their colleagues. Teacher leaders may alternately see themselves as reflective practitioners, action researchers, collaborators, mentors, instructional experts, or risk takers (Wynne, 2001). Teacher leaders, at times, perceive themselves as professional development trainers and curriculum innovators (Mimbs, 2002), while their colleagues may perceive them either in a positive light as teacher advocates (Beachum & Dentith, 2004) or in a negative light as elitists, harmful to teacher morale, or detrimental to accepted classroom practices (Smylie & Denny, 1990).

Allen (2004) examined teacher leadership in terms of their voice, pointing out that too often the teacher's voice focuses on everyday management issues rather than school renewal efforts. Moreover, teachers must believe that their voice will be respected, listened to, and acted upon. Otherwise, teachers will be unwilling to participate in any reform efforts. Allen categorized the types of voice in schools:

- Voting voice—which requires little time or risk

- Advisory voice—which requires time and some risk when the outcome is not a foregone conclusion

- Delegated voice—which may include teachers serving on a leadership team, thus requiring time and some risk in openly giving one's opinion

- Dialogical voice—which requires high levels of collegial interaction, a deep commitment, and a high level of risk.

Silva and associates (2000) noted that teachers' and principals' voices are missing from much of the literature advocating for teacher leadership, leading to the conclusion that teacher leadership has yet to be defined by those who actually practice the concept.

If teachers are the leaders, then what is the role of the principal? What are the conditions necessary for teacher leaders to flourish? What barriers might stand in the way of successfully encouraging teacher leaders at the school level? A reflection upon the National Middle School Association's beliefs (NMSA, 2003) provides a roadmap for the answers to these questions.

Principal Leadership and Teacher Leadership

Schools that embrace teacher leadership are those "successful schools for young adolescents [which] are characterized by a culture that includes … courageous, collaborative leadership" (NMSA, 2003, p. 7). Collaborative leaders recognize that in today's schools, one person cannot adequately address the needs of all members of the school community. Empowering others to lead alongside the principal builds collegiality and shares opportunities for active participation in the improvement of the school. This sharing of power by the principal is critical to the success of teacher leadership but does not come without some risk and sacrifice from the school administration.

In schools that are improving in terms of student achievement, leadership is fluid and emerging, rather than fixed (Harris, 2002). This blurring of leadership between leader and follower is alternately termed as leadership that is distributed (Harris, 2003), invitational (Stoll & Fink, 1996), constructivist (Fennell, 1999), and parallel (Andrews & Lewis, 2002). By and large, leadership strategies that foster teacher leadership (Harris, 2002; Katzenmeyer & Moller, 2001; Silins & Mulford, 2004) parallel those strategies found in the school effectiveness literature (Edmonds, 1979; Hallinger & Murphy, 1986; Mortimore, Sammons, Stoll, Lewis, & Ecob, 1988; Sammons, 1999; Teddlie, Kirby, & Stringfield, 1989; Teddlie & Stringfield, 1993) and may include:

- Empowering others in the organization

- Promoting a shared vision and communicating it to all stakeholders

- Structuring an organization that promotes collaboration

- Exhibiting high expectations for innovation and effectiveness

- Providing adequate resources

- Trusting, supporting, and caring for others and expecting trust, support, and care in return.

Empowering schoolteachers as leaders requires that principals relinquish some of their power while still retaining ultimate responsibility and accountability (Harris, 2003). Thus, embracing the concept of teacher leadership may prove difficult for some school principals. Others may accept the concept in principle but not in practice. Acker-Hocever and Touchton (1999) studied the power relationships of teachers and principals and concluded that conditions for successful teacher leadership call for principals to give up power, to release control, to offer respect and trust, and to set up conditions for teachers to practice their leadership. However, a caveat to these obligations from the principal is that teachers must be willing to take the power and leadership when it is offered to them. Teachers must also be willing to cross the invisible boundaries from follower to leader.

Anderson (2004) extended the notion of power boundaries between principals and teachers with three models of influence. The buffered principal is surrounded by teacher leaders who act as foot soldiers protecting the principal from the other teachers. In this model, teacher leaders are the "powers that be" and exert pressure to carry out the decisions of the buffered principal. The *interactive principal* is involved with and works closely with all teachers and staff. This model is one of distributed, shared decision-making. The third model of influence is the contested principal. This principal is outside the loop and works against the teacher leaders. The teacher leaders, in turn, attempt to undermine the decisionmaking power of the principal. This is a model of conflict. Leadership practices that promote and empower teachers to contribute to school improvement through their leadership create an organization where all stakeholders can learn and grow. This type of learning organization is built upon collaboration, professional relationships, high expectations, and continual learning.

School Culture and Teacher Leadership

The vision for middle schools encompasses learning, not only for adolescents, but for the adults in the school community as well. Schools that promote lifelong learning for all are "successful schools for young adolescents [which] are characterized by a culture that includes … high expectations for every member of the learning community … [with] students and teachers engaged in active learning" (NMSA, 2003, p. 7). Teachers who work in a culture of high expectations and continuous learning find that their leadership skills are actively called upon to contribute to the improvement of their school—leadership abilities that might otherwise wax stagnant in other environments.

The culture of continuous learning is sustained through ongoing, job-embedded professional development. Teacher leadership and learning are fostered through a teacher's role in planning and initiating professional development, where teachers work together to end professional isolation (Guiney, 2001).

Through opportunities to model, share ideas for reform strategies, and participate in team-building activities, teacher confidence is boosted, increasing the likelihood that future teacher leadership opportunities will be accepted (Thornton, Langrall, Jones, & Swafford, 2001). Sustaining the initial enthusiasm and extending the learning of professional development can be achieved through interaction with colleagues. This is particularly true if implementation of the professional development is difficult (Feiler, Heritage, & Gallimore, 2000). In addition to professional development, teacher leadership promotes professional relationships and a participatory work environment through consensus building (Fennell, 1999; Ryan, 1999).

School cultures that support teacher leadership approach problem solving with enthusiasm, focusing on students as the cornerstone for all decisions. Moreover, these schools foster a high level of trust between teachers, principals, and the community. Teachers believe they are competent and effective, embracing opportunities for leadership (Ryan, 1999; Short, 1998). Schools with these cultures are referred to as learning organizations, characterized by collaboration, risk taking, and shared mission (Silins & Mulford, 2004).

The context in which a teacher works is particularly critical to the success of teacher leadership. A healthy work culture of trust and support where both principal and teachers share a purpose or set of goals will lead to a growth in teacher leadership (Moller, Childs-Bowen, & Scrivner, 2001). Work environments where teacher leadership thrives are those that emphasize collegiality, communication, and collaboration. School cultures built around these relationships find that teacher commitment to the job and loyalty to the organization are enhanced (Fennell, 1999).

Organizational Structures and Teacher Leadership

Aspects That Mediate the Leadership Process

Learning organizations with cultures where teacher leadership can flourish require "organizational structures that support meaningful relationships and learning" (NMSA, 2003, p. 7). In addition, factors in the school that hinder teacher leadership should be avoided. The following sections outline these success factors and barriers that extend across school levels, including the building-level principal, the teachers who participate in leadership, and the colleagues who work alongside the teacher leaders.

Principals. Clear communication with the teacher leaders is a vital component to the success of teacher leadership in a school. Principals must not only communicate their boundaries for decision making and power sharing but also their expectations for the role of teacher leader. While assisting the teacher leaders in developing their leadership skills, the principal should also hold them accountable for decisions made. Time release to work with other teachers and keeping administrative duties to a minimum provide a structure that encourages success for teacher leaders.

Principals can offer support for teacher leadership both overtly and covertly. Through empowering teachers, including them in decision making, recognizing their efforts, relinquishing control, sharing responsibility for failure, and giving credit for success, principals can send the message to the school community that teacher leadership is important and accepted in the school culture. Acknowledging and supporting teacher leaders can ultimately contribute to the success of the principal (Barth, 2001). As Barth notes, the success of "those at the front of the line depends on the support of those behind them" (p. 446).

While principal support is critical to the success of teacher leadership, school building leaders also must be cognizant of their own boundaries for power surrendering and communicate this to the teachers. Principals should take on the role of fostering expertise in the teachers, not promoting their own expertise (Short, 1998). Principals cannot really give empowerment to teachers. Principals can only create the environments and opportunities that lead to and support empowerment. As teachers take on empowering roles, principals must clearly communicate the responsibilities that accompany the roles and the goals the empowered teacher should work toward; that is, toward school-level goals rather than personal goals (Short, 1998).

Resources and time are repeatedly cited as barriers to teacher leadership (Harris, 2003; Ryan, 1999; Smylie & Denny, 1990; Wynne, 2001). While principals are often constrained by these factors as well, attempting to alleviate these barriers to teacher leadership sends a message of support to the teacher leaders.

Teacher leaders. Tapping teacher leaders to serve involves consideration of appropriateness and willingness. Most schools have limited resources and time capacity; therefore, teachers who can meet the greatest need should be selected. Fully supporting a few leaders is better than partially supporting many (Feiler, Heritage, & Gallimore, 2000). Expertise and leadership skills should be considered; however, just as critical, is the teacher's ability to influence colleagues and take risks. Teachers placed in leadership roles should be those for whom student learning is the first and last priority (Feiler, Heritage, & Gallimore, 2000).

Once given the opportunity to serve, teacher leaders receive intrinsic benefits from their position. Teacher leaders have the opportunity to be exposed to new ideas and to engage in nontraditional roles. Moreover, teacher leaders are able to collaborate with colleagues. Opportunities afforded to teacher leaders lead to greater feelings of professionalism (Wetig, 2002). As teachers grow in confidence and a self-perception of professionalism, their sense of agency within the organization may also increase; that is, teachers will naturally develop a perception that they have the means to accomplish goals and a shared purpose. Frost and Durrant (2002) contended that teachers do not need autonomy to restore a sense of agency but need a work culture that provides the capacity to exercise leadership, coupled with the satisfaction of having an impact on facets of the organization. These facets include an impact on teachers (e.g., personal, interpersonal, instructional practice), on the school (e.g., the processes, the culture, the capacity), beyond the school (e.g., knowledge), and on the students (e.g., metacognition, achievement).

Teachers who have the opportunity to pursue leadership roles in the school do not always have the willingness to serve. Barth (2001) noted that the Coalition of Essential Schools found that teacher leaders rarely comprise more than 25% of a school faculty. Why are more teachers not involved in this positive path to school improvement? Several factors may be responsible for this hesitancy. Some teachers are not prepared to confront hard issues or ask tough questions that may be required for decisions that must be made in the leadership role (Bowman, 2004). Teachers may lack the confidence and belief that they actually have the ability to lead others (Barth, 2001).

Teacher leaders may begin their work with high levels of enthusiasm; however, as the realities of balancing leadership roles with classroom obligations and personal lives set in, enthusiasm often wanes. In addition, personal discouragement at the slow wheels of change may lead to stress and burnout. Facing the constraints of time, resources, and flexibility also dampens the spirits of teacher leaders accustomed to excellence (Beattie, 2002; Lanting & Jolly, 2001). DiRanna and Loucks-Horsley (2001) found that burnout was common in teacher leaders because they are responsible for their classrooms as well as school-level leadership. Recommendations from these findings included the need for a leadership pipeline so that initiatives can continue if teacher leaders vacate their positions.

Ryan (1999) found that one of the greatest barriers to successful implementation of teacher leadership came from the types of situations in which teachers were asked to practice their leadership skills. All too often, teacher leaders are called upon to decide technical issues such as textbook choices and grade book packages rather than administrative decisions such as hiring teachers and budget development. Teachers who are asked to determine the individual work assignments of their instructional teams will feel more empowered by the shared decision-making capacity than those teacher leaders who vote on whether caps can be worn by students on Fridays. Teacher leaders who are deprived of the ability to make decisions on what they perceive are critical issues report greater dissatisfaction with their job, more stress, and less loyalty to their principal (Ryan, 1999).

Colleagues and school environment. A school environment that supports teacher leadership includes quality professional development for the teachers, a culture of collegiality and collaboration, and a respect for the autonomy and abilities of teachers (Katzenmeyer & Moller, 2001). Unfortunately, the greatest resistance to teacher leadership may come from colleagues. Fellow teachers do not always embrace their colleagues as leaders. When teacher leaders attempt leadership roles, fellow teachers may chastise them for being power hungry or wanting control (Bowman, 2004). Too few teachers take on leadership roles because of contentment with inertia and complacency in their current work of teaching. Moreover, insecure colleagues may take on an "us/them" mentality, separating the teacher leaders from the larger faculty (Barth, 2001). Colleagues can provide the greatest challenge to teacher leadership through active resistance to decisions made, initiatives advocated, or simply to the teacher leaders themselves (Barth, 2001). In these cases, without the principal's support, the concept of teacher leadership will likely fail in that environment.

Conclusion

Teacher leadership is a phenomenon in which teachers daily walk on a balance beam, balancing their desire to influence and improve the school-wide organization with their calling to teach children and see them succeed. To ensure success for these teacher leaders, the school culture must value their work, the school principal must support their work, and their teacher colleagues must be willing to work alongside them as they strive for a more effective school. Collaboration, shared decision making, reflective practice, quality professional development, and shared goals are all part of an organizational culture that promotes the high expectations and school-wide learning necessary for successful teacher leadership. A courageous, collaborative leader willing to share power, extend boundaries, and provide support, respect, and appreciation is critical to a school embracing teacher leadership. Teachers who are willing to take risks, collaborate with colleagues, engage in nontraditional roles, and who are organized and committed to student learning will inspire excellence and contribute to school improvement as teacher leaders. Teacher leadership as a vehicle for implementing school reform requires a commitment from all members of the school community. Organizations that embrace leaders at all levels take the first step on the path to creating successful schools for young adolescents.

References

Acker-Hocever, M., & Touchton, D. (1999, April). *A model of power as social relationships: Teacher leaders describe the phenomena of effective agency in practice*. Paper presented at the meeting of the American Educational Research Association, Montreal, Canada.

Allen, L. (2004). From votes to dialogues: Clarifying the role of teachers' voices in school renewal. *Phi Delta Kappan, 86*, 318–321.

Anderson, K. D. (2004). The nature of teacher leadership in schools as reciprocal influences between teacher leaders and principals. *School Effectiveness and School Improvement, 15*(1), 97–113.

Andrews, D., & Lewis, M. (2002). The experience of a professional community: Teachers developing a new image of themselves and their workplace. *Educational Research, 44*(3), 237–254.

Barth, R. (2001). Teacher leader. *Phi Delta Kappan, 82*, 443–449.

Beachum, F., & Dentith, A. (2004). Teacher leaders creating cultures of school renewal transformation. *The Educational Forum, 68*, 276–286.

Beattie, M. (2002). Educational leadership: Modeling, mentoring, making, and re-making a learning community. *European Journal of Teacher Education, 25*(2), 199–221.

Bowman, R. F. (2004). Teachers as leaders. *The Clearing House, 77*(5), 187–189.

Coggins, C. T., Stoddard, P., & Cutler, E. (2003, April). *Improving instructional capacity through school-based reform coaches*. Paper presented at the meeting of the American Educational Research Association, Chicago, IL.

Crowther, F., Kaagan, S. S., Ferguson, M., & Hann, L. (2002). *Developing teacher leaders*. Thousand Oaks, CA: Corwin Press.

Davidson, B. M., & Dell, G. L. (2003, April). *A school restructuring model: A toolkit for building teacher leadership*. Paper presented at the meeting of the American Educational Research Association, Chicago, IL.

DiRanna, K., & Loucks-Horsley, S. (2001). *Designing programs for teacher leaders: The case of the California science implementation network*. Columbus, OH: ERIC Clearinghouse for Science, Math, and Environmental Education. (ERIC Document Reproduction Service No. 465590)

Edmonds, R. R. (1979). *A discussion of the literature and issues related to effective schooling*. St. Louis, MO: Central Midwestern Regional Educational Laboratory.

Feiler, R., Heritage, M., & Gallimore, R. (2000). Teachers leading teachers. *Educational Leadership, 57*(7), 66–69.

Fennell, H. A. (1999, April). *Encouraging teacher leadership*. Paper presented at the meeting of the American Educational Research Association, Montreal, Canada.

Frost, D., & Durrant, J. (2002). Teachers as leaders: Exploring the impact of teacher-led development work. *School Leadership and Management, 22*(2), 143–161.

Frost, D., Durrant, J., Head, M., & Holden, G. (2000). *Teacher-led school improvement*. New York: Routledge Falmer.

Guiney, E. (2001). Coaching isn't just for athletes: The role of teacher leaders. *Phi Delta Kappan, 82*, 740–743.

Hallinger, P., & Heck, R. H. (1996). Reassessing the principal's role in school effectiveness: A review of empirical research, 1980–1995. *Educational Administration Quarterly, 32*(1), 5–44.

Hallinger, P., & Murphy, J. (1986). The social context of effective schools. *American Journal of Education, 94*, 328–355.

Harris, A. (2002, April). *Building the capacity for school improvement*. Paper presented at the meeting of the American Educational Research Association, New Orleans, LA.

Harris, A. (2003). Teacher leadership as distributed leadership: Heresy, fantasy, or possibility. *School Leadership & Management, 23*(30), 313–324.

Hatch, T., White, M. E., & Faigenbaum, D. (2005). Expertise, credibility, and influence: How teachers can influence policy, advance research and improve performance. *Teachers College Record, 197*, 1004–1035.

Katzenmeyer, M., & Moller, G. (2001). *Awakening the sleeping giant: Helping teachers develop as leaders*. Newbury Park, CA: Corwin Press.

Lanting, A., & Jolly, A. (2001, April). *Leadership transformations of two teachers and their principal: A case study*. Paper presented at the meeting of the American Educational Research Association, Seattle, WA.

Leithwood, K., Jantzi, D., Earl, L., Watson, N., Levin, B., & Fullan, M. (2004). Strategic leadership for large-scale reform: The case of England's national literacy and numeracy strategy. *School Leadership and Management, 24*(1), 57–79.

Mimbs, C. (2002). Leadership development as self-development: An integrated process. *Action in Teacher Education, 24*(3), 22–25.

Moller, G., Childs-Bowen, D., & Scrivner, J. (2001). *Teachers of the year speak out: Tapping into teacher leadership*. Greensboro, NC: South Eastern Regional Vision for Education.

Mortimore, P., Sammons, P., Stoll, L., Lewis, D., & Ecob, R. (1988). *School matters: The junior years*. Wells, UK: Open Books.

Murphy, J. (2005). *Connecting teacher leadership and school improvement*. Thousand Oaks, CA: Corwin Press.

National Middle School Association. (2003). *This We Believe: Successful Schools for Young Adolescents*. Westerville, OH: Author.

Ogawa, R. T., & Bossert, S. T. (1995). Leadership as an organizational quality. *Educational Administration Quarterly, 31*(2), 224–43.

Ryan, S. A. (1999, April). *Principals and teachers leading together*. Paper presented at the meeting of the American Educational Research Association, Montreal, Canada.

Sammons, P. (1999). *School effectiveness: Coming of age in the twenty-first century*. Lisse, The Netherlands: Swets-Zeitlinger.

Sergiovanni, T. (2001). *The principalship: A reflective practice perspective*. Needham Heights, MA: Allyn & Bacon.

Short, P. M. (1998). Empowering leadership. *Contemporary Education, 69*(2), 70–72.

Silins, H., & Mulford, B. (2004). Schools as learning organizations—effects on teacher leadership and student outcomes. *School Effectiveness and School Improvement Journal, 15*(3–4), 343–366.

Silva, D. Y., Gimbert, B., & Nolan, J. (2000). Sliding the doors: Locking and unlocking possibilities for teacher leadership. *Teachers College Record, 102*, 779–804.

Smylie, M. A., & Denny, J. E. (1990). Teacher leadership: Tensions and ambiguities in organizational perspective. *Educational Administration Quarterly, 26*, 235–259.

Snell, J., & Swanson, J. (2000, April). *The essential knowledge and skills of teacher leaders: A search for a conceptual framework*. Paper presented at the meeting of the American Educational Research Association, New Orleans, LA.

Stoll, L., & Fink, D. (1996). *Changing our schools: Linking school effectiveness and school improvement*. Buckingham, UK: Open University Press.

Teddlie, C., Kirby, P., & Stringfield, S. (1989). Effective versus ineffective schools: Observable differences in the classroom. *American Journal of Education, 97*, 221–236.

Teddlie, C., & Stringfield, S. (1993). *Schools make a difference*. New York: Teachers College Press.

Thornton, C. A., Langrall, C. W., Jones, G. A., & Swafford, J. O. (2001). *The emergence of teacher leaders through professional development*. Columbus, OH: ERIC Clearinghouse for Science, Math, and Environmental Education. (ERIC Document Reproduction Service N0.465594)

Wasley, P. A. (1991). *Teachers who lead: The rhetoric of reform and the realities of practice*. New York: Teachers College Press.

Wetig, S. L. (2002, April). *Step up or step out: Perspectives on teacher leadership*. Paper presented at the meeting of the American Educational Research Association, New Orleans, LA.

Wynne, J. (2001). *Teachers as leaders in education reform*. Washington, DC: ERIC Clearinghouse on Teaching and Teacher Education. (ERIC Document Reproduction Service No. ED 462376)

York-Barr, J., & Duke, K. (2004). What do we know about teacher leadership? Findings from two decades of scholarship. *Review of Educational Research, 74*, 255–316.

CHAPTER 11

The Time Is Ripe (Again)

Roland S. Barth

Is this a promising time for teacher leadership? As someone who's been in education for 50 years, serving as both a teacher and a principal, I've found that it's *always* been a promising time for teacher leadership. It's just never been a *successful* time. It's never happened on a wider scale.

So what continues to stand in the way of teachers assuming serious leadership of schools? Five obstacles strike me as the most inhibiting.

First, many principals need to control what goes on in school. Principals are ultimately responsible. If I, as a principal, delegate or accept a teacher's leadership of something and it goes badly—say, staff development or developing the science curriculum—the superintendent isn't going to call that teacher. He or she is going to call me. So I have to be really careful about relinquishing control. And most principals just don't want to relinquish it.

There's also a taboo in our profession against one teacher elevating himself or herself above the others. You see it with merit-pay discussions, but you also see it when one teacher takes responsibility for something in the school and the other teachers are just worrying about their own 30 kids. The teacher who takes a leadership role can expect to be punished by fellow teachers.

It's just a very leveling profession. Teachers are, in a way, their own worst enemy when it comes to unlocking leadership because they don't welcome it, typically don't respect it, and often feel threatened by one of their own taking it on. Anyone who bumps above the level is subject to condemnation: "Who the heck do you think you are?!" I'm not talking about trends—I'm talking about people impeding teacher leadership. Some of the people are called principals, and some are called teachers.

Another big issue is that teachers' plates are full. Teachers already have a huge amount of responsibility for their students. With the increasing accountability we're seeing, they're going to be very careful about deflecting time and energy to that science curriculum committee rather than to getting their kids up to grade level in reading. It's an add-on for most teachers to assume additional responsibility for a school.

There's also the subtle and sometimes not-so-subtle adversarial relationship that exists between teachers and principals, between unions and management. If I'm a teacher who's taking on a part of what's seen as the principal's responsibility, I'm siding with the enemy. What teacher wants to be criticized for siding with management?

And finally, schools have been coopted by a business model over the years. We hear the language of business in school. I even heard a principal talk about "our product line here." Give me a break! By and large, the business model doesn't model leadership of the line workers—Toyota, Saturn, a few companies have tried—but mostly the job of the line worker is, know what's expected of you and do it fast and well. That business model does *not* favor teacher leadership.

Take any one of these obstacles, and they're pretty serious. Take them collectively, and they make realizing teacher leadership very hard indeed.

Three Promising Trends

Despite these formidable challenges, the time may be ripe for change. Three circumstances bode well for teacher leadership.

A Need to Share the Load

For a long time, people have realized that the principal alone can't run something as complex and enormous as a school. But now I think *principals* realize that. Principals are also beginning to understand that one way they can get teachers invested in what they're doing is to let them sit at the table with the other grown-ups and take on a leadership role.

When I was an elementary school teacher, I noticed there were two classes of citizens in the school: those who worried about their classroom and those who worried about the school writ large. By and large, it was the teachers in one place and the principals in the other. I vowed that if I ever became principal, I would change that.

And I did. Every September I used to ask every teacher, "What piece of this school do you want to take responsibility for?" I had a long list—the parent committee, staff development, and so on—and they could pick the one they cared passionately about. Usually they revealed their interest in one of two ways: Either they said, "I want to jump on this and make it better." Or they'd complain about something—like how the faculty meetings were run. I took those complaints as a hopeful sign that the teacher cared about that issue. So a few teachers would then get together to plan how those faculty meetings *should* be run.

Teachers were not just permitted to take on leadership roles in the school—they were *expected* to take them on. If all teachers are expected to be leaders, no one is breaking the taboo about standing higher than the others because everyone is on the same higher level.

In my lifetime, there has never been a better time for teacher leaders to emerge. Either these leaders emerge soon, or public education as we know it is gone.

When public education is under such vicious attacks and the public school system itself may be lost, for a teacher *not* to take a leadership role is tantamount to complicity. Are you willing to go along with the destruction of a wonderful profession? Are you willing to have your wages frozen, your job stability lost, your chance to teach kids what they might love to learn about highly restricted, your worth determined by a test of children who may be English language learners or in poverty or who may not quite qualify for special education services but are close? Sorry, but silence is agreement.

Did you really mean to be silent when they instituted high-stakes tests because your state needed to know how it was doing? What did you learn that you didn't already know about your students? What did the state learn that couldn't have been predicted from zip codes? How much does all that test data inform your teaching compared to your own classroom tests and knowledge of your students? Are you going to remain silent now, as they get ready to fire you because your test scores are not as high as someone wants them to be for your poor kids and your English language learners? Maybe you should have spoken out earlier and taken a leadership role before this all happened.

The fact is that teachers must lead and manage the political forces that now buffet them. Teachers have always led busy lives and worried more about their students and their families than the politics that surround them. But now politics needs their attention.

Today's teachers can no longer afford to be pawns. We need more teachers—in particular, more female teachers—on community boards, in state legislatures, and in Congress. We would probably have a better and more humane social system in the United States as a result.

Teachers should stand up for professional rights, as did the teachers in Seattle recently, who simply said, "No" to irrelevant high-stakes testing. Of course there needs to be accountability. Of course there have to be assessments. Of course schools need to improve. But they'll only improve if the lives of the children and families they serve improve.

It's time for educators to stop taking the rap for a society that has allowed a 30-year drift into poverty for so many families. Teacher leaders need to get into political positions and right these wrongs. Teachers who stand together in solidarity can force responsible changes in education.

A Curriculum to Create

The Common Core State Standards also represent an opportunity here. The standards specify what students should know and be able to do, but they don't specify how teachers must teach those things. They're intentionally leaving it up to each school to put together an effective curriculum that will lead to the accomplishment of those standards.

Principals aren't about to write a curriculum. They're inviting teachers to do this, to design the methods of instruction. Teachers have usually been told what they're going to teach and how they're going to teach it. This new development is a profound form of teacher leadership.

Already, over the Internet, teachers are sharing their experiences designing the curriculum. Teachers in other schools are asking them, "So how did you do this?" They're getting professional recognition for their efforts in this area—recognition they haven't received in previous years.

New Models of Leadership Today we see a proliferation of all kinds of alternative schools—charter schools and pilot schools, among others. If you look at their organizational and decision-making structure, you'll see that many accord teachers a major decision-making role, such as the ability to choose their new colleagues, evaluate one another, and design the curriculum.

First, Unlock the Passion to Teach

Promoting teacher leadership also means supporting teachers' passion to teach. Teachers tend to keep two sets of books. One lists what they have to do to comply; the other lists what they believe is best for their students. As a teacher, I learned what I had to do to be successful, and I jumped through those hoops. At the same time, the things I cared most deeply about—the reason I signed up for the profession—had little to do with jumping through those hoops. Most teachers sign up for different reasons than those they're evaluated on.

For example, a lot of teachers are committed to experiential education—taking kids on field trips, getting them involved in the community, or taking them to the park and having them pick up leaves and categorize them. Yet schools don't really acknowledge, let alone appreciate, the power of experiential learning. So you do the worksheets, the workbooks, the didactic instruction, enough to get the supervisors off your case, and then you've earned the right to take your kids on a field trip. But you've got to succeed on the first set before you can move on your own set.

There's great power in that second set of books, though, and here's how I discovered it. As a principal, I was convinced the teachers had all these interests and passions they were just locking in the car in the parking lot each morning before coming in to teach. So we organized what we called *optionals* once a week for two hours in the afternoon. Every teacher would teach something they really cared about. The students would choose which classes they wanted to attend.

Everyone got involved—the librarian, the custodian, the secretaries—so the class sizes were small. Everybody got a green light for their topic of interest. You want to teach kids how to build a model airplane?

In some ways, this is the best of times for teacher leaders. Because the quality of teaching varies widely from classroom to classroom, schools need skilled and dedicated teachers to extend their influence beyond their classroom—whether as instructional coaches, leaders of grade-level teams, induction coordinators, mentors, or peer reviewers. Principals' responsibilities continue to expand with every new policy, and they simply cannot do all they're expected to do. Expert teachers can use their specialized knowledge about curriculum and instruction to bridge the boundaries in the "egg-crate" school and thus ensure that the school will more effectively serve all students.

At the same time, teachers and their union leaders are developing new approaches to identifying, promoting, and rewarding teacher leaders. Baltimore, Maryland, and Cleveland, Ohio, have adopted performance-based career ladders that allow effective teachers to assume differentiated roles within their schools, thus supporting colleagues who have less experience or skill; in other districts, consulting teachers both mentor and evaluate fellow teachers in peer assistance and review (PAR) programs.

Formal positions for teacher leaders were widely adopted in response to No Child Left Behind, which required schools to succeed with all subgroups of students, but these positions encountered deep cuts following the recession of 2009. However, without an organizational strategy for supporting and developing all teachers, schools will never move beyond being a patchwork of separate classrooms, some excellent or good, others mediocre or poor. Teacher leaders can be the centerpiece of such strategies for organizational improvement, but few policymakers see that potential.

Many teachers serve as informal leaders within their schools, and although others may appreciate their contributions, their influence will remain limited until the school formally recognizes these teacher leaders' talents and authorizes their roles. Formal policies, whether passed in legislatures or negotiated locally through collective bargaining, provide the best route for establishing teacher leadership and ensuring its future.

Understand the subway system? Great—do it!

What I found was that teachers were bringing that second set of books to these classes. They suddenly came to life, recognizing that their second set of books had value and that kids thrived on things the teachers really cared about.

If you can unlock the second set of books, and not let it get locked up in the car each morning, or even merge the two sets of books, that's crucially important in supporting not only teachers' passion to teach, but also their passion to lead.

Lead—and Win

I've always been haunted by the phrase, "I'm just a teacher." It says that I'm not really so important, that I'm *just* a teacher. But if you're a teacher, you're already a teacher leader. Just ask your 28 students. They'll tell you who the leader in that classroom is. The teachers may be good leaders or bad leaders, but they're incontrovertibly leaders.

The shift comes when you also take on a piece of leading the school. There's tremendous satisfaction that comes from making that jump, from being an owner rather than a renter here. The thinking goes, "I'm taking ownership of my school and making my corner of it a little bit better."

Although higher education hasn't provided for me much of a model of inventive teaching over the years, it does offer a noteworthy model of teacher leadership. Professors lead major committees on matters such as program evaluation and curriculum. They participate in making decisions about finance, use of space, graduation requirements, and scheduling. And they're instrumental in selecting new colleagues—as well as their own school administrators. Indeed, few important decisions are made without them.

Another important outcome of teacher leadership relates to learning. We're always looking for conditions under which the learning curves of teachers, principals, or students go right off the chart. When you're responsible for something, whether it's the science curriculum or the supply closet, you're invested in making it work. You have to talk to other people and to other schools to get ideas, to figure things out. All of a sudden, you come alive as a learner. Teachers who aren't alive as learners start to percolate when they take on leadership roles.

Look at the beginning teacher or principal. Both have steep learning curves. All the energy they invest and the learning they experience get transferred to other areas like classroom management or curriculum. It's the same with kids. When students take responsibility for something important in the classroom or school, their learning curves go way up.

A school should be a community of leaders—not just a principal and a lot of followers. The principal, teachers, students, and parents should all be first-class citizens of that community. Our business ought to be to promote profound levels of learning in school—and teacher leadership is one of our most powerful assets for doing so.

CHAPTER 12

Teacher Leadership

Overcoming "I Am Just a Teacher" Syndrome

Valeri R. Helterbran

Eighteen Master of Education students sat in a class titled "Teacher Leadership" pondering how they could possibly be teacher leaders. One offered, "But my principal is our leader. He leads. I follow." Another said, "Teacher leadership is just a theory, I believe. It does not exist in real life—at least not in my school." A third said, "I think I have some leadership qualities, but I am just a teacher."

"I am just a teacher." This mantra is embraced by legions of teachers across the land. Principals lead; teachers follow. And so it goes. The guiding principles of teacher leadership date to antiquity and received renewed interest in the twentieth century. Over 60 years ago, Bahn (1947) charged administrators with the task of "exploring abilities, releasing creative powers, tapping experiences, and, consequently, developing the quality of teacher leadership" (p. 155). In addition, numerous reform efforts in the 1980s and 1990s recommended "teacher leadership" as a mechanism for widespread reform. Wasley (1991), too, almost two decades ago, led a clarion call for the necessity of teacher leadership and shared decision-making in school improvement. She rightly acknowledged, however, that the body of literature was absent in supporting this concept. Twenty years later, a body of literature has been developed and continues to grow, yet it is poorly understood and only intermittently practiced where it counts—in schools. Despite the many calls for teacher leadership in the literature over the years, the message has not reached teachers themselves in any large measure. School improvement ultimately will depend on teacher leadership—a factor largely untapped in schools today.

Principal leadership and teacher leadership

Sustained, effective school leadership substantially strengthens student achievement (Waters, Marzano, & McNulty, 2004) as does a positive school climate (Heck, 2000). Having engaged in numerous school reform efforts over the years, it is clear that traditional, top down leadership falls short of effecting the systemic, meaningful reform necessary to meet the needs of students in the new and challenging world they will face (Copland, 2003).

The principal has position, power, authority, and the responsibility of accountability for the total school program. However, the prevailing, role-bound model in schools depicting the principal as having the requisite set of leadership skills and teachers being passive recipients of directives or prescribed professional development must be examined. Both principal and teachers have important and reciprocal roles in the overall leadership quotient of a school, but to do so, an open and equitable relationship must be in place. Leadership at its best takes place in the interactions between people in the school and the situations they face; therefore for leadership to be effective, it must be shared or distributed (Gronn, 2000; Hargreaves & Fink, 2006); this takes certain leadership dispositions on both the part of the principal and the teachers.

Using Occam's razor, leadership can be succinctly defined as "making happen what you believe in" (Barth, 2001). Considering this, leadership can no longer equate exclusively with the man or woman in the principal's office and the tendency to focus on the managerial aspects of the job. Bolman and Deal (2003) assert:

> If an organization is overmanaged but underled, it eventually loses any sense of spirit or purpose. … The challenges of modern organizations require the objective perspective of managers as well as the brilliant flashes of vision wise leadership provides. (p. xvi)

So, in this age of accountability where no one person can possibly be omniscient, a "wise" principal will honor and support a distributed form of leadership, a philosophy put in action where others in the building are trusted and expected to bear the burden and pleasure of leadership, which far surpasses a few "brilliant flashes of vision."

To be clear, distributing or sharing leadership is not delegating responsibility. Historically this has entailed principals wooing teachers into accepting a certain professional responsibility or simply assigning a task. Likewise, it is not simply garnering extra help or providing a second set of hands for the principal. Teacher leadership rises from within the teaching ranks and expresses itself in a myriad of ways for the betterment of students, specifically, and school in general. Effective leadership can and should be infused among teachers. The principal, to be fully effective, must understand the importance and benefit of sharing leadership for without this understanding to support and foster teacher leadership, little good will come. According to Anderson (2004), a key purpose of leadership is "set[ing] directions and influence [ing] others to move in those directions" (p. 100), so principal leadership coupled with teacher leadership is a logical, rational, and productive model for school improvement. If it can be agreed upon that the spate of recent reform efforts has been largely ineffective, maintaining a culture where "just a teacher" states of mind prevail is a terrible waste of expertise, energy, and influence in the school community.

Taking the reins

Confidence is at the heart of any leadership role. Principals must have confidence in their own leadership skills to encourage and support leadership within the teaching ranks. Teachers, similarly, must have or build confidence in extant leadership skills they embody and seek ways to use them to strengthen their own professional practice. For the teacher, there are numerous formal and informal avenues to express leadership. The most familiar are the traditional, formal, and hierarchical roles in a school which may include departmental or grade level chair, subject area supervisor, mentor, or various instructional coaching roles. These important positions come replete with a job description and formal expectations; they also typically are associated with release time or monetary compensation. The other, more informal and emergent, type of teacher leadership runs much deeper, is self-generated, and holds the promise of serving as a mechanism for continual professional learning and innovation in the school.

Teacher leadership, in its truest sense, involves those informal aspects of leadership, where a teacher sees a need or identifies a problem and takes the reins to address it within his or her means. Danielson (2007) refers to these elements of leadership as "emerg[ing] spontaneously and organically from the teacher ranks" (p. 16). Because teachers are indispensable in improving student achievement (Gabriel, 2005), this "emergence" cannot and will not occur unless and until teachers recognize their own leadership potential and develop the confidence and skills to be effective teacher leaders. In doing so, teachers will come to realize that taking responsibility for their own professional learning and collaborating meaningfully with and among colleagues not only impacts their personal effectiveness in a school, but can produce results in the classroom nothing short of miraculous.

Awareness of leadership potential

No Child Left Behind requires that teachers be "highly qualified" in one or more content areas when they enter their first classroom. "Highly qualified" usually translates as "minimally qualified" in most states with certificate holders holding only a bachelor's degree and demonstrating competency on a Praxis or Praxis-type test. Armed with a quiver of ideas and the courage of their convictions, novice teachers often enter a profession woefully underprepared for the rigors of today's classroom. Teaching is a flat profession. Unless a teacher wants be a principal or guidance counselor, he or she will spend a career in the classroom with first-year teachers and 30-year veterans essentially carrying out the same functions.

Teachers have no trouble visioning themselves as leaders in their communities, churches, or other venues, but often tend to have great difficulty identifying themselves as leaders in their schools; the matter lies chiefly in whether or not teachers are willing to assume the role of "teacher leader." Becoming a teacher leader involves the breaking of stereotypical isolation familiar to most teachers. Collaborating among teachers is rare in the depth required to produce meaningful school improvement. It means eschewing what Tocqueville (1996) called *rugged individualism—a* principle revered as "the American way" to a culture where interdependence is valued and a collection of individual teachers melds into a community of learners with shared purposes, goals, and understandings (Harris, 2002).

When educators focus on who is the leader and *who* are the followers, only one person can contribute significantly to the overall well-being of the school. Teachers in this scenario are relegated to a sub-professional category likened much to baby birds in the nest that await as their mother goes to get a worm, then returns to the nest to feed them. Teachers need to get their own "worms," but knowing what to search for and where complicate the scenario. In the prevailing leadership model, teachers do not see themselves as meaningful contributors which reinforces the "just a teacher" mentality. Lambert (2003) discusses the importance of teachers owning a sense of purpose in their profession which elevates them into leadership as they must define their own instructional problems and seek ways to remedy them. This is a matter of awareness for teachers as they come to see that they have more control and influence over their destiny than they give themselves credit for and that this control can result in purposeful agency and positive results for students. Teacher leadership is typically not compensated leadership and certainly generates more work for a teacher, but this is true of most acts of professionalism and empowerment. Therefore, teacher leadership capacity in any school building is a melding of support and encouragement by the principal and the willingness of teachers to impact their own professional vocation.

Change is good

Nothing is permanent except change. These prophetic words of Heraclitus, Greek philosopher who lived around 500 BC, still ring true. Yet change is not comfortable for most teachers who have been asked to make changes in their teaching and other areas of their professional lives time and time again, most of which have yielded few measurable improvements. It is not surprising that teachers may resist a renewed call for teacher leadership thinking, and rightfully so, that this is simply a new way to extract more work from them—and unpaid work at that. Familiar with the aforementioned practice of *delegating*, teachers may see *teacher leadership* simply as "business as usual" with a new appellation. Teachers are exhausted with the many and varied reform efforts they have experienced knowing that before any new program or philosophy is firmly in place, another will replace it resulting, in the minds of many, in equally dismal results. Most reforms are done to teachers and are externally imposed; teacher leadership is a practice emanating *from* and *with* teachers and, due to this key difference, can be exquisitely tailored to teachers' needs and practice.

The profession of teaching is highly bureaucratic and often crippled by the ponderous influence of inertia. When reform efforts present themselves, the new roles are often "simply appended to a flat, compartmentalized school structure" (Johnson & Donaldson, 2007, p. 10) and despite being rallied to a point by the novelty of the reform *dujour,* we toy, we tinker, and the results remain much the same.

Our own worst enemy

Identifying and overcoming barriers is an essential component in encouraging and supporting teachers in their quest to share leadership. Leadership, according to Harris (2003), is an "interactive process of sense-making and creation of meaning that is continuously engaged in by organizational members" (p. 314) and as such, impact the four dimensions of teacher leadership as suggested by Day and Harris (2003). These include: 1) strengthening classroom practice; 2) encouraging teacher ownership in the change process; 3) assuming the mantle of teacher expert; and 4) engaging in collegiality for mutual learning. These facets are not without direct and corollary challenges. Collinson (2004) explains that exemplary teachers "seek, accept, or create leadership roles" (p. 383), but identifying exemplary teachers and harnessing or directing the expression of leadership can be problematic.

The principal is the lynchpin in creating and supporting a school climate in which teacher leadership can flourish. Climate is related to those shared values, interpretations of social and academic activities, and commonly held definitions of purpose (Kottkamp, 1984). As discussed earlier, if leadership remains vested in one person, the principal, teacher leadership is unlikely to develop in any great measure. It is certainly possible for teachers to engage in professional learning, be collegial, and work in ways to strengthen practice, but if the principal is resistant or unwilling to share leadership, it is highly unlikely the strivings of individual teachers will reach the critical mass necessary to impact the school as a whole.

However, even with the most supportive and enlightened principal, pitfalls abound. As an example, teachers are often suspicious of other teachers selected to spearhead tasks needed for the effective running of a school. Despite being identified due to their being "competent, credible, and approachable" (Katzenmeyer & Moller, 2009, p. 14), weaker teachers often ascribe the selection of others to favoritism, not capability. Whereas often appreciated by those selected, if for no other reason than to vary responsibilities, others harbor resentment and can easily thwart the best intentions of their colleagues. Keeping in mind that naysayers may not have any interest in being a mentor, coach, or any other permutation of leadership, but they can be bitter towards others who do. Kelley, Thornton, and Daugherty (2005) suggest that teachers desire consistent treatment, yet do not fully appreciate that "differential treatment is needed based on the developmental level of the teacher or the task in question" (p. 23).

Teachers may also openly question why one person was asked to assume leadership roles and others not. Foot-dragging, open opposition to change, the stifling of discussion or problem-solving, or outright subterfuge are common strategies to suppress or subjugate the change process. Collegiality, although one of the primary hallmarks and benefits of teacher leadership, may be met with resistance, too, as, despite the debilitation of isolation, some teachers find comfort nestled in their own classrooms and feel threatened by the expertise or actions of others. These teachers often lack the requisite skills, attitudes, and dispositions required to be a teacher leader and although every school building has individuals who meet this description, they cannot be allowed to thwart the process. Colonial patriot Thomas Paine's (1737–1809) truism, *Either lead, follow, or get out of the way* could not be more applicable in contemporary American education. We are, very often, our own worst enemies regarding change and school improvement. Obstructionists must be recognized and, if after every attempt has been made to secure their involvement fails, they need to be stepped over by those willing to lead.

Fostering teacher leadership

Teacher leadership can only flourish in a school culture that embraces "an optimistic and rigorous educational mission, and it must do so in an environment of respect and a culture of hard work and success" (Danielson, 2006, p. 126). This is no small consideration and must be grappled with first and foremost particularly in situations where faculty members cannot ascribe this description to their school. Vision, desire, and support are all necessary in shaping and inspiring teacher leaders. However, none of this is important if no plan is in place. Shared leadership provides coherence, stability, and is essential for innovation (Printy & Marks, 2006). To move schools in this direction, a plan to develop teacher leaders is necessary. These plans would be as idiosyncratic as the schools in which they were carried out, but several basic and common strategies must be addressed as follows:

Consideration One: An important consideration in cultivating teacher leaders involves the hiring of new teachers. The interview process provides an ideal opportunity to discuss the importance and merits of teacher leadership especially when a candidate's exposure to this concept may vary widely depending on the emphasis placed on it in their collegiate certification program. Every new hire provides an opportunity to increase leadership strength in a school building. "Autonomy need and achievement motivation consistently distinguish leaders from non-leaders …," according to Rogers (2005, p. 629). Knowing this, school administrators can design questions or scenarios to query prospective teachers in determining if indicators of these two criteria are present in an individual. Coupled with hiring practices is a carefully crafted induction program which highlights and reinforces the roles and opportunities for teacher leadership.

Consideration Two: Equally important, many schools have an established faculty having little turnover on a year-to-year basis. It is in these seasoned educators that the work of having them see themselves as leaders and conversely, seeing one another as leaders, is critical. This of course requires a paradigm shift and intentional acts focused on *the leader within* specifically aimed at the art and craft of learning, teaching, and collaboration. Identifying specific, measurable goals and approaches to achieve them is imperative in honoring teacher voice, empowerment, and ownership of the school. *Owners* take care of their "property" and seek to improve it! Similarly, there must be an ongoing commitment to professional inquiry where continuous personal and professional improvement is considered a point of pride and professional expectation.

Consideration Three: Model learning and collegiality. Learning is a social activity. Strengthening one's knowledge-base provides an excellent and non-threatening activity to build relationships with others on the faculty. Learning inspires confidence and the willingness to take risks in improving practice even if in the smallest, most tentative steps at first. Professional development is the cornerstone of improving practice and is essential to teacher growth, expertise, and skill development. It would be unimaginable to select a physician who does not study the latest medical or surgical advances or retain an attorney who does not keep abreast of current case law. Yet, many teachers spend an entire career devoid of meaningful, purposeful professional development with far too few recognizing their obligation to seek and engage in self-identified professional learning. Stigler and Hiebert (2000) assert that schools are places for teachers to learn, but that this is a concept almost lost in contemporary American schools. Teachers need high-quality, sustained professional development throughout their careers. Unfortunately, only 12–27% of teachers in 2000 believed that the professional development provided by their districts actually improved their teaching (National Center for Educational Statistics,

2001). If district-provided professional development is inadequate in promoting student achievement (Lee 2004/2005), it becomes vital that teachers at every level of experience take a proactive role in their own continuous improvement (Kent, 2004).

Closing thoughts

Teachers have always been leaders, but there is little evidence that a focused, collaborative movement exists in public schools designed to promote and support widespread teacher leadership in the profession. Unless the concept of teacher leadership is embraced by the *schools, just a teacher* will remain the prevailing habit of mind in the nation's schools.

Educators must decide who they are and how they want to be perceived in their schools and in their profession. Becoming a principal or teacher leader demands a commitment to change and grow as a person and as an educator (Helterbran, 2008a). Talk of career ladders, differentiated pay scales, master teacher designations, advanced certifications, and other incentive-based motivators for teachers abound with a goal to boost professionalism and leadership skills. However, none of this will matter unless there is a large-scale groundswell of intentional effort on the part of educators and teacher leadership will continue to be expressed only in fits and starts and schools will continue to achieve at current rates.

Educators are among the hardest workers in America. There is little doubt that American teachers are committed to the children of the land. However, teaching is the only profession where novice practitioners start anew every generation and are somehow expected to know how to teach expertly when entering their first classrooms. In addition, little preparatory and ongoing professional development (Helterbran, 2008b) is offered and goals tend to shift and change with political caprice. The frustration and exhaustion experienced by our nation's teachers is palpable.

As a profession, we seem to still be looking for that magic potion as a solution for all that ails education, that final bandwagon that we are so well-exercised in hopping on; it does not exist. However, what does exist is a yearning by teachers to be valued, relevant, and involved professionals. For this to occur, there needs to be a renewed effort to work and learn collaboratively with the knowledge that with a goal, a plan, and the perseverance to take small, incremental steps toward an ideal leadership arrangement where principals and teachers share the yoke of leadership. That first step requires the courage to ask tough questions of ourselves and our colleagues in purging *just a teacher* mindset and replacing it with *teacher leader*.

References

Anderson, K. D. (2004). The nature of teacher leadership in schools as reciprocal influences between teacher leaders and principals. *School Effectiveness and School Improvement, 5*(1), 97–113.

Bahn, L. A. (1947). Releasing teacher leadership. *Educational Leadership, 4*(3), 155–158.

Barth, R. (2001). Learning by heart. San Francisco, CA: Jossey-Bass.

Bolman, L. G., & Deal, T. E. (2003). Reframing organizations: Artistry, Choice, and Leadership (3rd ed.). San Francisco, CA: Jossey-Bass.

Collinson, V. (2004). Teachers caught in acts of leading, teaching, and learning. *Teacher Education and Practice, 17*, 363–385.

Copland, M. A. (2003). Leadership inquiry: Building and sustaining capacity for school improvement. *Educational Evaluation and Policy Analysis, 25*(4), 375–395.

Danielson, C. (2006). *Teacher leadership that strengthens professional practice.* Alexandria, VA: Association for Supervision of Curriculum Development.

Danielson, C. (2007). The many faces of leadership. *Educational Leadership, 65*(1), 14–19.

Day, C., & Harris, A. (2003). Teacher leadership, reflective practice, and school improvement. In K. Leithwood & P. Hallinger (Eds.), *Second International Handbook of Educational Leadership and Administration.* Norwell, MA: Kluwer Academic.

Gabriel, J. G. (2005). *How to thrive as a teacher leader.* Alexandria, VA: Association for Supervision of Curriculum Development.

Gronn, P. (2000). Distributed properties: A new architecture for leadership. *Educational Management and Administration, 28*(3), 317–338.

Hargreaves, A., & Fink, D. (2006). *Sustainable leadership.* San Francisco, CA: Jossey-Bass.

Harris, A. (2002). Improving schools through teacher leadership. *Education Journal, 59*, 22–23.

Harris, A. (2003). *Teacher leadership as distributed leadership: Heresy, fantasy or possibility, 23*(3), 313–324.

Heck, R. (2000). Examining the impact of school quality on school outcomes and improvement: A value-added approach. *Educational Administration Quarterly, 36*(4), 513–552.

Helterbran, V. R. (2008a). Professionalism: Teachers taking the reins. *The Clearing House, 81*(3), 123–127.

Helterbran, V. R. (2008b). Planning for instruction: Benefits and obstacles of collaboration. *International Journal of Learning, 15*(1), 893.

Johnson, S. M., & Donaldson, M. L. (2007). Overcoming the obstacles to leadership, *Educational Leadership, 65*(1), 8–13.

Katzenmeyer, M., & Moller, G. (2009). *Awakening the sleeping giant: Helping teachers develop as leaders* (3rd ed.). Thousand Oaks, CA: Corwin Press.

Kelley, R. C., Thornton, B., & Daugherty, R. (2005). Relationships between measures of leadership and school climate. *Education, 126*(1), 17–25.

Kent, A. M. 2004. Improving teacher quality through professional development. *Education, 124*(3), 427–435.

Kottkamp, R. (1984). The principal as cultural leader. *Planning and Changing, 15*(3), 152–159.

Lambert, L. (2003). Leadership redefined: An evocative context for teacher leadership. *School Leadership & Management, 23*(4), 421–430.

Lee, H-J. (2004/2005). Developing a professional development program model based on teachers' needs. *Professional Educator 27*(112), 39–49.

National Center for Education Statistics. (2001). *Teacher preparation and professional development 2000.* Washington, DC: U.S. Department of Education.

Printy, S. M., & Marks, H. M. (2006). Shared leadership for teacher and student learning. *Theory Into Practice, 45*(2), 125–132.

Rogers, J. (2005). Aspiring to leadership-identifying teacher-leaders. *Medical Teacher, 27*(7), 629–633.

Stigler, J. W., & Hiebert, J. (1999). *The teaching gap.* New York, NY: Free Press.

Tocqueville, A. (1966). *Democracy in America.* New York, NY: Harper & Row.

Wasley, P. (1991). Teachers who lead: The rhetoric of reform and realities of practice. New York, NY: Teachers College Press.

Waters, T., Marzano, R., & McNulty, B. (2004). Leadership that sparks learning. *Educational Leadership, 61*(7), 48–52.

CHAPTER 13

Understanding Teacher Leadership

Marilyn Katzenmeyer and Gayle Moller

Being a teacher leader means sharing and representing relevant and key ideas of our work as teachers in contexts beyond our individual classrooms so as to improve the education of our students and our ability to provide it for them.   —Ariel Sacks, Eighth Grade Teacher Leader

Hardworking educators struggle every day within a system that was not designed for the needs of today's students. In spite of the skepticism of the public and the ensuing policy reports that reveal failures within our educational system, most teachers are committed to searching for answers to improve student outcomes, although other demands compete for their attention. The unending need to find social services for students and their families, competitive challenges from advocates of charter schools and school vouchers, and the dwindling numbers of capable individuals who want to become teachers and school administrators create distractions from the challenge committed educators face in improving student learning.

Over the last 25 years, the massive number of reports on how to improve schools influenced policymakers to pass legislation placing pressure on educators to provide quality education for all students. Few would disagree with this goal. Many would argue, though, that the goal cannot be accomplished by simply raising standards, creating and implementing more outcome measures, and holding students, teachers, and administrators ever more accountable for test scores. Research on the impact of the accountability movement (Darling-Hammond & Prince, 2007; Wechsler et al., 2007) has helped us understand that investing in teachers and their learning, rather than creating more tests, is a better investment for improving student outcomes. Unlike well-intentioned policymakers who persist in their search for "silver bullet" legislation to reform schools, savvy parents already know that the focus of reform efforts should be on the classroom teacher, who can make the most difference in their children's learning.

After mixed results with accountability measures, externally designed reform programs, and reward/ punishment systems meant to exact higher test scores, the focus is turning toward individual classrooms and teacher quality (*Education Week*, 2008). To improve teacher quality, teachers need to learn to teach better. So attention has shifted to professional development, formerly an occasional experience for most teachers that is now a frequent obligation for every teacher regardless of the relevance for the teacher. Vendors, district administrators, school reform leaders, and others provide menus of professional development; some reflect quality, but many violate even the rudimentary standards for effective professional development. Wechsler et al. (2007), in a study of teaching in California, reported that this state does not have a coherent approach to ensuring that teachers have the knowledge and skills to be effective, and this conclusion would most likely also be true in every state.

Perhaps the answers to concerns about education rest in the potential of a leadership structure that taps into everyone's talents within the school community, especially the teachers. There cannot be significant progress within an educational system in which hierarchical control separates managers (school principals) from workers (teachers). Leadership must be "embedded in the school community as a whole" (Lambert, 1998, p. 5). The notion of the principal as the only leader is evolving into a clearer understanding of the leadership roles that teachers must take if our schools are to be successful.

Within every school there is a *sleeping giant* of teacher leadership that can be a strong catalyst for making changes to improve student learning. By using the energy of teacher leaders as agents of school change, public education will stand a better chance of ensuring that "every child has a high quality teacher" (Wehling, 2007, p. 14). We can call upon the leadership of teachers—the largest group of school employees and those closest to the students—to ensure a high level of teacher quality by bringing their vast resources to bear on continuously improving the schools. By helping teachers recognize that they are leaders, by offering opportunities to develop their leadership skills, and by creating school cultures that honor their leadership, we can awaken this sleeping giant of teacher leadership.

In order to do this, we begin in this chapter to examine how teacher leadership emerged. Then we share our expanded definition of teacher leadership. To illustrate the definition, we provide three examples of teacher leaders who struggle with universal dilemmas teacher leaders face. We next invite teachers to assess their inclination to be teacher leaders using the Readiness for Teacher Leadership instrument. Finally, we suggest that everyone has a responsibility to support teacher leaders, because teacher leaders cannot do it alone within the existing system.

Teacher Leadership Emerges

When we wrote the first edition of this book in the mid-1990s, the concept of "teacher leadership" was relatively unknown. We discovered the importance of teacher leadership in our work with principals and school improvement. Principals who learned with teachers about school reform were more likely to transfer their learning from professional development workshops to the work in their schools. Unfortunately, though, many of the principals were transferred to other schools, and the initiatives at their previous schools fell to whims of the next principal. The teachers who had been colearners with their former principals were disillusioned and powerless to sustain their work. We wondered how systems could be built to sustain school improvement initiatives over time in spite of who sat in the principal's office. We dreamed that in every school, there would be a critical mass of positive teacher leaders who had the knowledge, skills, and beliefs to maintain the momentum of school improvement that influenced student learning. The gap between our dream for teacher leadership and the reality of school leadership structures has been an obstacle for over 20 years.

In spite of these obstacles, today, teacher leadership is emerging, and in many schools teacher leaders are finding their voices. Previously, if we asked a principal to identify teacher leaders, most often there were long hesitations and tentative responses, finally principals responded by identifying the textbook chairperson or the team leader. Yet they did not consider these teachers as "real" leaders, and certainly the teachers in those positions did not see themselves as leaders. Currently, "teacher leadership" is a more familiar term as evidenced by the vast growth of the numbers of instructional leadership positions, the inclusion of teacher leadership in standards for teachers, collaborative work across states on licensure for teacher leaders, and the proliferation of teacher leadership literature.

A primary reason that teacher leader positions are emerging is that school systems recognize that the professional development offered to teachers does not result in changed teacher behavior in the classroom unless follow-up coaching and support are offered. Teacher leaders with titles such as literacy coach, mentor, and lead teacher provide onsite assistance for teachers. As teachers take on leadership roles, they are uniting and reaching out beyond their classrooms to influence educational policy through professional networks, such as the Teacher Leaders Network (www.teacherleaders.org) that spans the United States.

Meanwhile, the number of journals, research reports, and books focused on teacher leadership is growing (Mangin & Stoelinga, 2008). We hear from many doctoral students who are engaged in writing dissertations that study teacher leadership and its impact. Although important first steps are underway, we look forward to the unleashing of leadership talent within every school as the norm.

To tap into the potential of teacher leadership requires moving beyond changing policy, enforcing mandates, and offering professional development. These reform strategies are relatively easy compared to the challenges of guaranteeing teacher quality in every classroom, ensuring effective principal leadership, and engaging teachers in meaningful leadership responsibilities. To reach these goals, we must overcome three obstacles. First, the structure of school and school system leadership must be examined. Next, there must be a shift from the old norms of teaching in isolation and focusing on just "my students." Finally, many teachers must recognize that a broader role of teacher leadership is open and available to those who wish to assume the responsibilities. Teaching is basically a "flat" profession (Danielson, 2007, p. 14), in which a teacher's responsibilities can remain the same from the first day of teaching until retirement regardless of the level of expertise gained over the years. Although many teachers engage in collaborative work and practice shared decision making to expand their circle of influence to *all* students and *all* teachers in *their* schools, too many teachers and administrators work in parallel universes, where formal leadership still rests in the principal's office and teacher leadership is haphazard at best.

While teacher leadership is no longer an unknown idea, it is "sometimes touted, but [it is] rarely fully realized" (Berry, Norton, & Byrd, 2007, p. 48). In our work with teacher leaders, we wondered why teachers are hesitant to be called leaders even when they are active in leadership activities. Regardless of the region of the country, we found three major reasons for their reluctance. First, the quality of teacher leadership depends on the culture of the school. Teachers describe school contexts that do not encourage them to be leaders. Often teachers who are motivated to become leaders will leave these unsupportive school cultures and will seek out schools more conducive to their leadership aspirations. A second concern is that teachers feel they do not have the skills to lead other adults. While principals and other leaders are required to learn leadership skills, teachers rarely are engaged in building these skills. Finally, the egalitarian norms of school cultures suggest that all teachers should be equal. This strong norm discourages teachers from drawing attention to themselves. Fearing the reactions of their colleagues, teachers hesitate to be singled out of the group in an environment that has valued treating all teachers the same (Johnson & Donaldson, 2007). All of these factors impede the progress of teacher leadership. As teacher leadership becomes more widely accepted in some schools, the culture of teaching has more readily embraced leadership from peers (Mackenzie, 2007).

Teacher leadership is essential for the level of complex change schools face. In order to advance these roles for teachers, it is necessary for proponents to be clear about what teacher leadership is.

Definition of Teacher Leadership

There is common agreement that we are a long way from a widespread understanding of teacher leadership. Confusion about definitions and expectations of teacher leaders abound (York-Barr & Duke, 2004). Just what does teacher leadership look like? Who are teacher leaders? In the past, when we visited groups that were interested in teacher leadership, there was a request for time to clarify the concept of teacher leadership. Now we face a different predicament. Since teacher leadership is popular in the educator's professional jargon, there is a reluctance to examine the concept, because everyone believes he or she knows what it means. Regardless of the interest or lack of interest in defining teacher leadership, we believe a dialogue about the definition provides the foundation for a common understanding in order to promote and support teacher leaders.

We arrived at our definition of teacher leadership after a review of the educational literature, careful consideration of our experiences, and much conversation with teacher leaders, principals, and others. This definition continues to evolve as we continue our exploration and learning. Our definition is teacher leaders lead within and beyond the classroom; identify with and contribute to a community of teacher learners and leaders; influence others toward improved educational practice; and accept responsibility for achieving the outcomes of their leadership.

Lead Within and Beyond the Classroom

The professional teacher is first of all competent in the classroom through the facilitation of students' learning. Teacher leadership is allowed by other teachers when the teacher is perceived as a capable teacher of students. Little (1995) cited legitimacy for leadership as a prerequisite for teacher leaders in their influence of peers. This legitimacy can only be given by other teachers and not by a positional title. Teachers we meet clearly accept this part of the leadership role, and some even recognize that they can transfer many classroom skills to their work with peers. Teachers can be leaders of change beyond their classrooms by accepting more responsibility for helping colleagues to achieve success for all of the students and for the total school program.

The level of involvement in teacher leadership beyond the classroom depends on the context of the school and the school system as well as the teacher's willingness. Most important, teachers do not have to divorce themselves from focusing on teaching and learning to be leaders. In the past, a commonly held belief was that if you were a teacher, the only way to become a leader was to leave the classroom and possibly the school (Barth, 1988; Boyer, 1983). Few teachers are attracted to school administration, and if they prepare for this role, it is because administration appears to be their only option for affecting students more broadly. The goal of becoming an administrator as the only way of getting ahead in education is giving way to teachers finding other outlets for their leadership both inside and outside their schools.

There are differences of opinion about teachers becoming leaders by taking responsibilities outside classrooms they consider their own. When we first started working with teacher leadership, we advocated for teachers to continue to teach while contributing beyond the classroom. We feared that teacher leaders might lose their connection to the classroom. With the emerging formal roles for teacher leaders, such as those of math coach or full time mentor of new teachers, we acknowledge that teacher leaders may leave the classroom and remain quite effective in working with other teachers. Their work is still focused on the improvement of teaching and learning, but within their colleagues' classrooms. Time demands and increased workload make it difficult for some teacher leaders to remain full time in the classroom and also to take on demanding leadership roles. Formal teacher leader roles can enable teachers to be valuable contributors to school improvement as long as the teacher leaders are not pulled into quasiadministrative responsibilities that take them away from the focus on teaching and their authentic relationships with colleague teachers.

Leadership, of course, is not limited to a selected group of lead teachers or master teachers. Teachers who choose not to leave the classroom and instead to assume informal leadership roles within the school are equally valued and powerful. Drawing from their expertise and passion for teaching, these teachers influence other teachers informally through having casual conversations, sharing materials, facilitating professional development, or simply extending an invitation for other teachers to visit their classrooms.

Teacher leadership roles empower teachers to realize their professional worth while still maintaining the centrality of their teaching roles (Stone, Horejs, & Lomas, 1997). Although some teacher leaders may seek administrative roles, most teachers in leadership roles do not view these opportunities as steps up the ladder to the administrative ranks. These teachers want to remain close to students and are willing to assume leadership roles that will affect decisions related to their daily practice with those students.

Contribute to a Community of Learners and Leaders

Leading beyond the classroom provides an opportunity for teachers to interact with other adults in the school. Ackerman and Mackenzie (2007) suggested that teacher leaders "live for the dream of feeling part of a collective, collaborative enterprise" (p. 237). If this dream is realized, teachers learn within the school's professional community. Barth (2001) suggested that there is a "powerful relationship between learning and leading" (p. 445). Although the concept of professional learning communities emerged as a logical way to engage the adults in the school in their own learning, the realization of this type of school culture is relatively rare. Developing a professional learning community is more difficult than most people realize. Yet when teacher leaders do join a community of learners and leaders, in contrast to an elitist group, it opens up opportunities for every teacher to be a part of the community.

Teacher leaders, though, know the value of working with their peers in "communities of practice" (Lieberman & Miller, 2004, p. 22) or their own professional learning communities. Within these settings, teachers are learning in social context rather than only learning individually (Stein, Smith, & Silver, 1999). Teacher leadership develops naturally among professionals who learn, share, and address problems together.

When teacher leaders and principals expand professional learning communities to include the entire school, then all teachers are included in the professional learning. Hord's (2003) examination of professional learning communities reveals that teacher leaders are partners with the formal school leaders in their efforts to improve teaching and learning. Five dimensions emerge as attributes of schools that are professional learning communities. The dimensions are

1. Supportive and shared leadership: School administrators participate democratically with teachers—sharing power, authority, and decision making.

2. Shared values and vision: School administrators and teachers share visions for school improvement that have an undeviating focus on student learning and that are consistently referenced for the staff's work.

3. Collective learning and application of learning: Faculty and staff collective learning and application of the learning (taking action) create high intellectual learning tasks and solutions to address student needs.

4. Supportive conditions: School conditions and human capacities support the staff's arrangement as a professional learning organization.

5. Shared personal practice: Peers review and give feedback on teacher instructional practice in order to increase individual and organizational capacity. (Hord, 2003, p. 7)

Teacher leaders thrive in professional learning communities that exhibit these attributes. Credible teachers are empowered to assume leadership roles with the support of their peers. A critical mass of teacher leaders engaged in a professional learning community can often maintain momentum in a school's improvement efforts even during changes in formal, administrative leadership. The lack of continuity of leadership in schools and school districts makes maintaining reforms difficult (Fullan, 2005), but a professional learning community provides the best buffer we have to prevent this level of disturbance to sustainability of improvement efforts.

Teacher leaders also reach outside their schools to a wider professional community. Participation in national educational projects, professional organizations, and other external school reform movements provide teachers with networks of other teacher leaders who reinforce improved teaching practices. Lieberman and Wood (2003) documented the value of teacher involvement in external networks. These communities of learners and leaders can be the impetus for teachers to realize that their leadership skills are valuable and can give them the courage to lead within their own school while developing both professional expertise and leadership skills.

Finally, teacher leaders know how to build alliances and networks in order to accomplish their work (Crowther, 2008). These connections help them to pull together the necessary people, funding, and other resources to support their action plans. They know the social dynamics within the school and how to connect likeminded people as well as work with the skeptics. Depending on the health of the school culture, teacher leaders can build community and collaboratively find ways to make a difference for students.

Influence Others toward Improved Practice

Teacher leaders influence others toward improved educational practice. A key word in our notion of teacher leadership is *influence*. There is probably not another profession that provides more practice in influencing than teaching, in which students are influenced daily by their teachers. The art of transferring these skills into work with colleagues, although complex, can be learned by teacher leaders. Leadership is influencing. Teacher leaders are approachable and influence primarily through their relationships, which become the foundation upon which teacher leaders are able to share and learn with others. Silva, Gimbert, and Nolan (2000) found in their study of teacher leaders that building relationships was critical in their work. Also, Mooney (1994) reported descriptions of teacher leaders by other teachers. Teacher leaders were described as hardworking, involved with innovation, motivating students with a variety of abilities, and available to other teachers.

Formal positions are not necessary to influence others. In fact, teachers collaborating with their colleagues are just as effective in influencing others as are individuals with formal titles who carry the power of a position (Lambert, 2003). Motivating colleagues toward improved practice relies on the personal influence of competent teachers who have positive relationships with other adults in the school. In every school there are teacher leaders who show initiative, willingly experiment with new ideas, and then share their experiences with others.

Colleagues are influenced if leaders exhibit behaviors they advocate. Teacher leaders may engage in "reaching out to others with encouragement, technical knowledge to solve classroom problems, and enthusiasm for learning new things" (Rosenholtz, 1989, p. 208). Successful teacher leaders we know are consummate learners who pay attention to their own development and model continuous learning. Sharing information and visibly improving their own practice gives teacher leaders endorsement in their work with other teachers. Teachers who are credible to their peers, who are continuous learners, and who pass relevant information about best practices to others influence their colleague teachers. While teacher leaders are working in professional communities, they are, in turn, influenced by other teachers.

This attribute of teacher leadership is the most difficult to accomplish within a teacher culture that does not easily acknowledge that a colleague may have knowledge to share. The delicate balance of relationships is a constant challenge for teacher leaders who want to influence others to work together toward the goal of improved practice. Unless this balance is achieved, teachers can remain isolated except to share "war stories" about their daily interactions with students, parents, and even administrators.

Accept Responsibility for Achieving Outcomes

Leadership assumes accountability for results. This is a new component in our definition, and when we have shared it with different groups of leaders, there has been universal agreement that taking responsibility for one's leadership is crucial for teacher leadership to be taken seriously. One teacher shared, "If we design the leadership role, we are also obligated to accept the accountability that comes with it." As a result of these kinds of conversations with teacher leaders, the definition is expanded to include this component.

Teachers often enter leadership roles by recognizing an area for improvement and then addressing the issue. This passion for finding solutions can lead to multiple and extensive ideas that require a high level of energy and more time than is available. For these reasons and many others, teachers can become discouraged and desert the plans midstream. In contrast, teacher leaders take responsibility for follow through on commitments and for achieving outcomes.

An effective teacher leader sets the resolution of a pressing concern as a goal, gathers data to support the need for change, engages like-minded colleagues, and secures resources to make changes. Keeping the vision of a better world for students, teacher leaders persist to find ways to achieve their goals. Tichy warned us that "vision without execution equals hallucination" (Harris, 2003, p. 6). So teacher leaders move beyond vision, take action, and are responsible for the outcomes.

Persistence is the key to their success. With limited formal power, even in a formal role, teacher leaders know that they have to rely on their personal power to influence others, and they rarely let go of the desire to achieve desired outcomes. Ferren (2000) suggested that it takes "random acts of responsibility" committed each day to be a leader (p. 1). Teacher leaders may achieve only partial success, but they recognize that "half a loaf" is an incremental step and may lead to an ultimate solution (Barth, 2007, p. 25).

In a study of effective professional learning communities, teachers reported that one of the most important types of support the principal provided was consistent follow-through on decisions (Moller et al., 2000). If this is true for principals, then it also applies to teacher leadership. Trust is built through experience with how much you can depend on another person. Follow-through on leadership responsibilities is important for ensuring that the principal and other teachers have trust in a teacher leader. As we have discussed teacher leadership with principals, we have found that one of the primary reasons for hesitating to share leadership is that these principals experienced disappointment when teachers became excited about a project, made a commitment to take the lead, and then did not follow through. Not only are teacher leaders accountable, but they also hold the same expectations for their colleagues.

This definition of teacher leadership helps teachers to think differently about leadership and encourages teachers to consider leadership in their schools. In contrast to an authoritarian model of leadership, this definition more closely parallels what many teachers do already. It gives them confidence to acknowledge that they are or can be leaders and still maintain their relationships with their peers.

With this definition in mind, we share descriptions of three potential teacher leaders. Each teacher faces challenges to stepping up to a leadership role.

Three Potential Teacher Leaders

Descriptions of three potential teacher leaders illustrate the promise of rousing the giant of teacher leadership. Most educators will recognize these situations as typical.

Latonya

An elementary teacher for five years, Latonya experienced what she believed to be an excellent preservice preparation program at a nearby university. She entered the profession with knowledge of content, instructional strategies, and communication skills that help her interact effectively with students, parents, and her peers. Latonya works with experienced teachers in a school that is governed by a school leadership team that includes teachers, parents, and administrators as well as several local community members. Latonya plans and teaches with a team of fourth grade teachers whose students meet with success. She mentors preservice teachers from the nearby university on a regular basis. Her principal recognizes her competence and often recommends her to serve on committees in the school district. She has visited other schools to observe innovations. She is encouraged by the feedback she gets from parents on her work with their children. Often she visits families in their homes when parents find it difficult to attend parent-teacher conferences.

Currently, Latonya wrestles with the role she takes in the school's change efforts. She worries about how other teachers perceive her. Do they suspect that she is hoping to move into administration, even though her real motivation is to improve daily life at school for her students and her colleagues? Latonya wonders how other teachers will react if she offers to facilitate a study group so that teachers can share ideas and materials from the professional reading they are doing. Sometimes Latonya thinks she is too assertive in meetings and wonders if she may offend her colleagues by proposing too many changes. Last week she feared she was intimidating other teachers on the school improvement team. How much leadership she should exert is a concern for Latonya.

George

Recognizing the unlimited possibilities of teacher leadership would also be helpful for George, a music teacher who works in an urban high school. Two years ago, George left his vocation of performing with a band to become a teacher. A dedicated and competent professional teacher, George is pleased he made the switch but experiences frustration with the lack of change in the traditional high school where he teaches. George meets obstacles when he tries to persuade others that his music program should be expanded further to meet student needs. When he joined the school advisory committee, he found that little was accomplished. His experience in working outside the school in the community would, he thinks, really help facilitate the work of this committee.

After two years as a classroom teacher, he decided to pursue a master's degree. George would also like to share and to apply knowledge he is gaining in his graduate courses to the problems faced in his high school. Test scores at his school could be improved; student dropout rates are alarming. There is much improvement needed in his school. He feels that, except within the fine arts department, his colleagues will neither listen to his thinking nor value his expertise. He hesitates to step forward, though he thinks he has something to contribute. George ponders whether his principal and his colleagues will be supportive of his leadership on schoolwide issues.

Miranda

Miranda is a special education teacher in a middle school. Over 20 years ago, she started teaching with most of the same teachers in this school. Two new middle schools opened recently in the district, and attendance boundaries changed. Her school's student population also changed drastically. Rather than the middle class suburban population that Miranda and her colleagues have worked with for years, they are now teaching students from neighborhoods where poverty, unstable family structures, and substance abuse are prevalent. The students do not respond well to the curriculum and instructional strategies of the past. Miranda knows that the demands of a diverse student population require change in her school. She feels alone in this belief. She wants to help her colleagues cope with the new challenges they face rather than join them in doing things the way they have always done them. She recently was awarded certification from the National Board for Professional Teaching Standards and has gained confidence in her ability as a teacher leader.

Miranda would like to lead discussions with her colleagues to invite them to solve instructional problems they face. Possibly she will talk to her principal about trying to find time for professional development activities targeted to middle school strategies. She would like to initiate some coteaching inclusion strategies with a regular education colleague. She believes these approaches can help teachers cope with the changes in their student population. She feels ready to step out and exercise her leadership, but she wonders how much impact she will have on reluctant teachers who seem to value maintaining the status quo.

Dilemmas similar to those of Latonya, George, and Miranda are not unusual. These teachers can play an even broader leadership role in the improvement of teaching and learning in their schools. However, administrators, other teachers, and, most important, the structures of schools may not support the contributions such teachers could make. Not seeing teacher leadership as a legitimate activity supported by others may keep teachers like these from contributing in significant ways to change in their schools.

We view the roles available to teachers like Latonya, George, and Miranda broadly. The sheer number of possible roles for teacher leaders in schools and districts lends credence to the idea that there truly is a huge untapped resource in schools. Surprisingly, though, many of these teachers do not see themselves as leaders unless opportunities are provided for them to reflect on their potential to lead.

Readiness for Teacher Leadership

Teachers benefit from conversations designed to raise their awareness about teacher leadership. This discussion is a prerequisite to teachers thinking about their development as teacher leaders. In school systems, district staff members often ask us to help principals identify teacher leaders. How do we know who is a teacher leader or has the potential to be a teacher leader? It is easy to identify the formal teacher leaders, because they have titles and assigned responsibilities. The informal leaders are the teachers who practice their craft in subtle ways that may not be obvious to others. We use three adjectives to help teachers and administrators identify potential teacher leaders: *competent*, *credible*, and *approachable*. Teachers usually know which teachers are competent within their classrooms, and this naturally establishes them as credible. Being approachable is a critical characteristic. There are some teachers who are competent and credible but who choose to work as individuals rather than in collaboration with others. The ability to build positive relationships is critical to becoming a teacher leader.

A valuable conversation can be initiated by raising an individual teacher's awareness about his or her potential for leadership or about recognition of fellow colleagues as potential leaders. Am I a teacher leader? Do I have the potential to be a teacher leader? What characteristics do teachers need to have to become leaders? Which of my fellow teachers might also be identified as leaders? If answering these questions helps teachers more fully understand teacher leadership, then they may be ready to explore their own development as leaders and support the development of their colleagues.

One strategy to begin exploring teacher leadership is to use the instrument in Figure 1.1. on pp. 132–135 This is an instrument to measure readiness for teacher leadership. Once teachers are open to considering that it is their responsibility to be leaders, the checklist is a tool to generate conversation around the concept. We use this instrument as we work with groups of teachers who are relatively unfamiliar with the idea of teacher leadership. It is useful for groups of preservice teachers or experienced teachers.

Who Is Responsible?

The responsibility for the development of teacher leaders is not limited to a single individual or group. Too often, the entire obligation is placed on the shoulders of the school principal. Others share in this responsibility. Teachers, superintendents, and district administrators, as well as leaders in colleges and universities, can be excellent advocates for teacher leadership.

Teachers

Teachers are responsible for the support of teacher leadership. The giant cannot be awakened without teacher leaders inviting others to join together in a community of leaders. By establishing collaborative relationships among faculty members, teachers begin to take the first step toward establishing an environment in which teacher leadership can thrive. The social relationships of teachers within a school are powerful determiners of how teachers assuming leadership roles will be viewed. Members of powerful cliques within a school can encourage or inhibit teachers who are willing to take on leadership roles.

School Administrators

Principals or assistant principals can encourage or discourage teacher initiative. These formal schoolsite leaders are critical to empowering teachers as leaders. They are the primary models for teacher leaders in the school and may effectively model leadership strategies and skills that teacher leaders can use. A principal's willingness to share power and to be a colearner with teacher leaders to improve classroom practice provides support for teacher leadership. Removing barriers, providing resources, and actively listening can be the most important tasks a principal does for teacher leaders.

Superintendents and District Staff

The school rests within a larger organization, the school district. In a two-school district or a district with hundreds of schools, the decision makers at the district level influence the learning of the adults within the entire system. The influence can be tangible, such as resources allocated to professional development, or it can be intangible, such as setting the expectation that employees will learn. Just like in schools, where principals set the tone for change, superintendents and their staffs are responsible for providing the type of support that frees and encourages schools to prepare teachers as leaders. Superintendents and other staff in a school district can legitimize the efforts of developing teacher leadership by establishing appropriate policy and district culture and by being advocates for teacher leadership.

Colleges and Universities

The role of the colleges and universities in preparing teacher leaders is significant in the continuum of teacher development. The expectation that leadership is a teacher's responsibility can be cultivated early in the undergraduate preparation of the individual (Sherrill, 1999). Collaborative arrangements, such as professional development schools or learning consortia, connect teachers with university personnel. Standards and licensure for teacher leaders are being explored in many states, so professors are beginning to examine the content of their courses to assure they are preparing their graduates for leadership roles. Development of knowledge, skills, beliefs, and attitudes about teacher leadership begins with the university or college preparation programs for future teachers. Graduate programs and courses are emerging across the country specifically designed to prepare practicing teachers for leadership. The leadership skills are as important in these programs as the curriculum and instruction content. After the teacher leaves the university, the goal should be to encourage that teacher to be a leader.

Conclusion

The giant resource of teacher leadership must be unleashed in the support of improved student learning. When teachers recognize that they can be leaders and accept a leading role from among the array of roles available to them, positive results in schools will follow. Teacher acceptance of leadership roles, appropriate professional development, and advocacy from formal leaders in the school system can start building a critical mass of teacher leaders to improve schools. The importance of teachers in complex, ongoing, educational change efforts cannot be overstated.

Application Challenges

For Teachers

1. Help teacher colleagues to see the value of teacher leadership in improving student outcomes by opening the discussion in your school. Be positive, share your knowledge of the concept, and engage others in discussion. Emphasize the benefits to the improvement of teaching and learning for students, the retention of teachers, and the possibility to sustain change in the school setting. Work together to influence your principal's understanding of teacher leadership and its value.

2. Tap into the many resources available to develop yourself as a teacher leader. Professional reading, networking with other teacher leaders, and online communications can assist you in growing your understanding of teacher leadership and in building your own capacity.

For Principals

1. Build the confidence of teachers to be leaders. Make yourself available for regular interactions with prospective teacher leaders, and authentically listen to their ideas. Support teachers in initiatives they wish to lead, and remove barriers to their success. Find ways to give incentives (e.g., release time, resources, recognition, and problem solving assistance) to teachers who are willing to take on leadership.

2. Grow professionally yourself in understanding teacher leadership and its possible impact on student outcomes in your building. Assure that you model professional learning and collaboration, and then work toward empowering the teachers rather than controlling them. Share professional readings and resources with teachers. Engage them in meaningful dialogue about teaching and learning.

For Superintendents and District Level Administrators

1. Recognize that changes in schools are enhanced by a balance of efforts from the top down and the bottom up. Attempt to put policy and practice into place that pave the way for teacher leadership. Reflect on specific ways the school district can support teacher leaders, make resources available, and provide opportunities for networking.

2. Model leadership by working collaboratively with school administrators in ways that you would like to see principals and assistant principals work with teacher leaders. Create an understanding of teacher leadership among your building administrators, and encourage them to empower teachers in the same ways you empower your administrators.

For College and University Professors

1. Introduce the concept of teachers acting as leaders early in the preservice experience. Engage teacher education students in collaborative work, and build their skills to be fully functioning members of school cultures in which professional learning communities thrive. Emphasize the linkages between teacher collaboration and improved student outcomes.

2. Examine your curriculum and preparation programs for opportunities for preservice teachers to gain a broad perspective on formal and informal leadership opportunities for teachers. Assess the extent to which your programs are encouraging leadership rather than followership among your graduates.

Assessing Your Readiness for Teacher Leadership

Respond to the following statements in terms of how strongly you agree or disagree	Strongly Disagree	Disagree	No Opinion	Agree	Strongly Agree
1. My work as a teacher is both meaningful and important.					
2. Individual teachers should be able to influence how other teachers think about, plan for, and conduct their work with students.					
3. Teachers should be recognized for trying new teaching strategies whether they succeed or fail.					
4. Teachers should decide on the best methods of meeting educational goals set by policymaking groups (e.g., school boards, state departments of education).					
5. I am willing to observe and provide feedback to fellow teachers.					
6. I would like to spend time discussing my values and beliefs about teaching with my colleagues.					
7. It is important to me to have the respect of the administrators and other teachers at my school.					

(Continued)

Respond to the following statements in terms of how strongly you agree or disagree	Strongly Disagree	Disagree	No Opinion	Agree	Strongly Agree
8. I would be willing to help a colleague who was having difficulty with his or her teaching.					
9. I can see the points of view of my colleagues, parents, and students.					
10. I would give my time to help select new faculty members for my school.					
11. I try to work as a facilitator of the work of students in my classroom and of colleagues in meetings at my school.					
12. Teachers working collaboratively should be able to influence practice in their schools.					
13. I can continue to serve as a classroom teacher and become a leader in my school.					
14. Cooperating with my colleagues is more important than competing with them.					

(Continued)

Respond to the following statements in terms of how strongly you agree or disagree	Strongly Disagree	Disagree	No Opinion	Agree	Strongly Agree
15. I would give my time to help plan professional development activities at my school.					
16. My work contributes to the overall success of our school program.					
17. Mentoring new teachers is part of my responsibility as a professional teacher.					
18. School faculty and university faculty can mutually benefit from working together.					
19. I would be willing to give my time to participate in making decisions about such things as instructional materials, allocation of resources, student assignments, and organization of the school day.					
20. I value time spent working with my colleagues on curriculum and instructional matters.					
21. I am very effective in working with almost all of my colleagues.					

(Continued)

Respond to the following statements in terms of how strongly you agree or disagree	Strongly Disagree	Disagree	No Opinion	Agree	Strongly Agree
22. I have knowledge, information, and skills that can help students be successful.					
23. I recognize and value points of view that are different from mine.					
24. I am very effective in working with almost all of my students.					
25. I want to work in an environment where I am recognized and valued as a professional.					

Figure 1.1 Teacher Leadership Readiness Instrument

Assessing Your Readiness for Teacher Leadership
Scoring Protocol

1) Count the number of times you chose "strongly disagree." Multiply by minus two (–2), and write the number here:
2) Count the number of times you chose "disagree." Multiply by minus one (–1), and write the number here:
3) Ignore the number of times you chose "no opinion."
4) Count the number of times you chose "agree." Write the number here:
5) Count the number of times you chose "strongly agree." Multiply by two (2), and write the number here:
6) Write the sum of these four numbers here:

~ If the number on line 6 is between 35 and 50: Virtually all of your attitudes, values, and beliefs parallel those related to teacher leadership.
~ If the number on line 6 is between 20 and 34: The majority of your attitudes, values, and beliefs parallel those related to teacher leadership.
~ If the number on line 6 is between –5 and 19: Some of your attitudes, values, and beliefs parallel those related to teacher leadership. Several do not.
~ If the number on line 6 is –6 or below: Few of your attitudes, values, and beliefs parallel those related to teacher leadership.

Source: © Professional Development Center, 2004.

References

Ackerman, R. H., & Mackenzie, S. V. (Eds.) (2007). *Uncovering teacher leadership: Essays and voices from the field.* Thousand Oaks, CA: Corwin.

Barth, R. S. (1988). School: A community of leaders. In A. Lieberman (Ed.), *Building a professional culture in schools* (pp. 129–147). New York: Teachers College Press.

Barth, R. S. (2001). Teacher leader. *Phi Delta Kappan, 82(6),* 443–449.

Barth R. S. (2007). The teacher leader. In R. H. Ackerman & S. V. Mackenzie (Eds.), *Uncovering teacher leadership: Essays and voices from the field* (pp. 9–36). Thousand Oaks, CA: Corwin.

Berry, B., Norton, J., & Byrd, A. (2007). Lessons from networking. *Educational Leadership, 65(1),* 48–52.

Boyer, E. L. (1983). *High school.* New York: Harper & Row.

Crowther, F., with Ferguson, M., & Hann, L. (2008). *Developing teacher leaders: How teacher leadership enhances school success* (2nd Ed.). Thousand Oaks, CA: Corwin.

Danielson, C. (2007). The many faces of leadership. *Educational Leadership, 65(1),* 14–19.

Darling-Hammond, L., & Prince, C. D. (2007). *Strengthening teacher quality in high-need schools—policy and practice.* Washington, DC: Council of Chief State School Officers.

Education Week. (2008). *Quality counts 2008: Tapping into teaching: Unlocking the key to student success.* Bethesda, MD: Author.

Ferren, C. (2000). Become a leader by taking responsibility every day. *The Journal for Quality and Participation, 23(1).* Retrieved December 6, 2007, from http://0-web.ebscohost.com.wncln.wncln.org/ehost/pdf?vid=3&hid= 115&sid=8dda2d0d-4a71–48db-bald-79cb40978d4e%40sessionmgr106

Fullan, M. G. (2005). *Leadership and sustainability: System thinkers in action.* Thousand Oaks, CA: Corwin.

Harris, B. (2003). *Noel Tichy: Leadership beyond vision.* Missoula: Montana Associated Technologies Roundtables. Retrieved December 6, 2007, from http://www.matr.net/article-9269.html

Hord, S. (2003). Introduction. In S. Hord (Ed.), *Learning together, leading together: Changing schools through professional learning communities* (pp. 1–14). New York: Teachers College Press.

Johnson, S. M., & Donaldson, M. L. (2007). Overcoming obstacles to leadership. *Educational Leadership, 65(1),* 8–13.

Lambert, L. (1998). *Building leadership capacity in schools.* Alexandria, VA: Association for Supervision and Curriculum Development.

Lambert, L. (2003). *Leadership capacity for lasting school improvement.* Alexandria, VA: Association for Supervision and Curriculum Development.

Lieberman, A., & Miller, L. (2004). *Teacher leadership.* San Francisco: Jossey-Bass.

Lieberman, A., & Wood, D. (2003). *Inside the National Writing Project: Connecting network learning and classroom teaching.* New York: Teachers College Press.

Little, J. W. (1995). Contested ground: The basis of teacher leadership in two restructuring high schools. *Elementary School Journal, 96(1),* 47–73.

Mackenzie, S. V. (2007). (How) can a new vision of teacher leadership be fulfilled? In R. H. Ackerman & S. V. Mackenzie (Eds.), *Uncovering teacher leadership: Essays and voices from the field* (pp. 373–382). Thousand Oaks, CA: Corwin.

Mangin, M. M., & Stoelinga, S. R. (2008). Teacher leadership: What it is and why it matters. In M. M. Mangin & S. R. Stoelinga (Eds.), *Effective teacher leadership: Using research to inform and reform* (pp. 1–9). New York: Teachers College Press.

Moller, G., Pankake, A., Huffman, J. B., Hipp, K. A., Cowan, D., & Oliver, D. (2000). *Teacher leadership: A product of supportive & shared leadership within professional learning communities.* Paper presented at the annual meeting of the American Educational Research Association, New Orleans, LA.

Mooney, T. (1994). *Teachers as leaders: Hope for the future.* Washington, DC: National Commission on Excellence in Education. (ERIC Document Reproduction Service, No. ED 380407).

Rosenholtz, S. J. (1989). *Teachers' workplace: The social organization of schools.* New York: Longman.

Sacks, A. (2008). *Teacher leadership at the Ford Foundation.* Retrieved November 8, 2008, from http://teacherleaders.typepad.com/shoulders_of_giants/2008/10/teacher-leaders.html

Sherrill, J. A. (1999). Preparing teachers for leadership roles in the 21st century. *Theory into Practice, 38,* 56–61.

Silva, D. Y., Gimbert, B., & Nolan, J. (2000). Sliding the doors: Locking and unlocking possibilities for teacher leadership. *Teachers College Record, 102(4),* 779–803.

Stein, M. K., Smith, M. S., & Silver, E. A. (1999). The development of professional developers: Learning to assist teachers in new settings in new ways. *Harvard Educational Review, 69,* 237–270.

Stone, M., Horejs, J., & Lomas, A. (1997). Commonalities and differences in teacher leadership at the elementary, middle, and high school levels. *Action in Teacher Education, 19(3),* 49–64.

Wechsler, M., Tiffany-Morales, J., Campbell, A., Humphrey, D., Kim, D., Shields, P., et al. (2007). *The status of the teaching profession 2007.* Santa Cruz, CA: The Center for the Future of Teaching and Learning.

Wehling, B. (Ed.). (2007). Foreword. In *Building a 21st century U.S. education system* (pp. 13–21). Washington, DC: National Commission on Teaching and America's Future. Retrieved February 11, 2008, from http://www.ecs.org/html/offsite.asp?document=http%3A%2F%2Fwww%nctaf%2Eorg%2F

York-Barr, J. & Duke, K. (2004). What do we know about teacher leadership? Findings from two decades of scholarship. *Review of Educational Research, 74(3),* 255–316.

CHAPTER 14

What Does Leadership Capacity Really Mean?

Linda Lambert

Throughout this hemisphere, conferences, seminars, and academies are hosting events on leadership capacity. The Internet lists dozens of online courses about leadership capacity. Google reports more than 3 million hits under the title "leadership capacity."

What is really meant by leadership capacity? The term has been around for some time. What is my leadership capacity? What is the leadership capacity of individual teachers, our principal, our political figures? This personal usage, while central to school improvement, does not offer a framework or schema to sustain school improvement. Since the publication of *Building Leadership Capacity in Schools* (ASCD, 1998), educators use the term "leadership capacity" as an organizational concept meaning broad-based, skillful participation in the work of leadership that leads to lasting school improvement.

First, let's look closely at these terms.

Leadership—and therefore the work of leadership as used within the definition of leadership capacity—means reciprocal, purposeful learning together in community.

Reciprocity is essential to solving problems and working collaboratively. Purpose suggests values, focus, and momentum. Learning is mutually creating meaning and knowledge. Community is the essential environment for experiencing reciprocal, purposeful learning. These four ideas frame a definition of leadership in which all can see themselves reflected. It is the mirroring pool of a professional culture.

Broad-based participation refers to who is at the table, whose voices are heard, and what patterns of participation exist. These patterns form the structure through which the work of the school or organization is done. Also, it is within these patterns of participation (teams, cadres, learning communities, study groups) that individuals develop lasting and respectful relationships. To be effective, participation requires skillfulness.

Skillful participation is the understanding, knowledge, and skills that participants either develop or bring to their engagement in purposeful learning. The work of leadership involves developing skills in dialogue, inquiry, reflection, collaboration, facilitation, and conflict resolution. Leadership skills for adult learning parallel good teaching: A good leader is a good teacher who uses her knowledge and skills with colleagues.

By defining these terms and how they interact, we are able to understand schools' differing levels of ability to sustain improvement. Schools at varying stages of developing leadership capacity may be described as follows:

- Low leadership capacity schools tend to be principal-dependent, lack a professional culture and are significantly unsuccessful with children. Only the principal, serving as a top-down manager, is referred to as the "leader" in the school. Teacher leadership is not a topic of conversation, let alone interest. Educators in such cultures deflect responsibility while preferring blame; they avoid focusing on teaching and learning while holding fast to archaic practices. While professional relationships may be congenial, they lack the challenge of collegiality. Tests and test scores may be considered the only valid measures of student success, and promising products and performances revealed by students' work are neglected. Absent an internal accountability system, these schools are subject to the whims, demands, and pressures of parents, districts, and states.

- Moderate leadership capacity schools lack a compelling purpose and focus, are governed by norms of individualism, hold few conversations among members of the whole community, and suffer from fragmentation and polarization. Concerns regarding teachers who will "not buy in" may arise when a small group of more skilled educators form an isolated inner core of decision makers. Either scenario—dispersed and individual action or corralled and exclusive action by a few—will leave the school without a focused, professional culture. The first scenario calls for a concerted effort to create a shared sense of purpose. The second scenario requires using broad-based, inclusive strategies (e.g., norms, collaborative action research, dialogue, inquiry) to involve everyone in the work of leading the school. In a school with moderate leadership capacity, disaggregating student scores inevitably reveals a lack of success for its more vulnerable or challenged students.

- High leadership capacity schools are learning communities that amplify leadership for all, learning for all, success for all. These schools have developed a fabric of structures (e.g., teams, communities, study groups) and processes (reflection, inquiry, dialogue) that form a more lasting and buoyant web of interrelated actions. The principal is only one of the leaders in the school community and models collaboration, listening, and engagement. Each participant shares the vision, understands how the school is moving toward the vision, and understands how he or she contributes to that journey. The quality of the school is a function of the quality of the conversations within the school. Student success is revealed by multiple measures of contribution, products and performances, including the vivid presence of student voice. High leadership capacity schools hold great promise, but no guarantees, of sustainability. In other words, schools that include everyone within collaborative patterns of participation are able to develop greater levels of leadership skillfulness. This achievement can move a school closer to lasting school improvement than would otherwise be possible.

Six Critical Factors

If high leadership capacity schools are good, why are they not always able to sustain improvement? That question usually leads to issues of values, authority, dependence, and identity within schools and districts. A study of high leadership capacity schools (Lambert, 2004) found several critical factors must be addressed to fully realize leadership capacity's promise:

1. The school community's core values must focus its priorities. Democratization and equity must be foremost among these values and are interdependent. Democratization is the means through which staff experience and honor equity. Members of high leadership capacity schools accept responsibility for all students' learning and include all voices.

2. As teacher leadership grows, principals must let go of some authority and responsibility. When principals lead for sustainability, teachers and principals become more alike than different. They share similar concerns, blend roles, and ask tough questions. They find leadership and credibility within each other through frequent conversations, shared goals, and, ultimately, collective responsibility.

3. Educators must define themselves as learners, teachers, and leaders. How we define leadership determines who will participate. This broad perspective encompasses sharing and distributing leadership. Leadership becomes a form of learning—reciprocal, purposeful learning in community. To learn is to be able to lead. Like children, all adults can learn, all adults can lead.

4. We must invest in each other's learning to create reciprocity. When principals engage teachers in problem solving rather than render them helpless through directives and granting or withholding permission, natural capacities for reciprocity come to life. Dependencies cause us to ask permission, to abdicate responsibilities, and to blame. Learning communities require reciprocity.

5. The first tenet of leadership capacity is "broad-based participation." Schools must create the structures through which participation occurs. Structures for broad-based participation include teams, study groups, vertical communities, and action research teams. These are the settings in which people deepen relationships, alter their beliefs, and become more skillful in the work of leadership. Without these structures, reculturing is unlikely.

6. Districts must negotiate the political landscape to provide professional time and development, a conceptual framework for improvement, and tailored succession practices (fitting the principal to the school).

This work requires engaging the board and the community in conversations that build an understanding of lasting school improvement. Without this groundwork, schools continually fight the same battles for time, for professional development, and for selecting principals who can take a school from where it is to where it ought to be without losing momentum or denying the worthy experiences of teacher leaders.

These factors are particularly challenging because they challenge our beliefs and traditional conceptions of leadership, how we relate to each other and ourselves and how we distribute power and authority. We consistently have called on ordinary people to do extraordinary work, and many times we succeed. We can succeed more often if we understand and implement the tenets of leadership capacity for lasting school improvement. The notion of "lasting" or sustainable improvement may well represent today's major learning edge.

References

Lambert, L. (2004). *Lasting leadership: A study of high leadership capacity schools.* Oakland, CA: Lambert Leadership Development.

Lambert, L. (1998). *Building leadership capacity in schools.* Alexandria, VA: ASCD.

CHAPTER 15

Teachers, Learners, Leaders

Ann Lieberman

What if teachers ran their own professional development through projects? And what if teachers themselves received funding for these projects? What if the purpose of such projects was not only to spur individual professional learning, but also to develop leadership skills and initiate an exchange of knowledge among one's peers?

In Ontario, Canada, teachers pursue this kind of self-designed professional learning through the publicly funded Teacher Learning and Leadership Program (TLLP). Since the 2007–08 school year, 1,500 people—mostly teachers—have initiated 225 teacher learning projects through TLLP, 83 percent of which have been collaborations among several educators.

Part of the beauty of this professional learning structure is that it represents a successful joining of the education policy arm and teachers' unions. The program meshes education research, education policy, and teaching practice and is a prime example of how researchers, policymakers, and practicing teachers can work together instead of pursuing conflicting agendas.

The Context: Building a Collaboration

The province of Ontario serves 2 million students, and approximately 120,000 teachers work in Ontario's K–12 public schools. English, French, Catholic, and nonreligious K–12 schools all receive public funding through the provincial government. The Teacher Learning and Leadership Program was developed in 2003 in the context of a new Ontario provincial government. From the start, the new education minister deliberately avoided the kind of "top-down" approach to education policy that many Canadian teachers felt had characterized past approaches. The new administration was determined to create a professional development program for teachers that was supportive, collaborative, and sustainable.

In 2005, recognizing that all stakeholders needed to come together if they hoped to enhance education in Ontario, Ontario's education ministry called together a Working Table on Teacher Development. All groups who represented Ontario's schools—including the Ontario Teachers' Federation (OTF) and its affiliates—were included. This Working Table was charged with making recommendations for how the government and other bodies should support teachers' professional learning, keeping in mind that teacher quality is the single most important factor in student learning. To inform this work, the ministry assigned two university professors, Kathy Broad and Mark Evans, to write an extensive literature review on the best content and delivery modes of professional development for experienced teachers (Broad & Evans, 2006).

Defining Professional Learning and Opting for Choice

The Working Table first made distinctions among *training* (skills all teachers must learn to do their job, such as lesson planning); *staff development* (a systemwide set of learning activities driven by the system's needs, such as enhancing early literacy instruction); and *professional development* (self-chosen activities that teachers can do individually or as a group, such as action research). The Working Table participants decided that the ministry should focus on supporting the latter kind of learning. Teachers have different learning styles and professional needs, and they should have the chance to pursue those needs independently. At the same time, any ministry-supported program should give teachers choice and connect teachers' needs to the goals of the ministry of education and other official bodies. Effective professional development needs to positively affect students as well as teachers. Toward that end, the group concluded that a high-quality teacher learning program should be:

- *Built on the three Rs of respect, responsibility, and results.* The program must respect the complexity of teachers' learning and, ultimately, be responsible for boosting students' success.

- *Attentive to adult learning styles.* Teachers should have choices of meaningful, relevant, and substantive content and ways to learn.

- *Goal-oriented.* The program should be clearly connected to improved student learning as well as to changes in daily practice, remaining respectful of varied contexts.

- *Sustainable.* It should provide appropriate resources (including a clear support system from colleagues) and time for practice and self-assessment.

- *Supported by research and data.* This base in research would ensure that professional development reflects up-to-date theories and practice (Working Party on Teacher Development, 2007).

The Working Table affirmed that this program should tap into the tremendous resource of experienced teachers who can provide peer leadership and that grantees should be strongly urged to team up with fellow classroom teachers, resource teachers, or other players in the education field.

Creating a Teacher-Led Program

These ideas formed the basis for Ontario's teacher learning and leadership program. The program was designed and developed—and continues to be sustained—collaboratively by the ministry of education and the Ontario Teachers' Federation (OTF), who decide together which teacher projects of the many submitted will be funded.

At the beginning of the school year, teachers submit a description of their proposed project and a request for funds (most range from $1,000 to $10,000). All funding is used to cover costs for materials and teacher release time; lead teachers don't receive a stipend for spearheading their projects. Teachers must show how their project will address participants' professional learning and contribute to student learning; they must also delineate the experience that different teachers will bring to this effort. They outline a budget and show how they will measure both students' learning and their own, and they describe how they will share the learning with colleagues. Teachers are encouraged to expand their project to other schools, networks, and regions; 91 percent of projects have included other schools in the teacher leaders' boards (the Canadian equivalent of a district), and 43 percent have reached beyond their board—for example, by developing a conference or websites.

After a panel chooses the cohort of Ontario teachers whose projects will be funded that year, the ministry and OTF sponsor a conference to introduce essential leadership knowledge to these educators and show support for them. Presenters clarify any questions about finances and offer training sessions to draw out skills among project leaders (typical sessions include "Developing and Delivering a Dynamic Workshop" and "Persuasion, Not Pontification: Promoting Your Project").

As teachers from past cohorts describe their successful projects to those just starting out, teacher leadership multiplies. Meeting with other participants in the beginning not only motivates project participants, but also helps them realize they are part of something larger than themselves: Their learning can improve students' lives as they stretch themselves and become members of a developing professional community.

A Look Inside the Projects

A glance at TLLP-funded projects gives an idea of the breadth and depth of teacher learning that's possible when teachers organize professional development connected to their own contexts, strengths, interests, and needs. Projects range from "Working Together to Improve Boys' Literacy" (in both French and English) to "Engaging Young Readers with E-Books" to "A Plan for Work-World Readiness." There are projects focused on every subject in K–12 schools and projects that integrate music into language arts, science, and social studies. Teachers have devised support strategies for students falling through the cracks. In one project called "The Success Room," teachers work with any 7th or 8th grader who is struggling with academics or work habits; they sometimes bring the students' peers into the process. For example, if a student hasn't been handing in homework, a teacher in the Success Room talks with both the student and his or her classroom teacher and arranges a support system to help that student succeed.

To get inside the power of the program, let's look at two projects up close.

Fostering Math Talk

Math teacher Nicole Walter Rowan realized that she and other teachers at Agnew H. Johnston Public School, a K–8 bilingual school in Thunder Bay, Ontario, needed a deeper understanding of how to help students think and talk about math. Walter Rowan and a group of 12 colleagues—several of whom had earlier participated in an action research project on "math talk"—wanted to address students' weaknesses and uncertainties in math. The teachers decided to work on improving both their practice as teachers and their students' math awareness.

Four educators, forming the leadership team of the project, worked collaboratively with interested classroom teachers to deepen their collective understanding. They aimed to build a community of like-minded professionals. Supported by a university professor and a staff developer from a New York-based group called Math in the City, this leadership team helped their fellow teachers explore and practice math talk strategies.

In several workshops the team led during the school day, the teachers studied teacher talk and actions as portrayed on a video (part of Pearson's Young Mathematicians at Work series) that modeled actual teachers fostering student discourse during math class. The leadership team, along with outside consultants, identified exemplary teaching strategies appearing at key points in the video—for example "teacher asks students to apply one student's strategy that was different from their own to solve a problem"—and discussed these strategies with the learning community.

As teachers watched the video together, they practiced spotting instances in the lessons in which teachers modeled each of these effective strategies and students displayed heightened mathematical awareness. Teachers in the video prompted students to "turn and talk" about math understandings at pivotal moments in exploring math concepts, and the Agnew teachers saw how the experienced teachers sensed when to stop kids at a pivotal moment. Through these workshops, the group developed a shared vocabulary and began to envision what a classroom involved in collaborative mathematical problem solving could look like.

Two teachers from the leadership team then planned and cotaught lessons with other team members. Each coteaching session included planning, delivering instruction together, and debriefing. The focus of how lessons were planned and cotaught differed, depending on the needs of each teacher and his or her learners, but the focus generally centered on teacher and student talk and the effect of the chosen strategies on students' thinking.

The impact of this learning project was powerful. Teachers developed more confidence in how to question students and elicit responses that showed math understandings. Many went public with their teaching for the first time. Shared pedagogical knowledge and vocabulary made it easier to view one another's instructional practices with a critical lens and give feedback. The team members began to realize that their own practice was authenticating and expanding the research they were learning about. Eventually, a nearby school board took notice of the Agnew team's work, and this board is now supporting its own similar initiative.

Spreading the Graphic Novel Gospel

Matt Armstrong, Heather Murphy, and Anne Doorly, teachers at Adult High School focused on spreading a practice they had honed—using graphic novels to boost older struggling readers' literacy—throughout a wider circle. In Canada, an adult school is one in which students older than 18 can retake courses they must pass to pursue a diploma or take additional courses, such as English as a second language. Armstrong, Murphy, and Doorly had found graphic texts to be a promising resource with adult learners who need motivation to continue reading or who are still learning reading skills. They had developed extensive strategies for how to use graphic texts fruitfully, organized all their notes on how to use these texts into an easy-to-share binder, and were primed to provide workshops on this instructional practice to others.

The team started by introducing these materials to five English teachers in the team's own school. As a result of these workshops, all five began using graphic novels in their classes as well, and they saw struggling students become heavily engaged in reading.

At the school board's English professional development day, Heather Murphy and Anne Doorly shared strategies on using graphic texts with about 150 teachers from other schools. They provided participants with an electronic version of several graphic texts, including *Persepolis* by Marjane Satrapi and a version of John Steinbeck's *Of Mice and Men.*

The team expanded its presentations to additional groups of teachers that year and the following year. As they presented to each new audience, the team learned more about how to facilitate their peers' learning; for example, they learned their peers mostly wanted hands-on, practical ideas. A video produced by the Ontario Teachers' Federation shows this teacher learning in action.

Joining Learning and Leadership

Teachers teaching teachers is a powerful strategy for finding, developing, and using all talents. Teacher Leadership and Learning recently funded its fourth cohort of projects, and the ministry plans to keep the program going. TLLP shows what can happen when teachers propose professional development efforts centered on what they know, what they want to learn, and what they hope to share with peers. The program recasts the traditional paradigm that stresses compliance rather than collaboration, disparages teacher unions rather than builds shared solutions, and imposes research on teachers without rooting new knowledge in everyday teaching and learning. This program is also a robust example of how practice, research, and policy can join to change learning for both teachers and students.

References

Broad, K., & Evans, M. (2006). *A review of literature on professional development content and delivery modes for experienced teachers.* Toronto: Canadian Ministry of Education.

Working Party on Teacher Development. (2007). *Report to the Partnership Table on Professional Learning.* Ontario: Ontario Ministry of Education.

Questions for Reflection and Application

After reading the essays in Section Three, answer the following questions:

Think about both good and bad teacher leaders whom you have admired in the past.

1. What are the most important qualities and skills that define "good" teacher leadership?

2. Is there an ethical and moral dimension to teacher leadership?

3. And, most importantly, what is the impact of teacher leaders on the professional status of teachers?

4. What changes would have to occur in the teaching profession if teacher leadership became the norm in schools?

Answer these questions using both the ideas from the essays that we are considering as well as your personal experiences with the schools you have encountered during your life: as a student, parent, and/ or teacher. References to specific ideas found in the Section Three essays are expected.

SECTION 4
Teacher Leaders in Action

Introduction

I mages of teacher leaders in twenty-first-century schools are often contradictory and confusing. Teachers are important, tireless leaders and mentors to our children, and yet, simultaneously, they are held accountable for the demise of public education as measured by high-stakes tests and various accountability measures. Teachers are both heroes and villains in the theatre of public education. There are no winners in this scenario, and concessions to the lowest expectations for public schools seem to dictate that more control and regulation will somehow make schools better. And thus it is really no surprise that twenty-first-century teachers are often "locked" into arbitrary and strictly defined roles, where thinking and creativity are seldom rewarded and unquestioning obedience is considered an asset. Twenty-first-century teachers are considerably better educated than their twentieth-century counterparts; however, the circumstances of their work have not changed significantly. On a daily basis, teachers routinely enter a profession where they are given a curriculum that is measured by high-stakes tests that define teaching and learning efficacy as student scores on high-stakes tests and opportunities for teacher leadership are limited and strictly prescribed to ensure compliance to externally imposed mandates.

School reform that embraces notions about teacher leadership frequently focuses on superficial changes that redefine teachers' work as compliance, not advocacy. In lieu of creating spaces that accommodate the need for reflection, inquiry, and dialogue by teachers, schools are still designed around business models that focus on outcomes, not process or progress. Teachers as both learners and leaders possess a knowledge base that should contribute significantly to school improvement efforts; however, the chasm that exists among teachers and administrators and policymakers disrupts attempts to facilitate a process of negotiation and consideration of the many complex, and often messy, dimensions of public education that make "one-size-fits-all solutions" unacceptable. Teachers know what good teaching and good schools look like, but this knowledge has little value to those individuals and groups charged with the responsibility of reforming schools. In *Pedagogy of the Oppressed*, Freire (2000) discusses the relationship between knowledge and conceptions of absolute ignorance through the banking concept of education, where "knowledge is a gift bestowed by those who consider themselves knowledgeable upon those whom they consider to know nothing. Projecting an absolute ignorance onto others, a characteristic of the ideology of oppression, negates education and knowledge as processes of inquiry" (p. 72). Furthermore, he suggests a consideration of "the poles of contradiction" in the teacher–student relationship, which exacerbate the difficulty of challenging and changing a situation where "the teacher presents himself to his students as their necessary opposite; by considering their ignorance absolute, he justifies his own existence … . Education must begin with the solution of the teacher-student contradiction, by reconciling the poles of contradiction so that both are simultaneously teachers and students" (p. 72).

When I begin to consider the "poles of contradiction" as they would apply to the relationships that simultaneously exist between teachers and administrators, and between teachers and the politicians who are charged with creating school policies, it suddenly becomes clear how these relationships mirror those of teachers and students. Freire elaborates on the "attitudes and practices" between teachers and students that "mirror oppressive society as a whole" (p. 73). It is a fairly simple task to extrapolate Freire's ideas and apply them to the relationship that exists between teachers and those individuals in formal leadership positions, that is, politicians and administrators. For example,

a.   Leaders lead, teachers teach;

b.   Leaders think, reflect and have dialogue, teachers and teaching are thought about by others;

c.   Leaders make decisions, policies, rules and regulations, teachers enforce these decisions, rules and regulations;

d.   Leaders talk, teachers listen;

e.   Leaders reprimand and discipline, teachers are reprimanded and disciplined;

f.   Leaders choose and enforce choices, teachers comply;

g.   Leaders act and teachers have the illusion of acting through the actions of those in formal leadership positions;

h.   Leaders choose curriculum content, and the teachers adapt to it;

i.   Leaders make decisions about high stakes tests, teachers enforce those decisions;

j.   Leaders confuse the authority of knowledge with her/his own professional authority, which is then set in opposition to the freedom of teachers to establish and their own authority of knowledge; and finally,

k.   Leaders are the subject of most discussions of leadership, while teachers are merely objects to be led. (p. 73)

As a consequence of these oppressive practices, teachers are routinely expected to follow the rules and enforce the policies and practices that have been "handed down" to them. And Freire (2000) writes, the less likely they are to "develop the critical consciousness which would result from their intervention in the world as transformers of the world. The more completely they accept the passive role imposed on them, the more they tend simply to adapt to the world as it is and to the fragmented view of reality deposited in them" (p. 73). The realization that teachers function in roles very similar to those of students highlights the difficulties that they encounter in their pursuit of full professional status, and the obstacles they face in their attempts to successfully advocate on behalf of parents and students in public schools that fail to provide suitable environments for teaching and learning and leading.

Freire's ideas provide a context for the Section Four essays on teacher leaders in action. DuFour, Johnson and Donaldson, Peterson and Deal, Piercey, and Willis expand the discussion of teacher leadership to explore how teachers work together in professional learning communities to influence the culture of schools and overcome the obstacles to teacher professional growth and development. Embracing participation strategies that require transformative shifts in the ways that teachers' work intersects with the work of other key stakeholders is fundamental to lasting and sustainable change. These essays present a variety of perspectives on and examples of shared leadership that nurtures the emergence of teacher leadership as the norm in teachers' work.

Reference

Freire, P. (2000). *Pedagogy of the oppressed.* New York: Bloomsbury Academic.

CHAPTER 16

Professional Learning Communities

A Bandwagon, an Idea Worth Considering or Our Best Hope for High Levels of Learning?

Richard DuFour

I t should surprise no one that there are faculties throughout North America that refer to themselves as professional learning communities (PLCs) yet do none of the things that PLCs do. Conversely, there are faculties that could serve as model PLCs that may never reference the term. A school does not become a PLC by enrolling in a program, renaming existing practices, taking the PLC pledge, or learning the secret PLC handshake. A school becomes a professional learning community only when the educators within it align their practices with PLC concepts. Therefore, any valid assessment of the impact of PLC concepts on a school or the compatibility of those concepts with the middle school model would first need to determine if PLC practices were actually in place in the school. Only then would it be possible to determine the impact of those practices on the learning of both students and adults.

The May 2006 issue of the *Middle School Journal* included the article "Learning Communities in 6–8 Middle Schools: Natural Complements or Another Bandwagon in the Parade" (Patterson & co-contributors, 2006). The authors based the article on interviews and surveys of the staff members of two middle schools that considered themselves to be in the very early stages of implementing professional learning community concepts. In brief, the authors discovered there was widespread confusion regarding the term and that teachers saw little potential benefit in the PLC concept. They concluded the article by offering the caution that, while PLC ideas "are worth considering," educators should be wary about "jumping on the bandwagon" and following a "recipe-driven process."

If the educators in these schools are confused about the term, "professional learning community," they are not alone. As I observed in an earlier article, the term has been used "to describe every imaginable combination of individuals with an interest in education—a grade-level teaching team, a school committee, a high school department, an entire school district, a state department of education, a national professional organization, and so on. In fact, the term has been used so ubiquitously that it is in danger of losing all meaning" (DuFour, 2004, p. 6). As Fullan (2005) has cautioned, "terms travel easily … but the meaning of the underlying concepts does not" (p. 67). Thus, it is not surprising that some educators would express uncertainty regarding terminology.

The Wrong Focus

The authors of the "Bandwagon" article did not focus much on practices; instead they focused on terminology, structures, and perceptions. They described one school's structural change from "eight teams to four learning communities." Teachers were perplexed by the change, saying their learning communities "still act like teams" and merely represented the merging of two teams into one. The second school continued to assign teachers to one of seven "teams" but added two "learning communities" on the basis of the location of teacher classrooms. Teachers in this school focused on "the structural aspects of learning community" and saw it as "a way of organizing or containing students." In both instances teachers expressed confusion regarding vocabulary and a preference for the "team" format over "learning communities." The authors presented little evidence that the educators in these schools actually engage in PLC practices. Had they studied a school that was a PLC in fact rather than in name only, they would have found that teachers were organized into collaborative teams that focused their collective efforts on certain critical questions such as:

1. Are we clear on the knowledge, skills, and dispositions each student is to acquire as a result of this course, grade level, and unit we are about to teach?

2. Have we agreed on the criteria we will use in assessing the quality of student work, and can we apply the criteria consistently?

3. Have we developed common formative assessments to monitor each student's learning on a timely basis?

4. Do we use the formative assessments to identify students who are having difficulty in their learning so that we can provide those students with timely, systematic interventions that guarantee them additional time and support for learning until they have become proficient?

5. Do we use data to assess our individual and collective effectiveness? Do assessment results help us learn from one another in ways that positively affect our classroom practice?

6. Does our team work interdependently to achieve SMART goals that are Strategic (linked to school goals), Measurable, Attainable, Results-oriented (focused on evidence of student learning rather than teacher strategies), and Time-bound?

7. Are continuous improvement processes built into our routine work practice?

8. Do we make decisions by building shared knowledge regarding best practices rather than simply pooling opinions?

9. Do we demonstrate, through our collective efforts, our determination to help all students learn at high levels?

10. Do we use our collaborative team time to focus on these critical issues?

Researchers who have studied schools where educators actually engage in PLC practices have consistently cited those practices as our best hope for sustained, substantive school improvement (Darling-Hammond, 2001; Fullan, 2005; Louis & Marks, 1998; McLaughlin & Talbert, 2001; Newmann, 1996; Reeves, 2006; Saphier, 2005; Schmoker, 2005; Sparks, 2005). Those practices have been endorsed by the National Staff Development Council, the National Association of Secondary School Principals, the National Association of Elementary School Principals, the National Commission on Teaching and

America's Future, the National Board of Professional Teaching Standards, and the National Forum to Accelerate Middle-Grades Reform. They certainly "complement" the recent recommendations presented in *Success in the Middle* by the National Middle School Association (2006) and *Breaking Ranks in the Middle* by the National Association of Secondary School Principals (2006).

It would be inaccurate to portray PLC concepts as a fad, bandwagon, or recipe. We have known for decades that students benefit when the teachers in their schools work in collaborative teams (Little, 1990), establish a guaranteed and viable curriculum to ensure all students have access to the same knowledge and skills (Marzano, 2003), monitor student learning on a frequent and timely basis (Lezotte, 1997), use formative assessments to identify students who need additional support for learning (Reeves, 2006), and demonstrate high expectations for student achievement through a collective commitment to help all students learn (Brophy & Good, 2002). These concepts represent more than "ideas worth considering": they continue to represent best practices for meeting the needs of all students.

The Wrong Timing

Had the authors of "Bandwagon" set out to describe potential problems in the early stages of the implementation of the PLC concept, a case could be made for studying schools immersed in their first and second year of the initiative—if the schools were actually implementing PLC concepts. However, the authors proclaimed their purpose was to assess the potential of the concept by studying schools that did not have sufficient time to make valid assessments. As Fullan (2001) wrote: "One of our most consistent findings and understandings about the change process in education is that all successful schools experience 'implementation dips' … a dip in performance and confidence as one encounters an innovation that requires new skills and understanding" (p. 40). As a result, Fullan concluded, people are likely to feel anxious, confused, and overwhelmed in the early stages of innovation.

Another researcher put it this way: "Everything looks like a failure in the middle. Predictable problems arise in the middle of nearly every attempt to do something new … . Stop an innovation because of these problems, and, by definition, that initiative will be a failure … . Change-adept organizations support initiatives through the difficult middle period" (Kanter, 1997, p. 11).[1]

The schools studied in the Patterson and associates article (2006) had neither implemented PLC concepts nor had enough experience to assess the effectiveness of those concepts. Had schools been described that had pushed through the implementation dip to drive PLC concepts deep into the culture of their schools—the nationally recognized Freeport Intermediate School in Brazosport, Texas; the award-winning Adams Middle School in Westland, Michigan; Levey Middle School in Southfield, Michigan, which has not only closed but shattered the achievement gap between students of different races; Woodlawn Middle and Twin Groves Middle in suburban Chicago, where more than 90% of students meet state proficiency standards; or any of hundreds of other middle schools that actually do what learning communities do—they would have observed very different results and heard very different opinions regarding the potential for PLC concepts to make schools better places for learning for students and teachers.

Conclusion

School reform efforts in the United States have followed a predictable pattern. An improvement initiative is launched with great enthusiasm, only to be buffeted by confusion, criticism, and complaints. Many educators then abandon the initiative and continue their quest for the quick fix that will result in deep cultural changes that are unaccompanied by anxiety and concerns. Hosts of researchers, however, have concluded that substantive change inevitably creates discomfort and dissonance as people are asked to act in new ways (Marzano, Waters, & McNulty, 2005; Fullan, 2005; Sarason, 1996). We cannot avoid the discomfort, but we can determine how we will respond when the going gets tough. As Schlechty (2005), a veteran observer of school reform has concluded, "One of the most fundamental problems confronting those who would transform schools … is the problem of persistence of effort" (p. 23).

In his study of organizations that made the leap from "good to great," Collins (2001) found that the transformation was never the result of "a single defining action, no ground breaking program, no one killer innovation, no miracle moment" (p. 14). The improvement was always the result of "a cumulative process, step by step, action by action, decision by decision" (p. 165) and "pushing in a constant direction over an extended period of time" (p. 169). Greatness required persistence, fierce resolve, and consistent, coherent effort over the long haul. There were no shortcuts.

The professional learning community concept does not offer a short cut to school improvement. It presents neither a program nor a recipe. It does provide a powerful, proven conceptual framework for transforming schools at all levels, but alas, even the grandest design eventually degenerates into hard work. A school staff must focus on learning rather than teaching, work collaboratively on matters related to learning, and hold itself accountable for the kind of results that fuel continual improvement. When educators do the hard work necessary to implement these principles, their collective ability to help all students learn inevitably will rise. If they fail to demonstrate the discipline to initiate and sustain this work, their school is unlikely to become more effective, even if those within the school claim to be a professional learning community. The rise or fall of the professional learning community concept in any school will depend not on the merits of the concept itself, but on the most important element in the improvement of any school—the collective capacity, commitment, and persistence of the educators within it.

Note

1. The phenomenon where measurable success does not immediately follow the implementation of a new initiative is called the "J-curve" effect. For a more complete discussion of how the J-curve phenomenon applies to educational innovations, see Erb, T. O., & Stevenson, C. (1999). Middle school reforms throw a "J-curve": Don't strike out. *Middle School Journal*, 30(5), 45–47.

References

Brophy, J., & Good, T. (2002). *Looking in classrooms* (9th ed.). Boston: Allyn & Bacon.

Collins, J. (2001). *Good to great: Why some companies make the leap … and others don't.* New York: Harper Business.

Darling-Hammond, L. (2001). *The right to learn.* San Francisco: Jossey-Bass.

DuFour, R. (2004). What is a professional learning community? *Educational Leadership*, 61(8), 6–11.

Fullan, M. (2001). *Leading in a culture of change.* San Francisco: Jossey-Bass.

Fullan, M. (2005). *Leadership and sustainability: System thinkers in action.* Thousand Oaks, CA: Corwin Press.

Kanter, R. M. (1997). *On the frontiers of management.* Boston: Harvard Business School Press.

Lezotte, L. (1997). *Learning for all.* Okemos, MI: Effective Schools Products.

Little, J. W. (1990). The persistence of privacy: Autonomy and initiative in teachers' professional relations. *Teachers College Record*, 91, 509–536.

Louis, K. S., & Marks, H. (1998). Does professional community affect the classroom: Teachers' work and student experiences in restructuring schools. *American Journal of Education, 106*, 532–575.

Marzano, R. (2003). *What works in schools: Translating research into action.* Alexandria, VA: Association for Supervision and Curriculum Development.

Marzano, R., Waters, T., & McNulty, B. (2005). *School leadership that works: From research to results.* Alexandria, VA: Association for Supervision and Curriculum Development.

McLaughlin, M., & Talbert, J. (2001). *Professional communities and the work of high school teaching.* Chicago: University of Chicago Press.

National Association of Secondary School Principals. (2006). *Breaking ranks in the middle: Strategies for leading middle level reform.* Reston, VA: Author.

National Middle School Association. (2006). *Success in the middle: A policymaker's guide to achieving quality middle level education* [Electronic Version]. Retrieved November 26, 2006, from National Middle School Association http://www.nmsa.org/portals/0/pdf/advocacy/policy_guide/NMSA_Policy_Guide.pdf

Newmann, F. (Ed.). (1996). *Authentic achievement: Restructuring schools for intellectual quality.* San Francisco: Jossey Bass.

Patterson, J. A., & 16 co-contributors. (2006). Learning communities in middle schools: Natural complements or another bandwagon in the parade? *Middle School Journal*, 37(5), 21–30.

Reeves, D. (2006). *The learning leader: How to focus school improvement for better results.* Alexandria, VA. Association for Supervision and Curriculum Development.

Saphier, J. (2005). *John Adams' promise: How to have good schools for all our children, not just for some.* Acton, MA: Research for Better Teaching.

Sarason, S. (1996). *Revisiting the culture of the school and the problem of change.* New York: Teachers College Press.

Schlechty, P. (2005). *Creating the capacity to support innovations.* Louisville, KY: Schlechty Center of Leadership in School Reform.

Schmoker, M. (2005). No turning back: The ironclad case for professional learning communities. In R. DuFour, R. Eaker, & R. DuFour (Eds.), *On common ground: The power of professional learning communities* (pp. 135–154). Bloomington, IN: Solution Tree.

Sparks, D. (2005). *Leading for results: Teaching, learning, and relationships in schools.* Thousand Oaks, CA: Corwin Press.

CHAPTER 17

Overcoming the Obstacles to Leadership

Susan Moore Johnson and Morgaen L. Donaldson

Lacey's high school needed her talent and skills. Located in an urban, working-class community, the school was struggling to serve all students well and had failed to make Adequate Yearly Progress for two years running. As a social studies teacher, Lacey had developed considerable skill in teaching with a project-based format during her four years in the classroom, and her students were making steady progress as a result. But the reach of her expertise was limited by her classroom walls. Teachers in her school were dedicated to their students, but not to one another's growth. Whatever they had learned over time—how to do project-based learning, how to facilitate classroom discussions, how to effectively use technology—remained largely private. No one asked; no one told. As a result, the school's instructional capacity remained static, no more than the sum of individual teachers' strengths and deficits.

Tempered Enthusiasm

The standards and accountability movement has placed extraordinary demands on schools like Lacey's to improve instructional outcomes. To meet these demands, principals are appointing increasing numbers of teacher leaders to work with colleagues in such roles as instructional coach, lead teacher, mentor coordinator, and data analyst. Because recent large-scale retirements have left a shrinking pool of veteran teachers, principals often ask teachers in the second stage of their career, with 4 to 10 years of experience, to take on these specialized roles.

Second-stage teachers may find this opportunity attractive for several reasons (Donaldson, 2005; Johnson & the Project on the Next Generation of Teachers, 2004). First, many of them feel increasingly competent and confident in their work, and they want to share their acquired expertise with others. Lacey acknowledged, "I'm pretty good" at teaching social studies. She said that over time she had developed "a wider repertoire for teaching students at many levels" and had become more comfortable in her classroom and her school. Research confirms Lacey's sense of increasing skill and effectiveness. On average, students of fourth-year teachers learn more than students of first-year teachers (Rockoff, 2004).

Second, becoming a teacher leader promises to reduce isolation. When they begin their career, many of today's new teachers expect to work in teams but are dismayed to find themselves working alone day after day. Lacey expressed regret about the lack of collegial interaction in her school: "It's just you alone in your classroom. You don't get into each other's classrooms very often."

Third, becoming a teacher leader offers an opportunity to vary one's responsibilities and expand one's influence. Many second-stage teachers want to have a hand in making decisions about how their school operates. Lacey criticized "the way it's set up right now. You don't move up. You do the same thing the whole time." She liked the idea of using her growing expertise to help "change the bigger picture."

Thus, competent and confident second-stage teachers like Lacey welcome opportunities to collaborate with colleagues, learn, grow, and expand their influence. Having taken on these roles, how do second-stage teachers fare?

With colleagues at the Project on the Next Generation of Teachers, we interviewed 20 second-stage teachers who had assumed roles as teacher leaders (Donaldson et al., in press). These teachers worked in a range of settings: elementary and secondary schools, urban and suburban communities, and several metropolitan areas across the United States. We found that, although these teachers were initially enthusiastic about their new roles, they encountered unforeseen challenges. The schools in which they worked remained largely unchanged, with an egg-crate structure that reinforced classroom boundaries and a professional culture that discouraged teacher leadership. These findings suggest that, to reap the full benefits of teacher leadership, school administrators need to provide formal support structures and build leadership roles into the structure of the school.

Business as Usual

On the whole, few schools have reorganized to make the most of the expertise teacher leaders offer. Usually, the new roles are simply appended to a flat, compartmentalized school structure in which classroom teachers continue to work alone. Instructional coaches, for example, are expected to make periodic classroom visits and advise fellow teachers about their practice. But this model does little to change business as usual. The classroom teacher remains isolated and in charge, while the teacher leader arrives only occasionally as a visitor.

Teacher leaders' marginal status is underscored by the fact that their positions are typically funded with outside grants from year to year, rather than being built into a school's regular budget. Thus, the positions remain add-ons to the school program. When the funds run out, the school can eliminate these roles without seriously disrupting its operations.

In addition, teacher leaders' roles are seldom well defined. Principals often regard teacher leaders as a source of extra help in a school that is strapped for human resources. As a result, many teacher leaders spend their time as apprentices or assistants in administration—supervising the cafeteria, subbing for absent staff, or overseeing the logistics of testing—rather than using their instructional expertise to improve teaching at the school.

A Triple Threat

Teacher leaders' efforts to share their expertise can also be undermined by the culture of teaching. In fact, the professional norms of teaching present a daunting challenge to teacher leaders who are asked to improve their colleagues' instruction. Our interviews suggested that colleagues often resist these teacher leaders' work because they see it as an inappropriate intrusion into their instructional space, an unwarranted claim that the teacher leader is more expert than they, and an unjustified promotion of a relative novice to a leadership role. Thus, the norms of autonomy, egalitarianism, and deference to seniority that have long characterized the work of teaching remain alive and well in schools.

Protecting Autonomy

Teacher leaders said that they were often rebuffed when they offered to observe in colleagues' classrooms or made suggestions about teaching. Mai, a mathematics coach and fifth-year teacher, was responsible for organizing professional development meetings, demonstrating sample lessons for other teachers, and offering feedback on their teaching. She reported, "I can't even enter one teacher's room because he is not open to me coming to his room while he teaches." She explained further, "There are other teachers, especially teachers who have been teaching for a long time, who aren't comfortable with being observed, period." The school's teachers' union representative told Mai she could not "evaluate or make judgments, good or bad, on teachers or teaching practice. So I can't say, 'You did a great job with behavior management,' even though that's nice feedback to get." By denying her entrance to their classrooms and restricting the kind of feedback she could provide, Mai's colleagues asserted their right to decide what and how to teach.

Ensuring Egalitarianism

Teachers also questioned the premise that a peer could possess expert knowledge or presume to act on it. Clark, a 10th-year elementary teacher, reported that his colleagues assumed that he and the other instructional facilitator felt superior and avoided him. Frustrated, Clark contrasted his current, strained interactions with the relaxed, collegial relationships that he had enjoyed before he became an instructional facilitator.

Others told of being criticized by peers because their role granted them unusual privileges or special access. Anna, a math consultant and fifth-year elementary teacher, taught full time and ran afterschool classes on how to use the district's math curriculum. Several of her peers resented the fact that she could get substitutes to cover her classes so that she could observe and coach other teachers. Anna's role also required her to coordinate often with her principal, which seemed to create distrust and jealousy among her colleagues. It was, she said, "hard not to come off as the principal's pet."

Reinforcing Seniority

Teacher leaders in the second stage of their career often said that their colleagues viewed them as too young or inexperienced to have such a role. When Mai, age 29, tried to assist a veteran teacher in using the district's math curriculum, she was asked confrontationally, "And *how* old are you?" Even those who were not so young and had entered teaching after another career were criticized for their inexperience. Dave, a 45-year-old who had been teaching for seven years, was supposed to help others implement a new math curriculum and analyze student test data in his elementary school. Some of his colleagues, although younger, still questioned his appointment, asking, "Why him? Why didn't I get that job? I've been doing this for 18 years."

Teacher Leaders Cope

Such opposition was discouraging—sometimes demoralizing. To persist with their leadership work, the second-stage teachers devised strategies to minimize their colleagues' resistance and the emotional burden it placed on them. The following coping strategies often helped teacher leaders avoid provoking other teachers' fears, deflect opposition, and diminish tensions when they arose. But these strategies also tended to legitimize the traditional culture of teaching and its norms of autonomy, egalitarianism, and deference to seniority.

Wait to Be Drafted

Although teacher leaders were supposedly chosen for their special expertise, few roles came with explicit qualifications or procedures for selection. When no established process existed for choosing teacher leaders, colleagues often saw appointments as acts of favoritism by the principal. They raised objections on the basis of claims of seniority, the default mechanism for distributing special rights and privileges among teachers.

Anticipating that veterans might criticize them for their inexperience or question their qualifications, many of the teacher leaders whom we interviewed refrained from volunteering for leadership positions until they were drafted. For example, Eric, a 6th grade instructional coach, anticipated the problem of "coming in as some sort of hotshot." Although he wanted the position, Eric hesitated when the principal first offered it; he waited until his more experienced colleagues expressed no interest in the role and encouraged him to take it. He reasoned that with this approach he could counter any opposition by arguing, "You're the ones who didn't want the role, so I'm expecting you guys to give me a little bit more support." This strategy, he thought, would oblige them "to be on board."

Work with the Willing

Some teacher leaders who encountered resistance or opposition scaled back their efforts and worked only with their most willing colleagues. In doing so, they affirmed their colleagues' right to choose whether to accept their assistance. However, they also reduced their potential schoolwide influence.

Sarah had eight years of experience when she was appointed science curriculum coordinator for the two elementary schools in her district. In this role, she was supposed to help other teachers create and conduct inquiry-based science lessons. Other teachers had scant knowledge of her responsibilities, however, and administrators did little to help her gain access to classrooms and team meetings. Given this ambiguity and lack of support, Sarah chose to work with teachers who sought her out and ignore those who did not. She explained that she was on her own and limited by traditional boundaries: "I'm not an administrator, so I can't tell someone that they need to have me in their room." Therefore, she decided to help those who already welcomed her expertise. She found that working with these colleagues kept her busy, and she had little need to "drum up business" among other teachers.

Similarly, Lauren, an eighth-year teacher whose role as an elementary school literacy coordinator was also undefined and poorly supported, backed off from the challenges she encountered: "I've kind of given up the fight with the teachers who constantly cancel on me or don't want me in their room." Instead, she focused on improvements made by teachers who sought her help: "That's what inspires you and keeps you moving," she declared.

Work Side by Side

Other teacher leaders tried to foster joint ownership of the reforms their roles were designed to champion and support. They cast themselves as sources of support, not supervisors, permitting their colleagues to decide how to incorporate proposed changes into their classrooms. In doing so, they often reinforced the belief that teacher leaders are no more expert than their peers.

Anna, for example, said she was advised by more senior colleagues not to present information "in a way that feels suffocating." Anna believed that by casting herself as a collaborator, rather than an authority, she enabled her veteran colleagues to take some ownership over changes to their practice.

Similarly, Kelly—an elementary school literacy coach and sixth-year teacher—described herself to her colleagues as a "facilitator" who connected them to resources that they could use to improve their practice rather than telling them how to teach. By allowing the teachers they worked with to determine how the reforms would play out in their classrooms, Anna and Kelly recognized and reinforced other teachers' autonomy. Their role was to support each teacher's approach to reform, not direct it.

In summary, the teacher leaders whom we interviewed coped with a traditional school organization and a teaching culture that prized and protected norms of egalitarianism, seniority, and autonomy. Because their roles were ill defined, these teacher leaders had to devise ways to be seen as legitimate and to gain access to teachers and classrooms without being rejected or becoming disheartened.

Better Support for Teacher Leaders

Our interviews with teachers in the second stage of their career suggest that many want to vary their responsibilities, collaborate with peers, and influence teaching beyond their classrooms. In many ways, they are ideal candidates to provide the teacher leadership that schools urgently need. However, their accounts also reveal that their experience as teacher leaders often fails to fulfill their expectations and may do little to build their schools' instructional capacity.

Most teacher leaders we interviewed were left to define their own roles, which proved to be more of a burden than an opportunity. In the absence of any professional framework or established set of differentiated responsibilities to provide guidance or legitimacy for their roles, teacher leaders' offers of advice often strained their relationships with other teachers. No amount of skill, enthusiasm, or determination in these teacher leaders could fundamentally change the structure of schooling or culture of teaching.

We do not infer from this study that roles for teacher leaders are doomed. Rather, we conclude that the roles must be introduced deliberately and supported fully. Informal roles with unpredictable funding will never be taken seriously. To be viable, these roles must have well-defined qualifications, responsibilities, and selection processes.

In Peer Assistance and Review programs in districts such as Toledo, Ohio; Montgomery County, Maryland; and Rochester, New York, consulting teachers advise and evaluate all beginning teachers and some struggling veterans. The success and sustainability of these programs, the first of which was introduced in Toledo in 1981, suggests that school officials should focus on establishing and supporting a system of long-term, well-defined roles for teacher leaders.

Our interviews made it clear that the principal can make or break the role of teacher leader. It was not enough for the principal to be a passive supporter, as was the case for most of the teacher leaders we interviewed. Rather, he or she needed to anticipate the resistance that teacher leaders might encounter from colleagues and help them broker the relationships they would need to do their work.

A few teacher leaders said that their principals helped by having what one called a "big game plan," which explained to all the staff how teacher leaders would contribute to the school's effort to achieve its goals. Principals can build support for a teacher leader's role by explaining its purpose, establishing qualifications and responsibilities, encouraging applicants for the position, and running a fair selection process. They can work with the schedule and available resources to incorporate the work of teacher leaders into the structure of the school and provide common planning time, substitute coverage for peer observations, and use of faculty meetings for professional development. They can guarantee that teacher leaders are not diverted to take on administrative tasks. Because school culture is so crucial to the success of these roles, teachers must see the principal's practices and priorities as reinforcing a new set of norms that promote collaborative work, bridge classroom boundaries, and recognize expertise.

But principals' efforts alone will not enable teacher leaders to succeed. Fundamentally, the success or failure of teacher leaders will depend on their relationships with their colleagues. Teacher leaders need professional development that prepares them to respond to colleagues' resistance respectfully while helping these teachers improve their practice.

Redefining the Norms of Teaching

The traditional norms of teaching—autonomy, egalitarianism, and seniority—exert a powerful and persistent influence on the work of teachers. They reinforce the privacy of the individual's classroom, limit the exchange of good ideas among colleagues, and suppress efforts to recognize expert teaching. Ultimately, they cap a school's instructional quality far below its potential.

If these norms remain dominant, many talented teachers who desire collaboration and expanded influence will become frustrated and leave education in search of another place to build a fulfilling career. Even more troubling—if these norms persist, they will continue to dissuade teachers from sharing vital knowledge about teaching and learning with their colleagues.

Schools cannot afford to lose promising teachers or squander opportunities to better serve students. It will take the efforts of all educators—district administrators, principals, teacher leaders, and teachers themselves—to redefine the norms of teaching and support teacher leaders in their work so that every school's instructional capacity expands to meet its students' needs.

Note

This chapter is based in part on analysis and argument presented in "Angling for Access, Bartering for Change: How Second-Stage Teachers Experience Differentiated Roles in Schools," by M. Donaldson, S. Johnson, C. Kirkpatrick, W. Marinell, J. Steele, and S. Szczesiul, in press, *Teachers College Record.*

References

Donaldson, M. L. (2005, April). *On barren ground: How urban high schools fail to support and retain newly tenured teachers.* Paper presented at the annual meeting of the American Educational Research Association, Montreal, Quebec, Canada.

Donaldson, M. L., Johnson, S. M., Kirkpatrick, C. L., Marinell, W. H., Steele, J. L., & Szczesiul, S. A. (in press). Angling for access, bartering for change: How second-stage teachers experience differentiated roles in schools. *Teachers College Record.*

Johnson, S. M., & the Project on the Next Generation of Teachers. (2004). *Finders and keepers: Helping new teachers survive and thrive in our schools.* San Francisco: Jossey-Bass.

Rockoff, J. (2004). The impact of individual teachers on student achievement: Evidence from panel data. *American Economic Review, 94*(2), 247–252.

CHAPTER 18

How Leaders Influence
the Culture of Schools

Kent D. Peterson and Terrence E. Deal

Parents, teachers, principals, and students often sense something special and undefined about the schools they attend. For decades, the terms climate and ethos have been used to capture this pervasive, yet elusive, element we call "culture."

Although hard to define and difficult to put a finger on, culture is extremely powerful. This ephemeral, taken-for-granted aspect of schools, too often over looked or ignored, is actually one of the most significant features of any educational enterprise. Culture influences everything that goes on in schools: how staff dress, what they talk about, their willingness to change, the practice of instruction, and the emphasis given student and faculty learning (Deal & Peterson, 1994; Firestone & Wilson, 1985; Newmann & Associates, 1996).

What is school culture, and who shapes it? Culture is the underground stream of norms, values, beliefs, traditions, and rituals that has built up over time as people work together, solve problems, and confront challenges. This set of informal expectations and values shapes how people think, feel, and act in schools. This highly enduring web of influence binds the school together and makes it special. It is up to school leaders—principals, teachers, and often parents—to help identify, shape, and maintain strong, positive, student-focused cultures. Without these supportive cultures, reforms will wither, and student learning will slip.

We have learned about the importance of school culture in a variety of ways. Over the past dozen years, we have conducted studies of school leadership, restructuring, and culture building and we have consulted with educators in hundreds of schools in the United States and abroad. Although interviewing staff highlights the importance of culture, it has often been through site visits that we have seen the power of positive cultures in action.

The Blight of Toxic Cultures

Unfortunately, some schools have, over time, become unproductive and toxic. These are schools where staffs are extremely fragmented, where the purpose of serving students has been lost to the goal of serving the adults, where negative values and hopelessness reign.

For example, in one high school, disgruntled staff came to faculty meetings ready to attack new ideas, criticize those teachers concerned about student achievement, and make fun of any staff who volunteered to go to conferences or workshops. Teachers who support change talked about the meetings as battlegrounds, the Sarajevos of education, where snipers and attacks were the norm. Negative staff had effectively sabotaged any attempts at collegial improvement.

Even good schools often harbor toxic subcultures, oppositional groups of staff or parents who want to spread a sense of frustration, anomie, and hopelessness. Toxic schools are places where negativity dominates conversations, interactions, and planning; where the only stories recounted are of failure, the only heroes are anti-heroes.

No one wants to live and work in these kinds of schools. But it takes leadership, time, and focus to rebuild these festering institutions. Happily, most schools are not this far gone, though many have cultural patterns that do not serve staff or students.

The Opportunities of Positive Cultures

In contrast to the poisonous places described above, many schools have strong, positive cultures. These are schools

- where staff have a shared sense of purpose, where they pour their hearts into teaching;

- where the underlying norms are of collegiality, improvement, and hard work;

- where student rituals and traditions celebrate student accomplishment, teacher innovation, and parental commitment;

- where the informal network of storytellers, heroes, and heroines provides a social web of information, support, and history;

- where success, joy, and humor abound.

Strong positive cultures are places with a shared sense of what is important, a shared ethos of caring and concern, and a shared commitment to helping students learn. Some examples might illuminate the possibilities.

Ganado Primary School in Ganado, Arizona, was once identified as one of the worst schools in the state. Now the culture is one that supports learning for its Navajo students, professional innovation for its staff, and meaningful parent involvement for its community. The principal, Sigmund Boloz, and his staff regularly meet for "Curriculum Conversations" about new instructional techniques, and they discuss new books during "Teachers as Readers" meetings. The school acclaims student accomplishment of all types during the "Celebrating Quality Learning Awards." The building, whose architecture symbolizes the four directions of Navajo beliefs, has student work and the rugs of skilled Ganado weavers displayed everywhere.

Joyce Elementary School in Detroit, Michigan, has developed a strong, student-focused culture. The school is located in an economically depressed area, but its culture is rich with hope and support. Over the past 20 years, Principal Leslie Brown Jr. has worked with his staff and parents to build a place that values its students, encourages professional improvement, and celebrates success. Regular classes for parents support their interest in learning. Staff hold high expectations for themselves and students. Joy and caring fill the hallways. A special honors ceremony with speeches, medallions for the students, and time to reflect on personal achievement attracts hundreds of community members each year.

Powerful informal professional norms characterize Central Park East Secondary School in New York City. Under the leadership of Deborah Meier, the staff and students developed a school culture with a clear vision about schooling for secondary students, linked with the coalition for Essential Schools for ideas and support (Meier, 1995). Staff exhibit a passionate professionalism and enjoy extensive opportunities for collegial dialogue, problem solving, and community building. The culture encourages student involvement in community service and teacher commitment to continual instructional development and design. The final student performance assessment remains a powerful tradition that reinforces a dedication to excellence and allegiance to learning.

At Hollibrook Elementary in Spring Branch, Texas, ceremonies and traditions reinforce student learning. Under the leadership of Suzanne Still and staff, and supported through ties to the Accelerated Schools Model, the school developed numerous traditions to create and foster increased student success (Hopfenberg, 1995). For example, faculty meetings became a hotbed of professional dialogue and discussion of practice and published research. "Fabulous Friday" was created to provide students with a wide assortment of courses and activities. A "Parent University" furnishes courses and materials while building trust between the school and the largely Hispanic community. Norms of collegiality, improvement, and connection reinforce and symbolize what the school is about.

In many other schools, local heroes and heroines, exemplars of core values, provide models of what everyone should be striving for. These deeply committed staff come in early, are always willing to meet with students, and are constantly upgrading their skills.

How do these strong cultures come about? School leaders—including principals, teachers, and often parents and community members—shape and maintain positive values and shared purpose.

The Role of School Leaders

School leaders from every level are key to shaping school culture. Principals communicate core values in their everyday work. Teachers reinforce values in their actions and words. Parents bolster spirit when they visit school, participate in governance, and celebrate success. In the strongest schools, leadership comes from many sources.

School leaders do several important things when sculpting culture. First, they *read the culture*—its history and current condition. Leaders should know the deeper meanings embedded in the school before trying to reshape it. Second, leaders *uncover and articulate core values*, looking for those that buttress what is best for students and that support student-centered professionalism. It is important to identify which aspects of the culture are destructive and which are constructive. Finally, leaders work to *fashion a positive context*, reinforcing cultural elements that are positive and modifying those that are negative and dysfunctional. Positive school cultures are never monolithic or overly conforming, but core values and shared purpose should be pervasive and deep.

What are some of the specific ways school leaders shape culture?

- They communicate core values in what they say and do.

- They honor and recognize those who have worked to serve the students and the purpose of the school.

- They observe rituals and traditions to support the school's heart and soul.

- They recognize heroes and heroines and the work these exemplars accomplish.

- They eloquently speak of the deeper mission of the school.

- They celebrate the accomplishments of the staff, the students, and the community.

- They preserve the focus on students by recounting stories of success and achievement.

Examples abound in the schools we have already described. At Ganado Primary, Boloz and his staff constantly share stories of the many changes they have made in the school. At Joyce Elementary, Brown and his faculty celebrate the successes of their students and parents in ritual "clap outs" and larger ceremonies. At Central Park East, school leaders meet regularly with students to communicate caring and support for hard work. Hollibrook Elementary holds regular discussion groups in parents' homes to cement ties and build trust. In small and large ways, school leaders refashion the negative sides of school culture and reinforce the positive aspects.

The role of school leaders in the crafting of cultures is pervasive (Deal & Peterson, 1994). Their words, their nonverbal messages, their actions, and their accomplishments all shape culture. They are models, potters, poets, actors, and healers. They are historians and anthropologists. They are visionaries and dreamers. Without the attention of leaders, school cultures can become toxic and unproductive. By paying fervent attention to the symbolic side of their schools, leaders can help develop the foundation for change and success.

References

Deal, T. E., & Peterson, K. D. (1994). *The leadership paradox: Balancing logic and artistry in schools*. San Francisco: Jossey-Bass.

Firestone, W. A. & Wilson, B. L. (1985). Using bureaucratic and cultural linkages to improve instruction. *Educational Administration Quarterly, 21*(2), 7–30.

Hopfenberg, W. S. (1995). *The accelerated school resource guide*. San Francisco: Jossey-Bass.

Meier, D. (1995). *The power of their ideas: Lessons for America from a small school in Harlem*. Boston: Beacon.

Newmann, F., & Associates. (1996). *Authentic achievement: Restructuring schools for intellectual quality*. San Francisco: Jossey-Bass.

CHAPTER 19

Why Don't Teachers Collaborate?

A Leadership Conundrum

David Piercey

Only an accumulation of individunl changes will produce a collective solution.—Carl Jung

Teacher collaboration is a prime determinant of school improvement. Unfortunately, though we talk about it a lot, we don't do it as much as we might hope for. We take pride and feel confident when we see a few random acts of collaboration in our schools. But the *modal* behavior in schools has changed little over the years.

This is surprising because the professional literature, for many years, has provided strong evidence that collaboration works. Still, collaboration is more the exception than the rule.

Why should this be so? Why should something that's considered a best practice not be practiced as consistently as pedagogy demands? Why should we say we're doing something when, in fact, we may be resisting it? Why should our public pronouncements profess our support for these practices when our public behaviors sometimes seem to demonstrate the opposite?

Our natural reactions may sabotage our attempts at collaboration

Part of our problem may be our language. Collaboration may simply mean different things to different people. Without making our assumptions clear, we may never fully understand each other's meaning.

For example, we often use the word "teamwork" to describe collaboration. We expect that we should operate as "highly effective teams." Yet, when we define it in practice, we often discover that we hold many different assumptions about what is an effective team. For many Americans, thinking of "teams" calls up images of football, a sport in which a star quarterback calls the plays and other players succeed in their positions by knowing their place. However, sports teams are simply not apt metaphors for professional collaboration, despite their intuitive appeal, because there is something much more *democratic* about collaboration, with many voices as equal contributors.

Even if we can't always readily agree on a suitable definition of what teamwork should mean, and thus what *makes* a good team, we all seem to have an appreciation for what makes a *bad* team. Patrick

Lencioni (2002) describes five dysfunctions of an underperforming team: absence of trust, fear of conflict, lack of commitment, avoidance of accountability, and inattention to results.

Interestingly, Lencioni's characteristics of a healthy team—high degrees of trust, willingness to engage in conflict in open discussions, a commitment to clarity and purpose, holding one another accountable, and focusing on collective results—are strikingly similar to the characteristics of professional learning communities (DuFour and Eaker 1998). Unfortunately, these qualities are still not that common in our schools, even in schools that claim to have professional learning communities.

Of course, any change takes time, and any new behavior must overcome old attitudes. There are always early implementers of new practices; some are more enthusiastic and some are less enthusiastic

---

Six conditions are necessary for collaboration.

Collaboration:

- Is based on mutual goals;
- Requires parity among participants;
- Depends on shared responsibility for participation and decision making;
- Requires shared responsibility for outcomes;
- Requires that participants share their resources; and
- Is a voluntary relationship.

Source: Friend, Marilyn, and Lynne Cook. *Interactions: Collaboration Skills for School Professionals.* New York: Longman, 1992.

---

or even resistant. There also are many circumstances, particularly in the political arena, beyond our control that constrain our choices for school organization. Let us even acknowledge that our own skill sets in how to lead collaborative processes may be wanting. Still, even granting these realities, why don't teachers collaborate more?

Ordering Collaboration

The professional literature continues to exhort teachers to use more authentic collaborative practices. But notice that teachers *are being told* that collaboration is how they should act.

Martin (2002) argues that, when leaders take charge of a situation, they too often convey an attitude of "I'm in charge"—with its corollary, "*and you are not.*" This "heroic" or "take charge" leadership style leads to "the death of collaboration" because it can elicit passivity and submission by subordinates. Subordinates may, in fact, abdicate more and more of their own responsibility and even feel increasingly marginalized, leading to increases in cynicism and distancing of self from the process. Collaboration thus becomes the first casualty in take-charge leadership.

The dominance and submissiveness in this kind of leadership situation are natural behaviors. They're adaptations to conditions our early ancestors had to overcome. However, in today's society, such behaviors may no longer have an evolutionary advantage. Instead, our natural reactions may sabotage our attempts at collaboration.

Our organizational structures may also reinforce these behaviors. For example, teaching continues to be practiced within clearly hierarchical structures. Teachers report to department heads, vice principals, or principals; principals report to assistant superintendents, associate superintendents, or superintendents. Even the language of leadership with terms that emphasize superordinate and subordinate ranks—might inadvertently promote attitudes we no longer wish to support.

Conditions for Collaboration

Though it may not be feasible to reinvent the words or organizational structures we use, we need to reconsider the relationships they promote. If we're to achieve better collaboration, we will have to develop some common understanding, some significant attitudinal shift, and the applications of some specific skills and processes.

Marilyn Friend and Lynne Cook (1992) argue that six conditions are necessary for collaboration. Collaboration:

- Is based on mutual goals;

- Requires parity among participants;

- Depends on shared responsibility for participation and decision making;

- Requires shared responsibility for outcomes;

- Requires that participants share their resources; and

- Is a voluntary relationship.

Achieving all six of those conditions in our current hierarchical school systems seems difficult.

Nor is it likely that we'll have time in the current school day and school year for the required discussion and consensus building. Not that all this isn't possible, but it certainly appears daunting.

If leaders are to foster collaboration, they must first change their own attitudes toward leadership. The "Authentic Leadership" movement is based on the idea that the leader's self-realization and self-transformation are necessary before organizational transformation can occur. For this to happen, an attitude of servant leadership is necessary (Greenleaf 1977). The biggest obstacle is getting used to the idea that there is not just one chief and relinquishing some of the power one has in order to empower others.

Perhaps, then, the simplest answer to the question, "Why don't teachers collaborate?" is that their leaders *won't* collaborate or *can't* demonstrate and model the necessary attributes.

References

DuFour, Richard, and Robert Eaker. *Professional Learning Communities at Work: Best Practices for Enhancing Student Achievement*. Bloomington, Ind.: National Educational Service, 1998.

Friend, Marilyn, and Lynne Cook. *Interactions: Collaboration Skills for School Professionals*. New York: Longman, 1992.

Greenleaf, Robert K. *Servant Leadership: A Journey into the Nature of Legitimate Power and Greatness*. New York: Paulist Press, 1977.

Lencioni, Patrick. *The Five Dysfunctions of a Team: A Leadership Fable*. San Francisco: Jossey-Bass, 2002.

Martin, Roger. *The Responsibility Virus: How Control Freaks, Shrinking Violets and the Rest of Us Can Harness the Power of True Partnership*. New York: Basic Books, 2002.

CHAPTER 20

Teacher Leadership

Alive and Thriving at the Elementary Level

Sherry Willis

During the summer of 2007, thirty-four selected kindergarten teachers from across the state of North Carolina came together to begin a journey purposefully crafted to enhance their instructional practice and to build their leadership capacity. This group of teachers, identified as North Carolina Kindergarten Teacher Leaders, was a key component of the state's early childhood initiative known as The Power of Kindergarten (Power of K). The impetus for this initiative arose from concerns voiced by a number of kindergarten teachers, administrators, and members of the North Carolina Birth Through Kindergarten Higher Education Consortium. These educators were highly concerned that developmentally appropriate practices in North Carolina kindergarten classrooms were being diminished if not lost entirely.

Members of the Early Childhood Division of the North Carolina Department of Public Instruction (NCDPI) listened to the concerns and quickly responded. An eight-member Kindergarten Think Tank composed of kindergarten teachers, administrators, and other early childhood professionals was organized. The Think Tank first created a position paper that defined the purpose and requirements for North Carolina kindergartens in the 21st century. Next, plans were made for selecting a cadre of teachers to become leaders in implementing and sustaining the kindergarten program described in the position statement. Interest in the initiative was high—over two hundred kindergarten teachers from all regions of the state applied to become a Kindergarten Teacher Leader. Thirty-four teachers were selected to begin an intensive three-year process of professional development designed to expand their knowledge of child development, learning environments, instructional intentionality, developmentally appropriate practice, and leadership skills. These teachers were expected to assume leadership roles within their schools, in their local school districts/regions, and at the state level. Possible leadership roles included serving on school improvement teams and system-level committees; conducting local, district, and regional professional development; and developing demonstration classrooms.

Ten of the Kindergarten Teacher Leaders recently participated in a study (Willis, 2010) designed to understand the experiences of North Carolina kindergarten teachers as they worked to establish, sustain, or improve developmentally appropriate practices in their classrooms. Developmentally appropriate practices are those research-based teaching and decision-making practices that take into account how each child learns, each individual child's growth and development, as well as the child's cultural values (Copple & Bredekamp, 2006). The study served to identify sources of support for these teachers as well as any barriers they encountered in their jobs. The study also served to discover how teachers coped with or resolved any challenges they experienced. The results of this study were intended to inform administrators and central office personnel of the needs and concerns of teachers committed to a developmentally appropriate approach to teaching kindergarten. These needs could inform system-wide and local school allocation of resources, professional development plans, teacher recruitment and retention strategies, and school improvement plans.

The participants in the study proved to be quite passionate in their beliefs favoring a developmentally appropriate approach to teaching; they desired to be as developmentally appropriate as possible in their teaching practices. Acutely aware of the academic standards for which they are held accountable, the kindergarten teachers wanted to be able to teach those standards in ways that were relevant to children. More specifically, they wanted children to be engaged in rigorous, challenging, active learning experiences that honor the ways children learn best. Developmentally appropriate classrooms, which the teachers in the study highly regarded, are thoughtfully designed to include learning centers, movement, exploration, meaningful hands-on learning experiences, and projects that support children's curiosity, interests, and natural eagerness to learn. The teachers serve as both *guides to* and *directors of* learning (Copple & Bredekamp, 2006; Katz, 2000; Rushton, 2001). The teachers did not believe that a more academic approach, often favored by other kindergarten teachers in their schools, was the best practice. That approach placed children in learning environments that resembled traditional first-grade classrooms. Those settings placed a heavy emphasis on teacher-directed learning, isolated skills, whole-group instruction, and worksheets, with children spending extended time sitting at tables or desks. Children had little opportunity to engage in problem solving, decision-making, or self-initiated projects within authentic contexts.

Most of the teachers in the study reported being required to follow some kind of system mandate that ran counter to their philosophical beliefs about developmentally appropriate practice as a significant barrier. These mandates involved the use of scripted commercial reading and math programs with whole groups of children. The teachers, strong in their knowledge of developmentally appropriate practices, worked creatively to adapt the programs in order to provide more effective and meaningful learning experiences for children. Other barriers reported by the teachers included the lack of meaningful and differentiated professional development aligned with the needs of early childhood teachers; the lack of meaningful feedback from administrators; and the feeling of being ignored and undervalued as professionals. These barriers were most challenging as the teachers felt they had little control in trying to overcome them.

Implications for Administrators

Several implications for administrators in North Carolina can be drawn from the study. These implications relate to understanding and supporting the needs of teachers as well as nurturing their leadership capacity, recruiting and maintaining high quality teachers, and providing them with meaningful professional development.

The ten North Carolina Kindergarten Teacher Leaders in this study were quite adamant in their belief that using a developmentally appropriate teaching approach was the best practice for educating young children. These Kindergarten Teacher Leaders truly wanted the help and support of administrators in order to be most effective in their practice. Teachers in the study found this source of help to be lacking or reported passive support from their administrator at best. Passive support occurred when administrators basically left the teachers alone, trusting them to do what they thought was best. Though the teachers appreciated any kind or means of support, they preferred active support from informed administrators. Active support included having the administrator in their classrooms frequently and for extended lengths of time; receiving meaningful feedback related to their practice, with knowledgeable suggestions for improvement; and recognition or praise for worthy endeavors.

It would not be a stretch to say that the number of North Carolina principals who are highly knowledgeable in the areas of early childhood education and child development is relatively low. If administrators are to be true instructional leaders in their schools, they must know and understand what is going on at every grade level and in every classroom and why. Being well informed is the only way they can meaningfully coach teachers to improve their practice. This level of knowledge also informs the administrator when celebrations of success are warranted. I have illustrated this point with principals during a professional development session with them. Using the analogy of a golf game, I described a scenario that included unheard of practices in the game of golf, but "golf-like" enough to someone not familiar with the game. These practices included driving the golf cart up on the green and placing a tee on the putting green. At the end of the scenario I asked the audience of principals if they saw any problems with the scenario I described. Only two principals, the golf-pros of the group, raised their hands wildly. "Don't ever drive your cart on the green!" one exclaimed. The other one said, "You don't use tees on the putting green!" The analogy was then applied to observing a kindergarten classroom. An administrator, who is not knowledgeable about what is observed, cannot tell the difference between appropriate practice and inappropriate practice; can make no meaningful suggestions for improvement; and has no idea what to consider praise worthy.

Principals must have available to them some means for gaining knowledge about child development and early childhood education. They must learn how the practices used in a developmentally appropriate kindergarten classroom impact a child's success beyond kindergarten. They should know what to look for in developmentally appropriate kindergarten classrooms—what teachers should be doing and what children should be doing—so that the integrity of this teaching approach is upheld. Few, if any, educational leadership programs provide such coursework related to early childhood education. Until that happens, it will be up to administrators to seek out this important information. Online courses could be specifically designed for this purpose with special emphasis on how the administrator can support instruction and teachers at the primary level.

Many administrators practice classroom "walk-throughs" designed to collect and document information about what teachers and students are doing. The administrator looks for evidence of specific researched-based strategies proven to have a high impact on student achievement. It would be helpful to administrators to have the checklist of practices "translated" to show how the practices might be represented in a developmentally appropriate kindergarten classroom. It is highly interesting to note that many of the research-based practices administrators are to look for in all classrooms at elementary, middle, and high school levels are the very practices they would find in a developmentally appropriate kindergarten classroom—differentiated instruction instead of whole-group instruction, student learning projects, small-group instruction, cooperative learning, and active, meaningful learning experiences.

A new state teacher evaluation instrument in North Carolina was fully implemented during the 2010–2011 school year. A small group of educators is actually working on a principal-support document for this instrument—a document specifically designed to inform principals of how the new evaluation instrument aligns to practices in Pre-K and kindergarten classrooms. Principals who are new to the instrument and not strong in early childhood knowledge will be grateful for this information. They need to make all efforts to secure and use the document once it becomes available.

Teacher Recruitment and Retention

Recruiting and retaining quality teachers is a high priority for all school systems. Once excellent teachers are recruited for specific positions, it then becomes important to retain those teachers for as long as possible. It is helpful to know what factors keep teachers in the classroom.

In the study, four teachers at one time or another considered leaving the classroom because of high levels of dissatisfaction. The teachers experienced low levels of esteem and lacked a sense of belonging. Curriculum decisions made at the system level often did not take into account input provided by the kindergarten teachers. Some of the teachers shared experiences indicating that no attempts were ever made to seek out their teacher voice. When mandates were issued requiring that teachers follow scripted teachers' manuals, the kindergarten teachers felt they were being given the message that the school system did not consider them competent to plan and teach based on the known needs of children.

If states are serious about keeping good teachers who have the knowledge and disposition to dedicate their lifework to young children, then school systems and local schools must act to honor the work of these teachers and to meet their needs. Administrators must demonstrate by word and action that they believe kindergarten has a valuable place and purpose within the school program. Kindergarten and kindergarten teachers cannot be relegated to a lower level of importance when it comes to providing resources, making schedules, and offering teachers support in terms of professional development. They cannot be ignored to accommodate the needs of teachers and students in tested grades. Kindergarten teachers are often the most knowledgeable teachers in the school in the area of child development. Their expertise is needed when critical instructional decisions affecting children have to be made.

Primary teachers do want to have a voice in making decisions at school and system levels that will affect them and their students. Teachers want their input to be seriously considered rather than just being a moot exercise. When their ideas are taken seriously, teachers' esteem is raised; their sense of autonomy is increased; they feel their opinions are valued and appreciated. School systems and schools would be very smart indeed to make it a standard practice to solicit opinions from and involve teachers in decision making as much as possible. Decisions are more likely to be supported if a feeling of ownership and involvement has been established.

Professional Development

The teachers in the study experienced a high level of support, esteem, and sense of belonging through their involvement with the Power of Kindergarten. All school systems should use this model to organize and support their kindergarten teachers as a professional learning community. Regularly scheduled meetings would afford teachers opportunities to network and learn from each other, to gain knowledge through professional development designed to meet the differentiated needs of kindergarten teachers, and to provide teachers the opportunities to share and discuss concerns with school and system-level administrators. Teacher leadership would be supported when the teachers are encouraged to lead the professional development or discussion sessions.

The North Carolina Kindergarten Teacher Leaders could not be more glowing in their descriptions of the positive impact the Power of Kindergarten initiative has had on their professional lives. The word "empowered" was used again and again to explain the effects of their increased knowledge and leadership skills. The teachers reported that they were better able to implement developmentally appropriate practices without fear of reproach from colleagues or administrators; they were also much stronger in effectively articulating their philosophy and their classroom practices to administrators, colleagues, parents, and other stakeholders.

The current participants are at the end of the three-year initiative. Plans are underway to sustain the powerful network that has been established. Demonstration classrooms are being discussed and developed. The Kindergarten Teacher Leaders are now available to provide support and professional development for teachers in their regions. Administrators have been encouraged to seek out these leaders and use their expertise to support their own kindergarten teachers.

Nurturing Leadership

No one should think that primary teachers are unable or uninterested in assuming leadership roles at the local, district, or state levels. Teacher leadership at the primary level is alive and thriving. This dynamic was certainly evident in the case of the teachers involved in the North Carolina Kindergarten Teacher Leader initiative. These teachers have been, in their own words, "empowered" to serve as models for teaching kindergarten in a way that honors how children learn best and makes learning meaningful; they stand ready to share their knowledge with others through professional development. The teachers are also assuming leadership roles in their schools, their school districts, regions, and even at the state level to make sure that the kindergarten teacher-voice is heard.

It is important to remember that over two hundred kindergarten teachers from all corners of the state initially applied to be selected as a Kindergarten Teacher Leader. They eagerly pursued the opportunity to assume the role of being a leader. For some, it was the first leadership opportunity ever extended to them. Changes must be made in the way some people view teacher leadership—it is not a role reserved only for upper elementary, middle, and high school teachers. Administrators are key players in this process.

Administrators must be fully knowledgeable about how to develop and nurture the leadership capacity in all teachers—*at all levels*. In other words, administrators must know, understand, and value, the contribution each teacher makes to the total school program; they must identify and enhance teachers' strengths; they must identify and meet teachers' needs. Having this information, administrators can help teachers craft the leadership skills needed in their classrooms, in the school, and in other places.

As a former kindergarten teacher, and now as an elementary school principal, I have experienced both sides of teacher leadership. While teaching kindergarten, I was encouraged and supported to assume leadership roles in the school system. Resources were provided so that I could develop a demonstration classroom for area kindergarten teachers to observe. I do understand what primary and elementary teachers need in order to feel professionally valued and supported. As principal, I am charged with the responsibility to provide all teachers—primary and elementary teachers—with opportunities for professional growth designed to build their leadership capacity. It is a responsibility I take seriously. I must also provide opportunities and encourage teachers to apply their leadership skills within the school setting and beyond. These opportunities often translate into teachers engaging in shared decision-making, leading parent meetings and professional development sessions, and actively serving on school and system-wide committees. School then becomes a true learning community where everyone works in tandem to support student achievement in the 21st century, as well as teachers' professional growth.

References

Copple, C., & Bredekamp, S. (2006). *Basics of developmentally appropriate practice*. Washington, DC: National Association for the Education of Young Children.

Katz, L. G. (2000). Another look at what young children should be learning. *ERIC Digest*, Retrieved April 28, 2007, from http://www.ericdigests.org/2000–1/look.html

Rushton, S. P. (2001). Applying brain research to create developmentally appropriate learning environments. *Young Children*, 56(5), 76–82.

Willis, S. R. (2010). *North Carolina kindergarten teachers and developmentally appropriate instructional practices: A phenomenological study* (Unpublished doctoral dissertation, Western Carolina University, 2010).

Questions for Reflection and Application

After reading the essays in Section Four, answer the following questions:

1. How can teacher leadership and the use of Professional Learning Communities change the culture of an entire school?

2. How can teachers work within the bureaucracy to ensure that teachers' voices help shape policy?

3. Whose support is necessary to facilitate these changes?

4. Is it likely that such support will be available?

Answer these questions using both the ideas from the essays that we are considering as well as your personal experiences with the schools you have encountered during your life: as a student, parent, and/ or teacher. References to specific ideas found in the Section Four essays are expected.

SECTION 5

Teacher Leadership in the Twenty-First Century: Changing the Culture of Schools

Introduction

Discussions of teacher leadership are not new. Teacher leadership is not a panacea for the educational problems of the twenty-first century; however, teacher leadership that involves putting teachers on the front line of school reform has the potential to transform schools and classrooms. Katzenmeyer and Moller (2009) refer to teacher leadership as "a sleeping giant," and that image is exciting within a context of considering the potential changes that could occur if teachers were awakened to the real possibilities of teachers' work that functions to support teachers acting as leaders to influence change and promote relevant innovation. Twenty-first century schools are being defined daily by the transformative changes that are arising from demographics, politics, and geography. Schools are responding to demands that they simultaneously respond to both local and national needs as well as global imperatives that require students to be technologically savvy consumers of both old and new knowledge. It has never been more important for teachers to simultaneously be leaders in the classroom, school, and community. The structure of educational innovation and progress cannot be defined by external forces ignorant of the complex dimensions that shape the parameters of teaching and learning. Teachers, and only teachers, have the training, experience, and knowledge to begin to define what twenty-first-century schools and learners need within an ideological context that acknowledges the important role a commitment to social justice and equity in teaching and learning plays in any school improvement plan.

One-dimensional attempts to articulate and mandate school reform efforts without a prerequisite understanding of the interconnectedness of myriad and broad-reaching factors are doomed to failure before they even get started. School failure, and more importantly, student failure, is not an option. However, a general acceptance of educational failure is what we find in too many communities, particularly those communities that serve poor and minority children. Many individuals may feel discomfort and even express scorn regarding the failure of public education, and yet nothing is done to fix the problem. I propose that authentic teacher leadership could fix the problem. Teacher leadership represents an opportunity to redefine what and how teachers work in schools. Teacher leadership represents the possibility of redefining teachers' roles to include teachers as activists, scholars, and change agents. Under the right circumstances and with appropriate training and professional development, teachers are the most likely heirs to leadership opportunities that could create dynamic schools capable of seamlessly responding to the needs of diverse and challenging teaching and learning conditions. In this arena, there would automatically be multiple roles for teachers as scholars-practitioners-leaders charged with the responsibility of re-creating schools and classrooms in new images—transformative images.

And yet teacher leadership is a dream because it is not a reality in most schools. Unfortunately, most discussions of twenty-first-century school reform are notable for the chaos and lack of direction that defines attempts at school improvement. Rather than opening the door for discourse and debate, this confusion often presents opportunities for external agents—corporate and political or both—to dominate the conversation, and, ultimately, mandate policies and procedures that support agendas that ignore the issues associated with equity and social justice and instead use children as pawns in a match where the most vulnerable populations are sacrificed for the good of a few.

As such, the essays in Section Five examine the relationship between teacher leadership and the changing culture of educational institutions faced with rapidly changing demographics and demands for global accountability. In the essays by Hess, Hurley, the Institute for Educational Leadership, Inc., Searby and Shaddix, Sherrill, and Wise and Usdan, the work of teacher leaders is connected to the realities of twenty-first-century initiatives. These varied perspectives contribute to an assessment of the status of teacher leadership and its potential for transforming both the profession and conceptions of teaching and learning in contemporary schools. However, it has been suggested throughout this book that attempts to foster teacher leadership are regularly challenged by a culture that is ambivalent, if not openly hostile, towards the empowerment of teachers. Thus, teacher leadership that challenges the status quo or causes discomfort between managers and their clients (students) is frequently discredited as inappropriate and not a viable option as a dimension of teachers' work. One is forced to ask if there is a place for teacher leaders in twenty-first-century schools? Or, perhaps, the better question might be whether teachers are ready for teacher leadership? I often struggle with these two questions. Teacher leadership has always been about school improvement, and not so much about teachers. However, it seems a natural evolution of thought to consider that teacher leadership can lead not only to school improvement but an improved profession and better working conditions for teachers. Obviously, this is the vision, not the reality, and therein lies the problem. Is this a vision that teachers are committed to achieving? Is it possible for teacher leadership to emerge as a key component of improved schools and a stronger profession? The answers to these questions are not clear. Teacher leadership requires conditions and opportunities that facilitate the work of teacher leaders, but, simultaneously, teachers must be prepared to make commitments and take risks that will lead to new definitions of what it means to be a teacher today. As such, the future is unknown and holds exciting possibilities for schools and teachers. This book will, I hope, contribute to critical reflection and discussion on these issues and others, and, as always, the debate is as important as the resolution.

Reference

Katzenmeyer, M., & Moller, G. (2009). *Awakening the sleeping giant: Helping teachers develop as leaders* (3rd ed.). Thousand Oaks, CA: Corwin.

CHAPTER 21

Busting out of the Teacher Cage

Frederick M. Hess

Teacher leadership is popular today for a simple reason—it's a terrific thing. And lots of people, from Secretary of Education Arne Duncan to your corner grocer, have been telling teachers that they deserve to lead and to be heard. The harsh truth, though, is that no one deserves these things—whether one is a doctor, lawyer, cop, or teacher. While everyone can desire them, leadership and a seat at the table always must be earned.

This matters—a lot. Frustrated by schools and systems that consume their time and passion, teachers can find it all too easy to retreat to their classrooms. But doing so leaves them trapped in a classroom cage, stuck with systems and policies that they find frustrating or incoherent. Cage-busting teachers reach out in ways that identify the problems and surface workable solutions.

There are problems of policy and practice that befuddle teachers and need to be addressed. Consider the example of Alex Lopes, Florida Teacher of the Year in 2013. The state's new teacher evaluation system mandated that 50% of a teacher's evaluation be based on student achievement, with teachers in nontested grades scored using schoolwide achievement. As a preschool autism teacher, Lopes had no tested students; thus, he was judged using schoolwide results from his high-poverty, low-performing school. His score was predictably poor, with the result that he was deemed ineffective and rendered ineligible for teacher leadership roles. In the midst of this, Lopes mused to colleagues that if he taught at a more successful school, he'd be classified as an effective teacher and free to be a mentor, coach, or teacher leader. No one meant for this to happen. But no one prevented it either.

Passion has its price

When confronted with these kinds of troubling policies, it's all too easy for teachers to speak up in destructive ways. Passionate people tend to be sure of their convictions and in a hurry to act on them. That can be good and admirable. But passion also can have real costs. It can leave us impatient, make us strident, and lead us to dismiss the views of others. It can make us better at talking than at listening. Passionate people aren't always great at understanding why others might disagree, which can make it hard to win over people or assuage their concerns. Michelle Shearer, a high school chemistry teacher in Maryland and the 2011 National Teacher of the Year, said, "That passion can be good and bad. Teachers often feel that they have no voice, so when they do speak up, all of that emotion comes to the surface. And it can come across as complaining or whining." Passion can lead people to say things that erode their credibility, making it harder to address their concerns. In early 2014, Michael Mulgrew, president of New York City's United Federation of Teachers, told 3,400 union delegates, "We are at war with the reformers. … Their ideas will absolutely destroy—forget about public education—they will destroy education in our country."

It can be all too easy for teachers to let their frustration get the better of them. "Everybody thinks they're an educational expert because everybody went to school," as the saying goes. Well, no. For one thing, most people don't think they're educational experts. For another, lawmakers have a job to do—write laws about how to spend money and provide services. More to the point, many advocates and policy makers do have some expertise when it comes to schooling. They've spent years talking to educators, studying schools and school systems, examining data, crafting education laws, and wrestling with implementation challenges. They frequently bring real knowledge to the table. If practitioners want outsiders to acknowledge their passion and expertise, they'd benefit from modeling that same respect.

A sympathetic ear

This should be easy advice to heed because teachers enjoy a sympathetic audience. People care what teachers think. The most recent PDK/Gallup Poll of the Public's Attitudes Toward the Public Schools found that two-thirds of Americans say they have "trust and confidence" in public school teachers (Bushaw & Calderon, 2014). After all, the public knows that teachers are closer to the classroom than anyone else. The question is what teachers do with this influence. Greg Mullenholz, a 2011 Washington Teaching Ambassador Fellow, said, "What fascinated me was this perception that folks at [the U.S. Department of Education] would look at us and think, 'They're just teachers.' But the high-level folks actually had a lot of respect for what we had to say. We would meet with them regularly to discuss the feedback we were getting from teachers in the field, and they'd use it to inform what they were doing."

There are lots of opportunities, even if you don't feel ready for them. Jay Hoffman, a technology education teacher in Vermont who has served on the state standards board for professional educators, suggests that teachers "Call your local legislator cold and say, 'Hey, I'd like to get together with you.' Teachers have more credibility than they might think. Don't worry about being blown off a few times. It's the nature of what they [legislators] do—they're pulled in a thousand different directions. Stick with it, and eventually you'll get an audience. It's just a matter of being a hound dog."

Wendy Uptain, a former kindergarten teacher and now director of teacher engagement for the Hope Street Group, a national nonprofit that helps teachers advocate for policy change, said, "We talk about meeting legislators like a first date. Set up a meeting, and make it a short and sweet introduction. Introduce yourself, and ask for some suggestions and advice. Listen. Don't race to offer recommendations on how to fix something or tell them you need more money. Ask if there's anyone else you should talk with. Use email to keep in touch. They're much more likely to take you seriously because you're not just someone from out of the blue."

Tapping teacher authority

Teachers are often unsure how they can effectively change schools, systems, and policy—and are skeptical that anyone will actually listen to them. After all, teachers don't have a lot of formal authority in schools. This means it's especially important that they be clear and strategic about tapping the authority they do have. After all, while teachers lack *positional authority*, they have two powerful sources of authority at their disposal: the *authority of expertise* and a potentially powerful *moral authority*. Teachers rarely employ these to their full extent. Many aren't even aware of the power they possess.

The authority of expertise derives from teachers knowing more than anyone else about how policies and decisions actually affect students and classrooms. Teachers know what's working, what's not, and what's really going on. They know how evaluation systems play out and how new technology gets used. They know where well-intended reforms are falling flat. If teachers share this knowledge clearly and constructively, they can profoundly influence policy and practice. In all walks of life, there's a deep-seated desire to trust the expertise of professionals. People want to lean on the advice of their dentist, plumber, or mechanic. The same holds true for teachers.

Moral authority is a different animal: It comes when professionals are seen as the guardians of the public interest. This can be confusing because there are lots of efforts to sloganeer one's way to moral authority—by saying things like "we're for the kids." But true moral authority doesn't come from saying anything. It comes with a track record of clear, consistent action to promote professional excellence. It derives from a record of doing things to help teachers get better, to get systems to stop wasting time or money, and to ensure that mediocre employees (whether they work in the central office or in classrooms) are dealt with appropriately. Moral authority is earned. It's the product of teachers convincing parents, voters, and policy makers, "We've got this." The authority of expertise is only effective when professionals are deemed trustworthy. If people grant the expertise of auto mechanics but believe that too many are ripping off their customers, then that undermines the moral authority of all mechanics. The result is a public that second-guesses mechanics and asks elected official to do something to rein in the bad apples. The authority of expertise is bolstered by moral authority, and moral authority isn't about what people think of this or that mechanic—it's about what people think of mechanics in general. For teachers, moral authority is not what people think of you but what they think of the teachers at your school, in your district or state, or throughout the profession. Moral authority is a team sport. That's why retreating to the classroom is so debilitating.

Tell policy makers

Even when teachers have done a good job marshaling both expertise and moral authority, they can stumble. In particular, when educators do get the chance to speak to system leaders or to policy makers, they can fall into self-defeating habits. On the other hand, if you understand where policy makers are coming from, it gets a lot easier to focus on what might influence them.

This means doing three things, in particular:

#1. ***Don't demand more money***. Everybody asks lawmakers for money. If policy makers had more money to give, they'd give it. But mostly what they hear from teachers is that schools need more. This is true even in places where districts are spending more than $20,000 per student each year.

#2. ***Emphasize shared concerns***. In other words, presume that they care about the same kids that you do—and explain the idea with a view to how they might see things.

#3. ***Offer them workable solutions***. Wendy Uptain, of Hope Street, offers some terrific advice: "Propose solutions that work beyond your classroom. If you show a policy maker that you have your eyes set beyond just the four walls of your classroom, they'll listen accordingly."

I remember meeting a group of accomplished North Carolina teachers who'd been disheartened by the state's decision to abolish tenure, eliminate hundreds of millions of dollars annually in pay for advanced degrees, and use only a small portion of the savings to create a tiny annual bonus for a quarter of the state's teachers. The teachers were angry. I totally got that. But here's the deal: Those legislators also had valid concerns. They were concerned that tenure too often protected the undeserving and that paying for advanced degrees was subsidizing course taking that didn't improve instruction. Disagreement on these things was not a good reason to dismiss legislators as misinformed or hopeless.

Those legislators may not want to pay for education degrees, but that doesn't mean they're wedded to cutting teacher pay. If you take the policy makers' concerns seriously, agree that the current system doesn't do enough to reward excellence or address mediocrity, and propose a viable alternative, you can alter the debate. Rather than arguing whether to pay for the old credentials or to cut pay, the question can be how those dollars might best attract, retain, and energize great teaching. Framed that way, it's tougher for anyone to argue that the money should simply go away.

Schooling is so complex that how education policies play out tends to be more a matter of practice than words on a page. This means that you can still shape policies long after they've been formally adopted. Laws are brought to life by hundreds of decisions made by federal, state, and local officials. Those decisions are made out of the spotlight, can be readily influenced, and often have more practical effect on classrooms than the formal law itself. This means teachers can have enormous effect on policy without hanging around statehouses if they stick to what they know and apply their expertise.

Taking sides

In recent years, the education debate has featured two warring camps: "reformers" and "antiprivatizers." On one side are those who embrace test-based accountability, merit pay, school choice, and a commitment to closing "achievement gaps." On the other are those who broadly reject such measures while demanding more support for teachers and kids, more professional autonomy, and more emphasis on peer assistance and portfolios.

Teachers can feel pressed to pick a camp. They attend conferences where state and district officials invite them to play leadership roles by championing this or that reform. They get emails from colleagues or union officials urging them to support or oppose particular initiatives. Through it all, there's a sense they're supposed to pick sides—to be for or against school accountability or charter schooling. Teachers should resist that pressure. If the goal is to create schools and systems where they can do their best work, teachers should judge each proposal accordingly, with an eye to its potential and its practical frailties.

Teachers should take inspiration from an unlikely source: Treebeard, the wizened, ancient Ent who befriends a couple of lost young hobbits in J. R. R. Tolkien's *Lord of the Rings*. Upon meeting Treebeard in the midst of a savage war, the wide-eyed young hobbit Pippin asks him, "And whose side are you on?" Treebeard ponders the question and then laconically replies, "Side? I am not altogether on anybody's side because nobody is altogether on my side."

Professionals should be accountable. It's also the case that many reforms intended to promote accountability may be half-baked or dependent on unreliable metrics. It's easy for teachers to look at today's scorched-earth education reform debate and, in good conscience, conclude that no one is altogether on their side. The funny thing is, by saying that clearly, firmly, and respectfully, teachers can make it more likely that they'll get a serious hearing from serious people on both sides.

Takeaways

So, what does this all mean for teachers who want to speak up? There are at least three things that are especially useful to keep in mind.

Teachers and policy makers have an asymmetrical relationship. Teachers who want a major role in shaping education policy need to earn the trust of lawmakers. In response, teachers will say, "Fine, I hear you. But we're the ones in the classrooms with the kids every day. Don't they need to earn our trust?" The short answer: Yep, they do. The longer answer, though, is that educators are in an asymmetrical relationship with the lawmakers who control budgets, write policy, and legislate accountability systems. Think of a teacher dealing with students. Both teacher and student ought to try to earn the other's trust. But the teacher gets to set the rules, which means students stand to gain more by winning the teacher's trust than vice versa. Such is life.

Pay close attention to where the power lies in your school and system. Jacob Pactor, a high school English teacher in Indianapolis, said, "When I went into a big school, my first priority was to know who the players are. Usually, that's going to be your department chair, the special ed chair, and the guidance counselor. If you build good relationships with them, when you go to your principal it's a whole new game. Rather than just me coming up with an idea, I can now tell my principal, 'I've been talking this over with A, B, and C, and we are all thinking …' and it's like you have the full force of the faculty behind you because you've secured the key players." Cage busting is a team sport, and that requires knowing your teammates, their individual strengths, and how to put those strengths to work.

Make it easy for policy makers or administrators to say "yes." In doing this, four steps are paramount. First, give leaders something they can say yes to. You need to give them a concrete, precise problem and solution. Second, give them something they'll want to say yes to. You need to explain why your idea is going to help solve a problem that they care about. Third, help them understand how they'll justify their yes to parents, school board members, or their supervisors. Let them know what they can say to those who might be skeptical of the decision. Fourth, reassure them that they won't regret saying yes. Explain how they can be sure that your request won't become a headache for them. It's the job of school and system leaders to help you solve problems, but it's your job to make it easy for them to do so.

A lot of advice presumes that if teachers are positive, passionate, and committed to their craft, things will work out. Yet teachers can do remarkable work only to wear themselves out as they slam again and again into the bars of their classroom cage. Teachers have it in their hands to change all of that. But it requires more than leadership; it will require that teachers apply outside their classroom the same savvy and patience that they value within it.

Reference

Bushaw, W. J. & Calderon, V. J. (2014). 46th annual PDK/Gallup poll of the public's attitudes toward the public schools. *Phi Delta Kappan, 96*(2), 48–59.

CHAPTER 22

Teacher Leadership

A New Foundation of Education?

J. Casey Hurley

Educational history, philosophy, politics, and sociology are the traditional foundations of American public education. They are "foundations" because they address how schools strive to achieve public education's purposes and ideals. Historians chronicle the struggle to achieve fundamental ideals. Philosophers explore the purposes of schools. Political pundits analyze the educational policies of state and local governments. And sociologists describe how schools mirror society as they struggle to achieve the ideals of its citizens. Teacher leadership is a new foundation of education because it explains how schools organize themselves for continuous improvement.

Teacher leadership has not been recognized as a foundation because, until recently, more popular ideas competed for the best ways to organize schools. Structuring schools around teacher leadership competes with the beliefs that the principal ought to be the school's instructional leader, and central office administrators ought to direct improvement efforts from a district-wide perspective. The whole point of recent teacher leadership literature, however, is that teachers must be engaged in continuous school improvement, and their leadership is needed to ensure its success. How else could a school's continuous improvement cycle be successful? Schools structured around the premise that principals or central office personnel lead the continuous improvement cycle see the cycle broken whenever a new principal or superintendent is hired. Teacher leadership literature simply argues that continuous improvement requires organizational structures that tap into the power of both teacher followership and leadership.

This chapter reviews the images of teacher leadership in recent literature. Then it traces our beliefs about leadership back to our beliefs about how to structure schools for improvement. Then it goes beyond descriptions of teacher leadership to a definition of teacher leadership—what it always is and what it never is.

Images of What Teacher Leaders Do and What It Is About

According to Katzenmeyer and Moller (2009), teacher leaders do four things: (a) lead within and beyond the classroom, (b) contribute to a community of learners and leaders, (c) educate others toward improved educational practice, and (d) accept responsibility for achieving the outcomes of their leadership. They present an image of teachers as classroom leaders who also accept responsibility for school and district goals.

Similarly, Barth (2001) said teacher leaders are engaged in "10 areas in which teacher leadership is essential to the health of a school":

- choosing textbooks and instructional materials;
- shaping the curriculum;
- setting standards for student behavior;
- deciding whether students are tracked into special classes;
- designing staff development and in-service programs;
- setting promotion and retention policies;
- evaluating teacher performance;
- selecting new teachers; and
- selecting new administrators.

These duties coincide with the principal's instructional functions (Lipham & Hoeh, 1974). Barth is describing how teacher leaders partner with principals to improve instruction.

Schlechty (1993) offered several metaphors for teacher leadership. He said they are often "trailblazers," "pioneers," and "settlers:"

Those who take the first steps are trailblazers. They are willing to go without maps to places where no person has gone before them …

Like the trailblazers, pioneers are an adventurous and hardy lot and willing to take considerable risks …

Settlers are bold, but they are not adventurers …

They want to be sure they know how to do what will be required of them. Many potential settlers will not move until they are assured that the requisite knowledge and support are available for them. (pp. 37–38)

Trailblazers and pioneers step out first. Settlers lead later, when they tell others to follow where trailblazers and pioneers are going.

These images and metaphors say teacher leaders take responsibility for classroom and school improvement, partner with principals, trail blaze, pioneer, and settle new territory. The images are as varied as the activities engaged in by teacher leaders.

Another way to look at teacher leadership is to describe what it is about. In *Redefining the Teacher as Leader* (2001), the Institute for Educational Leadership (IEL) emphasized that

Teacher leadership is not about "teacher power." Rather "it is about mobilizing the still largely untapped attributes of teachers to strengthen student performance at the ground level." This can happen through "real collaboration—a locally tailored kind of shared leadership—in the daily life of the school." (p. 4)

Teacher leadership is about working collaboratively on school projects to improve student performance.

What else is teacher leadership about? Is it about improving test scores, turning a school around, graduating more students, reaching high and low achievers, building a positive school climate? Of course it's about all these things, and more. Multiple descriptions of "what teacher leadership is about" suggest that teachers lead in many situations, but, according to this report, it is still largely untapped.

No Definition Yet

Multiple definitions and descriptions of what teacher leaders are distract us from seeing that teacher leadership is a foundation of public education. York-Barr and Duke (2004) wrote:

> These validity concerns are discussed subsequently, in part to highlight the dilemmas raised throughout the present article about what teacher leadership really is and how it is defined. In the absence of a valid definition, measurement and analysis are problematic. (p. 286)

Scholars struggle to explain what we know about teacher leadership because we lack a shared definition.

Teacher leadership literature is in its infancy and emerged only in the mid-1990s. In comparison, the principal-as-instructional-leader literature goes back to the early 1980s. And bureaucratic organizational structures, which are the strongest barrier to all forms of teacher leadership, were introduced in the early 1900s. According to York-Barr and Duke (2004, p. 260), "In writing about teacher leadership, many authors readily assert its importance and describe its various forms, but they usually fail to define it."

Katzenmeyer and Moller (2009) wrote: "There is common agreement that we are a long way from a widespread understanding of teacher leadership. Confusion about definitions and expectations of teacher leaders abound (York-Barr & Duke, 2004). Just what does teacher leadership look like?" (p. 5). And Hilty (2011) said: "Herein lies the problem with teacher leadership: it is often misunderstood by teachers and administrators, and thus, teachers are reluctant to seek out leadership roles and administrators prefer to retain all the power and authority they presently have in schools (p. xviii)."

Not only does teacher leadership, as a foundation of public education, suffer from a lack of definition, but it also creates misconceptions about teachers' roles in school organizational structures. Teachers who aspire to school leadership routinely confront the following kinds of questions: (a) Should I define a new leadership role for me? (b) Should I reluctantly lead? (c) Should I simply follow? The answers always depend on how teacher leadership is defined. Scholars have described teacher leadership and struggled to alter misconceptions, but we still have no definition.

Deductive thinking has led to the current state of the teacher leadership literature. Figure 1 illustrates thinking in this direction—from the central belief that teacher leadership improves education to all the specific ways that can happen.

The arrows represent deductive thinking. We start with a belief (in the center) and the arrows point to the research studies that describe specific images of teacher leadership in specific situations (at the periphery). Because we use deductive thinking, we have an infinite number of teacher leadership images and descriptions of what it is about, and we continue to describe more (Teacher Leadership Exploratory Consortium, 2011). We ought to start with a definition of teacher leadership that says what it always is and what it never is.

Beliefs About the Structure and Improvement of Public Schools

Our beliefs about how to structure public education also cause us to overlook the significance of teacher leadership in the continuous improvement cycle. We currently believe two things about teacher leadership in public schools: (a) Bureaucratic hierarchy must be its context; (b) research findings are needed to assure us that it improves student outcomes. What is the evidence for saying we hold these beliefs?

The first belief is so strong, and it is taken so much for granted, that we don't see how it affects everything about school organization. We can see it, though, if we contrast the belief in bureaucratic hierarchy with the communitarian beliefs that drive parochial and some charter schools.

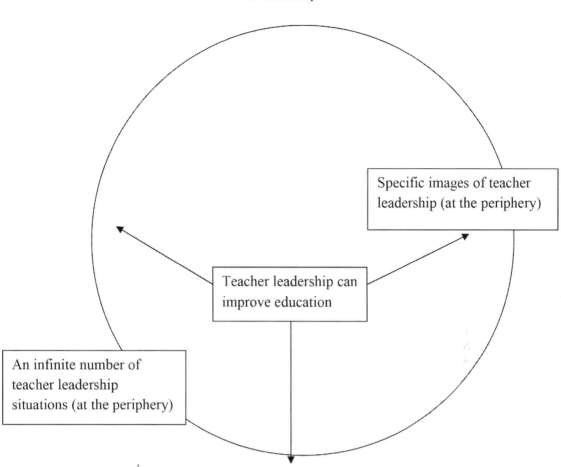

Figure 1

Parochial schools have little reason to exist unless they are communities. Most of them, when compared with public schools, have lower teacher pay, and fewer supplies, equipment and programs. They appeal to families, however, because their children will be part of a community, not a bureaucracy.

Communitarian charter schools have the same appeal. They are more like private schools than public schools, even though they are (a) free, like public schools, (b) funded by state governments, like public schools, and (c) chartered within a state system of public education. Regular public schools can be communities, too, but few are because we believe they must organize themselves bureaucratically.

Teacher leadership literature provides evidence for this belief. Teacher leadership in the classroom has never been contested. Classroom teacher leadership is not Katzenmeyer and Moller's (2009) "sleeping giant" because it has not been sleeping, and bureaucratic rules make the teacher the classroom leader.

The "sleeping giant" image says teacher leadership is a powerful, untapped resource in efforts to improve schools and districts. In these cases, bureaucratic superiors should harness teacher leadership for the benefit of school and district improvement. This is where it becomes contested. Teacher leadership in schools and districts generates conflict because of the belief that schools and districts should be bureaucratically structured, with teachers in followership, not leadership roles.

Hilty (2011) says teachers have learned they are *not* the leaders in schools and districts. Bureaucratic principles tell them so. She believes that, if the giants are awakened, they should be ready for battle because the bureaucratic context tilts toward the prerogatives of principals, district administrators, and policymakers. Similarly, Schlechty's (1993) images suggest that teachers lead in hostile territories (trail blazers, pioneers, and settlers). The norm is for administrators and policymakers to defend their prerogatives and make specific territories off-limits to teacher leaders.

York-Barr and Duke (2004, p. 264) also cite scholars' concerns about teacher leadership within the public education bureaucracy. They cite Darling-Hammond, Bullmaster, and Cobb (1995), who propose that "teacher leadership can be embedded in tasks and roles that do not create artificial, imposed, formal hierarchies and positions … such approaches may lead to greater profession-wide leadership as the 'normal' role of teacher is expanded" (p. 89).

They also cite Yarger and Lee (1994) and Coyle (1997): "teacher leadership requires some coherent reordering of the workplace among schools. This reordering helps to create a climate that encourages teacher collaboration and involves teachers in making decisions" (Yarger and Lee, p. 234). Stated more forcefully, Coyle asserts that "unless we flatten the present hierarchies … and create structures that empower teachers to collaborate with one another and to lead from within the heart of the school, the classroom, we will … discourage true educational leadership" (p. 239). Scholars recognize that teacher leadership challenges the belief that schools must be bureaucratically structured.

Finally, this was recognized by the Teacher Leadership Exploratory Consortium (2011, p. 12), which also called for new school structures: "Teacher leadership necessitates new organizational structures and roles in schools in order to successfully meet the needs of 21st century learners." This group argued that collaborative cultures are needed for teacher leadership to fulfill its potential as a force for school improvement.

In summary, teacher leadership within the bureaucratic structure of schools and districts is like a salmon swimming upriver. Swimming upstream is necessary for the species to survive, but the water's flow makes it a difficult feat. Teacher leadership is necessary for school improvement, but the bureaucratic structure of schools and districts makes it a difficult feat.

Research Findings Are Needed to Describe How Teacher Leadership Improves Student Outcomes

This second belief emerges from the social science paradigm for improving education (Hurley, 2009). Cochran-Smith (2002, p. 284) calls it the "research as foundation" metaphor. As a graduate student at the University of Wisconsin-Madison during the 1970s and 1980s, I was taught that schools improve as teachers and administrators apply the research findings of what was effective at improving student outcomes.

This is still the dominant paradigm for improving education, which is why York-Barr and Duke (2004) wrote in their "Closing Perspective":

> This article began by offering Smylie and Denny's (1990) view that the resurgence of interest in teacher leadership is due, in part, to new hope that teacher leadership will contribute to the improvement of schools. One could conclude this review of the literature, however, with a pessimistic view of the prospects for teacher leadership, correctly claiming that there is little empirical evidence to support its effects. An equally defensible conclusion, however, is the reasonableness of advancing teacher leadership and doing so with an informed spirit of hope. A long view of the findings from our review, we believe, substantiates this more optimistic view. Clearly, a large number of teachers and their administrators have ventured forth courageously into the uncharted waters of shared leadership, genuinely hoping to improve teaching and learning for the children and youth in their charge. Furthermore, many have persevered in their explorations despite being thwarted by centuries-old structures and conditions of schools that resist change. (p. 292)

The authors want teachers to continue to lead, even though "there is little empirical evidence to support its effects," and these efforts are sometimes "thwarted by centuries-old structures and conditions of schools that resist change." Still, they believe research findings may eventually describe how teacher leadership improves student outcomes.

Even after describing the debilitating effects of the social science improvement paradigm, the authors continue to hope for empirical evidence to support the effectiveness of teacher leadership. Beliefs are difficult to change and paradigms are difficult to shift.

When it comes to teacher leadership, the second belief combines with the first to restrict the leadership of teachers in schools and districts. In other words, when bureaucratic superiors approve, teachers are allowed to lead in situations like those described in the research.

Eleven years after York-Barr and Duke's (2004) literature review, there have been no breakthroughs on the effectiveness of teacher leadership. This is not surprising. Research cannot determine the effectiveness of what is not defined. Still, teacher leadership is gaining as a popular idea, and proponents *believe* research will continue to describe how it leads to improved student outcomes.

Evidence of this belief is *Teacher Leader Model Standards* (2011), written by The Teacher Leadership Exploratory Consortium, an ad hoc group of 51 educators holding positions in universities, teacher unions, school districts, the Educational Testing Service, and other education organizations. This group was formed to develop standards for evaluating teacher leadership effectiveness.

The report's vision statement includes much of what we already covered. Teacher leadership involves (a) sharing with principals, (b) achieving higher student test scores, and (c) flattening school hierarchies.

The heart of the report describes standards by which teacher leadership can be assessed. Standards are presented in seven domains. The details are not as important as the premise, namely, that teacher leadership should have standards by which it can be assessed. This is a common premise within the social science improvement paradigm, but it takes us further away from a shared definition and it adds more images, and situations, at the periphery of teacher leadership.

According to this report, teacher leaders should be assessed across seven domains on (a) 25 understandings, (b) 24 skills, and (c) 37 competencies. And that is just the beginning. The report poses 5 questions to be explored, recommending that educators should address 6 issues and complete 35 tasks to properly evaluate the effectiveness of teacher leadership.

The report concludes with two appendices. The first one "summarizes the cross-walk between the InTASC 2011 Standards and the Teacher Leader Model Standards." Of the 178 InTASC descriptors, the Teacher Leader Model Standards "cross-walk" on all but 9. That means we have 169 descriptors of things teacher leaders should be able to do. The second appendix shows how Teacher Leader Model Standards are also included in the ISLLC standards for education leaders. That makes 37 more descriptors of what teacher leaders do.

This report is another example of deductive thinking. The authors begin with a belief in the effectiveness of teacher leadership. Then they list all the understandings, skills, competencies, questions, issues, and tasks that can become standards for evaluating it.

There is nothing wrong with deductive thinking. In this case, however, it starts with a belief about an undefined concept, and nothing gets clearer, no matter how many images and situations are listed at the periphery. For teacher leadership to be regarded as the way schools structure themselves for improvement, we must develop a shared definition.

Figure 2 illustrates how these two beliefs lead to multiple definitions and images at the periphery.

We believe schools should be bureaucratically structured and that research findings are needed to describe how teacher leadership improves student outcomes. The result is that some administrators and policymakers allow teachers to lead, others do not. And the research supports both positions because these beliefs give this prerogative to teachers' bureaucratic superiors. We need to replace those beliefs with one that says teacher leadership is the way we structure schools for improvement.

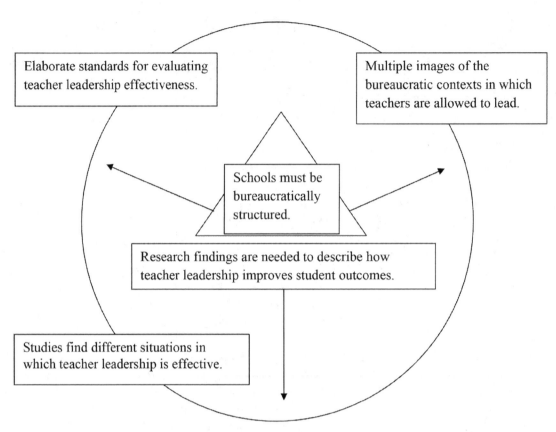

Figure 2

What Is the Essence of Teacher Leadership?

Starting with the multiple images and multiple situations at the periphery of Figure 2, we can think inductively to find the essence of teacher leadership. Teacher leadership can take many forms, but what must it always be?

A Third Type of Definition

The *IEL* (2001) definition began by saying teacher leadership is *not* about power. We sometimes say what leadership is *not* about to distinguish it from management. The most famous of these distinctions is Bennis and Nanus's (1985, p. 21): "Managers are people who do things right and leaders are people who do the right thing."

This definition says leadership always has a moral dimension. It addresses the question of whether or not Hitler was a good leader. According to this definition, he may have been a good manager, but he was not a good leader because he did not do the right thing.

Based on my own administrative experience, I offer a second distinction between managers and leaders. As a high school principal, I was consumed by management responsibilities, but I knew of colleagues who provided inspiring leadership. Listening to those principals, I concluded that "managers confront human vice; leaders cultivate human virtue." This distinction says leadership always has an aesthetic dimension. Principal "managers" (like me) addressed the ugly situations created by human vice. Inspiring principal "leaders" cultivated the human virtues that create beautiful school situations. (Regarding the "Hitler leadership question," in the aesthetic dimension he was neither a good manager nor a good leader because he failed to confront human vice or cultivate human virtue.)

Specifically, the aesthetic dimension says leaders cultivate the six virtues of the educated person—understanding, imagination, strong character, courage, humility, and generosity (Hurley, 2009). Some schools already lean toward this perspective. Parochial schools often stand for some of these virtues. And some public schools have a dean of discipline, whose purpose is to confront student vice, freeing teacher and principal leaders to cultivate virtue among students and other school personnel.

Figure 3 illustrates the inductive thinking that says what teacher leadership always is. Arrows point from the specifics at the periphery to the essence at the center. Managing schools involves many different functions addressing many different situations, but leading a school always involves doing the right thing, as educators model and cultivate the six virtues of the educated person.

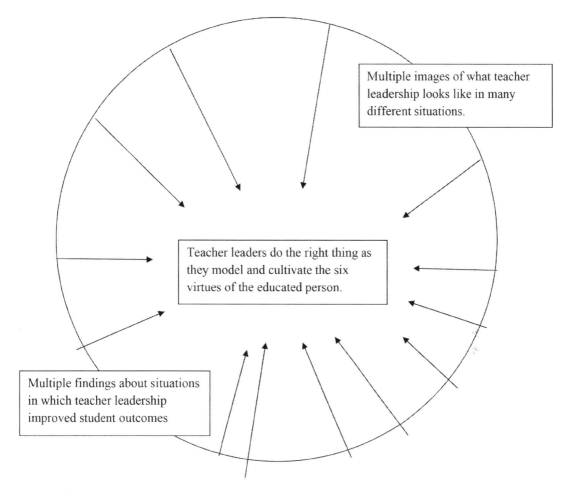

Multiple images of what teacher leadership looks like in many different situations.

Teacher leaders do the right thing as they model and cultivate the six virtues of the educated person.

Multiple findings about situations in which teacher leadership improved student outcomes

Figure 3

Old Beliefs and a New One

Figure 2 has our current beliefs in the center: (a) schools must be bureaucratically structured; (b) educational research findings are needed to describe how teacher leadership improves student outcomes. These drive our current thinking. This chapter has so far described the teacher leadership literature that reflects both beliefs. Scholars describe multiple images of teacher leadership in multiple situations, and some bemoan the bureaucratic contexts that make it unwise, or even dangerous, for teachers to lead.

Scholars, policymakers, educators, and parents have been calling for the reform and improvement of public education for a long time. Regardless of whether we believe public education needs a complete overhaul, or a little tweaking, we believe public education can be improved in many ways. The rest of this chapter explains why all of them require teacher leadership.

We start by challenging the beliefs at the center of Figure 2: (a) Must schools be bureaucratically structured?; (b) Are educational research findings needed to describe how teacher leadership improves student outcomes? These beliefs need to be challenged because they block the reform and improvement of public education.

Bureaucracy is an organizational structure built for stability, not change or improvement. Bureaucracy's stabilizing purpose is undisputed. A policymaker might believe that bureaucracy can be used for change and improvement, but organizational scholars know its fundamental purpose is stability. A stable organization is a good thing. Its very nature, however, stifles change and improvement.

The argument against this first belief is that as long as we believe schools must be bureaucratically structured, we will foster the development of the school and district hierarchies teacher leadership scholars warn against. This is already happening with the advent of math and literacy coaches, and other instructional supervisors in schools and district offices. When positions are created for teachers who do not have classrooms, and whose work is the improvement of classroom instruction and schools, the message is clear—classroom teachers are *not* the drivers of school improvement, and many of them need to be driven. The only way *not* to send this message is to replace this belief with one that says school improvement requires teacher leadership within a school community.

When people join a community, they agree to share responsibility for everything, which means all the adults in the school are responsible for doing the right thing and modeling the six virtues of the educated person. Teachers can lead and children will learn the virtues that lead to more knowledge and skills in a school that is a community, instead of a bureaucracy.

The second belief needs to be challenged because the social science improvement paradigm values the ideas of researchers outside the school more than those of the professionals inside it. Research findings inform us of the effectiveness of a method or idea, when all other things are equal. In real life, however, all other things are never equal. Therefore, we can never know if a method or idea will work in a specific school situation. (The argument against the social science improvement paradigm is explained more, and an alternative paradigm is offered by Hurley (2009) in chapter 8 of *The Six Virtues of the Educated Person*.) The point is, as long as we believe educational research findings are needed to describe how teacher leadership improves student outcomes, we will be looking in the wrong place for how to improve schools. We will be looking outside, instead of inside, the school.

Since No Child Left Behind famously legislated that teachers use "research-based" methods, the assumption that student achievement improves with the application of research findings has been strengthened. It does not matter that our 60-year experiment with educational research has not improved education. We simply believe this is how education *should* be improved. When it does not, we don't change our belief, we add another. We recently added the belief that schools have not improved because teachers don't apply research with fidelity. How many more beliefs will we add to explain why the application of research findings does not improve education?

Discarding these two current beliefs will not be easy, even though both are false. Schools do not have to be bureaucratically structured, and we don't need research findings to describe how teacher leadership improves student learning. Look at your own school and classroom experiences. Did you learn more in schools and classrooms that were bureaucratic or communitarian? Were your best teachers those who modeled and taught the six virtues, or those who applied research findings?

Beliefs are difficult to discard because they have a powerful hold on us. They are our frameworks for interpreting experience. The two beliefs we now hold are fundamental to how we think about structuring schools for improvement. We sincerely believe teachers should follow bureaucratic superiors' directives, and research findings are needed to describe how teacher leadership improves student outcomes.

But those beliefs don't hold up to scrutiny. Principals and policymakers can drive school improvement without teacher leaders, but the result will always result in failure or short-lived success. Teacher leadership is always needed for successful, long-term school improvement.

Discarding the first belief does not create an upside-down hierarchy. Instead, it creates community, where everyone is responsible for everything, including leading. Teachers work closely with students and their needs, so they share an improvement responsibility with students and parents, as well as with principals, central office administrators, policymakers, or consultants.

This is hard to imagine for those who have only taught in public schools, but the best parochial schools not only organize themselves this way, they define themselves this way. Being a community gives them their reason to exist. Community members are responsible for doing the right thing as they model and teach the six virtues of the educated person. Public schools can structure themselves as communities, too. The best ones always have.

Regarding the second belief, communitarian schools rely little on research, and more on the dedication, imagination, and talent of teachers. "Effectiveness" is not what research says it is, but what students, parents, and teachers say it is.

If we discard our current beliefs in bureaucracy and the social science improvement paradigm, nothing is lost. If we replace them with a belief in school community and a belief in teacher leadership as the way to structure a school for improvement, the results are likely to be school improvement.

Conclusion

This chapter has defined teacher leadership as doing the right thing as teachers model and teach the six virtues of the educated person. No matter what teacher leadership looks like in different schools and districts, if it does not have both the moral and aesthetic dimensions, it is not teacher leadership. It might be management of some sort, but it is not teacher leadership. With this inspiring, useful definition of teacher leadership, we have a much greater likelihood that student outcomes will improve. It all depends on the definition of teacher leadership.

On the other hand, if we insist on multiple definitions and multiple images of teachers leading in multiple situations, we will continue to wonder if teachers should lead in schools without empirical data supporting its effectiveness. And some of these situations might be hazardous to the careers of teacher leaders who step forward.

I don't care about empirical evidence, but I care if teacher leadership is suppressed because we believe schools must be bureaucratically structured and research findings are needed to describe how teacher leadership improves student outcomes. I care because neither belief is true.

Teacher leadership is a foundation of public education because it is the way schools structure themselves for improvement. That has always been true.

References

Barth, R. S. (2001). Teacher leader. *Phi Delta Kappan, 82*(6), 443–449.

Bennis, W., & Nanus, B. (1985). *Leaders: The strategies for taking charge.* New York: Harper & Row.

Cochran-Smith, M. (2002, September–October). The research base for teacher education: Metaphors we live (and die) by. *Journal of Teacher Education, 53*(4), 283–285.

Coyle, M. (1997). Teacher leadership vs. school management: Flatten the hierarchies. *The Clearing House, 70,* 236–239.

Darling-Hammond, L., Bullmaster, M. L., & Cobb, V. L. (1995). Rethinking teacher leadership through professional development schools. *Elementary School Journal, 96,* 87–106.

Hilty, E. B. (Editor). (2011). *Teacher leadership: The "New" foundations of teacher education.* New York: Peter Lang Publishing, Inc.

Hurley, J. C. (2009). *The six virtues of the educated person.* Lanham, MD: Rowman & Littlefield Education.

Katzenmeyer, M., & Moller, G. (2009). *Awakening the sleeping giant* (3rd ed.). Thousand Oaks, CA: Corwin Press.

Leadership for Student Learning: Redefining the Teacher as Leader. Institute for Educational Leadership (IEL). Retrieved on January 5, 2016, from http://iel.org/sites/default/files/Leadership-for-Student-Learning-Series-2-Teacher-04-2001.pdf

Lipham, J. A., & Hoeh, J. A. (1974). *The principalship: Foundations and functions.* New York: Harper & Row.

Schlechty, P. C. (1993). On the frontier of school reform with trailblazers, pioneers, and settlers. *Journal of Staff Development, 14*(4), 46–51.

Teacher Leadership Exploratory Consortium. (2011). Teacher Leader Model Standards. Retrieved on June 20, 2011, from http://www.teacherleaderstandards.org/downloads/TLS_Brochure.pdf

Yarger, S. J., & Lee, O. (1994). The development and sustenance of instructional leadership. In D. R. Walling (Ed.), *Teachers as Leaders: Perspectives on the professional development of teachers* (pp. 223–237). Bloomington, IN: Phi Delta Kappa Educational Foundation.

York-Barr, J., & Duke, K. (2004). What do we know about teacher leadership? Findings from two decades of scholarship. *Review of Educational Research, 74*(3), 2004, 255–316.

Leadership for Student Learning

Redefining the Teacher as Leader

Institute for Educational Leadership, Inc.

The Initiative

Of the myriad problems that have plagued American public education in recent years, few have resisted resolution more stubbornly than the complex of issues surrounding school leadership. While we sense that it is not working as well as it must, there has been no concerted national call to find out why—and to suggest how to improve it. Yet without richly qualified, dedicated, and enlightened state-of-the-art professional and political leadership, efforts to bring about genuine reform to enhance student learning are destined to suffer, possibly even to fail. Sadly, the American public and the nation's political leaders have yet to acknowledge the intrinsic seriousness of this matter.

This is the backdrop to the *School Leadership for the 21st Century Initiative*, a national effort led by the Institute for Educational Leadership (IEL) to clarify the issues of school leadership, shepherd them into the spotlight of public policy, and debate where they belong. To prod the process, the Institute created four task forces of experts, practitioners, business leaders, elected and appointed government officials, and others who met for a day and a half each in 2000 to probe one of four levels of school leadership—state, district, principal, and teacher—and examine ways to improve it as part of a massive, long-needed upgrading.

Not surprisingly, the task forces yielded differences in ideology and in how to approach the considerable dilemmas of leading public education. Had such differences not risen to the surface, the national debate about school leadership that the Initiative hopes to spark would be less spirited and robust than we expect it to be.

Introduction

No single principle of school reform is more valid or durable than the maxim that "student learning depends first, last, and always on the quality of the teachers." Experts may disagree about how highly to value the size of a class or school, how the system functions, or whether it is adequately funded—but nobody's list of education's priorities fails to place teacher quality at or very near the top.

As a front-running national concern, the issue of improving teacher quality has taken on a controversial life of its own that extends beyond the world of public education and into our political culture, where it was a spotlighted feature of the presidential campaign of 2000. On a seemingly nonstop basis, this core element of schooling in America has become an editorial staple, the rationale for countless legislative debates, and the subject of numerous books, reports, and commentaries by commissions, task forces, councils, working groups, scholars, and journalists.

Typifying this concern most recently is *Investing in Teachers*, an analytical dissection of public school teaching in early 2001 complete with a package of recommendations by the National Alliance of Business in conjunction with the U.S. Chamber of Commerce, the National Association of Manufacturers, and the Business Roundtable.

Any issue of public policy that can arouse the concern of the nation's media, politicians, scholars, and business interests—and have most of them on or near the same page—clearly demands more than just the rhetoric it usually receives.

How much good such attention is doing teachers and student learning is debatable. Indeed, a strong case can be made that its yield has been relatively modest, that, in fact, it has resulted in fewer tangible gains for teachers than those produced by the National Education Association (NEA) and the American Federation of Teachers (AFT) in helping to raise teachers' salaries and benefits, while working to stimulate the recognition and political backing that an undervalued line of work deserves.

In the early years of the new century, public school teaching still lags behind its nominal professional peers, both within and outside of public service, in public esteem. It is a dignity-challenged profession that often is more reviled than praised or even appreciated, and its members have few legitimate opportunities to defend it. It is no secret (but, rather, a national shame) that average salaries for teachers remain at or near the bottom of professional wage scales, while prospects for advancement in the conventional, career-oriented sense are all but shut off. Except through the teacher organizations, most of the profession's members normally have little or no effective representation in the key organizational, political, and pedagogical decisions that affect their jobs, their profession, and, by extension, their personal lives. These indispensable professionals to whom the nation entrusts its children daily rarely even have their own offices, computers, or telephones.

Mischaracterized though they often are as incompetent know-nothings, teachers are, paradoxically, also widely viewed as education's "franchise players," its indispensable but unappreciated leaders in the truest meaning of the word. It is unarguable that they instill, mold, and ultimately control much of the learning and intellectual development of the young people in their charge. It would be difficult to find a more authentic but unacknowledged example of leadership in modern life.

Yet we are loath as a nation to consider whether our roughly 2.78 million public school teachers should have any consequential role in schooling beyond that of closely controlled human mechanisms for funneling information into schoolchildren—and then getting out of the way. The infinite potential the nation's teachers possess for sharing their hard-earned knowledge and wisdom with players in education's decision-making circles—or even for becoming part of these circles—remains largely unexploited. There are a growing number of glittering exceptions, but they do not add up to much in American public education's universe of 46-plus million students, 15,000-odd school districts, and 100,000-plus schools. If they constitute a trend toward recognizing the teacher as leader, it is surely a slowly developing one.

Even as some of education's smartest people try to explain how the term "teacher leader" can have real meaning, their message is too often lost in the Byzantine maze of educational governance that runs our schools. The notion that classroom teachers should be part of education's policy-shaping, decision-making system—and that they may actually be able to help redefine it and their own role—is hardly new, but the record nearly a generation after the current incarnation of school reform began refutes any serious claims that this is happening on a significant or measurable basis.

Throughout their discussions, Task Force members consistently underscored two linked themes: 1) the vital role of the teacher in providing instructional leadership, especially at a time when the demands of up-to-date management, political pressure promoting tests and standards, and the near-universal obsession with across-the-board accountability are making principals more conscious of what happens in classrooms; and 2) the constantly reiterated proposition that well-prepared professional teachers are central to the decades-long push for school reform. In these pages, we will attempt to sift the evidence that emerged from the discussions of the IEL Task Force on Teacher Leadership, highlight the dilemmas that seem to surround the issue, and make the case that it is not too late for education's policymakers to exploit a potentially splendid resource for leadership and reform that is now being squandered: the experience, ideas, and capacity to lead of the nation's schoolteachers.

Teacher Leadership at Ground Level

Within the Task Force on Teacher Leadership there was strong sentiment that "the system has not been organized to treat teachers as leaders." The main paths to leadership for teachers who were interested have been 1) becoming an administrator—an obstacle-strewn route entailing added academic work, closely watched training, and tough competition for the few available slots; 2) organizing or hooking up with activist-type teacher movements (mainly in urban settings); and/or 3) becoming involved in local union affairs, thereby helping to improve conditions of work in the profession. As a group, however, the Task Force was more inclined to believe that, despite many impediments, the existing system is ripe for teacher-driven change from within—that is, for "teacher leadership" intrinsic to the role of teachers in the classroom, school, and larger policy environment.

Given a reinforcing school culture and a self-confident principal willing to experiment and to share some power, the raw potential for teachers to become a serious force in local school policy would appear to be enormous. Writing in the *Phi Delta Kappan* of February 2001, Roland Barth, a strong supporter of teachers as movers and shakers in schools, notes that, although "something deep and powerful within school cultures … seems to work against teacher leadership," there are at least ten areas, all of them having an impact on teacher-student relationships, where teacher involvement is actually essential to the health of a school:

- choosing textbooks and instructional materials;
- shaping the curriculum;
- setting standards for student behavior;
- deciding whether students are tracked into special classes;
- designing staff development and in-service programs;
- setting promotion and retention policies;
- deciding school budgets;
- evaluating teacher performance;
- selecting new teachers; and
- selecting new administrators.

To professionals in other fields, exercising responsibilities comparable to these would usually be "no brainers," mere starting points leading to the serious participation in the affairs of their organization that they had come to expect. It has long been part of the accepted wisdom in most sectors of the economy and the human services, certainly since the information age became a reality, that vertical hierarchy in organizations is giving way to horizontal information-sharing networks and collective decision-making. Rigid structures are becoming an anachronism, while organizational fluidity is taken for granted. In the human services model of 2000 (except, in most cases, education), leadership is conceived as being more transformational than transactional. And hearing all sides of an issue before setting policy and making final judgments is a fact of life, not a distant goal, as is still the case in most of public education's executive corridors.

Although the literature on the teacher as leader is thin, and some critics would argue that the products of today's teacher training institutions are not really qualified to take on more than the day-to-day responsibilities of managing a classroom full of children, contrary anecdotal evidence abounds. Across the country, teacher leaders have been making their presence felt beyond the classroom walls. These are teachers who seek and find challenge and growth. Writing almost ten years ago, Meena Wilson of the North Carolina-based Center for Collaborative Leadership, who interviewed high school teachers their peers had judged to be leaders, reported that such individuals support their colleagues, are "risk-oriented and collaborative," are often role models for students (although less so for their teacher colleagues), and are especially effective in mentoring or "peer-coaching." In the absence of valid statistical data, that is probably about where things stand in 2001.

In his *Phi Delta Kappan* article, Roland Barth states, "Few schools operate democratically." But when teachers take on leadership roles beyond the classroom their schools can become more democratic than dictatorial, and everyone benefits. The more democratic a school culture, "the more students come to believe in, practice, and sustain our democratic form of governance." In similar ways, teachers, principals, and the school itself will be strengthened in their roles. A more participatory ambiance is unlikely to materialize in settings where teachers' daily lives are overloaded with a staggering list of obligations, time is a precious commodity, and a climate of circumspection rather than creativity prevails in the school.

Teacher leadership is not about "teacher power." Rather, it is about mobilizing the still largely untapped attributes of teachers to strengthen student performance at ground level and working toward real collaboration, a locally tailored kind of shared leadership, in the daily life of the school. Teachers must be an essential part of that leadership, never more so than when issues of instructional leadership are at stake. Teacher leadership can be a big part of the answer to questions like the following:

- How can we create the "professional community" that research shows is essential to peak school and student performance?

- How can we create school environments where each student is known and treated as an individual?

- What can be done to increase the quality of teachers and enhance the professionalism of teaching and teachers?

- How can the necessary bridge be made between challenging academic standards and accountability and what goes on in the classroom?

- What can be done to ensure that state and national policies to reform education are informed by the realities of the school and classroom and to enhance the probability of successful policy/reform implementation?

Teacher leadership is no fantasy. The case is too strong that it is becoming an increasingly visible presence in our schools and that it can contribute much to improving their health and performance. But implying that the teacher as leader is poised to become a controlling force in the near future is delusional.

If there is one urgent requirement that cannot be emphasized too often as teacher leadership inevitably becomes more influential, it is that teaching must become a genuine profession rather than one still seeking public legitimacy. Without greater recognition of them as partners in making schools work better rather than as semiskilled functionaries, too many teachers are fated to remain second-class citizens in their workplace. School districts are becoming aware of these needs through reports such as Public Agenda's "Just Waiting to Be Asked?" and other sources, even if many schools, colleges, and departments of education may pay them too little attention.

There is no single path to enlightened teacher leadership, but there probably has never been a better time to examine ways to make it a positive fact of life. With 2.2 million teachers slated to leave the field in the next ten years, the American school can become a different—and better—place in the second decade of the 21st century. There is no shortage of models of teacher leadership; the job now is to choose what might suit a particular school or district and set about making it happen. Education's decision-makers must now make up their minds to do exactly this.

Clashing Images

In *Choosing Excellence*, the prize-winning veteran education journalist John Merrow describes teaching as "the noblest profession" and "the heart and soul of a school." In the same pages, though, he quotes a teacher's description of his world as "rushed, crunched, and isolated." And to this characterization, Merrow suggests, could be added "distrusted" and "undervalued."

Underscoring and expanding Merrow's observations, Stanford University's Linda Darling-Hammond, a member of the Task Force, adds, in "Educating Teachers: The Academy's Greatest Failure or Its Most Important Future?", that the ability of teachers is one of the most powerful determinants of student achievement—more influential, in fact, than poverty, race, or the educational attainment of parents. But if they are to do the job right, she points out in *The Right to Learn: A Blueprint for Creating Schools That Work*, teachers must have help in the form of "more intensive teacher training, more meaningful licensing systems, and more thoughtful professional development." In other words, the systems that support teacher development need to be much better than they are.

These comments by two thoroughly credentialed, nationally respected observers who want public education to succeed encapsulate a lot of the prevailing wisdom about teachers and their profession. Perhaps unintentionally, they also cast a shadow of doubt on the proposition that teaching is yet, in fact, a *bona fide* profession comparable in most ways to such stalwarts as, for example, medicine, law, and architecture. Even though most parents of schoolchildren (one-fifth of the population) like their children's teachers, it would be hard to find another supposedly professional field that triggers such consistent overall criticism and so many reminders of its alleged shortcomings.

Clearly, teaching lacks many of the qualities that stamp a real profession. Income, one of the more reliable determinants of professional status, still presents a discouraging picture. Data from the federal Bureau of Labor Statistics and other sources put elementary and secondary school teachers in roughly the same wage bracket as telephone installers, nurses, and mail carriers, below that of police officers, detectives, and firefighters, and, when employee benefits are factored in, at a level of income comparable to that of senior noncommissioned or lower-level commissioned officers in the military services (who, however, have the option of retiring in their upper thirties or low forties with 20 years of service and of going on to second careers).

The debate over whether teaching is a legitimate, full-fledged profession whose members can or should be part of public education's leadership ranks evokes mixed responses. Vocal support for their inclusion, especially by the NEA and AFT, is generally strong though too often as a generality rather than as a reality. But those who doubt that teachers belong in the councils of leadership have a bulging arsenal of arguments such as the menial indignities of much of the work, the lack of independence, the still-inadequate reward system, and the possibility that teacher leadership might actually mean union control. Indeed, many of the hard realities of public school teaching tend to undercut the satisfying features of a career in the classroom. Some of the demeaning facts of the teacher's work life are so routinely accepted as natural features of the job that they are usually not even discussed when teacher issues appear on the agendas of school boards, editorial meetings, or campaign platforms. But they remain sizable burrs under the saddle of a line of work that strives for professionalism while tolerating practices that few, if any, professions would countenance.

Examples of how seriously the American teacher is being "rushed, crunched, and isolated"—and generally disrespected—pervade the field. With some exceptions, the very nature of today's schools militates against innovation, much less relatively free expression or professional "leadership" by anyone other than statutory supervisors. Teaching is a "flat" career lived out in jobs and schools that Vivian Troen and Katherine C. Boles described in *Teacher Magazine* as "legacies of their 19th-century industrial-style origins, with principals viewed as bosses and teachers as replaceable workers on an assembly line. This history has bred a school culture of isolation and egalitarianism that effectively stymies all attempts at reform." This is not the stuff of leadership-in-waiting.

The teacher who may lack the healthy self-respect that sustained encounters with energetic young people demand is destined to be additionally frustrated by the strictures that too often epitomize daily life at work. Disillusioned by daily, even hourly, indignities such as ceaseless interruptions by public address announcements, being ordered to "teach to the test," and a legion of others, 30 percent of all new teachers now last less than five years, while half of those in urban schools are gone within three. They see little hope of gaining the respect and relative autonomy that a true professional usually expects. And some, routinely assigned as new teachers often are to a district's worst schools, leave during or at the end of their first year—frustrated, disillusioned, and often self-doubting. Teaching is no longer a lifetime career. And that weakens it—immeasurably.

At the day-to-day level, the career itself has always had deflating qualities. To succeed within it, teachers in many systems have traditionally needed only to do enough to get by and, if ambitious, take off-duty courses in almost any field, even irrelevant ones, in order to ensure relatively regular pay hikes and occasional bonuses within a carefully calibrated salary schedule. As in most taxpayer-supported endeavors, it is not easy to fire anyone for inadequate performance. In most settings, little or no credibility is given to the experience-based judgments or opinions of teachers. To do their jobs right, responsible teachers in many systems lay out as much as $1,000 annually for essential equipment and learning materials that budget-conscious school officials decline to provide.

As for the "shared decision-making" that, in one form or another, typifies the workplace in many professions, one teacher summarized his and his peers' reaction to how it works in education with the pithy observation that "as soon as they make a decision, they share it with us."

But for every, or nearly every, shortcoming in the vastness of teaching there is usually a mitigating plus or at least a plausible cause or explanation. If they don't step forward to challenge existing leadership or harbor ambitions of their own beyond the classroom, many teachers contend, it is because they prepared and signed on to work directly with schoolchildren, not bureaucrats. Whatever the ambiance in the school may be, this is what they are most satisfied doing. Although most appointed school officials began as teachers, numerous studies indicate that teachers generally have little interest in succeeding them; they have found the niche in the classroom where, depsite agonizing and demanding days that can sometimes seem like weeks, the satisfactions can be genuine and personal.

This is not to imply that teachers do not value recognition. They do. Rewards such as cash bonuses, awards, and various kinds of incentive grants are always welcome. But they are not always enough. Teachers are the core professional resource in every school in the nation, and they must be involved wherever possible in policies and decisions affecting how that resource is deployed. Such participation is a practical application of what Richard Elmore of Harvard calls "distributive leadership."

Some researchers have made the case that, as a matter of personal choice rooted in their own personalities and value systems, teachers crave neither the limelight of public attention nor the responsibilities and headaches of leadership of any kind outside their classroom fiefs. Most have not attended prestigious, high-pressure colleges and universities where competition and careerism may be campus-wide preoccupations. But any stereotype of today's teacher as what the education writer Harriet Tyson, in *Who Will Teach the Children?*, calls "the noble, literature-loving spinster of earlier eras" also has no validity today. John Goodlad, one of the most esteemed oracles of public education, contends that, contrary to popular impressions, education is actually attracting idealistic, bright, and able people who are "alert to the stupidity of much of the simplistic reforms that are being proposed, which they know won't work. Their bosses don't want bright people around who are going to resist when they impose things on them. So the schools lose the best, and who can blame them for leaving?" (Merrow 2001).

These clashing images of our nearly three million teachers do not seem at first glance to leave much room or hope for them to take on a conspicuous role in school leadership, especially in an ambiance of high-stakes testing and the ever-increasing politicization of education. To buy into this perspective is to underrate a huge and diverse population of caring Americans. Some of the very characteristics that shape informed leadership are exactly what our teachers possess—in abundance.

Rationales and Roadblocks

Beleaguered Bosses

As it is presently constituted, educational leadership needs all the help it can get. Whether at the level of the school building, district, or state, today's education leaders have few admirers, many skeptics, and a lot of tough critics. Media commentators, both print and electronic, as well as reformers of various ideological leanings, dismiss them all too glibly as comprising an obstructive "establishment," while others simply label public education's front offices and its inhabitants "the blob." Whatever it is called, and whether or not it is performing well, this guiding force in America's schools, its leadership, no longer enjoys the necessary trust of much of the larger population.

Since the principals, district leaders, and school board members who are the subjects of this criticism are reluctant to fight back in public, even though most of the negative judgments of them are unwarranted, the idea that existing forms of school leadership are failing us has gained traction. And it goes beyond that. With some signal exceptions, incumbents are often savagely labeled by the media, in particular, as (pick one or a combination) unimaginative, dictatorial, risk-averse, imperious, regulation-addicted, initiative-squashing, power-hungry, anti-intellectual, time-serving bureaucrats wedded to a past that modern leadership doctrine outgrew decades ago. These charges are bandied about with little regard for the real-world problems that plague education's top brass. They are mostly wrong, and they hurt. They also complicate efforts to bring teachers into leadership roles.

Democracy Sidelined

As the discussions of the Task Force on Teacher Leadership proceeded, it was clear to this representative group of educators and concerned lay leaders that they were confronting a concept—the teacher as a vital part of the policy-framing and governing processes—that may have been around for a long time but which has somehow never loomed large in the nation's school systems. Given the problems that teachers are experiencing at the turn of the century and the popular impression that they need badly to take care of their own house, it is perhaps understandable that becoming part of the structure of leadership at this time is a back-burner issue. It deserves better.

As long as school leadership remains mostly top-down and hierarchical, there is little chance that teachers will ever be more than fringe players—available as a resource when called upon, but seldom directly and continuously involved in decisions of substance. School district leaders often trot out the buzzword of teacher leadership as an established reality in their domains, but, Troen and Boles contend, touting participation by teachers in routine matters in the school rather than just in their classrooms is "somewhat like calling a banana republic a democracy if a few of its citizens are allowed to vote." Authoritarian governance styles may have fallen out of favor in most sectors of society since these words were written in 1993, but what appears to have replaced them is sometimes neither better nor appreciably more democratic, notably in the schools.

As leadership in business, technology, various professions, and public institutions has become more participatory and representative over the past 30 years, education has also taken to boasting of the inclusion of teachers, its lowest-ranking professionals, in its policy-creation and management processes. But the level of inclusion ordinarily does not deserve to be bragged about. True, classroom teachers in many schools are at least tangentially involved in their principals' and district leaders' concerns about curriculum, supplies, discipline, testing and standards, student and family problems in the school, and a few other classroom-specific concerns. In addition, some schools promote at least a veneer of participation though principal-led "leadership councils" or their equivalents. And most principals, especially those in middle and high schools, ask classroom teachers to take on the posts of department chairs, team and grade leaders, heads of curriculum committees, and others—often with extra pay and/or slightly reduced teaching schedules.

The greater likelihood, though, is that the teacher's role in school leadership is still limited to what goes on in or directly affects the classroom: how to teach creatively within narrow curricular specifications, how to organize class time, how to assess progress, how to deal with troubled children and their families. The expertise and good judgment of classroom teachers in all of these matters patently strengthen a school's capabilities, but they do not constitute leadership as it should be defined—or, in the case of teachers, redefined.

What Teachers Can Contribute

Teachers offer something beyond expertise. But at a time when nearly all of public education is in the grip of the rush to politically mandated tests, standards, and accountability, they may be under heavier pressure than they have ever known. The special qualities that the excellent ones possess—knowledge of children and subject matter, empathy, dedication, technique, sensitivity to communities and families, readiness to help, team spirit, ability to communicate, and many more—should be in even greater demand than ever.

These attributes also are an essential side of school leadership. But in the realm of school wide policy as distinguished from what happens in the classroom, the unique voice of teachers is too seldom heard or their views even solicited. Addressing this point, *The Metropolitan Life Survey of the American Teacher, 2000: Are We Preparing Students for the 21st Century?* found that many secondary school faculty members felt alienated, that substantial numbers felt "left out of things going on around them at their school" or that "what they think doesn't count very much at their school." It is readily apparent that, except in unusual cases, the basic decisions that affect the work lives of teachers, as well as the performance of their students, come from on high, from top-down leadership in its most pristine form. In most settings, teachers have little or no say in scheduling, class placement, how specialists are assigned, decisions on hiring new teachers, and, perhaps most telling at ground level, the preparation of budgets and materials. This is not the stuff of professionalism.

How They Are Prepared

Today's teachers are coming into the job market as the unevenly prepared products of some 1,300 schools and colleges of education that have historically constituted a largely change-resistant system. Reports about the escalating number of teacher preparation institutions that are breaking with tradition are refreshing, but they are still exceptions in a carefully preserved corner of academe that abhors revolutionaries, discourages mavericks, and is not too comfortable with mild dissenters. Organizations such as the revitalized National Council for Accreditation of Teacher Education (NCATE) have their hands full trying to help transform these institutions into the modern, first-class learning centers they must become if our teachers are to resist a beckoning slide into mediocrity.

The professionalism (and the beginnings of a consciousness about the teacher as leader) that should be a core feature of teacher training is not easily acquired in these settings. Though most teacher-training institutions claim to be making their curricula more responsive (and several hundred appear to be succeeding), many parent universities have few qualms about treating them as what John Merrow describes as "cash cows," that is, revenue-suppliers for other parts of the university where expenses are higher, such as programs in law, medicine, engineering, and nursing. Linda Darling-Hammond adds, "If you are preparing to be a teacher, you can expect about half of the tuition money that you put into the till to come back to support your preparation." This is training on the cheap, and it carries no guarantees of success.

While a heavy concentration on classroom teaching methods (to the detriment of substantive academic subjects) often appears to be the *raison d'être* of teacher training faculties, more institutions need to think about exposing future teachers to discussions of the larger policy issues of education. Although a growing number of institutions have made progress in this area, too many new teachers still report for duty largely uninformed in the essentials of the professional, cultural, and political worlds they are to inhabit—and what they do know they have often acquired on their own. There is a growing and encouraging realization that teachers need practical knowledge about contemporary family life, immigrant and minority group children, and the political and social currents that swirl about public education. However, too few teacher training institutions offer courses that treat these subjects in sufficient depth, and practically none below the graduate level scratch the surface of training in management and leadership.

On-the-Job Frustrations

Teacher training is not the only obstacle. Once hired and in the pipeline, young teachers often find that what they have learned in their four or more years of preparation has not equipped them for what they may encounter in their new classrooms. In a few districts, although hardly the norm, there are horror stories: freshly minted teachers assigned to instruct high schoolers in out-of-subject content areas, decaying and unsafe buildings, students with daunting family problems, neighborhoods with scarcely controllable violence, facilities comparable in some grotesque cases to those in their cities' jails. Newcomers come to realize all too soon that their education professors were either poorly informed about the downsides of teaching or that they simply didn't bother to share their knowledge and perspectives. More than they ever would have anticipated, new teachers too often enter a world in which administrative orthodoxies repeatedly combine with indifference in confronting often overwhelming problems. Rocking these boats is all but impossible when personal survival becomes the newcomer's mantra.

As policy analyst Denis Doyle observed in the March 2001 issue of *The School Administrator,* modern workers are "self-guiding problem solvers and troubleshooters. No longer … is passivity valued. To the contrary, independence and initiative are." Except, he might have added, in a huge swath of the country's classrooms where "go along to get along," a favorite slogan of Sam Rayburn, a longtime Speaker of the U.S. House of Representatives, normally sets the mood and tempo. This may have been the path to political success in a bygone era, but it is no prescription for school leadership or reform—or even a miniscule role in them—in the 21st century.

Unions and Teacher Leadership

A frequently cited barrier to grass roots teacher leadership is the supposedly pervasive, even controlling, role of the National Education Association and the American Federation of Teachers in the work lives of the nation's teachers. This description may apply in some districts and political settings where union functionaries may appear to rule the roost, but it distorts reality. Although the literature on the teacher as leader usually downplays the teacher organizations and the mass media are seldom kind to them, the inescapable fact is that most of the tangible gains teachers achieved in the second half of the 20th century would not have materialized without union activism and leadership. Many critics and analysts conveniently forget that the relatively decent salaries teachers now receive (decent, that is, compared to what they might be earning without successful union-led negotiations), their employee benefits packages, and their success in lobbying in Washington, state capitals, and local districts for increased funding for education owe much to union leadership. All have had a positive impact on how teachers are treated and perceived. They also strengthen the potential of teachers as leaders.

The commonly heard accusation that the unions have been so focused on bread-and-butter concerns that they have shown little interest in educational content is also mostly spurious. Admittedly, there are periods when strikes and other political-type concerns are dominant and professional matters must take a back seat—way back, sometimes. And members do have legitimate complaints about the overly bureaucratic style and operational methods of some union headquarters. But the long-run effect of the unions' presence has been to elevate the professional stature and self-regard of teachers, and this can only be positive. If further proof were needed, it came in a study revealing that states with a higher percentage of teachers represented by unions tended to report higher SAT and ACT schools than those with less representation. Based on their research as summarized in the Winter 2000 issue of the *Harvard Educational Review*, the three coauthors of the study (Steelman, Powell and Carini) said, "That we found such a strongly consistent positive relationship across so many permutations of analysis should give pause to those who characterize teacher unions as adversaries to educational success and accountability."

The Push for Professionalism

Happily, the quest for professionalism and the stature that goes with it—without which the idea of the teacher as leader would be a far-off dream instead of an achievable reality—finally appears to be gaining serious momentum. There are now countless examples scattered around the country, many of them in the form of intensified but greatly broadened teacher training programs, of institutions where visionary educators simply refuse to kowtow to established ways of doing things. Many are altering the balance between method and substance in preparing teachers. They are strengthening their content preparation as well as preparation for content pedagogy, curriculum development, and assessment. Several hundred of these programs blend undergraduate and graduate programs into five-year regimens from which the student gains two degrees while experiencing protracted involvement in school life far beyond the minimal opportunities that conventional practice teaching affords. Others offer teaching internships, often in a growing number of professional development schools, that provide sustained exposure while enabling the candidates as individuals and in teams to decide whether teaching really is their best career option. Promising though these examples of progress may be, they are still a minority in the 1,300-institution domain of teacher preparation. Less dramatic but likely to be equally effective in the long run, notably in helping to pave the way to teacher leadership, are broader kinds of influences such as these:

The National Commission on Teaching & America's Future

The 1996 report of the prestigious National Commission on Teaching & America's Future (NCTAF) called for no less than a thorough revamping and restructuring of the teaching profession, which, it declared, had suffered from decades of neglect. Likening itself to the Flexner Report of 1910, which led to the transformation of the medical profession, the Commission's report, *What Matters Most: Teaching for America's Future*, provided a detailed blueprint for recruiting, preparing, supporting, and rewarding excellent educators. Such terms as "overhaul," "reinvent," and "call to action" dot this historic report, which lays out a detailed agenda for restructuring the world of the American teacher. Unlike so many "blue ribbon" commissions, the NCTAF has also been able to monitor progress and to assist 20 states and nine school district partners in reaching its goals.

The NCATE Effect

In a quietly effective fashion, and with the backing of numerous education organizations, the reform-minded National Council for Accreditation of Teacher Education (NCATE) has helped get all but a few states to raise the standards bar for classroom teachers. Working with state agencies and teacher training institutions, NCATE is leading the way in insuring that colleges have a content-oriented system in place to facilitate assessment and that state licensing requirements are aligned with accreditation standards—a tough, thankless task destined to generate few headlines. Participation in the State/NCATE Partnership Program vaulted from 19 states in 1990 to 46 in 2001—proof that at the least, as the National Conference of State Legislatures asserted, NCATE "is a cost-effective means to upgrade teacher preparation in the states." In practice, it is much more. Though probably not yet fully quantifiable, the effects of these NCATE-guided steps toward accountability and measures to upgrade the profession are almost certainly being felt across the country in the early years of the new century. They exemplify education reform in action in a manner that should benefit both the quality of the teaching enterprise and the institutional and governmental infrastructure that supports it.

National Board Certification

The respected National Board for Professional Teaching Standards (NBPTS) epitomizes the ideal of the high-quality American teacher. Established at the recommendation of *A Nation Prepared: Teachers for the 21st Century* of 1986, a product of the Carnegie Foundation's Task Force on Teaching as a Profession, the NBPTS has established nationally applicable qualifications and procedures for certifying teachers that may be the most rigorous yet sensible of recent times. Those who survive a lengthy, costly, and demanding process are widely recognized as embodying all the attributes of topflight professional teachers. The roughly 10,000 who have successfully completed the NBPTS regimen (4,727 of them in 2000—the admittedly slow pace has been quickening) achieve almost instant recognition, usually receive tangible rewards such increased pay and advisory roles, and inevitably become role models for their colleagues.

Alternative Certification

Alternative certification, that is, credentials awarded teacher candidates who have not spent four or five years training to become teachers, has beckoned for over three decades to diverse groups and individuals. It has taken different forms and exposed public education to different breeds of aspiring teachers. Frowned upon by many mainstream educators and institutions, alternative certification nevertheless does represent something new and possibly invigorating in the field. The National Commission on Teaching & America's Future recognized that the aggressive policies needed to put a qualified teacher in every classroom include developing different approaches to preparation including alternative pathways to teaching for mid-career professionals, college graduates with no teaching certification, and paraprofessionals.

Although they are numerically miniscule in terms of the numbers of teachers prepared, alternative certification programs have been around, in one version or another, since at least the mid-1960s. The possibility exists that some of them may over time embody a different, more venturesome style of leadership than that which the products of conventional teacher training generally provide.

As a rule, the backgrounds of these nontraditional teachers reveal more diversity than is found in the teaching force in most typical schools. When Teacher Corps, the Johnson Administration's then-revolutionary program to prepare young people to serve in urban districts, began in 1965, it drew recent Peace Corps volunteers, liberal arts majors already working in non-teaching jobs, professionals from other fields, and a broad mix of public service-oriented young people. These roughly 3,500 feisty recruits survived an obstacle course that combined low-paying two-year internships in inner-city classrooms, "volunteer" work in low-income communities, and course work in schools of education—all of which usually led to a legitimate graduate degree and certification. The national Teacher Corps effort cost the federal government roughly $500 million from 1965 to 1981. It produced a lot of committed leaders for education, especially teachers (and future leaders) from minority groups.

Subsequent "alternative" programs have dotted education's landscape in 40 states. By 2000, according to the American Association of Colleges for Teacher Education, as many as half of the group's member institutions offered at least one alternate route, and *Education Week* and the Pew Charitable Trust's *Quality Counts 2000* estimated that 80,000 people had been licensed in nontraditional ways, 8,000 of them in New Jersey alone. Teach For America, a heavily publicized 12-year-old program to place liberal arts graduates of elite colleges and universities in inner city classrooms for two years before they start their "permanent" careers in other fields, now has 4,000 alumni. Although critics cite the lack of adequate preparation for the program's graduates, it has been claimed that more than half of TFA teachers have stayed in public education, where many of them are well regarded. Some who have left the classroom have gone into administrative posts, several have become charter school founders, and one, Sara Mosle, has been an outstanding writer for the *The New York Times Magazine* and *The New Yorker*, mostly on education, as well as a mentor of inner city children after leaving teaching.

Though statistically insignificant in the nearly three million-person behemoth that is America's teaching force, these and other unconventional programs now include former military officers, business people, police officers, government employees, and professionals from other sectors. Many were successful but "unfulfilled" in their previous careers and bring "leadership personalities" to the school. Others, such as those in paraprofessional career ladder programs that eventually lead upward to teaching posts in urban areas, come at teaching from a different job perspective, that of classroom aide. Often sponsored by the American Federation of Teachers, these "para-educators" usually live near the schools in which they work, know how their students live and what they endure daily, and, quite often, are also seasoned advocates and activists. This brand of leadership is not always welcome in the schools, but it surely helps keep policy-framers' feet to the fire.

Business Speaks Up

In *Investing in Teaching*, the 2001 report calling for "a renaissance in teaching," the National Alliance of Business and three of the most potent national organizations representing both large corporations and small business focused heavily on "an agenda that will elevate teaching to a profession" through improved preparation and professional development, NBPTS certification, higher pay, and, among others, access to job-related opportunities for growth such as mentorships, peer assessors, and possibilities of becoming adjunct university faculty members. With the understandable exception of its emphasis on readying students for success in the workplace (and then for higher education and life, in that order), *Investing in Teaching* could have been issued by a coalition of distinguished educators and policy-makers rather than business leaders.

The simple fact that a coalition of powerful business groups produced a thoughtful and constructive document in 2001 on teaching in America underscores the critical importance of the subject. The form and direction of the sponsors' follow-up will merit close watching. Exercised properly, the clout of such giants as the U.S. Chamber of Commerce, the Business Roundtable, and National Association of Manufacturers behind this NAB product could be enormously helpful in promoting and nurturing teacher leadership.

Material Rewards

The salary structure for teachers has historically been a disincentive for young people to enter the field. In the booming economy of the 1990s and early 2000s, in particular, the urge to teach has been squelched to an unknown degree by the explosive growth of salaries for young college graduates almost everywhere else in society. While teacher salaries are rising, they still do not suffice, as Public Agenda pointed out in 2000 in *A Sense of Calling*, which found that three-fourths of a cross-section of teachers it polled agreed "strongly" or "somewhat" that they are underpaid. But change is in the air. In early 2001, *Education Week* reported that at least 39 governors and legislators in 28 states from Alabama to Washington were making pay raises for teachers a high priority. Reflecting the mood of the times, their proposals were usually made in one or a combination of three forms: across-the-board raises, performance-pay plans, and cash bonuses.

Tying wage increases directly to teacher leadership, NEA President Bob Chase said, "we need to look at how we induct people into the profession and let them be part of the decision-making process in schools." Decision-makers or not, many teachers still double as late shift and weekend waiters and waitresses, bartenders, supermarket and department store cashiers, and sales clerks. There is a long way to go, even in places such as affluent Montgomery County, Maryland, where starting salaries for teachers are rising to $38,683 annually, but where most of the system's teachers still cannot afford to own houses. This jurisdiction had ten applicants for every vacancy in 2000, while the less prosperous neighboring Prince George's County was still scrambling to fill vacancies even after the 2000–2001 school year began. Selfless though many teachers may be, money and agreeable working conditions still matter very much.

Taking Ownership

As the nation comes to recognize the need to involve teachers more directly in shaping policy and contributing their knowledge and perceptions to decision-making processes, it is clear that concerned groups must do their part (and more) to make this happen. Situated as they are on the lowest rungs of education's professional hierarchy, teachers need a lot of help if their voices are to be heard and heeded. Therefore, to a large degree it is up to players and groups such as these to pitch in:

Teachers: Across the country, teachers are fully aware of the larger demands of school reform, and most are looking for ways to do their job better. Part of the quest for improvement must come from within. As one Task Force member indelicately put it, "Get in the game." Leadership is not handed out like blue books for a college examination. It is largely up to teachers themselves to locate and exploit opportunities for the professional growth and personal development that will increase their qualifications and credibility for leadership. Teaching is admittedly an exhausting, demanding job and a huge time-devourer, but people in many other professional fields are under similarly ferocious pressure. Yet they somehow manage to get published, to take on advocacy roles, to volunteer time and expertise, and otherwise improve themselves, their profession, and, most important, the products they may be developing, serving, or processing.

School Districts: Of the multitude of services school districts can provide or support to better the performance of teachers (and therefore of their students), none quite matches that of resources—pertinent, up-to-date materials for schools, for classrooms, for students, and, too often lost in the shuffle, for teachers themselves. Resources include increased pay (where clearly and fairly merited) as a district-wide priority, adequate allowances for otherwise unprovided classroom materials, and, of special significance, advanced training that bears on the teacher's job. Too many districts are content to support (at least partially) offerings for "advanced" training that have no realistic connection to the needs and responsibilities of the teacher but that represent a bureaucratic step toward salary hikes and improved status. With occasional exceptions, school systems assign a low priority to in-service training, which too often consists of a couple of days off during the school year and a few days of "planning" in late August or early September. No career field pays less attention to enhancing the qualifications of its professionals or their development than does public education.

Teacher Unions: Solidarity is important, but achieving it within unions should not mean discouraging members from launching independent initiatives to help improve school performance (or that of teachers). Too, unions have been asserting a more active presence in matters affecting instruction and school-wide matters rather than limiting themselves to the bread-and-butter issues that have traditionally been their bailiwick. Local union leaders, in particular, should explore specific ways to capitalize on the still largely untapped strengths of their members, especially those whose specialized knowledge could contribute to developing more competent and enlightened school leadership in the instructional realm.

Higher Education: As described earlier, NCATE, the National Board for Professional Teaching Standards, and the National Commission on Teaching & America's Future, among others, are doing much to professionalize teaching. But most of higher education, specifically the huge majority of mostly prosperous colleges and departments that do not consider themselves to be trainers of future public school teachers, is notably absent from any aspect of school reform. This may be a tired issue, but that does not mean that it should not be addressed. It may take political pressure on state legislatures or trustees, but at least some of the seemingly limitless intellectual and physical resources of the nation's great universities should be used to help fulfill the academy's implicit civic obligation to play a strong role in such obvious areas as development, leadership training, and instructional content.

Business Organizations: Thousands of corporations and business leaders, as well as the national and local organizations that represent their interests, have long been directly involved in trying to make schools more productive and efficient. Their support is becoming, on the whole, a welcome ingredient in contemporary school reform, especially in promoting achievable academic standards, different kinds of evaluation, and maximum feasible accountability—and, equally important, in aligning all three. Although corporate experience in these areas does not always transfer easily to public institutions, the business community should promote its basic premises and be prepared to offer a helping hand. At the same time, businesses that have developed (and applied) systems of shared responsibility in management should come forward to share their experience with school systems.

Mass Media: Both the print and electronic media have been ambivalent in their treatment of teachers. Locally-based media often run positive stories about the achievements of innovative teachers, while the national media tend to be critical of the performance of the profession as a whole. With rare exceptions, however, neither has paid much attention to the enhanced role that teachers can and logically should play as part of a school or district's policy apparatus. Yet large and middle-size school systems have media relations specialists whose job is to provide timely and accurate information on such topics. (Smaller systems do not customarily have the resources to employ public relations specialists, but the need there is ordinarily not as great. Teachers in small districts tend to get more respect, and they are often more involved in deliberations of policy issues.) There are countless ways to draw attention to the leadership potential of teachers, and public relations professionals should be able to help build a public climate sympathetic to the idea.

Leadership in Your Own Backyard

Leadership in public education is a matter of guiding a community to realize its potential to do the best job it can for its children. There are many priorities but only limited resources with which to succeed. And no action can really succeed without consensus for a focused, shared vision of what must be done. IEL encourages you to:

- *Gain consensus* on and backing for your community's vision and goals for its schools. If held strongly enough, they will help guide the community in a constructive fashion, especially when the issues become complicated and controversial, and the going gets rough.

- *Involve* representatives from as many different sectors as possible—education, government, business from both the "old" and "new" economies, the communications media, and others.

- *Do your homework* by collecting as much data and information as possible about teacher leadership issues in your community—challenges, opportunities, previous performance, the goals you have set, and the situation in communities with characteristics generally similar to yours.

- *Examine teacher leadership issues* within the broader framework of the community's shared education goals. Analyze your teacher leadership structures with a view to improving them if they appear to fall short.

- *Discuss and debate* the particular teacher leadership challenges, opportunities and options for action described in this report, using your community's shared education goals as the framework.

- *Plan* specific teacher leadership actions that will work for your community, so that your friends and neighbors are aware of the significance of school leadership issues.

Many of these actions are basically political, and leaders must engage the general public in this work. Taxpayers want good schools and generally agree that this will require investment. But most people have little or no understanding of the importance of teacher leadership. This means you will need to start building public awareness for the concept and support for options and approaches such as those described in this report.

Suggested Questions

To provide a starting point for discussion in your community, this report provides a number of questions that you might want to examine. Expect that differences of opinion and temporary impasses will surface in your discussions, just as they did in the task force meeting. Maintaining focus on group goals and respecting all participant perspectives will keep your discussions on track.

Recruiting Quality Teachers for Our Schools

- Are we facing a shortage of qualified, motivated teachers in our community?

- What kind of teacher turnover rate does our community have? What reasons do teachers give for leaving the profession?

- Do teachers in our community feel isolated and alienated or do they feel their input is valued in school decisions?

- Are the teacher salaries in our community competitive? Are the schools clean, safe, and well maintained?

- What recruitment efforts are in place to ensure an adequate supply of qualified and effective teacher-leaders?

- Do teacher demographics in our community mirror the demographics of the student body? If not, how can we support more representative recruitment practices?

- From what sources do we recruit our teachers? Are we satisfied with the results?

- Does our community recruit teachers from alternative preparation programs?

Supporting Quality Teachers

- Are new teachers in our schools provided instructional support, technical resources, and mentoring? What about a community orientation and assistance finding affordable housing?

- Do teachers in our community have frequent and meaningful opportunities for peer networking and collaboration? Do our schools encourage action research and the sharing of effective instructional approaches?

- Do the preparation and professional development our teachers receive expose them to policy issues, management and leadership skills, and the pedagogic implications of demographics, politics, and cultures?

- Are there adequate numbers of substitute teachers and other incentives for teachers to participate in professional development activities outside the school building?

- Are the roles of teachers differentiated?

- Is teaching in our community a "flat" career or is there a ladder for professional advancement?

Ensuring Leadership Opportunities for Teachers

- What opportunities for teacher leadership do our schools and our district support?

- Which unions or groups, if any, represent our teachers in salary discussions? Are they open to examining a greater leadership role for teachers?

- Are skilled teachers positioned to provide instructional leadership?

- Are teachers in our community actively involved in designing curricula and selecting textbooks and instructional materials?

- Are teachers actively involved in professional development activities such as developing and presenting in-service training, mentoring, peer coaching and the like?

- Do teachers have meaningful input into the school budget process? Do teachers in our community supplement the school budget from their own pockets?

- Do teachers have active roles in selecting and evaluating administrators and teachers in our community?

- Are teachers actively involved in setting school and district policy for student behavior, promotion, retention, and discipline?

Evaluating and Recognizing Quality Teachers

- Does our community or school district have professional standards for teachers? How do they relate to student performance standards?

- Are our community's teachers evaluated on a regular basis? How do these evaluations provide teachers with the information they need to grow professionally?

- How are accountability measures applied to teachers? Are principals, teachers, and students provided with the resources and supports needed to meet rigorous accountability measures?

- What incentives are built into our teacher evaluation and accountability systems to encourage lifelong learning and to recognize teacher leaders for their contributions and accomplishments?

Ensuring Community Support for Quality Teachers and Teacher-Leaders

- How can we promote better public understanding of teacher leadership roles?

- What community members, resources, and organizations are potential partners in supporting quality teachers and teacher-leaders?

- How do we communicate with the community and our stakeholders? How can we improve our communications strategies?

- Do we have a strong, positive relationship with the media serving our community?

References

Abrams, D. (2001, February 21). Hiring teachers gets trickier for other counties. *Montgomery County Gazette.* Available at http://www.gazette.net/search/

Barth, R. S. (2001, February). Teacher leader. *Phi Delta Kappan 82*(4).

Blair, J. (2001, February 2). Lawmakers plunge into teacher pay. *Education Week.* Available at http://www. edweek.org/ed-search.cfm

Bradley, A. (2000, April). Presto, change-o. *Teacher Magazine.* Available at http://www.edweek.org/edsearch.cfm

Darling-Hammond, L. (1999, January-February). Educating teachers: The Academy's greatest failure or its most important future? *Academe 85,* (1).

Darling-Hammond, L. (1997). *The right to learn: A blueprint for creating schools that work.* San Francisco, CA: Jossey-Bass.

Darling-Hammond, L. & Loewenberg Ball, D. (1998). *Teaching for high standards: What policy-makers need to know and be able to do.* Philadelphia, PA: National Commission on Teaching & America's Future and Consortium for Policy Research in Education.

Doyle, D. (2001, March). A liberal education. *The School Administrator.* Arlington, VA: American Association of School Administrators. Available at http://www.aasa.org/publications/sa/2001_03/doyle.htm

Education Week & Pew Charitable Trust. (2000). *Quality counts 2000: Who should teach?* Bethesda, MD: Education Week. Available at http://www.edweek.org/sreports/qc00/

Elmore, R. F. (2000). *Building a new structure for school leadership.* Washington, DC: Albert Shanker Institute.

Farkas, S., Foley, P. & Duffett, A. with Foleno, T. & Johnson, J. (2001). *Just waiting to be asked? A fresh look at attitudes on public engagement.* New York, NY: Public Agenda. Available at http://www.publicagenda.org/specials/pubengage/pubengage.htm

Farkas, S., Johnson, J. & Foleno, T. with Duffett, A. & Foley, P. (2000). *A sense of calling: Who teaches and why.* New York, NY: Public Agenda. Available at http://www.publicagenda.org/aboutpa/aboutpa7.htm

Koppich, J. E. (2001). *Investing in teaching.* Washington, DC: National Alliance of Business.

Merrow, J. (2001). *Choosing excellence.* Lanham, MD: Scarecrow.

Metropolitan Life Foundation. (2000). *The Metropolitan Life survey of the American teacher, 2000: Are we preparing students for the 21st century?* New York, NY: Metropolitan Life Insurance Co. Available at http://www.metlife.com/Companyinfo/Community/Found/Docs/2000pdf.html

Milken, L. (2000). *Teaching as the opportunity: The Teacher Advancement Program.* Santa Monica, CA: Milken Family Foundation. Available at http://www.mff.org/publications/publications.taf

National Commission on Teaching & America's Future. (1996). *What matters most: Teaching for America's future.* New York, NY: Author. Available at http://www.nctaf.org/publications/whatmattersmost.html

Perez-Rivas, M. (2001, March 26). Teachers moving beyond paychecks. *The Washington Post.* Available at http://www.washingtonpost.com

Steelman, L. C., Powell, B. & Carini, R. M. (2000, Winter). Do teacher unions hinder educational performance? Lessons learned from state SAT and ACT scores. *Harvard Educational Review, 70*(4).

Task Force on Teaching as a Profession. (1986). *A nation prepared: Teachers for the 21st century.* New York, NY: The Carnegie Foundation.

Terry, P. M. (1999–2000). Empowering teachers as leaders. *National Forum of Teacher Education Journal 10E,* 3. Lake Charles, LA: National Forum Journals. Available at http://www.nationalforum.com/TERRYte8e3.html

Troen, V. & Boles, K. C. (1993, November 3). Teacher leadership: How to make it more than a catch phrase. *Teacher Magazine.* Available at http://www.edweek.org/edsearch.cfm

Tyson, H. (1993). *Who will teach the children?* San Francisco, CA: Jossey-Bass.

Urbanski, A. & Erskine, R. (2000, January). School reform, TURN, and teacher compensation. *Phi Delta Kappan 81,* 5. Available at http://www.pdkintl.org/kappan/kurb0001.htm

Wilson, M. (1993, March). The search for teacher leaders. *Educational Leadership, 50,* 6.

CHAPTER 24

Growing Teacher Leaders in a Culture of Excellence

Linda Searby and Lisa Shaddix

How do you create a district pool of future principals who understand and honor the culture of a school community? How do you also increase the leadership capacity of teachers so that they can effectively lead from the classroom? The central administration and elected board of the Mountain Brook, Alabama school system sought to answer this question as a continuity plan for leadership that was being developed. The answer was to continue to shift the paradigm about the concept of leadership in the school system and intentionally promote a culture that would empower teachers to lead at all levels. The Teachers as Leaders program of the Mountain Brook, Alabama Schools represents that shift and is training teachers to utilize their leadership skills and contribute to the system as it fulfills its mission to offer education to its students that is effective, challenging, and engaging. This article describes their exemplary program.

Background

Growing teacher leaders needs to be an intentional act in our nation's school systems. The principal's job in schools is becoming more complex, and it has been established that school leadership can no longer reside in one person (Ballek, O'Rourke, Provenzano, & Bellamy, 2005). Further evidence for the urgency to grow teacher leaders is the fact that public school principals are leaving the profession in increasingly high numbers. According to the Educational Research Service, nearly 40% of all principals will retire or leave the position for other reasons before 2010, causing vacancy numbers to soar (Ballek et al., 2005). Principals nearing retirement must prepare to pass the torch of leadership to those who come after them (Weller & Weller, 2002); those who will carry the torch in the future are the classroom teachers of today. It is imperative that schools invest in the leadership capacity of the teaching staff.

Schools that have high leadership capacity are those that amplify leadership for all. The guiding paradigm is that the principal is only one leader in the school community (Lambert, 2005). Schools in which teachers are becoming significant leaders have structures in place that provide opportunities for broad participation in teams, study groups, vertical communities, and action research teams. According to Danielson (2007), there are three main areas of school life in which teacher leaders can have a role: within a department, across the school, and beyond the school. In an extensive study on the work of teacher leaders, Lieberman, Saxl, and Miles (1988) focused on what teachers actually did when they took on leadership positions. While the evidence proved that the work of teachers as leaders was varied and highly dependent on the individual context of the school, Lieberman et al. did discover that it was necessary for teachers to learn an array of leadership skills while on the job. These skills include the ability to build trust and develop rapport, diagnose organizational conditions, deal with learning processes, manage the work itself, and build skills and confidence in others. Lambert, Collay, Dietz, Kent, and Richert (1996) examined the importance of "leader behaviors" that classroom teachers can exhibit, even though they are not in formal leadership roles. "Teachers emerge into new and continually expanding roles by the very nature of learning to see themselves differently and therefore behaving differently. They also do not sabotage those in other leadership roles" (p. 29). Extending this concept, Dr. Charles Mason, superintendent of Mountain Brook Schools, developed a list of how teachers could lead without being in a formal leadership position:

1. Leaders ask the right, tough questions.

2. Leaders can set the tone for meetings and discussions with their energy level, attitudes, and encouragement.

3. Leaders are mentors, one-on-one, to others.

4. Leaders anticipate needs and meet them without being asked.

5. Leaders support other leaders emotionally and professionally.

6. Leaders establish their own credibility through competence.

7. Leaders learn what they need to know and are willing to share it.

8. Leaders interpret reality for others.

9. Leaders always ask, "What is our purpose?"

10. Leaders ask the question, "Is this consistent with our values and beliefs?" (C. Mason, personal communication, October 16, 2006).

The Teachers as Leaders program sought to encourage teachers to see themselves in those expanding roles of leadership.

The District's Rationale for Growing Teacher Leaders

The Mountain Brook school district, desiring to enhance the leadership capacity of its teaching staff, initiated a program that will prepare teachers for leadership roles both now and in the future. The Teachers as Leaders program was established in order to develop continuity in leadership as many administrator retirements were predicted for the near future. The program, however, was not designed primarily as a "Teachers as Future Administrators" program. Rather, it was an intentional plan to prepare teachers for continual leadership, whether that would be in their classrooms or in administration. In the Mountain Brook school system, the teacher-leader program was part of an aggressive plan developed to enhance the expectation of excellence that exists in this school system. According to Mason, the origination of the Teachers as Leaders program was conceptually tied to the culture of collaboration in the district. "All the important work we do in our district depends on teachers, and this forms our philosophy behind the Teachers as Leaders program. In our culture, there is a belief that the experts are those that are doing the job; thus, teacher leadership is extremely important. If teachers are going to collaborate effectively in groups, teacher leadership is necessary.

Therefore, we needed a structure to intentionally help teachers develop their leadership skills" (C. Mason, personal communication, January 16, 2008).

The Mountain Brook Schools have been recognized with a number of state and national awards for excellence, but the culture of the district does not allow it to become complacent. Under the leadership of Mason, the district has developed a strategic plan for boosting the achievement of students who are already performing at the highest levels in the state of Alabama. The district's continuity plan acknowledges that the teachers are the most important players in that pursuit of continued excellence. The Teachers as Leaders program was designed to ensure that there would be outstanding leaders in each of the schools who would take the initiative with their peers in preserving this culture of high expectations and bring to life the three words that characterize that culture: effective, challenging, and engaging.

However, the program was also set in the context of a district with leaders who have given thought to the fact that there are principals in the school system who are getting older. The district is intentionally planning for how to retain the culture that has been developed so carefully over the last decade when those who created and fostered it start to retire. District leaders want to look for individuals who have the potential to be future administrators and have an understanding of the vision and mission of Mountain Brook Schools. According to Mason, "the district is challenged to hire the best new leaders we can, and we want to encourage teachers to consider formal leadership roles such as reading coaches and assistant principals" (C. Mason, personal communication, January 16, 2008). The three goals of the Teachers as Leaders program, therefore, were:

1. to develop a cadre of teachers who have a deep understanding and commitment to the vision of the school system—that it would be effective, challenging, and engaging.

2. to give participants the opportunity to assess and develop their own leadership skills.

3. to encourage participants to provide positive leadership wherever they find themselves serving.

Description of the Teachers as Leaders Program

District principals were asked to nominate two or three teachers from each building who demonstrated leadership potential. Belinda Treadwell, principal of Mountain Brook Elementary, shared her criteria for selecting teachers from her building to be involved in the program:

> I listened to the comments of teachers in my building when they talked about what they want to do in the future. I looked for the pioneers and those who were engaged in continuous action research, trying new things in their classrooms. I watched for who was comfortable with collaboration. I chose teachers who were risk takers (B. Treadwell, personal communication, October 20, 2006).

Treadwell also concurred with research that cited the fact that exemplary teachers bring certain skills to the leadership role, which make it easy to for others to trust them. Such skills include relational skills, assistance in maintaining a school's sense of purpose, and the ability to improve instructional practices (Donaldson, 2007). This criterion further influenced her selection of the teachers who would become a part of the 2006–2007 Teachers as Leaders cadre.

The 2006–2007 cohort of 15 teacher leaders consisted of 13 females and 2 males, representing each of the six schools in the district. Three participants were early in their teaching careers (1 to 5 years of experience), five were mid-career teachers (6 to 15 years of experience), and six were veteran teachers (16 to 30 years of experience). There were five elementary teachers, three junior high teachers, and three high school teachers. Their ages ranged from 24 to 55, with a large cluster between the ages of 26 and 31. Eleven of the 15 participants had earned master's degrees; two had educational specialist certificates, and two were National Board Certified teachers.

Dr. David Stiles, director of Organizational Development for the Mountain Brook Schools at the time, was charged with developing the Teachers as Leaders program. He designed a protocol through which the selected teacher leaders met six times during the year for full-day experiences in understanding themselves and expanding their awareness of leadership issues. The district provided substitute teachers for the participants in the Teachers as Leaders program, allowing the participants to leave their classrooms during the school day. The first four sessions were devoted to activities that led to a great deal of self-awareness for the participants. They each completed an extensive personality inventory, and a trained consultant led the group of teachers in learning about their relationship styles, how they behaved when they were most productive, how they operated under stress, and how they would typically lead. One participant, responding anonymously in the program evaluation, shared the following:

> I am amazed at how much I learned about myself. I have always considered myself a motivated, energetic person. Going through this personality inventory, I learned that while I would make a good leader, I have so much to learn about how to "become" a good leader. This process really made me more aware of how I think of myself and how others view me as a leader.

In addition to the intense personality inventory activities, the participants had informative sessions such as an education legislation update and a presentation on how the power of personal reflection assists in developing leadership skills. Team-building activities were also an integral part of the Teachers as Leaders training. The teachers met in the summer to experience a ropes course, during which a trained facilitator led them through the challenges of working together to achieve difficult physical feats. The culminating team-building activity was a cooking challenge, held at a local restaurant that housed a corporate cook-off kitchen designed for organizations to practice working in teams. The teachers divided into two groups and were given instructions to prepare an elaborate Italian meal together in 90 minutes. They were judged on how well they cooperated, how creative they were with the recipes, and on the presentation and taste of the food. Of course, their reward was the opportunity to enjoy the gourmet lunch they had prepared! In both of these activities, the concepts of teamwork, negotiation, compromise, time management, delegation, handling crises, and dealing with multiple perspectives were explored and discussed by the teachers under the leadership of a facilitator.

Evaluation of the Teachers as Leaders Program

An evaluation of the Teachers as Leaders program was conducted by one of us (Dr. Searby), a professor of Educational Leadership at the University of Alabama at Birmingham. A survey was given to each participant at the conclusion of the 2006–2007 cohort activities to gather qualitative data on how the participants perceived the program. The survey consisted of a series of 11 open-ended statements for participants to complete, such as "Since participating in Teachers as Leaders, I …"; "The most significant learning occurred for me when … ." Teachers who participated in the program gave it high marks; in fact, there were no negative comments made about the program at all. Participants shared comments on how much they had grown both personally and professionally through the program. Many noted that they had changed their opinions about leadership. One participant shared the following in her survey:

> Having been in the classroom for more than 15 years, I have seen teachers move from teaching in isolation to being true leaders who enact change. In the past, teachers have thought that becoming a leader in their building meant that they must come out of the classroom and become an administrator. The Teachers as Leaders program made me realize that not only can I be a leader in the classroom, but through my professional development, my sphere of influence can reach beyond the classroom and into schoolwide leadership activities.

This teacher realized that her previous opinion of leadership was based on a faulty philosophy that leaders are born, not made (Lunenburg & Ornstein, 2004). "I have always looked at leadership as something that people had or didn't have. I hadn't ever really thought that leadership is something that can grow in a person. This process really made me more aware of how I think of myself and how others view me as a leader."

As a part of the final evaluation survey, participants in the Teachers as Leaders program were asked to identify where their leadership abilities were currently being demonstrated, as well as where they would like to extend their leadership work in their school or the system. They set 1-to 5-year goals for themselves and stated what encouragement and support they would need to reach those goals. Over half of the 2006–2007 group of 17 participants stated a desire to pursue a leadership position at a different level than their current assignment.

The teachers were extremely appreciative of being selected for this program, as is depicted in the following survey comments:

> Teachers as Leaders is the best professional development I have been to in a long, long time. It has been a privilege to be a part of this group. I hope we can continue as a group—a think tank—on other projects. Put us to work for the system!

> Thank you for giving me the opportunity to learn more about myself and my leadership abilities. Affirmation of these skills is important to me and has presented the need to use them more in my school and system.

Although the Mountain Brook school system has graduated just two cohorts from the Teachers as Leaders program, it has already reaped the benefits of encouraging teachers to take more responsible leadership roles. For example, several National Board Certified teachers have emerged from the first cohort of Teachers as Leaders. Others have become new teacher mentors, chairpersons of their grade levels or departments, chairpersons of professional learning community committees, or student teacher supervisors. In addition, one teacher became a staff development specialist; two were chosen to work on statewide curriculum committees, and one became an assistant principal. One of us (Shaddix) was a 2006–2007 Teachers as Leaders participant and has demonstrated leadership by becoming an advisor/mentor to new teachers, facilitating professional development activities, serving on school-based leadership teams, and serving on instructional support teams. Shaddix noted that, "by serving in these various leadership roles, I have noticed that my skills and knowledge about best practices in education have increased. I am much more confident, and I feel a renewed commitment to teaching and learning."

Schlechty (1990) defined teachers as leaders when they strive to influence peers to become more effective in classrooms and when they themselves become active in school governance. Shaddix advised teachers about how to take leadership roles by stating:

> I would encourage teachers who are looking to revitalize their careers to become more involved in leadership opportunities. Obtain a clear picture of the vision at your school, and take the initiative and become a vital part of that vision. Use your expertise and support and encourage other teachers. Facilitate reflection among your coworkers. Help your team make better decisions about teaching and learning. Be patient and realize that not everyone will be on the same learning curve as you, but the time you invest in people will be well worth it.

The Future of the Teachers as Leaders Program

Viewing teachers as leaders requires a paradigm shift about the concept of leadership in a school system. As DuFour, DuFour, Eaker, and Many (2006) state, these shifts often make teachers uncomfortable. Such paradigm shifts associated with developing teachers as leaders may include moving from isolation to collaboration, from privatization of practice to open sharing of practice, and from independence to interdependence. The designers of the Teachers as Leaders program of the Mountain Brook Schools acknowledged that these paradigm shifts are important, and they will continue to refine the program components as Teachers as Leaders will be offered every other year in the district. Mason, dedicated to the continuous improvement of the program, stated, "in future years we need to make sure that the components of the Teachers as Leaders program more tightly align to the goals of our system and that we help participants grasp the big picture and overarching purpose of the program, seeing the connectedness in all that we do" (C. Mason, personal communication, January 16, 2008).

We would like to make some additional suggestions for refining the Teachers as Leaders program in subsequent years. First of all, although it is important to spend time helping future leaders enhance their self-understanding through a personality inventory, we would advise that the time spent on the accompanying interpretive activities be reduced so that a varied list of leadership topics can be covered in the course of the year's program. A possible list would include how to lead the change process, how to conduct action research in a school, and how leaders can develop resiliency. Each of these topics could be translated into creatively designed, practical experiential activities.

Secondly, teachers who are considering expansion of their leadership need opportunities to stretch their skills. We would suggest that the designers provide teachers with authentic problem-based leadership tasks that have the potential to make a significant difference in the work of the system. It was noted that one participant in this cohort said, "Put us to work for the system!" Teacher leaders want to contribute; they welcome new challenges. Perhaps each cohort of teacher leaders could be given a specific assignment that they could work on collaboratively, developing their teamwork skills and making a significant impact systemwide.

Finally, we would suggest that teacher leaders receive coaching in how to develop a professional portfolio that would highlight their leadership abilities. We would also suggest that these teachers be given the option of participating in a mock interview for an administrative position. Teachers who aspire to leadership at the principal level need encouragement to start thinking like an administrator.

The Mountain Brook school system has demonstrated its commitment to growing teacher leaders in a culture of excellence. The Teachers as Leaders program will likely continue to empower teachers to utilize their leadership skills and contribute to the Mountain Brook Schools at a higher level as it fulfills its mission to offer education that is effective, challenging, and engaging.

Appendix

Teachers as Leaders
Participant Evaluation

Your Demographic Information:

M_____   F_____

Career Stage: _____   Early (1-5 years)   Elementary_____
              _____   Mid (6-15 years)   Middle School_____
              _____   Late (16-30 years)   High School_____
                                                    Other_____

Your age_____
Your highest degree_____   In what area?_____
Do you plan to pursue a higher degree? ___Yes ___No
If yes, what degree or certification?_____

Check all that apply:
Before participating in Teachers as Leaders, I.....

_____   didn't really see myself as a leader
_____   always/usually thought of myself as a leader

_____ always planned to be a classroom teacher/ counselor, etc., my entire career

_____ thought I might someday be an administrator

_____ knew myself well, including knowing my strengths, weaknesses, giftedness, personality style, leadership style, etc.

_____ did not know myself well in the above areas

_____ thought I was a good team member and knew how to work cooperatively in a group towards a common goal

_____ had not thought much about my role as a team member on teams I was involved in

_____ thought quite often/reflected about what leaders do

_____ seldom gave much thought to what leaders do

Write your responses to the following open-ended statements:

Since participating in Teachers as Leaders, I...

The one thing I'll never forget about Teachers as Leaders is...

The most significant learning occurred for me when...

One thing I could have done without in Teachers as Leaders was...

Something that surprised me was...

As a result of participating in Teachers as Leaders, I have had a change of heart/mind in regard to...

My leadership abilities are currently being demonstrated in...

I have the interest and expertise and would like to be given time to engage in the following leadership work in my school or in the Mt. Brook system...

My 1-5 year goals include...

I would like to pursue a leadership position at a higher level than my current position:
_____ yes _____ no _____ undecided Possibilities:_____

I need the following support/encouragement to reach my goals:

My advice to future Teachers as Leaders participants would be...

I would like to nominate the following Mt. Brook staff member(s) for future Teachers as Leaders programs:

Feedback I wish to give Dr. Mason and Dr. Stiles about Teachers as Leaders is...

Additional comments:

_____ you have my permission to use any of my comments in presentations or articles about Teachers as Leaders

_____ Please do not use my comments

Your Name is Optional

References

Ballek, K., O'Rourke, A., Provenzano, J., & Bellamy, T. (2005). Keys in cultivating principals and teacher leaders. *National Staff Development Council Journal, 26*(2), 42–49.

Danielson, C. (2007). The many faces of leadership. *Educational Leadership, 65*(1), 14–19.

Donaldson, G. A. (2007). What do teachers bring to leadership? *Educational Leadership, 65*(1), 26–29.

DuFour, R., DuFour, R., Eaker, R., & Many, T. (2006). *Learning by doing.* Bloomington, IN: Solution Tree.

Lambert, L. (2005). What does leadership capacity really mean? *National Staff Development Council Journal, 26*(2), 39–40.

Lambert, L., Collay, M., Dietz, M., Kent, K., & Richert, A. (1996). *Who will save our schools? Teachers as constructivist leaders.* Thousand Oaks, CA: Corwin Press.

Lieberman, A., Saxl, E., & Miles, M. (1988). Teacher leadership: Ideology and practice. In A. Lieberman (Ed.), *Building a professional culture in schools.* New York: Teachers College Press.

Lunenburg, F. C., & Ornstein, A. C. (2004). *Educational administration: Concepts and practices.* Belmont, CA: Thomson/Wadsworth Learning.

Schlechty, P. C. (1990). *Schools for the twenty-first century: Leadership imperatives for educational reform.* San Francisco: Jossey-Bass.

Weller, L. D., & Weller, S. J. (2002). *The assistant principal: Essentials for effective school leadership.* Thousand Oaks, CA: Corwin Press.

CHAPTER 25

Preparing Teachers for Leadership Roles in the 21ˢᵗ Century

Julie A. Sherrill

The many calls for educational reform in the last 15 years have shared several common themes, including increasing recognition of the importance of teacher quality and teacher leadership to school improvement efforts (The Holmes Group, 1986, 1990, 1995; National Commission on Excellence in Education, 1983; National Commission on Teaching and America's Future, 1996). New teacher leadership roles are emerging as educators and policymakers seek to improve the three major phases of the teaching career continuum: teacher preparation, induction, and ongoing professional development.

However, the new teacher leadership roles remain ill defined and unclear to both researchers and teacher leaders (see Conley & Muncey, this issue). The expectations attached to the new roles can be confusing, demanding, and overwhelming to teacher leaders, as well as to their colleagues and administrators (Collinson & Sherrill, 1997; Sherrill, 1993a; Wasley, 1991). Teacher leaders are literally forging their roles on site.

I have often desired a more clear and concise description of teacher leadership roles, coupled with a greater understanding of the foundational skills and knowledge teachers need to fulfill their roles successfully and of ways teachers are supposed to attain them. My desire for clarity stems from having studied emerging teacher leadership roles at the teacher preparation phase at a major research university (see Sherrill, 1993a), and having held positions of responsibility for induction and ongoing professional development programs for teachers in adjacent school districts. Universities and state are quickly adopting changes and altering requirements for teacher preparation, but they are not simultaneously developing and offering programs to prepare the teacher leaders who are expected to implement the changes. Teachers are expected to assume leadership roles with little or no preparation (Zimpher & Howey, 1992).

The complexity of the issues surrounding new roles for teachers cannot be ignored, but the development of common expectations of teacher leadership roles at the teacher preparation, induction, and ongoing professional development phases could prove helpful in setting high expectations, filling leadership positions with qualified individuals, and contributing to the continuous improvement efforts underway in many of today's schools.

Recognizing that any role assumed by a professional educator is influenced by local context, this article argues that basic expectations for teacher leadership roles can be drawn from existing research generated during the past decade. Like the teaching and learning standards initiated nationwide to provide common benchmarks and consistent expectations for teachers and students, similar guideposts for teacher leadership positions could enhance the reforms underway in teacher preparation programs and K-12 schools across the country. This chapter draws on existing research to outline common expectations for teacher leadership roles within three major phases of the teacher career continuum—teacher preparation, induction, and ongoing professional development.

The Teacher Leadership Challenge

Wasley (1991) offers a generic definition of teacher leadership as "the ability to encourage colleagues to change, to do things they wouldn't ordinarily consider without the influence of the leader" (p. 170). However, as Wasley (1991) notes, the realities of practice for teacher leaders are much more challenging and complex than the rhetoric on reform suggests. Her case studies illustrate that teachers have been unresponsive to top-down efforts to improve their instruction through administratively created teacher leadership positions. Not only must teachers be full participants in any discussion about leadership roles, they must also feel supported and understood by administrators in order for any new leadership role to make a positive and lasting contribution to the improvement of teaching and learning in a given setting (Wasley, 1991).

Additionally, Zimpher and Howey (1992) note widespread acknowledgment that the expertise and the catalyst for change has to be embedded in a continuing way at the school site. However, the still common reality of staff development efforts in school districts reflects the notion that outside experts are best suited to encourage professional growth (Jilek, Loadman, & Derby, 1998). This deeply-rooted habit of thinking persists despite teacher reports that the best way to go about improving the quality of their professional practice is to spend more time learning from and working with colleagues (Bacharach, 1986; Wasley, 1991), and despite research indicating that collegial interactions are necessary to build the collaborative cultures associated with school improvement (Hargreaves, 1991; Little, 1990; Rosenholtz, 1989).

Studies that focus on school-university partnerships have underscored the many challenges in defining new leadership roles and responsibilities (Miller & Silvernail, 1994). Specific challenges include resolving conflicting fundamental interests (Snyder, 1994), establishing inter-institutional authority and fiscal responsibility (Neufeld, 1992), and providing long-term rewards for teacher leaders (Lieberman, 1992; Sandholtz & Merseth, 1992).

Many authors have pointed to the critical role of "boundary spanners" (Sandholtz & Finan, 1998), teacher leaders who have assumed roles created with the expectation that they will bridge the complex cultures of K-12 schools and higher education. The sheer diversity of titles illustrates the wide range of possibilities and expectations: Teacher leaders are referred to as clinical faculty, clinical educators, and clinical supervisors (Zimpher & Sherrill, 1996).

Zimpher and Howey (1992) point out that even the best of teachers are not prepared for such an assignment. Recent case studies have reported high levels of frustration from teachers piloting new leadership roles. The reported frustrations of these teachers and their lack of self-efficacy indicate that teacher leader roles called for in reform efforts need to have greater definition, and teachers need to have more purposeful preparation (Cornbleth & Ellsworth, 1994; Sandholtz & Finan, 1998; Sherrill, 1993a; Snyder, 1994).

Targeted selection and preparation for such roles may increase the visibility among colleagues and alleviate the types of feelings experienced by a clinical educator who stated:

> I don't think I should have to keep saying to the principal, "Aren't you at all interested in what I do half the day?" I mean, this district does share me with the university a half day. Most of the staff still don't know what I do. They know if I leave school it is somehow associated with the university and PDS

(professional development school) work. They may not know I even have a title. More importantly, they don't recognize that I'm supposed to be doing things that should facilitate improvements in their own classroom and professional lives. I guess I just feel invisible. (Sherrill, 1993b)

The following section attempts to categorize the types of knowledge, responsibilities, and skills needed by teacher leaders as they assume leadership roles throughout the three major phases of the teacher career continuum: teacher preparation, induction, and ongoing professional development.

The Teacher Career Continuum

Teacher Preparation

In the report of the National Commission on Teaching and America's Future (1996), one of the five major recommendations is a reinventing of teacher preparation and professional development. The report recommends that teacher education and professional development programs be organized around standards for students and teachers. Additionally, the report suggests that extended, graduate-level teacher-preparation programs provide preservice students with a year-long internship in a professional development school.

Of the more than 1,200 schools of education in the nation, over 200 have created professional development schools. Each PDS is incorporating some variation of teacher leader roles for classroom teachers working with university faculty and preservice students (National Commission on Teaching and America's Future, 1996). The new roles require teacher leaders to link the experience of the school setting to university coursework for preservice students and to work with university faculty at school sites (Cornbleth & Ellsworth, 1994). Such "clinical faculty roles" are being interpreted more broadly than the traditional notion of cooperating teacher.

These new teacher leadership roles in a PDS are demanding. One clinical educator articulated her beliefs about her new role and the characteristics she modeled as follows:

A clinical educator is a person who values collaboration generally and school-university collaboration specifically and has demonstrated an ability to work toward professional development and instructional improvement; demonstrates that he/she is an expert classroom practitioner who can articulate his/her beliefs about children, teaching and learning; takes risks and works at the edge of his/her knowledge; has a strong commitment to his/her own professional development and is willing to engage in continuing preparation for the role. And by the way, they must be able to tolerate a high degree of ambiguity too. (Sherrill, 1993a, p. 147)

Teachers assuming leadership roles that are integrally tied to the initial preparation of teachers will need training in collaborative planning and implementation as well as instructional and developmental supervision (Reiman & Thies-Sprinthall, 1998). Critical abilities for teacher leaders engaged in teacher preparation will include demonstrating expert classroom instruction and sound knowledge of effective teaching and learning strategies, facilitating conferences with preservice teachers in a differentiated and reciprocal manner, analyzing approaches to their work via adult learning theory, and providing feedback tied to theory and research.

Induction

Research into the beginning years of teaching describes the transition years following preservice preparation as a period of chaos, often marked by a lack of support (Howey, 1988). In response to beginning teachers' concerns and high attrition rates in the first years of teaching (Heyns, 1988), entry year or induction programs for new teachers have evolved across the country. As a consequence, a number of teacher leadership roles, especially mentoring, focus specifically on emerging entry-year programs and other activities that support beginning teachers (Zimpher & Sherrill, 1996).

Teacher leaders cannot be expected to assume new mentoring roles armed with the skills necessary to work with peers. Teachers are not accustomed to "teaching" adults. However, their new roles can be enhanced through specific training. For example, Odell (1986) found that training clinical support teachers in supervision, relationship skills, and coaching techniques dramatically improved their effectiveness (see also Reiman & Thies-Sprinthall, 1998). The assignment of a well-trained support teacher or mentor to a beginning teacher was also found to be the most powerful and cost-effective intervention in an induction program (Huling-Austin, Putman, & Galvez-Hjornevik, 1986).

Classroom teachers assuming mentoring roles with entry-year teachers should have the opportunity, therefore, to acquire skills that enable them to develop relationships and nurture the growth and development of beginning teachers. They should learn how to systematically observe classroom instruction and coach beginning teachers, consulting as the need arises on classroom management, lesson development, and instructional strategies.

In addition to the skills required to work with beginning teachers individually and within cohorts, teacher leaders should also be adept at facilitating the conditions for mentoring. They need to know how to impact on the school building and district environments so that beginning teachers have opportunities to meet and talk with each other, observe other classrooms where outstanding teaching and learning is taking place, experiment with new instructional methods, and develop a sense of truth with their mentors and colleagues.

Ongoing Professional Development

Rosenholtz's (1989) study of collaborative elementary schools indicated that "teachers from collaborative settings described their leaders as those who initiated new programs, tried new ideas, [and] motivated others to experiment and brainstorm solutions to teaching problems" (p. 24). Since teachers, in general, do not share a tradition of leadership or collaboration, Zimpher and Howey (1992) called for highly selected teachers to be prepared for a variety of school-focused leadership roles to meet the vision of school leadership described in the Rosenholtz study. Zimpher and Howey (1992) argue that these uniquely trained teachers should undertake a variety of leadership roles at the school site while maintaining some instructional responsibilities. As teachers, they would enjoy more peer credibility than "outsiders." As leaders on site, they could encourage and support more effective and job-embedded professional development than found in most traditional professional development programs.

Standard prerequisites for leadership roles that focus on the ongoing professional development of teachers in the school setting should include the following knowledge domains: knowledge of classroom processes and school effectiveness; knowledge of interpersonal and adult development; knowledge of instructional supervision, observation, and conferencing; knowledge of local district needs; and a disposition toward inquiry (Zimpher & Howey, 1992). Additionally, tangible examples of the skills and knowledge needed by teacher leaders assuming such roles would be demonstrated by: expanding and improving colleagues' basic teaching methods, modeling how to enable students to better monitor their learning and take greater responsibility for their actions in the classroom, improving the working climate of both individual classrooms and schools as a whole, and documenting in a more accountable fashion the effects of their teaching in order to provide parents and community with precise and relevant data about learning than standardized tests allow (Zimpher & Howey, 1992).

A particular challenge for individuals assuming this teacher leadership role is the relationship established with school administration. Ideally, school administrators would have the time and skills required to carry out much of the above, but the reality of school administration in today's schools makes it nearly impossible to devote the time and energy required to carry out these aspects of teacher professional development. As such, a relationship of trust, cooperation, and respect between identified teacher leaders and school administrators will be critical to the success of roles targeted at the ongoing professional development of teachers in a building or school district. The dynamics of these relationships could be the greatest facilitator, or barrier, to change.

Table 1 captures, in summary form, a core set of expectations for leadership roles across the teacher career continuum, combined with specific expectations for teacher leaders working with peers in leadership roles at the teacher preparation, induction, and ongoing professional development phases.

The table is not intended to be all-inclusive, but rather to be illustrative of the clarity necessary for better defining expectations for the new teacher leadership roles called for in today's education reform efforts. The mere attempt to compose such a categorization of expectations raised a number of questions for further consideration. Just who will be responsible for providing the prerequisite training needed for teachers to carry out these roles successfully? Who will pay for teacher leader training? What is being done relative to the preparation of school administrators to complement and enhance teacher leadership roles? Should there be prerequisites for leadership roles in certain phases (i.e., National Board Certification prior to assuming a leadership role in the ongoing professional development phase)?

Core Expectations for All Phases:
Demonstrate exemplary classroom instruction and sound knowledge of
    effective teaching and learning strategies.
Understand theories of adult development.
Demonstrate knowledge of clinical supervision models and processes that
    support effective descriptions of classroom practices.
Cultivate desired dispositions in teachers.
Guide colleagues by a reflective and inquiry-oriented posture.
Possess research based knowledge about teaching and learning.

Teacher Preparation	Induction	Ongoing Professional Development
Articulate knowledge of the university teacher preparation curriculum.	Understand the unique needs and concerns of beginning teachers.	Demonstrate ability to assess, interpret, and prioritize local district and teacher needs and concerns.
Value collaboration generally and school-university collaboration specifically.	Demonstrate effective relationship skills and coaching techniques.	Recognize how to positively affect the broader culture of the school and establish positive relationships with administrators.
Facilitate conferences with preservice teachers and university faculty in a differentiated and reciprocal manner.	Develop relationships and nurture the growth and development of beginning teachers.	Understand action research and practice-centered inquiry.
Analyze their approach to work via adult learning theory.	Collect data related to classroom observations and provide constructive feedback.	Expand and improve colleagues' basic teaching methods.
Provide feedback tied to theory and research.		Possess skills needed to facilitate effective workshops and presentations.

Table 1. Teacher Leader Expectations for Three Phases of the Career Continuum

Conclusion

New teacher leadership roles are emerging as a result of educators and policymakers seeking to improve the three major phases of the teaching career continuum: teacher preparation, induction, and ongoing professional development. Data collected from Venture Capital schools in Ohio (Jilek, Loadman, & Derby, 1998) point to the fact that "previously prepared and newly prepared teachers and administrators are not and have not been prepared to take on the roles and functions which they are being asked to assume … both in preprofessional and professional development activities" (p. 16). This article argues that basic expectations for teacher leadership roles at the teacher preparation, induction, and ongoing professional development phases can be drawn from existing research. By completing such a task, courageous educators attempting to improve their profession could begin with a common framework, a blueprint from which to embark on important work. Clearly identifying expectations for teacher leadership roles needed now and in the 21st century—and determining how educators will acquire the knowledge and skills needed to assume those roles successfully—are critical steps in the continuous reform efforts to improve public education in this country.

References

Bacharach, S. B. (1986). *The learning workplace: The conditions and resources of teaching*. Washington, DC: National Education Association.

Collinson, V., & Sherrill, J. (1997). Changing context for changing roles: Teachers as learners and leaders. *Teaching Education, 8*(2), 55–63.

Conley, S. & Muncey, D. E. (1999). Teachers talk about teaming and leadership in their work. *Theory into Practice, 38*(1), 46–55.

Cornbleth, C., & Ellsworth, J. (1994). Clinical faculty in teaching education: Roles, relationships, and careers. In K. R. Howey & N. L. Zimpher (Eds.), *Informing faculty development for teacher educators* (pp. 213–248). Norwood, NJ: Ablex.

Hargreaves, A. (1991, April). *Restructuring restructuring: Postmodernity and the prospects for educational change*. Paper presented at the annual meeting of the American Educational Research Association, Chicago.

Heyns, B. (1988). Educational defectors: A first look at teacher attrition in the NLS-72. *Educational Researcher, 17*(3), 24–32.

The Holmes Group. (1986). *Tomorrow's teachers*. East Lansing, MI: Author.

The Holmes Group. (1990). *Tomorrow's schools: Principals for the design of professional development schools*. East Lansing, MI: Author.

The Holmes Group. (1995). *Tomorrow's schools of education*. East Lansing, MI: Author.

Howey, K. R. (1988). Why teacher leadership? *Journal of Teacher Education*, 39, 28–31.

Howey, K. R., & Zimpher, N. L. (1991). Patterns in prospective teachers: Guides for designing preservice programs. In F. B. Murray (Ed.), *The teacher educator's handbook* (pp. 465–503). San Francisco: Jossey-Bass.

Huling-Austin, L., Putman, S., & Galvez-Hjornevik, C. (1986). *Model teacher induction project study findings* (Report No. 7212). Austin: University of Texas at Austin, R&D Center for Teacher Education.

Jilek, J., Loadman, W., & Derby, L. (1998, February). *Ohio's P-12 systemic educational reform: Implications for the preparation of teachers and administrators*. Paper presented at the annual meeting of the American Association of Colleges for Teacher Education, New Orleans, LA.

Lieberman, A. (1992). School/university collaboration: A view from the inside. *Phi Delta Kappan, 74*, 147–155.

Little, J. W. (1990). The persistence of privacy: Autonomy and initiative in teachers' professional relations. *Teachers College Record*, 91, 509–536.

Miller, L., & Silvernail, D. (1994). Wells Junior High School: Evolution of a professional development school. In L. Darling-Hammond (Ed.), *Professional development schools: Schools for developing a profession*. (pp. 28–49). New York: Teachers College Press.

National Commission on Excellence in Education. (1983). *A nation at risk*. Washington, DC: U.S. Government Printing Office.

National Commission on Teaching and America's Future. (1996). *What matters most: Teaching for America's future*. New York: Teachers College Press.

Neufeld, B. (1992). Professional practice schools in context: New mixtures of institutional authority. In M. Levine (Ed.), *Professional practice schools: Linking teacher education and school reform* (pp. 133–168). New York: Teachers College Press.

Odell, S. (1986). Induction support of new teachers: A functional approach. *Journal of Teacher Education, 37*, 26–29.

Reiman, A. J., & Thies-Sprinthall, L. (1998). *Mentoring and supervision for teacher development*. New York: Addison Wesley Longman.

Rosenholtz, S. (1989). *Teachers' workplace: The social organization of schools*. New York: Teachers College Press.

Sandholtz, J. H., & Finan, E. (1998). Blurring the boundaries to promote school-university partnerships. *Journal of Teacher Education, 49*, 13–25.

Sandholtz J. H. & Merseth, K. K. (1992). Collaborating teachers in a professional development school: Inducements and contributions. *Journal of Teacher Education*, 43, 308–317.

Sherrill, A. (1993a). *A qualitative case study of the clinical educator role during a pilot year of implementation.* Unpublished doctoral dissertation, The Ohio State University, Columbus.

Sherrill, A. (1993b). {A qualitative case study of the clinical educator role during a pilot year of implementation}. Unpublished raw data.

Snyder, J. (1994). Perils and potentials: A tale of two professional development schools. In L. Darling-Hammond (Ed.), *Professional development schools: Schools for developing a profession* (pp. 98–125). New York: Teachers College Press.

Wasley, P. A. (1991). *Teachers who lead: The rhetoric of reform and the realities of practice.* New York: Teachers College Press.

Zimpher, N. L., & Howey, K. R. (1992). *Policy and practice toward the improvement of teacher education.* Oak Brook, IL: North Central Regional Educational Laboratory.

Zimpher, N. L., & Sherrill, J. A. (1996). Professionals, teachers, and leaders in schools, colleges, and departments of education. In J. Sikula, T. J. Buttery, & E. Guyton, (Eds.), *Handbook of research on teacher education* (pp. 279–305). New York: Macmillan.

CHAPTER 26

The Teaching Profession at the Crossroads

Arthur E. Wise and Michael D. Usdan

The teaching profession and the unions that represent it are at a crossroads in their history. What happens to public schools in the future depends on a confluence of trends surrounding teachers unions, teacher accountability, and curriculum.

Declining Union Power

Recent efforts to curb the power of teachers organizations, even in traditionally strong pro-union states like Wisconsin, Ohio, and Illinois, highlight how vulnerable these once-powerful groups have become. Examples of the dilution of union political influence abound. Sacrosanct tenure and seniority rights have been challenged in dozens of places, even in bastions of unionism like New York City, Chicago, and New Jersey. Unions face criticism not only from traditional Republican opponents but also from "progressive" elements of the Democratic party. Both the National Education Association (NEA) and the American Federation of Teachers (AFT) reportedly have suffered significant losses in membership, and there is little doubt that they are on the defensive.

Those who support teachers unions are increasingly concerned that the lack of respect for teachers and the decline in public sector unions will affect the morale of today's teachers and tomorrow's recruits to teaching. In the meantime, many education reform advocates in the political, business, and philanthropic sector, as well as substantial segments of the U.S. public, believe that the teachers unions have not pursued professional reform with the urgency required to improve student performance.

Teacher Accountability: Professional—or Bureaucratic?

Currently, the major point of contention between reform leaders and teachers organizations is the use of standardized testing as the primary basis for teacher evaluation. The future of public education may hinge on how teachers are evaluated and held accountable. Every reasonable person believes that teachers should be accountable for the performance of their students. The controversy is about the accountability mechanism and its consequences.

Throughout the 20th century, those who favored viewing teaching as a profession promoted accountability mechanisms intended to engender public trust in teachers. In the 1950s, teachers organizations and others established an accreditation system for teacher preparation institutions; today, the majority of such institutions, but not all, are accredited. States, with the support of teachers organizations, have established and regularly upgraded requirements for a state teaching license. However, the enforcement of these requirements has been highly uneven and often ignored. And the decision to grant tenure, which could and should be the definitive judgment of a teacher's competence, is too often made hastily and by default.

The path to bureaucratic, test-based teacher accountability began in the 1960s with state-imposed accountability systems that effectively supplanted teachers' judgment and grades with standardized tests. To the extent that standardized tests limit instruction to what is tested, they prescribe the content and form of teaching and reduce teaching to a bureaucratic routine. Thus, the education system demands less of teachers, requires less teacher preparation, and treats teachers as bureaucratic employees who, because the public has no basis for trusting them, must be micromanaged.[1]

In the 1980s, teachers organizations and other groups took another step toward professional accountability when they sponsored the National Board for Professional Teaching Standards to establish a system of advanced certification for teachers. But policy-makers' support for National Board certification has been uneven: Incentives for certification have periodically been given and taken away by states and districts. For the most part, National Board–certified teachers have been confined to their classrooms and have not been employed in leadership roles, such as working with novices or other teachers who need assistance. The partial and uneven implementation of these and other quality-control measures has not unexpectedly left the public wondering just how much to trust teachers.

Advocates of bureaucratic and professional accountability have been battling each other for decades in a war that has barely been acknowledged. Each approach leads to a different vision of teaching and learning. Occasionally the war breaks out into the open—for example, when middle-class parents object to "too much testing" or teachers protest the unfairness of being judged by student performance on standardized tests. Yet, for the most part, advocates for professionalization have operated in stealth while state and federal legislators promote test-based accountability without input from parents or teachers.

How Accountability Choices Affect Curriculum

If accountability mechanisms were neutral in their impact, it might not matter which side wins the accountability "war." Yet the choice has unmistakable practical consequences.

Here are the activities that we've observed in two different science classrooms. The difference between these two typical learning experiences indicates how accountability mechanisms determine what teachers teach and what students learn.

5th Grade Science in a Virginia Public School

Each week, students learn a specific scientific concept through the study of related scientific vocabulary. What is a hypothesis? What are the parts of a plant? Students learn how to spell, define, and use these words. Each Friday, students are tested on their knowledge of these words. A comprehensive textbook with appropriate photographs, charts, and graphs is provided to each student, although time permits only limited use. After the state administers the SOL (Standards of Learning) science examination in late spring, teachers and students may do science experiments.

5th Grade Science in a Virginia Private School

Students first learn about simple machines. Each student then designs a practical instrument that makes use of these simple machines. After the teacher approves the design, students build the instrument.

Students write a paper describing their projects and make an oral presentation to their classmates. On parent/grandparent visiting day, students display their projects in a science fair setting, explaining them to the visiting adults.

What the Examples Show Us

Both the public school and the private school treat teacher accountability for student learning as essential. Yet here we see in stark relief how the *mechanisms* of accountability determine the content of instruction. Virginia is a state with a history of test-based accountability in public schools that precedes No Child Left Behind. In the mid-1990s, the state developed its Standards of Learning (SOL), clearly describing what students should learn in each grade in the major school subjects. Standardized examinations fully aligned with the standards made clear to educators and parents that everyone—students, principals, and teachers—would be held accountable for performance on these examinations.

Within a few years, classroom instruction changed to ensure optimal results on the SOL. Teachers understood what now counted: Whatever other learning goals they may have entertained for their students, these were now clearly subordinate to strong performance on the state examination. The message to those contemplating teaching as a career was equally unmistakable: Prepare for a job in which test scores are what matter most. The message to students was also clear: Science is memorizing lists of science words.

The private school uses a very different accountability mechanism, which allows teachers to teach something closer to real science. Accountability is based not on an examination about science but on performance on real-world scientific tasks and communication skills. The student must acquire knowledge about machines, but then must put that knowledge to work building something that can be seen and judged by peers, teachers, parents, and others. The display is public and self-evident. The requirement to describe the project in writing and orally not only reinforces these real-world skills but also enables others to determine the degree to which the student has mastered the content of the instruction.

The message to the teacher is clear. Create challenging instruction, but know that your students and you will be publicly evaluated. (Music teachers and coaches have always lived under this accountability mechanism.) Under this approach, instruction and assessment can be what teachers, boards, parents, and administrators think it should be. This kind of accountability does not distort instruction; instead, instruction comes first, and the accountability mechanism comes second. The message to teachers is, Teach to high standards, knowing that you will be evaluated in ways that support authentic instruction. The message to would-be teachers is, You will face a challenging environment in which the tools used to appraise you are appropriate to the task. The message to students is, You are learning real-world skills and not simply learning to perform well on a test that is a poor reflection of the real world.

The Role of Teachers Organizations

The development of each of these accountability mechanisms has been, and will continue to be, advanced or hindered by the leadership provided by teachers organizations. A brief look at the history of the two national teachers organizations shows that both have experienced tensions as they have tried to promote teacher professionalism while protecting teachers' jobs and benefits.

From its beginning in the 19th century until the 1960s, the National Education Association (NEA) was a professional advocacy association encompassing all educators working toward the advancement of education. In the 1960s, in response to the belief that the NEA did not advocate aggressively for teachers' rights, the American Federation of Teachers (AFT) began to assert itself as a labor union. As the AFT gained traction, the teacher members of the NEA felt obliged to divorce themselves from school administrators and to add union organizing and collective bargaining to the NEA agenda. At the same time, the AFT added advocacy of professional and education issues to its agenda. From the 1960s to the present, both the NEA and the AFT have behaved as both professional associations advocating the advancement of education and unions pressing for higher salaries and increased job protection for teachers.

Given the current position and status of teachers and their unions, how will a decline in union power generally, and teachers union power in particular, affect the course of professional accountability?

One possibility is that as union power declines, the move to professional accountability will further decline, leaving bureaucratic teacher accountability to fill the void and test-based accountability to continue unabated. In this scenario, schools will become even duller factories, producing students who can do better and better on standardized tests and worse and worse on real-world skills. Teaching will become an even more bureaucratic job, one that is not appealing to the best and brightest, who seek a measure of control over their work and career prospects.

Another possibility is that teachers organizations will turn back to their original missions of strengthening teaching and learning. They will be advocates for a teaching profession that appeals to the best and brightest, for high-quality teacher preparation and meaningful mentoring of beginning teachers, and for a career progression in teaching in which novices are supported and veterans take on greater leadership roles. They will be advocates for systems that remove underperforming teachers. They will be advocates for a system that generates sufficient public confidence that competent professionals are allowed to teach real-world skills that meet the needs of all students. The problem with this scenario, however, is that unless teachers organizations retain some characteristics of unions, they may be unable to influence legislators and other policymakers to pay teachers sufficiently to compensate them for increased rigor in teaching and better results for students.

A New Direction in Teacher Professionalism

As teachers unions and public education come to this crossroads in their history, we must address a number of important questions. Does a merger between the National Education Association and the American Federation of Teachers make sense at a time when both organizations confront serious threats to their influence and even existence? What can teachers organizations do to build more public understanding and credibility? Do reform efforts endorsed by teacher unions—such as differentiation of educator roles and responsibilities and peer evaluation—merit greater acceptance?

Should academic credentials and entry requirements be elevated to provide greater prestige to teaching, as has occurred in Finland and Singapore? Can better preparation and stronger peer supervision enhance the quality of the teaching force enough to meet the United States' needs in a competitive global economy? Will the National Board for Professional Teaching Standards play a more active role in elevating the teaching profession? Will educators and parents join forces to insist that schools teach real-world skills rather than test skills?

Supporters of the teachers unions contend that the organizations are already in the process of reinventing themselves and embracing approaches that call for mutually agreed-upon standards for performance pay and more rigorous requirements for tenure. Will these efforts to ensure quality be sufficient to ward off the powerful bipartisan political forces insisting on more rapid change and a bureaucratic view of the teaching profession?

The future of teachers and their organizations may well depend on the recognition that some form of test-based accountability is inescapable. The next generation of teachers already accepts this reality. It will be incumbent on future union leaders to collaborate in developing a synthesis of top-down, test-based reform and professional norms that allows for greater professional discretion, attention to the needs of individual students, and authentic teaching and learning.

This synthesis may well determine the future relevance of teachers unions—and the future shape of public education. Without teacher and union leadership, test-based accountability systems will dominate and continue to narrow the learning process. This trend may well compel families who can afford it to leave the public schools and thus further exacerbate the growing economic, demographic, and social polarization between the haves and the have-nots in U.S. society. The nation at large has a collective stake in ensuring that teachers have a voice in shaping the teaching profession, thus preserving public schools' traditional role as engines of social mobility and democracy.

Note

1.   Wise, A. E. (1979). *Legislated learning: The bureaucratization of the American classroom.* Berkeley: University of California Press.

Questions for Reflection and Application

After reading the essays in Section Five, answer the following questions:

1. Identify key trends and issues that you believe will have an impact on twenty-first-century schools and classrooms.

2. Discuss how these trends and issues will influence schools and the changing roles, responsibilities, and work of teacher leaders.

3. Consider how teacher leadership would look from the perspective of a politician, a school administrator, and a parent. Discuss which of those individuals will have the most to gain and/or lose from emerging teacher leadership.

Answer these questions using both the ideas from the essays that we are considering as well as your personal experiences with the schools you have encountered during your life: as a student, parent, and/or teacher. References to specific ideas found in the Section Five essays are expected.

Contributors to Teacher Leadership Book (2ⁿᵈ Edition)

Ann S. Allen is an assistant professor in Human Services and MSA Program Director at Western Carolina University. A graduate of the University of Kentucky, she has experience as an elementary teacher, junior high teacher, and elementary principal. Her doctoral degree is from the University of Cincinnati in Urban Educational Leadership. Her research agenda includes public schools and leadership preparation.

Pamela S. Angelle is an associate professor and Program Coordinator in Educational Leadership and Policy Studies at University of Tennessee, Knoxville. Her research interests include school reform, with a focus on distributed leadership and those organizational conditions and contexts that contribute to a collegial school community.

Roland S. Barth is a former public school teacher and principal. He was founding director of the Principals' Center at Harvard University and the author of several books: *Open Education and the American School, Run School Run, Improving Schools from Within, Cruising Rules,* and *Learning by Heart.* He is an educational consultant who lives in Maine and Florida.

Eleanor J. Blair is an associate professor at Western Carolina University, Cullowhee, North Carolina. She has a PhD from the University of Tennessee, Knoxville, and teaches both undergraduate and graduate foundations of education courses to students in the United States, Jamaica, and South America. Her research and writing focus on the many dimensions of teachers' work.

Nelda Cambron-McCabe is a professor in the Department of Educational Leadership and Chair, Department of Educational Psychology at Miami University (Ohio). As an advisory board member and a facilitator of the National Superintendents Roundtable, she works closely with Roundtable superintendents in planning programs to support them as they pursue educational change in their school systems.

Paul Carr is a professor in the Département des sciences de l'éducation at the Université du Québec en Outaouais in Gatineau, Quebec, Canada. He is a prolific writer, passionate about social justice, transformational change, "conscientization," counter-hegemonic democracy, and "radical love." He is the author of the award-winning *Does your vote count? Critical pedagogy and democracy*, and coeditor of some 15 academic books, in addition to having roughly a hundred articles and book chapters on diverse topics, including the sociology of education, racism, democracy, peace, media, and the environment.

Elizabeth Craig is a fifth-grade teacher in the Greenwich Public Schools, Greenwich, Connecticut.

Terrence E. Deal is the Irving R. Melbo Professor at University of Southern California's Rossier School. He is an internationally known lecturer and author who has written numerous books on leadership and organizations. In addition to those written with Lee Bolman, he is the coauthor of *Corporate Cultures* (with Alan Kennedy, 1982) and *Shaping School Culture* (with Kent Peterson, 1999).

Morgaen L. Donaldson is an associate professor of Educational Leadership at the University of Connecticut and Director of the University's Center for Education Policy Analysis. She is also a research associate at the Center for Policy Analysis and a research affiliate of the Project on the Next Generation of Teachers at Harvard University. Dr. Donaldson began her career as a high school teacher in urban and semi-urban schools and was a founding faculty member of the Boston Arts Academy, Boston's public high school for the arts. She also served as a Project Director in a Gates Foundation – funded effort to replicate the best practices of small schools successfully serving low-income and minority populations.

Richard DuFour was a public school educator for 34 years, serving as a teacher, principal, and superintendent. During his 19-year tenure as a leader at Adlai E. Stevenson High School in Lincolnshire, Illinois, Stevenson was one of only three schools in the nation to win the United States Department of Education Blue Ribbon Award on four occasions and the first comprehensive high school to be designated a New America High School as a model of successful school reform. He received his state's highest award as both a principal and superintendent.

David Gabbard is professor in the Department of Curriculum, Instruction, and Foundational Studies in the College of Education at Boise State University. He is author of "Not Too Big to Fail: How Teacher Education Killed the Foundations" (*Critical Questions in Education*; Spring 2013, Vol. 4 Issue 2, p. 181) and numerous other articles and books on how compulsory schooling fails the collective learning needs of our species.

Valeri R. Helterbran writes a weekly column for the Ligonier Echo and is professor of Education at Indiana University of Pennsylvania. She lives in Ligonier, PA.

Frederick M. Hess is director of education policy studies at the American Enterprise Institute, Washington, D. C., and author of *The Cage-Busting Teacher* (Harvard Education Press, 2015).

J. Casey Hurley is a professor of educational administration at Western Carolina University. He earned a bachelor of arts in English from St. Norbert College, DePere, Wisconsin, and a master's degree in educational administration from the University of Wisconsin–Madison, after which he served as an assistant principal and principal in three Wisconsin public high schools. He earned a PhD from UW–Madison in 1989. He is the author of *The Six Virtues of the Educated Person*, published in 2009.

Institute for Educational Leadership, Inc. (IEL) has worked for half a century to equip leaders to rise above institutional barriers and to build effective systems that prepare children and youth for postsecondary education, careers, and citizenship.

Susan M. Johnson studies, teaches, and consults about teacher policy, organizational change, and administrative practice. A former high school teacher and administrator, Johnson has a continuing interest in the work of teachers and the reform of schools. She has studied the leadership of superintendents and organization of school districts; the effects of collective bargaining on schools; the priorities of local teacher union leaders; teacher evaluation; the use of incentive pay plans for teachers; and the school as a context for adult work. Currently, Johnson directs the Project on the Next Generation of Teachers, which examines how best to recruit, develop, and retain a strong teaching force. She is the author or coauthor of six books and many articles. She served as academic dean of the Ed School from 1993 to 1999. Between 2007 and 2015, Johnson was co-chair of the Public Education Leadership Project (PELP), a collaboration between Harvard's Education and Business Schools.

Marilyn Katzenmeyer is president of Professional Development Center, Inc., and she currently engages in consultation, instructional design, and professional writing. She most recently served as a faculty administrator at the University of South Florida, where she was responsible for the development and implementation of the Executive Leaders Program, a leadership development opportunity for school-based administrators and teacher leaders who were transitioning into district-level leadership roles, and for the coordination of a Transition to Teaching project with a local school district.

Brad W. Kose is an assistant professor at the University of Illinois at Urbana-Champaign, USA. Both his teaching and research center on the integration of leadership for learning with leadership for social justice. He is particularly interested in how school leaders promote and support teaching for social justice and environmental sustainability. Recently, he has examined the impact of this type of leadership, professional learning, and teaching on student outcomes.

Linda Lambert is professor emeritus from California State University, East Bay. She is founder of the Center for Educational Leadership at California State University, Haywood. She is the author of dozens of articles and lead author of *The Constructivist Leader* (1995, 2002), *Who Will Save Our Schools* (1997), and *Women's Ways of Leading* (2009); she is the author of *Building Leadership Capacity in Schools* (1998) and *Leadership Capacity for Lasting School Improvement* (2003).

Ann Lieberman was previously a senior scholar at The Carnegie Foundation for the Advancement of Teaching and is professor emeritus of Education at Teachers College, Columbia University. Lieberman is widely known for her work in the areas of teacher leadership and development, collaborative research, networks and school-university partnerships, and the problems and prospects for understanding educational change. Lieberman received her BA and EdD at UCLA and her MA at California State University at Northridge, where she also received an honorary degree.

Martha M. McCarthy was previously director of the Indiana Education Policy Center and the High School Survey of Student Engagement. McCarthy has also been a public school teacher and administrator. She has authored or coauthored nine books and more than 200 articles on educational law and leadership preparation programs. She has served as president of the Education Law Association (ELA) and the University Council for Educational Administration (UCEA) and vice-president for Division A of the American Educational Research Association. In addition to being inducted into the University of Kentucky Alumni Hall of Fame for the College of Education in 1990, she was named an Alumna of Outstanding Achievement to celebrate the University of Florida's fiftieth anniversary of admitting female students (1997).

Gayle Moller is a retired associate professor in the Department of Educational Leadership and Foundations at Western Carolina University, Cullowhee, North Carolina. She was formerly executive director of the South Florida Center for Educational Leaders. The center served large, urban school systems in

South Florida that provided staff development for school leaders. Gayle worked in the Broward County Public Schools (Fort Lauderdale, Florida) for 19 years as a teacher, school administrator, and staff development administrator. She received her doctorate from Teachers College/Columbia University. Teacher leadership and professional learning communities are her research interests.

Kent D. Peterson is an emeritus professor at the University of Wisconsin–Madison. He is the founding director of the Vanderbilt Principals Institute and has worked with schools and institutes that serve school leaders in the US and around the world in both public and independent school settings. Over the past two decades he has written extensively about school leadership, school culture building, and successful improvement practices.

Bree Picower is an assistant professor at Montclair State University in the College of Education and Human Development. Her book, *Practice What You Teach: Social Justice Education in the Classroom and the Streets*, available from Routledge, focuses on the continuum of development toward teacher activism. She is the coeditor of the annual Planning to Change the World: A Planbook for Social Justice Teachers published by the New York Collective of Radical Educators (NYCoRE) and the Education for Liberation Network, and her recent scholarly articles have appeared in *Teachers College Record, Teacher Education Quarterly*, and *Race, Ethnicity and Education*. Currently, as a core leader of NYCoRE and founding member of the national Teacher Activist Groups network, Bree works to create multiple spaces for educators to sharpen their political analysis and take action for educational justice.

David Piercy is an organizational psychologist in Edmonton Public Schools, Edmonton, Alberta, Canada.

Lystra M. Richardson is a professor in the Department of Educational Leadership & Policy Studies at Southern Connecticut State University, where she teaches courses in the Sixth-Year Program, the Doctoral Program and the Superintendents' Program. Dr. Richardson is the author of several articles and one book, *The Power of Poetry for School Leadership*. Dr. Richardson holds a PhD in school leadership from The University of Connecticut.

Phillip C. Schlechty was one of the nation's foremost authors and speakers on school reform and was the founder and chief executive officer of the Schlechty Center. His intensive work—promoting the Schlechty Center's vision for public education—is a reflection of his dedication and commitment to public education. He passed away on January 7, 2016.

Linda Searby is an associate professor in the Educational Foundations, Leadership, and Technology Department at Auburn University. Her research interests include women and leadership, mentoring, and reflective practice. She has been in the field of education for over 25 years. Her passion as an administrator was leading her schools in staff development and systemic change. Transitioning from public school administration into higher education in 2003, Linda began focusing on preparing preservice teachers and aspiring administrators to meet the changing challenges of today's schools. She has taught both teacher education and educational administration courses at the undergraduate and graduate levels.

Lisa Shaddix was a participant in the Teachers as Leaders program of the Mountain Brook, Alabama School system, which represented an attempt to facilitate the empowering of teachers to utilize their leadership skills and contribute to the system as it fulfills its mission to offer education to its students that is effective challenging, and engaging.

Julie A. Sherrill is an educational administrator at Upper Arlington High School, Upper Arlington, Ohio.

Christopher Steel is the director of Curriculum, Instruction, and Technology, Emerson Public Schools, Emerson, N. J.

Holly J. Thornton is a professor in the Department of Curriculum and Instruction at Appalachian State University. She has received National Board Certification as an Early Adolescence Generalist. She currently serves on the Association for Middle Level Education Board of Trustees. Holly has served on the board of examiners for the National Association of Colleges of Teacher Education and as a lead reviewer and auditor for the National Middle School Association/National Council for Accreditation of Teacher Education Program Review Board. She served on the executive board of the Georgia Middle School Association, acted as Executive Director of the South Region for National Professors of Middle Level Education (NAPOMLE) and was president of the North Carolina Professors of Middle Level Education. Her research interests include teacher dispositions, responsive pedagogy, school reform, and collaboration with school partners.

Kathleen Topolka-Jorissen is an associate professor and director of the EdD Program in Educational Leadership in Human Services at Western Carolina University in Cullowhee, North Carolina. She teaches and advises doctoral students in the Educational Leadership program and conducts research related to educational policy and capacity building. Prior to joining the WCU faculty in 2006, she spent 25 years as a school and district level administrator in Minnesota. She also taught in educational leadership programs at the University of Minnesota, Winona State University, and Bowling Green State University. She earned her PhD from the University of Minnesota.

Sherry Willis was a school administrator with Hickory City Schools in Hickory, North Carolina for 20 years after serving 19 years as classroom teacher in the primary grades.

Arthur E. Wise is an education policy consultant based in Potomac, Maryland, and president emeritus of the National Council for Accreditation of Teacher Education.

Michael D. Usdan is a senior fellow at the Institute for Educational Leadership and its former president.